The Last Generation

The Last

Civil War America

Gary W. Gallagher, editor

Generation

Young Virginians in Peace, War, and Reunion

Peter S. Carmichael

The University of North Carolina Press | Chapel Hill and London

303 17 5077

© 2005 The University of North Carolina Press
All rights reserved

Designed by April Leidig-Higgins
Set in Ehrhardt by Copperline Book Services, Inc.
Manufactured in the United States of America

The paper in this book meets the guidelines for permanence
and durability of the Committee on Production Guidelines
for Book Longevity of the Council on Library Resources.

Library of Congress Cataloging-in-Publication Data
Carmichael, Peter S.
The last generation: young Virginians in peace, war,
and reunion / by Peter S. Carmichael.
    p. cm. — (Civil War America)
Includes bibliographical references and index.
ISBN 0-8078-2948-x (cloth: alk. paper)
1. Men, White—Virginia—Social conditions—19th
century.   2. Young men—Virginia—Social conditions
—19th century.   3. Whites—Virginia—Politics and
government—19th century.   4. Youth—Virginia—
Political activity—History—19th century.   5. Virginia
—Politics and government—19th century.   6. Virginia
—Social conditions—19th century.   7. Nationalism—
Southern States—History—19th century.   8. Southern
States—Politics and government—19th century.
9. Virginia—History—Civil War, 1861–1865—Social
aspects.   10. United States—History—Civil War,
1861–1865—Social aspects.   I. Title.   II. Series.
F235.A1C37 2005
975.5'03—dc22   2004022034

09 08 07 06 05   5 4 3 2 1

For Gary W. Gallagher

Contents

· ·

Illustrations and Map

· ·

MAP

Acknowledgments

· ·

EIGHTEEN YEARS AGO Dr. Gary W. Gallagher
stopped at the Spotsylvania battlefield exhibit shelter when I was a seasonal
historian with the National Park Service. We walked around the "Bloody
Angle" with his dog, Nipper, and talked history; by the end of our conver-
sation I knew that I wanted to study under him at Penn State University. I
could not have made a better decision at such a formative time in my career.
Dr. Gallagher's seminars set an unbelievably high standard for teaching that I
will always strive to emulate. He raised challenging questions, demanded that
his students master the historiography, and then allowed them to reach their
own interpretations. His own work on Confederate nationalism and Stephen
Dodson Ramseur prompted me to think about the lives of student youth in
the 1850s and their fervent expression of Confederate nationalism during the
Civil War. This book began as a dissertation under Dr. Gallagher's direction
in 1993. At every step of the way he has been a compassionate critic, a wise
mentor, and a good friend. I am honored that *The Last Generation* is part of
his Civil War America series.

At Penn State I found a very collegial and engaging intellectual community. Elizabeth Woodruff, Daniel Letwin, William Pencak, Richard Garner,
and Carol Reardon gave more of their time than I had any right to expect.
Among my fellow graduate students I developed important relationships
with Charles Holden and William A. Blair. Chuck's insights into nineteenth-
century Southern conservatism have helped me to think more broadly about
the intellectual context of the last generation. He read a number of rough
drafts and listened patiently when I tried to sort out one of my many inco-
herent ideas about young Virginians. Through it all he has been a trusted
colleague and superb friend. Bill's work on Confederate identity has been
crucial to how I understand slaveholder authority during the Civil War. Our
conversations were some of the most intellectually stimulating discussions
that I had while preparing this book. I am thrilled that he is back at Penn

State, where he edits *Civil War History* and oversees the George and Ann Richards Civil War Center.

I was very fortunate to land my first job at Western Carolina University in Cullowhee, North Carolina. The history department set high standards for publishing and teaching, and my colleagues were very empathetic to the innumerable pressures that a new faculty member faces. I received plenty of peer encouragement to expand and deepen my research on young Virginians. I also had an opportunity to work with a talented group of graduate students —Kevin Barksdale, Steve Nash, Bruce Stewart, and Rod Steward—all of whom contributed to important discussions about religion and Confederate nationalism that ultimately shaped this book.

My move to the University of North Carolina at Greensboro in the fall of 2000 enabled me to transform my dissertation into a book. The institutional support of UNCG exceeded what I had any reasonable right to expect. Chancellor Patricia A. Sullivan, Provost Ed Uprichard, and Dean Timothy D. Johnston have created an academic environment where both research and teaching flourish. I received a new faculty grant from the Office of Research that was critical to completing my research at the University of Virginia. My colleagues in the history department have been a tremendous source of creative energy and wisdom. Robert Calhoon, Phyllis Hunter, Lisa Tolbert, and William Link took time from their busy schedules to critique the manuscript. Bill, in particular, was extraordinarily generous with his time and research. Fortunately for me he was finishing a manuscript on slavery and politics in Virginia when I arrived at UNCG, and I have incorporated many of his ideas into my book. Bill also thoroughly read the entire draft of *The Last Generation* and offered much-needed advice on issues related to publishing in the academic world. Not only has Bill been an important steward of this project, but he has also become a trusted friend. I am very sorry to see him leave UNCG.

Cheryl Junk of the University of North Carolina at Chapel Hill is one of the best editors I have ever encountered. She brought focus to the book's overall thesis without rebuilding the architecture of the manuscript, sharpened the interpretive edge of many of my chapters without forging entirely new arguments, and offered stylistic improvements without overhauling the prose. I benefited enormously from her extensive comments and suggestions, all of which were made in the most positive way imaginable. I simply cannot thank her enough for all that she has done to improve this book. Eugene D. Genovese has been a tireless supporter of this project. As a graduate student

I did not always find senior scholars to be accessible. That simply was not the case with Dr. Genovese, who immediately offered his help after hearing me deliver a paper at the St. George Tucker Society. We have shared many sources and ideas over the years, and it has been gratifying to work with a man whose scholarship I admire so much. Dr. Genovese critiqued a number of chapters and was brutally honest in his assessment. His tough criticisms, however, have made this study a much better book. My understanding of the religious and intellectual life of the Old South has also benefited enormously from conversations with Beth Barton Schweiger. I draw heavily from her ideas about the modern impulses of Protestantism in antebellum Virginia.

Keith Bohannon of the State University of West Georgia and Robert E. L. Krick of the Richmond National Military Park have been indispensable in every historical endeavor that I have undertaken since college. This project was no exception. They provided countless research leads and read portions of the manuscript. I value their historical advice and friendship more than they can imagine. If it had not been for David Perry this manuscript would not have landed at the University of North Carolina Press. Although we did not quite mesh as weight-lifting partners, David is all that anyone could ever want in an editor. Paul Betz took on the formidable task of cleaning up my prose and clarifying my ideas. I was very fortunate to have him as a copyeditor. He did a superb job and improved this book in innumerable ways. Mark Simpson-Vos and Ron Maner have also been very helpful at the press. While living in Chapel Hill, I met Matthew Fellowes, now of the Brookings Institute in Washington, D.C. We quickly became good friends and intellectual companions. Matt did a wonderful job of transforming my rough statistics into readable tables.

I was very fortunate to have a number of colleagues either read portions of this manuscript, comment on paper presentations, or provide general advice on some important historical issue. They include Michael C. C. Adams, John Coski, Lesley Gordon, John T. Kneebone, Robert K. Krick, James McPherson, David Moltke-Hansen, James Tice Moore, T. Michael Parrish, J. Tracy Power, George Rable, William Kauffman Scarborough, Mitchell Snay, Patricia Walenista, and Bertram Wyatt-Brown.

In a previous book I wrote that there is no better place to study the history of the Old Dominion than the Virginia Historical Society. I now believe that it is the premier institution in the South, and I would argue that it ranks as one of the finest repositories in the country. The collections and facilities are first rate, and Dr. Charles F. Bryan Jr. should be commended for building an incomparable staff. Francis Pollard and her colleagues in the library and reading room are extremely knowledgeable, helpful, and amazingly efficient. Graham Dozier's steady efforts on my behalf are deeply appreciated. He authored an impressive guide to the Civil War collections at the Virginia Historical Society. Nelson D. Lankford organized a valuable colloquium during the summer of 2002, where I aired some of my ideas while doing research funded by a Mellon grant. A number of other archival institutions have been helpful. I wish to record my gratitude to Laura Clark Brown, of the Southern Historical Collection, Wilson Library, University of North Carolina at Chapel Hill; and to Michael Plunkett, of the Albert and Shirley Small Special Collections Library, Alderman Library, University of Virginia. More generally, my thanks go to the many helpful individuals I encountered at the Rare Book, Manuscript, and Special Collections Library, Duke University; the Virginia State Library; the National Archives; Special Collections, James Graham Leyburn Library, Washington and Lee University; Special Collections, Virginia Polytechnic Institute and State University; the Virginia Military Institute Archives; the Eleanor Brockenbrough Library, Museum of the Confederacy; and the Birmingham Public Library Archives, Birmingham.

Closer to home I have a bullpen of family members who provided me with a much-needed boost during those long, difficult stretches of writing. My mother and father, Lowell and Charlotte Carmichael, have never wavered in their support over the years, even when I was an irrepressibly whiny graduate student. Now that I am a boorish academic, their unconditional love continues unabated, and their enthusiasm for my work amazes me. In the summer of 2003 I married the incomparable Elizabeth A. Getz of Westfield, New Jersey. Her beauty, intelligence, and wonderful sense of humor can easily be traced to her parents, Janet and Jack Getz, and her grandmother Florence Getz. Janet, Jack, and Grandma Flo have embraced me as one of their own. I am grateful to be part of their family, and the only way I know to express my heartfelt appreciation is to simply say: "My best to you."

Every day my wife, Beth, brings indescribable joy to my life. She, more than anyone else, deserves the lion's share of credit for this book's publication. Beth read and edited a number of drafts, hunted down obscure sources, and transcribed countless theses from the University of Virginia. I will always cherish our collaboration on this project. Now that I have spent so many years working on *The Last Generation*, I am no longer part of "young America." I am on the cusp of becoming an old fogy, but with Beth by my side the years ahead are filled with unimaginable promise.

The Last Generation

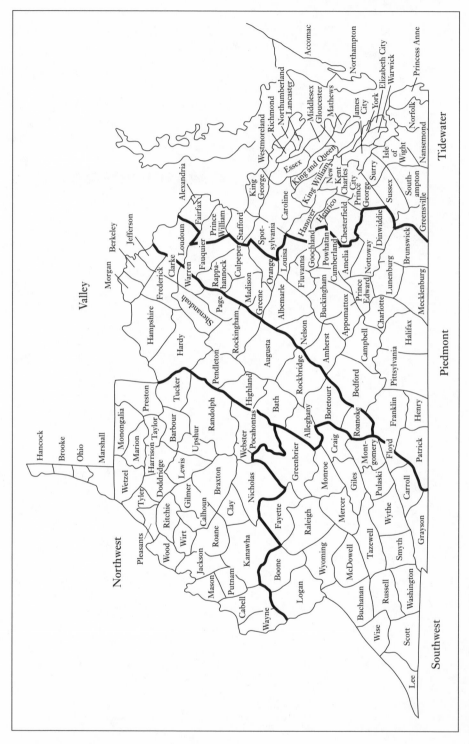

Counties and Regions of Virginia, 1860

Prologue

· ·

THE APPLAUSE OF THE veterans gave way to an uneasy silence as ex-Confederate William Roane Aylett assumed the podium. This fifty-two-year-old lawyer from King William, Virginia, was the first Southern speaker at the 1887 Gettysburg reunion. Everyone knew that hostility and bitter sectionalism lurked beneath the pageantry and ceremony of American unity. Correspondents from major newspapers, including the *New York Times*, had gathered to see if such a meeting could produce a true expression of reconciliation. Up to this point, the former combatants had engaged in plenty of flag waving, handshaking, and patriotic speeches, transforming the reunion into a lovefest of Americanism. But could these gestures withstand an authentic rendering of the Confederate experience in Pennsylvania? When Aylett served in the Army of Northern Virginia during the summer of 1863, he endorsed and executed a hard policy of war against the state's civilians; he tried to shoot Union prisoners as an act of retaliation, and at the end of the failed campaign he promised his wife that "I'll fight them as long as I have a leg to stand on or an arm to strike . . . for God cannot intend that such wickedness should succeed."[1]

Although the audience was filled with the men who had fought in Pickett's Charge twenty-four years earlier, Aylett decided to do a great deal of forgetting at the expense of history. He ignored his own personal history during the Gettysburg campaign while purposefully avoiding any controversial topic relating to Northern and Southern relations, except for the return of the Confederate flags to the South. Aylett diffused this issue at the onset of his address: "Southern men don't care who keeps the flags," he announced, "the past went down in war, and we recognize now the banner of our fathers." This cued one of Aylett's old comrades to raise the national banner, and, according to one observer, the "audience sprang up and gesticulated wildly."[2] Aylett filled the rest of his address with patriotic rhetoric, assuring his Northern hosts that "there is not a true man at the South to-day, but who feels as if he would like to stand at the tombs of Lincoln and Grant to plant a flower there and to water it with a manly tear."[3]

Aylett's transformation from a fight-to-the-death Confederate into a post-war crusader for reconciliation is truly remarkable when considering the trajectory of his life from his 1850 enrollment at the University of Virginia to Robert E. Lee's 1865 surrender at Appomattox. A deep concern for the South's future animated Aylett's actions from the moment he entered the university. As a first-year student, he helped organize the school's Southern rights' association. A few years later, in his final address before the Jefferson Literary Society, Aylett spoke passionately about the duties that each student should fulfill to the Union, Virginia, and the South. He warned, however, that radical action might be necessary if the South ever lost political equality with the North. Aylett lived up to his words during the political crisis that followed Abraham Lincoln's election in 1860. He embraced secession at a time when most Virginians preferred to remain in the Union. His strong sense of being Southern and Virginian, evident during the secession crisis, matured into a strident expression of Confederate nationalism while serving as an officer in the Army of Northern Virginia.

Military defeat forced ex-Confederates like Aylett to renounce earlier beliefs, recognize federal authority, and reinvent themselves as free-labor capitalists. Although Aylett's postwar Americanism should come as no surprise, the ease with which he changed his opinions is astonishing, and his intellectual journey deserves explanation. His experience was not exceptional among his peers—Virginia men born between 1831 and 1843—who also made a speedy journey back to the Union. These men were the last generation of white Southerners to grow up with the institution of slavery. All were ideologically and materially connected to the master class. They grew up politically in the tumultuous 1850s, lobbied for secession when their conservative elders preached Union, and served as secondary officers in Lee's army, distinguishing themselves as some of the most devoted sons of the Confederacy.

Reconstruction marked the ascension of the last generation to a position of authority in Virginia. Virtually every one of Aylett's peers capitulated to the Northern creed of free labor and industrialization. A desire for home rule and economic power does not capture the complexities as to why this age group embraced reconciliation. To understand how Aylett and members of his generation reconstructed their identities, one must turn to the dilemma that faced them in the 1850s: how to stop the Old Dominion's decline and restore the Commonwealth to a position of prestige and leadership in the Union. Their response to this question resulted in a battle with the "old fogies" over the meaning of progress in a slave society. The war interrupted their mission, but their vision prevailed, forging the nexus between Old and New South thought in Virginia. For men like Aylett, Reconstruction provided a second chance to instill in Virginia a spirit of innovation, reform, and prosperity, even if it came at the price of having to return to Pennsylvania and worship the Star-Spangled Banner on the sacred ground of Gettysburg.

Introduction

· ·

IN THE 1966 CLASSIC "Mother's Little Helper,"
the Rolling Stones' Mick Jagger belted out the verse: "Kids are different
today, I hear every mother say." Although the Stones' young listeners probably thought these sentiments were uniquely suited to their generation, there
is an unmistakable timelessness to Jagger's words. Throughout history adults
have charged that young people have morphed into unrecognizable creatures
who lack respect for traditions and authority. This has led some observers to
conclude that generational tension does not originate in particular events or
social movements but inheres instead in the universality of the youth experience. The turbulent "nature" of young people explains all. Contemporaries as
well as scholars have portrayed young people as restless by nature, impetuous
in their actions, predisposed to challenge authority, and eager to irritate their
more conservative elders.

Although it is true that young people of different times and places exhibit
similar behavior while making the transition to adult society, we should not
conclude that the experience of coming-of-age is a universal one. Young people have not always confronted the same questions, the same problems, or the
same obstacles in trying to become independent free thinkers. If anything,
a generational approach should remind us that the experience of each group
has a unique historical context specifically rooted in the political and material
conditions of a particular time period.[1] Moreover, young people have usually
reaffirmed their loyalty to long-standing traditions, mores, and institutions
while criticizing those in power for the failings of the adult world. It cannot
be emphasized enough that exceptionalism, whether in beliefs or actions, does
not have to be present in every facet of young peoples' lives for a generational
perspective to be valid. Indeed, it is not uncommon for younger people to
express fidelity toward their families, to defend community traditions, and to
uphold the dominant values of their society while at the same time condemn-

ing the older generation for its mismanagement of public affairs. Such was the case with the last generation of Virginians during the 1850s.[2]

Seeing the experience of Southern young men as a universal one surfaces with disturbing regularity in the historiography of the Old South. The popular, but one-dimensional image of Southern youth as lazy, immoral, and hotheaded overlooks the changing nature of what it meant to be a young man in the slave South.[3] Moreover, the scholarly perception that young Southern men could only bond by fighting, drinking, or gambling has made it difficult for us to take them on their own terms, to see them as political beings who could think as much as they could feel. Discounting the powerful impact of emotions would be a serious mistake, but the emotional history of Southern men must be understood within the context of the religious and intellectual life of the Old South. If that essential context is not considered, the stereotype of the Southern man as an unthinking brute will unfortunately prevail.

The issue of Southern manliness is central to this project, which began as an examination of Confederate nationalism among Virginia men born between 1830 and 1842. Members of this age group largely served as second-echelon officers in the Army of Northern Virginia. On the surface, they seemed to fit the stereotype of the warlike Southerner, for it appeared that the violence they craved during secession could not even be satisfied by a bloody civil war. I discovered instead that this age group and class of Southern men articulated a version of masculinity based on Christian gentility, not raw physical aggression; that they were highly ideological, not just men of feeling; and that they were remarkably savvy as the Confederacy's front-line negotiators, not the brutal enforcers of the slaveholders' political will.

A case study of this age group best explains how young Southerners of a certain class exerted authority during the Civil War and why they identified so strongly with the Confederacy. I turned to Virginia because it was considered the most important of the Confederate states and housed the nation's capital. The Commonwealth was also the most populous state; it contained impressive industrial resources; and it was arguably the decisive theater of the Civil War. To develop a sample of consequence, I selected 121 men who resided in the counties that represented the state in the Confederacy. These young men — the last generation to grow up with the institution of slavery — were highly educated, closely aligned with or part of the slaveholding class, and came of age in the 1850s. In that decade they formed their political identities as a group because they had the same experiences at the same historical moment. A "typical" member of the sample group in 1860 was a twenty-three-year old son of a slaveholder, had attended the University of Virginia, and stayed in the state upon graduation. Although he took a deep interest in national and state politics, his party allegiance could not be determined. Antebellum voting records reveal local patterns of group behavior rather than individual affiliation. In other words, it is very difficult to determine the party affiliation of these young men unless they were part of prominent Whig or Democratic families; they did not run for or hold office. The typical Virginian in the sample was single before the war and not considered a head of household. He was most likely a lawyer, teacher, or student. During the Civil War, he served in the Army of Northern Virginia as either a staff or a field officer. If he survived the war (28 percent of the sample did not), he married, became a head of household, and gravitated toward the fields of either law or education.[4]

This book should be seen as a generational study, not as a group biography. This is a crucial distinction as I do not provide a detailed examination of a few individuals from cradle to grave. Rather, I have drawn from anything written about or by a member of the last generation. A random approach was necessary as sources from young people, regardless of their class standing, were difficult to locate. With a few exceptions, the research material did not permit me to follow an individual from his student days through Reconstruction. I had no choice but to collect a collage of snapshots—a master's thesis written at the University of Virginia, a single letter from the Petersburg trenches, or a postwar speech calling for reconciliation—with the idea that I could piece together a collective portrait of young Virginia. I should also add that I selected these men because I could explore their private lives through their letters, speeches, master's theses, and published writings.

My sample of the last generation decisively favors young people who attended Virginia universities, although I have included a smaller group of men who studied at Northern and European institutions. Although the more highly educated men tended to be part of or closely aligned with the state's slaveholding class, my study group was not exclusively affiliated with the planter elite or the state's wealthiest circles. Many of the young men in the sample did not come from privilege, and they struggled financially to remain in school. Despite economic differences among these educated men, they all looked at the world within the broad intellectual framework of the dominant slaveholding class. Whether a young Virginian's family owned two slaves or twenty did not matter. They grew up in a slave society, and this forged a consensus on vital political and social matters among whites of all classes and age groups. Some might question whether this book is a true generational study because my sample disproportionately favors elites. Limited manuscript material made it difficult to find suitable candidates from the largest component of the last generation—nonslaveholders. I did find a subgroup of nonelite young men who either came from nonslaveholding families or never entered Virginia universities. Within this smaller cohort, the prominent example of John Buchanan, a nonslaveholder from western Virginia, reveals the master class's influence during the antebellum period as well as the shared perspective of young people coming of age in the 1850s.

I have emphasized the points of generational agreement among young Virginians sometimes at the risk of creating a flat, homogeneous cohort. The use of the term "last generation" contributes to this problem as it creates the impression that I see complete unanimity among young people throughout the state. I use "last generation" and "young Virginians" knowing that there existed a variety of experiences and perspectives within the sample group as well as among other young people across the state. For the sake of style and readability, I employ these terms without always adding qualifiers such as "many" or "most." I have tried to acknowledge differences in outlook without obscuring the fundamental unity that young Virginians expressed in their views of progress, slavery, secession, and the Confederacy. Moreover, I have avoided any hint of generational determinism. Age does not become the universal explanation or the overriding factor that determines human motivation. I have tried to incorporate age as a category of analysis within the framework of race, class, and gender that has served historians so well.

The last generation's importance becomes apparent with Abraham Lincoln's 1860 election to the presidency. Young Virginians embraced secession against the wishes of their Unionist elders, but historians of the secession crisis have generally overlooked the role of young people in promoting the disunionist cause.[5] As secondary officers in Robert E. Lee's Army of Northern Virginia, members of the last generation earned a reputation as the Confederacy's most devoted sons. These young Southerners, even those who lived outside Virginia, were recognized as the most desperate class of Confederates. In 1863, Union general William T. Sherman described these "young Bloods of the South" as "bold to rashness, and dangerous subjects in every sense." "They hate Yankees 'Per se' and don't bother their brains about the Past, present or Future," he added. "This is a larger class than most men suppose, and are the most dangerous set of men which this war has turned loose upon the world." The tough-minded Sherman did not see how these young men could ever be subdued. He concluded that "they must all be killed, or employed by us before we can hope for Peace."[6]

Sherman saw these young Southern warriors as the children of war, their rage fueled by the killing and destruction of rampaging armies. Many historians have reached similar conclusions in their studies of Civil War soldiers because they fail to consider the life experiences of Americans prior to 1861. There were conversations, political acts, dramatic events, and cultural developments that influenced the last generation's reaction to Lincoln's call to arms and continued to shape their actions long after they entered Confederate ranks. In order to understand why young Virginians gave themselves so completely to the Confederacy, I needed to explore their formative years in the 1850s. I expected to find men who possessed a weaker attachment to Union than their elders. Unlike their parents' generation, they did not participate in a great national event like the Mexican War. They were also farther removed in time from the Revolutionary generation and most likely did not have contact with anyone associated with the struggle for independence. Young Virginians also became political beings in the 1850s, when discord over slavery destroyed the two-party system. No other period in American history witnessed such political divisiveness or extreme expressions of Southernism. It is tempting to assume that the decade of sectionalism weakened the bonds of Union to such an extent that my study group had no difficulty imagining an independent Southern nation.

Such an assumption is built on the premise that young Virginians saw themselves as Southerners first, Americans second. To test this hypothesis I set out to understand the origins of their Southern identity, a line of inquiry that could best explain their radical political action during the secession crisis and the Civil War. The antebellum sources, however, did not fully support this premise. Members of the last generation did not believe that they had to pick either the wardrobe of Americanism or that of Southernism. Rather, they felt comfortable putting together an eclectic outfit that reflected their diverse attachments to their local environs, the state, the region, and the nation. The central challenge of the book came to be that of explaining how the last generation assembled such a uniform.

Although events and cultural trends of the 1850s influenced their regional identity, members of my study group adopted a more Southern perspective in response to internal issues and debates relating exclusively to Virginia. These young men were not Southern radicals or rabid defenders of slavery. This was an important discovery, but it made it more difficult to explain why young people challenged their elders over secession. My desire to understand the secessionist impulse of young Virginians revealed a series of generational struggles that played out in 1850s Virginia. I should make it clear that the last generation's sense of mission did not lead to cultural warfare between young and old. The members of my study group upheld the dominant values and slaveholding ethic of their parents' generation, but they also believed that the legacy of the Revolutionary heroes had been betrayed and that their elders were responsible for Virginia's decline. This was not a new complaint. Since the 1830s, Virginians had lamented the Old Dominion's economic and political fall in the Union. Nonetheless, it became my belief that the last generation's critique of Virginia society deserved attention in its own right because of its implications for secession, Confederate loyalty, and, as I would discover later, even Reconstruction.

From these generational battles, a story line began to crystallize. It was centered on the problem of young Virginians' being caught between two competing cultural forces. A desire for membership in the slaveholding class pushed them inward toward a more traditional version of Southern culture—one that valued the ownership of land and slaves, community obligation, and a life of aristocratic ease. Surprisingly, many young people questioned this as the dominant ideal. Owning a handful of slaves while practicing law at the county courthouse or serving as the local doctor had once commanded a respectable financial reward and social recognition. This seemed unrealistic to the last generation in the 1850s, for there were too many physicians and lawyers. An entire generation of young Virginians came of age deeply troubled that they would never achieve the professional standing that would earn them community recognition as men. To make matters worse, members of the last generation believed that their elders had allowed the state to wallow in economic misery while they fancied themselves as grand cavaliers who lived off the glories of departed ancestors. These young men blamed their personal difficulties on the state, accusing their elders of falling under the sway of "old fogyism."[7] Such a philosophy, according to young Virginians, encouraged unthinking opposition to change, even at the expense of economic or educational reform.

The criticisms leveled at the older generation reveal the pressures of a transatlantic Victorian culture that pushed the last generation to look outward. Young Virginians were not a bunch of provincial sons of slaveholders whose view of the world never extended beyond the Blue Ridge Mountains. Instead, they craved bourgeois respectability, hungered for professional success, followed personal ambition, and desired the material trappings of a middle-class lifestyle—all of which they believed could only come from a diversified state economy rather than from slavery alone. I doubt their aspirations were entirely unique, but what stands out is the last generation's perception that Virginia was being passed by as the rest of the world reaped the amazing material rewards of an age of progress. Personal frustrations intensified these fears about the Commonwealth's decline. Struggling for their livelihood left the young men wondering if society could accommodate their dreams.

The idea of the Christian gentleman helped young Virginians negotiate between the aristocratic traditions of Virginia's slaveholding class and the bourgeois spirit of the times. The Christian gentleman harkened back to an eighteenth-century code of behavior that slaveholders had tried to emulate, although often unsuccessfully, since William Byrd. He was to be pious, self-controlled, educated, and the master of his household. This version of manliness was central to the slaveholders' hierarchical worldview in which relations between men and women, rich and poor, and black and white were considered inherently unequal. Since young Virginians subscribed to the same ideas, I wondered if they were any different from their elders. The letters and diaries of these young men make clear that they too believed in Christian gentility, male dominance, and inequality. Despite such important similarities, they put their own spin on the eighteenth-century model of Christian manliness, which reveals that the last generation looked forward, not backward; that they wanted to transform their society into a progressive land of economic prosperity and intellectual vitality, not return to the "golden age" of Revolutionary Virginia; and that they wanted the Old Dominion to become a leader in the age of progress, not insulated from the Atlantic world.

The point of departure between young and old centered on the last generation's celebration of individual ambition as the distinguishing trait of a respectable man. In this, they were no different from their bourgeois counterparts above the Mason-Dixon Line. Although young people still emphasized the importance of duty to family and community, the last generation's model of the Christian gentleman shifted the scales in favor of individualism and away from communal obligations. Young people reshaped manhood and their relationship to society because they came of age when an aggressive market economy made impressive gains in the state.[8] This insight should not obscure the fundamental fact that members of the last generation were part of a slave society and consequently were committed to the idea of inequality as a guiding principle of society. But individualism no longer remained subservient to the household or community when young Virginians came of age in the 1850s.

The rise of individualism did not spark a reckless youth rebellion in the Old Dominion. In fact, an older generation of youth cultivators (religious leaders and educators) was quite successful in reaching the hearts and minds of young Virginians with their Christian message. Young people listened, and while not all became saints or even converted for that matter, a noticeable change in student behavior did occur. The epidemic of student rioting that began in the 1820s came to an end in the 1850s. Virginia campuses in the decade before the Civil War also witnessed a wave of revival activity and the rise of student-led religious organizations such as the Young Men's Christian Association.[9]

I needed to explain why generational tension flourished in Virginia at a time when young people acknowledged adult authority by trying to emulate the eighteenth-century idea of the Christian gentleman. From this perspective it became clear that young Virginians turned the message of the youth cultivators against the state's political class by connecting the problems of the day to the sins of their fathers.[10] What did the idea of the Christian gentleman and Virginia's decline have to do with the last generation's actions during the secession crisis and the Civil War? It was tempting to reduce my study group's eagerness for secession to youthful ardor or romantic visions of soldiering; many, but not all, young Virginians felt a powerful urge to prove their manhood on the battlefield. A more useful approach, however, would frame this historical moment as a convergence of the personal struggles of the last generation—their desire for reputation as full adults and their dream of returning Virginia to a position of leadership—with their ironclad political belief that the South must always have political equality in the nation. Although some of the most prominent advocates of disunion were "grey heads" such as Edmund Ruffin and Henry Wise, most of the state's elders preached moderation. Waiting for the Republicans to enact their policies ensured Virginia's eventual subjugation to Northern interests. Many of these young men did not understand why the state's leaders would allow the Northerners to light the fire first.

Young Virginians believed that their state was kept out of the Confederacy by decrepit leaders who were morally bankrupt and out of touch—the very men who were responsible for the state's decline in the Union. They argued that leaving the Union would not only free the Old Dominion from domination by an aggressive, abolitionist-led North, but would also serve as a moral cleansing agent at home, purging the Commonwealth of its dissolute class of leaders while elevating the state to a position of leadership in a new Southern nation. In their minds, entering the Confederacy would resolve many of the internal problems that had plagued the state since the Revolution. The last generation saw themselves as redeemers saving Virginia from the dishonor of living under an abolitionist regime produced by corrupt party politics. They did not imagine themselves as Southern radicals. Their public campaign for secession coincided with their private desire to satisfy personal aspirations. They hoped to secure positions of authority and prestige in the Confederacy that had eluded them during the 1850s because of their age and limited opportunities. The prospect of earning adult status by freeing Virginia from the grasp of the "Black Republicans" and thus returning the state to a position of uncontested leadership in a new Southern nation drew them to secession and war.[11]

Lincoln's call for troops brought unity between young and old. Even though young Virginians had blamed the state's political leaders for allowing Virginia to decline, they followed their elders into a bloody civil war and willingly sacrificed themselves for the principles of a slave society. Explaining this paradox required that I return to the issue of manliness. Young Virginians felt the need to prove themselves in war, to show the older generation that they were worthy of being considered Southern men. During the secession crisis the state's Unionists had alleged that young Virginians were silly, emotional, and stunted sexually, all of which were metaphors for weakness. In the wake of these public attacks, young Virginians were in part motivated to join the Confederate war effort to prove that their generation possessed manly courage and self-discipline. Consequently, they saw war as an opportunity not only to redeem their native state but also to gain personally in self-improvement. Wartime journals were filled with rhetoric about the war as a means of maturing rather than as an aggressive response to an insult against honor. Ministers and politicians helped push this idea by depicting combat as a chance for young people to purge their internal weaknesses. By constructing the war as a path for achieving individual "manhood," young Virginians became eager to sacrifice themselves physically. The idea of the Christian gentleman coalesced into a new, wartime version of masculinity based on raw courage and heroism. The human consequences were tragic. This generation of young Virginians sustained horrific losses on the battlefields of its native state.

It was hardly surprising that young Virginians became devout Confederates. As members of the master class, they had everything to lose in a war over slavery. Consequently, my attention shifted to nonslaveholder allegiance and the role that members of the last generation played in promoting Confederate loyalty. Much of the secondary literature portrays the Confederate ruling class as insensitive to the demands from below, but the junior officers were far more responsive than has usually been thought.[12] As mediators between the rank-and-file and the Confederacy's top brass, they astutely diffused dissent by undercutting official military policy concerning leaves. Soldiers demanded brief visits home to care for families or handle urgent personal issues. Even in the most extreme cases of need, however, high-ranking officers generally refused permission. These restrictions created a volatile situation for men on the front lines. Secondary officers eased class tension by granting "French furlough," thus giving them tremendous power in determining the men's welfare. Private soldiers appreciated gestures made on their behalf and responded by doing their duty under fire. They also forged a bond with secondary officers in battle and in the shared religious experiences in camp, and by assisting in welfare relief efforts for the home front. In the end, the last generation successfully furthered the power of the Confederacy's ruling class by representing themselves as the guardians of nonslaveholder interests. My intention is not to vindicate the actions of the last generation, but rather to show how effective they were in representing their class interests in a war over slavery. It would be a mistake to conclude that young Virginia officers manipulated enlisted men. There was a give-and-take relationship between the two groups in which members of the last generation almost always had to compromise in order to earn the consent of those below.

How these young officers understood themselves as Confederates, the gateway question to this project, still remained unanswered. Whether or not young Virginians possessed a strong sense of Confederate nationalism has been answered by Gary W. Gallagher and William A. Blair.[13] Both scholars have demonstrated that Virginians of all ages might have been some of the Confederacy's most loyal subjects, even though the Old Dominion was one of the last states to secede. I thought it would be more fruitful to try to understand the nature of their loyalties and how they changed over the course of the war. The letters and diaries from my study group reveal that Virginians displayed a remarkable capacity to channel cultural upheaval into familiar patterns of beliefs. The war, in their minds, merely confirmed antebellum assumptions about the inherent differences between Northerners and Southerners. Union depredations, civilian sacrifices, and the symbolic image of Robert E. Lee erased any fears that God would forsake Southerners. Regardless of the military situation or the immense suffering and dislocation on the home front, the thought of God siding with the enemy seemed ludicrous to the last generation. Even when Southern speculating and other moral crimes suggested cause for divine wrath, these men found ample reasons to expect divine favor. Losing faith in the Confederacy or rejecting the worldview of the planter class constituted a direct challenge to God's will—a step most Southerners refused to take. By 1864, members of the last generation were unable to distinguish between their religious beliefs and their political nationalism. A spirit of vengeance, a blinding trust in Providence, and a controlling sense of honor transformed these young men into fanatics. Throughout the 1850s and even during the secession crisis, they were thoughtful, deliberate, and self-critical, but war narrowed their perspective and caused them to lose touch with the military reality of the Confederacy.

Ending the story at Appomattox would miss a rich opportunity to understand the impact of the Civil War on a group of men who figured prominently in the development of a Lost Cause mythology and the New South creed. Much of the secondary literature on Reconstruction posits that a Southerner could either be a modernizer or a reactionary Lost Cause fanatic. The veterans of the last generation created a hybrid ideology combining both types. Their antebellum campaign to bring economic diversity to Virginia largely provided the intellectual punch to their postwar message. Ironically, the war interrupted the last generation's progressive plans for the Old Dominion. The industrial might of Northern armies did not suddenly awaken the last generation to the ideas of economic innovation and development; they had advocated an energizing of the state before Fort Sumter. As Paul Gaston has argued, a white Southerner could be both a Lost Cause champion and a New South booster.[14]

Reconstruction provided a second chance to instill into Virginia a spirit of innovation, reform, and prosperity. Although most of the last generation had been unyielding Confederates during the war, they reconfigured their identities as Americans with remarkable ease. A desire for home rule goes a long way toward explaining this transformation, yet more than power was at stake. The last generation's postwar vision cannot be fully understood without an examination of the intellectual connections to the 1850s. In the end, I argue that the last generation's antebellum mission to modernize Virginia might explain why many of these young men had minimal difficulty in accepting the realities of reunion and industrial capitalism. Rather than seeking refuge in the "moonlight and magnolias" view of the Old South or a strident defense of Confederate principles, the last generation's Lost Cause message revived their antebellum dream of bourgeois progress.

To tell this story required that I employ a chronological narrative, but within this structure I also found it necessary to examine my subject topically. The hybrid approach allowed me to look at the last generation's experience from a more analytical perspective. At the same time, I thought it was important for me to broadly describe their inner thoughts, emotions, public behavior, and personal relationships. I decided that a series of narratives within this analytical framework would humanize my subject matter by providing a more holistic view of individual lives while conveying change over time. I realize that this approach came at the expense of tightly argued chapters. If my method of exposition succeeds, however, the complex relationship between the ideas and actions of my study group will become clearer as I move the last generation forward toward Civil War and Reconstruction. Chapter 1 explores the attitudes of these young men toward the "age of progress" and why they did not share the concerns of many slaveholders who worried about a world moving toward free-labor capitalism. Chapter 2 shows how the last generation's desire for progress encouraged many young men to believe that a spirit of "old fogydom" prevented Virginia from advancing materially or intellectually. The perception that Virginia was in decline intersected with the personal struggles of these young men. Many complained that the road to respectability through landownership and slavery was no longer possible for young Virginians. Professional frustrations reinforced their belief that something had gone wrong in the Commonwealth, and generational tensions consequently intensified. Chapter 3 examines the last generation's solution to Virginia's decline. They called for reforms in Virginia character based on the model of the Christian gentleman, and in trying to live up to this ideal they engaged in benevolent campaigns across the state. Chapter 4 builds upon the previous chapters by focusing on how young Virginians could simultaneously see themselves as Virginians, Southerners, and Americans. Their disunionist activities are detailed in chapter 5. I also use this chapter as an opportunity to explain how the secessionist campaign resolved many of the internal dilemmas that had confronted the last generation in the 1850s. The next two chapters deal with the Civil War years. Chapter 6 discusses how young Virginians exercised authority as subordinate officers, and chapter 7 explains their transformation into Confederate zealots. In the final chapter, I analyze how these men drew from their antebellum experiences and reconstructed their identities as Americans.

It is important to clarify that this is a study about identity formation within the context of power relations in Virginia and the nation as a whole, but it is not intended to be a political history of Virginia. Members of the last generation were not prominent in partisan politics until Reconstruction. For most of their lives they were critical observers who often felt alienated from sources of

power and authority. Therefore, throughout the book I move beyond the cul-
turally descriptive to reveal how these young men challenged, accepted, or asserted authority within the grand political events of secession, Civil War, and
reunion. The book, moreover, is deeply concerned about how power operated
at a variety of levels—generational, gender, class, military, state, and national.
I also make no pretense that the last generation's experience speaks for young
people throughout the South. Coming of age in Virginia meant something
special in the 1850s, when a remarkable market and transportation revolution
altered the household economy. Market forces gradually shifted economic and
political power away from small rural communities led by a slaveowning elite.
In other words, structural changes in the economy weakened the ability of
households to restrict labor and its attendant social relations to the private
sphere. This initiated sweeping social changes that reconfigured gender, class,
slave, and age relations in the state. Many white males believed that slaves, free
blacks, and women had become unruly, and older Virginians were particularly
incensed by the "fastness" of young people.[15] The ensuing debate regarding
the last generation's proper place tells us a great deal about Southern identity,
secession, the Civil War, and Reconstruction in the Old Dominion.

The changes in the self-identities of the last generation cannot be understood
in isolation from power relations inside Virginia and within the nation at large.
In fact, their sense of being Virginian and Southern did not dictate the political action of these men. They constructed and remodeled ideas about what
it meant to be a man, a Virginian, a Southerner, and a citizen of the United
States in relationship to their membership in the South's ruling class and that
class's struggle to maintain economic and political power. The case study of
the last generation demonstrates that the search for a Southern identity can
become a pointless endeavor if one is simply trying to locate a distinctive set
of traits, habits, and values, or a mystical feeling of Southernness. Culture, as
David Potter rightly warns, does not equal nationality, nor can it offer a comprehensive answer to a critical line of historical inquiry: what has compelled
some groups of people to form a nation and then to go to war and die for that
abstraction? The experience of the last generation reaffirms Potter's indispensable argument that a feeling of oneness or imagining a shared identity within a
larger group is not sufficient reason for people to risk their lives for a political
cause or entity. Shared political and economic interests must be present, for
they knit together a wide array of local, regional, and national attachments into
a powerful expression of group loyalty. The experience of young Virginians

further supports Potter's important observation that loyalties and interests are constantly in motion, ebbing and flowing in relationship to the political currents and material conditions within a specific time and place.[16]

Any cultural identification that the last generation might have felt with the South in the 1850s did not well up inside of them and turn members of this age group into fiery radicals. In other words, a mystical feeling of Southernness did not animate their political acts. Only when the institution of slavery came under Republican attack did they call for Southern unity to defend the region's "institutions." It took an unmercifully bloody civil war to transform young Virginians into Southern nationalists — not because honor, manliness, race, or Christianity triggered such a response, but because they recognized that the very existence of the slaveholders' world was at stake. They explained secession and their extreme political devotion to the Confederacy through the language of honor, manliness, and Christianity.[17]

A generational approach also reveals how specific classes and age groups adopted their own particular ideas of Southernness to advance a variety of political and social goals. Because young Virginians came of age in the 1850s when the state underwent seismic market changes, their expressions of Southern identity originated within a slave society moving toward a bourgeois vision of progress. They called for an alliance with the rest of the South in the 1850s as a means of bringing intellectual and material improvement at home. For the state to gain recognition, young Virginians emphasized Southern interests and adopted a more extreme Southern point of view, especially when it came to educational and economic reform. This interpretation departs from most studies of Southern identity and nationalism, which focus almost exclusively on sectional issues or slavery.

In the end, the last generation's claims of being Southern should remind us that when looking across Dixie, the cry of Southern rights and Southern distinctiveness has had various meanings and political purposes. The story of the last generation demonstrates that the rhetorical shield of Southern unity encompasses a wide range of political interests, sentiments, and motivations. It also can be as much an offensive weapon as a defensive one to preserve and protect. In the case of the Virginians of the last generation, the language of Southernism simultaneously inspired admirable acts of progressive reforms and self-improvement and spurred them to fight to the death for a cause that was inescapably devoted to human bondage.

 **Progressives All**

· ·

How in the world can any man
read the history of these times
and subscribe to the theory of anti-
progress?—Lancelot Blackford,
Lancelot Blackford Diary

AFTER GRADUATING FROM THE University of Vir-
ginia in 1854, in his very first speech upon returning to his native King William County, William Roane Aylett proclaimed: "The mighty winds which
sweep by us on their way to distant lands tell us, at every blast and every whis-
per their moving principle is progress. And shall not we be governed by progress also [and] the law of nature and of God? Yes ladies and gentlemen," Aylett
averred, "it *must* be so."[1] Aylett and his contemporaries held an unshakeable
faith in progress's ability to improve man's material and moral condition. But
his sweeping endorsement of progress overlooked some hard questions: How
could Virginia pursue progressive economic, political, and educational reforms without sacrificing Christianity and slavery? What would prevent the
Commonwealth and the rest of the South from following the North into spiritual experimentation, radical egalitarianism, and an obsession with materialist
values? Virginia's move toward a diversified market economy and political
liberalism might even diminish slaveholder status and influence within the
South.

Only a few of Aylett's contemporaries probed these questions, and not a
single member of my sample group expressed concern about slavery's future
in a world driven by free-labor capitalism. Renowned intellectuals such as
John C. Calhoun, Thomas Roderick Dew, Robert L. Dabney, James Henley Thornwell, and Albert Taylor Bledsoe, on the other hand, warned of an
impending crisis in free-labor societies that would ultimately threaten lib-

erty and republicanism in the South.[2] When it came to the linchpin of their argument—that the South represented an alternative social system in which the laboring classes were subordinated, society was stratified, and an organic vision of mutual dependence and obligation bound all people—they exerted little noticeable influence on the last generation. Very few young Virginians made reference to this line of argument, and even fewer idealized the plantation economy as an organic, pastoral community. Slavery was so ingrained in their way of life that they rarely examined the institution as an abstract social system. Quite simply, their minds were just opening to the complexity of the problems to which Southern intellectuals had applied so much time and talent to unravel. When Professor William Smith of Randolph-Macon College asked Fredericksburg's Moncure Conway to name "the principle of slavery," the latter bluntly replied that "it has no principle." Smith was deeply disappointed with Conway's response and only wished "I had you in my senior class" where "I lecture on this subject every week." For Conway and many others in the last generation, slavery had always appeared "to be as permanent a fact as the Rappahannock River."[3]

Even though Conway and his contemporaries took slavery for granted, they never underestimated its value in their own lives and in those of other white Southerners. The status and authority of their families, not to mention the power of the region's ruling class, depended on its continuation, and they were understandably devoted to the institution. Why then did young Virginians move closer, in substance as well as style, to the bourgeois world even though they feared the immorality and "radicalism" that accompanied its advance? The material conditions in which these men lived changed in the 1850s, as the Old Dominion made unprecedented strides toward a market economy. Of all the sweeping changes, the movement of labor from the control of Virginia households to commercial agriculture, mining, railroads, light industry, and small businesses proved the most decisive. This structural shift sent tremors through the household economy and weakened its ability to restrict labor and its attendant social relations to the private sphere. Subsequent social changes reconfigured gender, class, slave, and age relations in the state, making the Old Dominion a decidedly less hierarchical place to live in—although it still remained, at the most fundamental level, a modern slave society committed to human inequality. In the end, these economic and social changes signified to the last generation the dawning of a new era, and the young Virginians were eager to push the Old Dominion to the head of the pack in the global race for progress.

Young Virginians did not applaud all of the changes that ensued, particularly the spread of mass democracy and the expansion of suffrage enacted by the constitutional reforms of 1850–51.[4] Despite their qualms about mass democracy, however, they generally welcomed any sign of the liberal, bourgeois spirit in their native land, and rejected any attempt to make Virginia into a reactionary, corporatist society. The influence of Whig political culture must have shaped the thinking of many young Virginians, even those who came from Democratic families such as Henry Clay Pate and John L. Buchanan, both of whom endorsed economic reforms that would have pleased the staunchest Whig supporter. Unfortunately, it is impossible to say how many young Virginia Democrats shared Pate's and Buchanan's views, largely because of the difficulty in establishing party affiliation for the vast majority of their peers in the last generation. It is striking, however, that so many members of the last generation articulated the principles typically associated with the Whig Party. Scholars generally agree that the Whigs were more cosmopolitan, more interested in economic development, and more inclined to support manufacturing. Although the Whigs collapsed on the national scene in the 1850s, the party survived in the Old Dominion. Ex-Whigs drifted to the Know-Nothings before turning themselves into the Opposition Party. Despite their diluted political presence in the state, it appears that the Whigs' ideological legacy offered young men, regardless of partisan affiliation, a credible economic platform that complemented their program of progress for Virginia.[5]

Young Virginians shared with free-labor societies a belief that progress represented an increase in material prosperity, individualism, and bourgeois liberalism. They championed economic development as the first step toward the promised land of progress. Like most Southern thinkers, young Virginians welcomed these improvements as long as they advanced in tandem with Christianity. "As soon as the doctrines of Christianity were brought to bear on society, moderating the passions of men," Richard M. Venable of Prince Edward County argued in the *Virginia University Magazine*, "this march was commenced, and it has gone on until liberty and order have become compatible, and will continue until *perfect* liberty and *perfect* order become compatible." Most of Richard Venable's peers would have agreed with his belief that anyone who tried to stand in the way of progress challenged the will of God. "This progress," Venable wrote, "although it may seem slow, is nevertheless inevitable, and whoever shall attempt to oppose it will reap his own destruction."[6] Venable, who survived the Civil War as a Confederate staff officer, believed it was impossible to separate moral and material progress. On this point there was widespread agreement between young Virginians and their fathers.[7]

These young men believed that they were coming of age when new and powerful forces had been unleashed in the world, creating a special moment in history when the possibilities of human endeavor appeared endless. Their concerns about the age of progress did not center on the potential radical effects that free-market capitalism and individualism could have on a slave society. Rather, the last generation appeared most troubled by those Virginians who were the enemies of progress. They derisively called their opponents "old fogies." Although this generational battle will be explored in the next chapter, it is worth noting that many young people embraced progress as a reaction to the ideas of old fogyism. This backward philosophy, the last generation charged, had kept Virginia out of touch with the demands of the modern world. In his 1851 University of Virginia thesis, J. Latane of Essex County determined that the old fogies were incapable of distinguishing between "immobility and stability," making it impossible for them to appreciate the universal truth that "immobility is antagonistic to progress." To prove this assertion, he offered a historical survey of the "Indo-Chinese world" in which he found that life had been stationary for centuries with no progress, no innovation, and no advance under the "great despotism of Asia." Latane concluded his analogy with a rather narrow interpretation of Chinese history and culture, but one he thought applicable to Virginia. "Their history like that of animals and vegetables is but the history of one generation — it needs but be written once." Latane worried that future Virginians would become mired in the deep ruts cut by previous generations if the Commonwealth did not open itself to change.[8]

The last generation's offensive against the old fogies and their excessive cheerleading for progress did not lead them to see man as morally perfect, and consequently they never flirted with any notion that smacked of egalitarianism. As Christians, they believed that man was born into sin, making him more than qualified to commit inconceivable crimes against humanity. The University of Virginia's James M. Boyd, the son of a Lynchburg tobacconist, rejected the charge that Catholic doctrine naturally bred corruption while other religions were thought to be immune from such evils. Any system or institution that bore "marks of humanity," he argued, was liable "to such a fate." Boyd shared with most Southerners a dark view of human nature that anchored a worldview committed to human inequality as an essential principle of any slave society. "If . . . meant by all men being born free and equal, . . .

[that] they are born with the same qualities and in the same condition, it bears an absurdity on its face," wrote a student in the *Hampden Sydney Magazine*. He concluded that "all men are not capable of attaining to or enjoying the same things, and no one can be said to have a right to what he is altogether incapable of attaining and unfitted for enjoying." Of a similar mind, Culpeper's Henry Coons suggested that "there are very few things which cannot be over done, or carried too far. . . . For we can go so far as to grant men rights and liberties which instead of doing them good will tend to lower them on the scale of enlightenment and civilization."[9] A tension existed within the minds of many young Virginians, as was true of most Southerners, in trying to explain the bright prospects for world progress when they considered man inherently sinful and believed, to varying degrees, in human inequality.

This belief in human inequality did not undercut the last generation's faith in the power of the individual as an agent of change. The idealism of youth, coupled with their elitist view of themselves as the "chosen" men in Virginia, encouraged them to embrace a powerful strand of individualism. This notion flowed into and strengthened their belief that civilization's advance ultimately resided in man rather than God. On November 23, 1857, Robert Taylor Scott confided to his fiancée that "it is a delightful thing to think we are in part the architects of our fortunes, that we are endowed with free will not the creatures of chance or subject merely to circumstances."[10] A few young Virginians, it should be noted, warned that a growing faith in science was deluding people to believe that man could unravel all of life's mysteries. Most, however, felt comfortable taking a seemingly contradictory position. They defended the supremacy of God's authority while asserting that an individual, not a higher power, determined the course of life. Those members of the last generation who rejected predestination took an important step toward the self, albeit they were inching their way toward that dominating individualistic spirit of New England and other free-labor societies. Their faith in man's moral judgment never reached Emersonian heights. Young Virginians wanted it both ways. They believed that their native land could retain its allegiance to God and hierarchy while creating an open society that celebrated individualism and intellectual innovation. Placing so much power in the individual had led to spiritual experimentation and other "radical" philosophies in the North. Awareness of these developments troubled the South's intellectual class, but members of the last generation avoided the logical outcome of their vision of progress and slavery.

Why then did these young men entertain an extraordinarily optimistic view of progress when the region's leading minds warned that disaster awaited any society that failed to rein in the excesses of individualism, materialism, and mass democracy? The Commonwealth appeared tired and worn out, physically as well as intellectually. The age of progress instilled in these young men a deep faith in the regenerative powers of youth. "Youthful ambition" and "youthful energies" would revive the state, proclaimed a Virginia Military Institute cadet in 1857.[11] Widespread agreement existed within the last generation that youth possessed the unique power to revive the state's intellectual and moral energy. Culpeper's Henry Wilkins Coons typified those members of the last generation who believed that the spirit of youth would reinvigorate old-stock Virginians. Leaving his father's plantation in Culpeper, Coons entered Richmond College in the fall of 1857. He remained there until the spring of 1860, during which time he penned a number of essays about the meaning of youth and its role in the future. Coons recognized that the habits he formed in school would follow him through life. He did not romanticize youth, bluntly acknowledging that "young persons generally prefer doing wrong rather than right."[12] Although Coons feared that the self-destructive genes of youth might be lurking in his own body, such knowledge did not make him fatalistic. The optimism and energy of his peers proved that the supposedly immutable laws of youth were false and that a person's place in life was not fixed. Coons, although no advocate of free-soilism, advocated a broad philosophy of social mobility for white men. Everyone except women and blacks should have a chance of rising up. Even if a young man lacked the advantages of a "higher birth" and wealth, Coons knew that he could overcome any obstacle with the proper habits. "Hence we see the importance of being diligent and dutiful while we are young," he concluded, "and by these means winning for ourselves a name which shall last us through life and still be remembered by men when we have departed."[13]

Coons's broader vision of the world elevated young people as the saviors of society. He wanted his peers to remember that in this "age of improvement . . . we are young Americans" destined to make a unique contribution to the Union. He could not imagine that "all the stars of America" had risen and refused to "depend upon those who are beneath the sod"; his generation should "seek to write our names even higher upon the mountain of fame than they did."[14] Joseph M. Logan of Emory and Henry College also thought that the future rested with his peers. The progressive spirit of the times empowered his fellow youth, and Logan noticed that many set off in the world without seeking guidance from above. They spurned "with contempt any compromise with the manners and customs of the past generation." Logan did not voice any complaints against a young man who "neither perceives any obstructions in his path, nor apprehends any difficulties to surmount."[15]

William P. Louthan of Winchester also agreed that a new generation could remake Virginia. In his master's thesis submitted to the University of Virginia in 1859, he described a new age dawning for his generation, a time in which youth would play a key role in advancing society toward the perfection of man. A glorious era of peace and prosperity would ensue, he believed, but this destiny could only be reached if every individual performed his assigned role in the advancement of society. While Louthan, who would become a professor at Richmond College just before the Civil War, placed his ideas within a hierarchical religious framework—always careful to acknowledge the importance of promoting God's glory first—he distanced himself intellectually from a world in which Providence controlled and manipulated human events. God remained the architect of the Universe, but humans functioned as the engineers who possessed the capacity to follow His blueprint to earthly perfection. Not all young Virginians diminished the role of Providence as Louthan did, but most were so enthused by the spirit of the time that they believed that God had empowered humans to storm every obstacle along the road to progress. The Civil War would shatter their faith in man's capacity to control his environment without divine assistance. When death and destruction suddenly filled their world, young Virginians found solace in the belief that Providence would preserve the righteous and strike in favor of the Confederacy.[16]

The last generation, it appears, also embraced progress with few reservations because they subscribed to an optimistic reading of world history. History imparted many somber lessons, and young Virginians knew that any nation would face an early mortality if it did not learn from past civilizations. Despite occasional relapses, the last generation thought history confirmed that human society was marching forward, an inevitable advance that would ultimately fulfill the promise of progress. The sins of an individual or the crimes of an entire people did not necessarily result in a society's demise. Young Virginians interpreted dark periods of world history as moments of purification. After studying the Crusades at the University of Virginia, for example, Albemarle's Robert Rives deemed the slaughter of thousands of Christians necessary and beneficial. Those who manipulated the Bible for radical purposes were deserving of death, even at the hands of the Muslims. "When we consider the character of the majority of those [Christians] that fell in this war, and reflect that they formed for the most part the very scum of society," Rives knew "it was surely at least a step towards a better state of things." Rives applauded the Crusades for ushering in a more enlightened age by stirring up and then eliminating "the corrupt state of society in the middle ages."[17] Rives believed that the Crusades, like every great human catastrophe, were temporary moments in history that cleansed society.

What could easily have appeared as an irreversible decline to some was often viewed by young Virginians as a springboard for the future. The advantage of hindsight, they argued, enabled each succeeding generation to learn the hard lessons of history, to become wiser, and to improve on the past. Though a number of young men cautioned that even the United States could suffer a collapse reminiscent of what happened to ancient Greece or Rome, they pointed out that they lived in a radically different world and were not vulnerable to the same vices, not burdened by the same depths of ignorance. Christianity and republicanism guaranteed world enlightenment. "To sum up the whole argument," concluded Leesburg's Powell Harrison in his 1855 thesis on the perpetuity of the Union, "we not only differ from those [ancient] nations from which the analogy is taken, but we are far superior to them, superior in morality, education, and refinement, superior in local position and form of government and finally superior in the fact that we have laid out before us the experience of all nations."[18] Sifting through the layers of history gave young Virginians irrepressible hope for the future. They realized that every generation improved on the work of its elders, infusing society with new ideas and a spirit of innovation that would result in a unique and lasting contribution.

More than any other factor, the bitter sectionalism of the 1850s turned the last generation into disciples of progress. In this acrimonious environment, young Virginians felt an intense desire to prove that a slave society could become a leader in the world of progress. They wanted to show that the Commonwealth's golden age, when economic prosperity and intellectual creativity flourished in the eighteenth century, could come again. It cannot be emphasized enough that the last generation came of age when the reputation of their state and region endured an intense and an unrelenting assault from outsiders. Northern charges of Southern backwardness struck the raw nerve of private assessment that often drove Southern men wild with rage and humiliation. Surprisingly, the last generation responded to outsider attacks in a composed and thoughtful manner. Some took the easy way out and simply claimed the moral high ground over the North as a land of radical "isms." But most looked inward and acknowledged the problems of their society. Significantly, they refused to invoke the cavalier tradition to justify their way of life. Such a shallow defense would have only confirmed the state's deficiencies in the eyes of the world. A more effective response, the last generation realized, must show that Virginia was preparing its citizens to compete in this new age of progress.

When Northern attacks intensified against the South, condemning everything in the region from slavery to speech habits, young Virginians felt an overpowering need to defend Virginia's honor. Antislavery agitators ridiculed Virginians as modern-day Don Quixotes who hallucinated about becoming chivalrous knights while economic and intellectual stagnation silenced their state's voice in the nation. *Harper's* contributor David H. Strother, "a Virginia Yankee," found the Commonwealth in a shocking state of disrepair. "I have myself considered the Old Virginia people as a decadent race," Strother opined. "They have certainly gone down in manners, morals, and mental capacity. There seems to be nothing left of their traditional greatness but a senseless pride and a certain mixture of dignity and suavity of manner, the intelligence of a once great and magnanimous people." Strother predicted that the Civil War would "wipe out this effete race" and give the Old Dominion "a more active and progressive generation." He expressed a basic Northern assumption that Virginia had fallen from national grace and become a decrepit, degenerate place. Members of the last generation also had to endure Northern attacks on Southern youth for their supposed violent manners, excessive emotionalism, and sterile minds. An intellectual firewall, outsiders charged, prevented young people from engaging in an open and free exchange of ideas. Without the air of academic freedom, Southern institutions of higher learning were little more than finishing schools for the pampered sons of the slaveholding class. After a Northern paper depicted student life at the University of Virginia in 1860 as a veritable orgy of sin and violence, a Charlottesville newspaperman responded in disbelief: "Our friends at the North seriously regarded it as a sort of lawless rendezvous, to which the young tyrants of the cotton-field transferred their unrestrained and ill governed passions."[19]

Northern criticisms forced young Virginians to confront the indisputable fact that Virginia lagged behind most states in the race for progress. They accepted the North's challenge without considering that the "spirit of the times" could result in the undoing of their own society. The last generation should not be criticized too hastily for its short-sightedness. Few people have the prescience to see the long-term consequences of their philosophy or actions. Although they were not intellectually lazy, young Virginians were naive. They glossed over the disastrous effects that a free-market economy and the rising tide of individualism posed to a slaveholding Virginia. Only a few members of the last generation fired a warning shot about seeking membership in a world obsessed with progress, but even then they were not concerned about the potential dangers to slavery or the demise of slaveholder power. They worried about how Virginians could join the crusade for progress without becoming soulless, practical people, indistinguishable from the stereotypical Yankee. A number of young people also feared that Virginians were trying to outdo Yankees at being Yankees. This vocal subgroup of the last generation denounced utilitarianism for suffocating imagination, stifling emotion, and preventing people from appreciating the beauty of life. Yet they did not associate utilitarianism with radical individualism or any other philosophy that might threaten the peculiar institution. In the *Virginia University Magazine*, James McDowell Graham, the son of a Lexington minister, lamented that young people were subjected to a scientific education that crammed their heads with mountains of dull facts. An indignant Graham could not understand why children's books "are no longer now the tales of fairy-land . . . but in their stead useful and practical lessons are conjured up for their amusement. This is but an example of the spirit of the age," he asserted, "which deifies the practical and useful, and wholly ignores the poetic and imagination." Graham understood this trend through the lens of sectionalism, blaming New Englanders for trying to turn Virginia into a sterile land devoted only to machines and profits. Instead of appreciating the intrinsic beauty of the state, Northerners "saw in Virginia only a magnificent water-power for turning wheels and driving spindles." This "pernicious philosophy" that reduced life to the cash nexus, Graham admitted, had infected some of his peers who wanted economic opportunity at home regardless of the cost.[20]

Even as the last generation's most outspoken critic of utilitarianism, Graham wanted his readers to know that he would not stand against the winds of progress. Such a gesture, he realized, would have been futile. Although it is tempting to see young Southerners as hopeless romantics, Graham and his peers recognized the hard reality of progress and the necessity of confronting, not escaping, this new world. Graham never evoked a pastoral landscape with knightly cavaliers who would turn back the clock to an insulated way of life. His prescription for the Commonwealth was to move forward, even if that meant risking the core values that had long defined Virginia as a civilized land. Graham never came up with a solution as to how young Virginians could preserve their unique sense of aesthetics. He weakly concluded that his peers should not cut themselves off from a past that had once made Virginia great.[21]

Henry Mason Mathews of Greenbrier County also worried that the quest for practical knowledge might annihilate man's capacity to appreciate the purer elements of life. Yet Mathews, who survived the war as a Confederate staff officer and would become governor of West Virginia, accepted the decline of fine taste and cultivation as an inevitable casualty in civilization's advance. In his 1854 University of Virginia thesis, "Poetry in America," he criticized his peers for their infatuation with science and technology and their lack of interest in literature and poetry. If his fellow Virginians were losing their love of fine arts, however, Mathews did not believe all was lost. His irrepressible confidence in progress enabled him to grudgingly accept the decline of poetry. Even if the arts were sacrificed on the altar of progress, Mathews held firm to his belief that the world was entering an epoch of vast improvement, a time when "civilized" notions of Christianity and republicanism would bring prosperity and peace across the globe. "Man's intellect is now developed," Mathews boldly concluded, "and whilst we may regret to see the art of poetry declining; . . . yet we know also that this very fact is an evidence of the continual improvement of the mind of man, and of the advancement of the world in the accomplishment of its destiny."[22] When forced to choose between preserving a sense of high aesthetics and progress, young Virginians such as Mathews were willing to take their chances with progress, even if that meant risking the mechanization of man.

What does the last generation's campaign for progress ultimately say about their loyalties to Virginia, the South, and the United States? It would be ridiculous to claim that young Virginians challenged the intellectual hegemony of the proslavery theorists and theologians. Young and old subscribed to the fundamental principles of slavery, but many elder Virginians worried (with just cause) that members of the last generation were recklessly lobbying for progress without considering its dangerous effects on the "peculiar institution" and other sources of authority. Young Virginia loathed abolitionism, but it is crucial to note that they did not believe that this radical movement was a direct outgrowth of progress or endemic to a free-labor society. Rather, young Virginians explained abolition as a perversion of the mind and heart. Moreover, they wholeheartedly agreed with the region's intellectual class that the South was a distinctly Christian society pitted against a radical and godless North. The message of Southern moral superiority and Northern depravity resonated with the last generation and gave them a strong sense of regional identity, but it cost the South's intellectual class dearly. Instead of seeing the potentially lethal consequences that progress posed for a slave society, young

Virginians were supremely confident that the uniquely religious nature of their civilization would forever serve as a bulwark against the wild and unpredictable forces of progress.[23]

The widespread acceptance of progress among the last generation also attests to the beginning of a convergence of the antebellum Southern mind with its bourgeois Northern counterpart. This was a glacial move in intellectual thought, but one with powerful consequences, as it would prepare young Virginians for the demands of the New South. To varying degrees of intensity, members of the last generation embraced a fundamental principle of all free-labor societies: that the source of society's improvement and knowledge resided in the individual. Yet these same young men rejected the extreme individualism of the New England Transcendentalists because it elevated the Self above God as the arbiter of moral truth.[24] As long as the presence of Christianity was felt, the last generation possessed a nearly unshakeable faith in the powers of man. As Carter Louthan bluntly put it in the *Virginia University Magazine*: "The watchword of man is 'onward and upward,' and God has given him power to storm every bastion."[25]

How did this intellectual wrangling over progress play out in the lives of young Virginians away from the classroom and debating halls? Lynchburg's Lancelot Blackford makes for a valuable case study. Blackford's writings reveal the dilemma of his generation: young people were caught between two competing cultural forces. As a member of a prominent Virginia family, Blackford undoubtedly felt a desire to be a part of the dominant slaveholding class. The most important and influential people in his society owned other human beings; that was the inescapable reality of the last generation's existence. As a young man trying to find his way in the world, Blackford aimed for community respect and status that could only be fulfilled by becoming a member of the slaveholding class. Such a yearning pushed young Virginians like Blackford inward toward a more traditional version of Southern culture, one that valued owning land and slaves, acting on community obligation, and achieving a life of aristocratic ease. Blackford and his peers also felt the outside pressure of a transatlantic Victorian culture that accompanied the advance of free-labor capitalism. As a result, they craved bourgeois respectability, hungered for professional success, and desired the material trappings of a middle-class lifestyle. While these goals were not inimical to a slave society, it is significant that young Virginians believed that their aspirations could only be fulfilled if the Commonwealth developed a diversified economy, rather than languished in one based on slavery alone.

Lancelot Minor Blackford (1837–1914). Blackford shared his age group's enthusiasm for material progress, writing in his diary: "How in the world can any man read the history of these times, and subscribe to the theory of anti-progress?" (From John Hampden Chamberlayne, *Ham Chamberlayne — Virginian*, ed. C. G. Chamberlayne, 1932)

In *Leisure and Labor* (1858) artist Francis Blackwell Mayer contemplates the meaning of the cavalier in Virginia. The last generation was also moved to critique the state's aristocratic traditions within the context of a slave society moving ever closer toward a bourgeois world of progress. (Courtesy of Corcoran Gallery of Art, Washington, D.C.)

It appears that Blackford envisioned Virginia's moving away from the dominant plantation economy as part of the state's rebirth as a progressive society. Such a transformation, he and other like-minded youths believed, would again make Virginia an intellectual leader, an innovator, the admiration of the world, just as the Old Dominion had been during the Revolutionary era. But neither Blackford nor his peers fully appreciated the role of slavery in Virginia's Golden Age in the mid-eighteenth century, nor could they fully divorce themselves from that intellectual and religious heritage. There was no way to break away from the traditions of their elders or slavery, even though they held the "old fogies" responsible for the state's decline.

Blackford typified his generation by paying little attention to those who warned of the dangers of progress. "How in the world can any man read the history of these times," he scribbled in his diary on March 23, 1855, "and subscribe to the theory of anti-progress?" Blackford also raved about any sign of the modern spirit appearing in Virginia.[26] He took a deep interest in the technological inventions of the time, routinely informing his diary about the completion of new railroads near his Lynchburg home, the opening of mechanical fairs in Richmond, and the construction of gas works, telegraphs, and other modern conveniences. At an early age, Blackford tinkered in a laboratory constructed by his father, the editor of the *Daily Virginian*, Lynchburg's leading paper. His intense fascination with science and the mechanical arts did not exclude other interests. When he was not playing with test tubes and beakers in his chemical playground, Lancelot spent much of his time in his father's well-stocked library. Before his seventeenth birthday, he had read Caesar, the *Aeneid*, the *Bucolics*, Cicero, Livy, Tacitus, and Herodotus. Like so many of his peers, Blackford found nothing incompatible between his deep love of the classics and his desire to acquire and spread scientific knowledge.

Blackford worried at times that his fellow youths cared only for the practical, but he never feared for the master class's authority in a utilitarian age. Any concerns that he entertained about the spread of utilitarianism were cast aside in favor of the economic development of Virginia. Whenever Blackford encountered improvements in the state, he interpreted such innovations as tangible proof of recovery. After visiting an 1854 exposition in Richmond, he proclaimed that Virginia contained some of the leading progressive minds in the country. "The first feeling that thrilled my breast on entering the grounds (comprising I was told, nearly 20 acres), was State pride," wrote Blackford. He almost could not believe the fair was "the product of the energy and industry of [the] Old Dominion alone." "If the *men* of Virginia had much to be proud of in the Exhibition," Blackford concluded, "the *women* not less so, for really it seemed to me that the tent for 'Domestic Manufactures' was worthy of attention in the whole Fair."[27] Blackford's diary entry reveals the tangled relationship between honor, progress, state loyalty, and personal identity. Blackford's self-worth and reputation hinged on the creative genius of his fellow citizens and their ability to make a unique contribution that would bring the glow back to Virginia. While historians now understand how honor commanded Southern allegiance to the institution of slavery and often encouraged twisted, Faulknerian behavior from whites in everyday life, the experience of the last generation reveals that this same ethic could also drive Southerners to crave bourgeois respectability.[28]

Blackford, furthermore, did not mourn the passing of Old Virginia with its insulated agrarian life and its aristocratic pretensions of ease and refinement. Like his peers, he embraced the possibilities that the age of progress might bring to Virginia. He shared his generation's ambition for the state to rank among the most progressive societies in the world. The optimism that pervaded young people, however, created unrealistic expectations in their own lives. When they faced life away from home for the first time, their abstract ideology confronted the material reality of daily life. They quickly discovered that their hopes might not be attainable in the Old Dominion. Their ensuing struggles reinforced the belief that something had gone wrong in Virginia, because the once formidable state could no longer provide for its young people.

**United by a Problem**

. . . .

My native state seems to be doomed
to the rule of enemies of progress.
—Henry Clay Pate, *The American
Vade Mecum*

IN THE SUMMER OF 1850, after two promising years
at the University of Virginia, Henry Clay Pate of Bedford County packed his
bags, withdrew from school, and left for Kentucky. His desire to go west arose
out of financial necessity, not a spirit of youthful adventure. After reaching
Louisville, Pate dabbled in a variety of careers that eventually led him to Cincinnati. Two years later, he pulled up stakes again, heading to Missouri where
he remained until the outbreak of the Civil War. When he was not fighting
John Brown in neighboring Kansas—which nearly resulted in his death after
he fell captive to the fiery abolitionist—he found time to write and publish *The
American Vade Mecum; or, The Companion of Youth, and Guide to College*. In
this slim volume, Pate paid tribute to the University of Virginia for producing
well-educated Christian gentlemen. Unfortunately, the Old Dominion struggled to retain this rising generation. Many graduates were leaving for distant
lands, continuing a destructive pattern of out-migration that had plagued the
Commonwealth since the 1830s. With the best and the brightest fleeing the
state, Pate could not dispute the popular notion that ignorance and economic
neglect had rendered the Old Dominion obsolete. Virginia, he sadly admitted,
was on the decline.

Pate, however, refused to blame young people for the state's sagging reputation. Responsibility rested with Virginia's governing class for allowing the
glow of the Old Dominion's distinguished past to blind them to the future.
In *The American Vade Mecum*, Pate asked his readers to take their blinders
off and see the unlimited possibilities for developing the Commonwealth into
a leader of progress. To make this argument, Pate recounted a recent trip

Henry Clay Pate (1832 – 64). Like many of his peers, Pate was disillusioned with Virginia's political class because of its failure to develop the state's resources and keep pace with the progressive spirit of the times. Pate, who had fought against and was captured by John Brown in Kansas, also blamed the North for inhibiting the South's economic development. He was killed in 1864 in a cavalry battle outside Richmond. (From *A Guide to Virginia Military Organizations, 1861 – 1865*, comp. Lee A. Wallace Jr., 1986; attributed to the Illinois State Historical Society)

through western Virginia that took him into the heart of Appalachia. Wherever he looked, he saw the wasted potential of the state—towering stands of trees waiting for harvest, rich veins of coal in need of mining, and powerful rivers to make steam. Taming nature, Pate believed, would bring civilization to the locals. These roughnecks could have become respectable citizens generations ago, Pate claimed, if only the Virginia legislature had pursued internal improvements with sufficient vigor. Negligence could be seen in the wretched appearance of the people, who obviously lacked "an enlightened spirit of enterprise." Pate, who would give his life to the Confederacy in an 1864 cavalry battle outside Richmond, felt a mixture of humiliation, anger, and sadness after his foray into the wilderness. Yet he remained hopeful about the future. In the western part of the state, with its abundant resources and energetic citizens, he thought that "Old Virginia" could transform itself into a "seat of wealth and learning." "But my native state," he harshly concluded, "seems to be doomed to the rule of enemies of progress, who say daily—let us rest at our ease, and live upon the glory of departed ancestors. Must it be thus forever?"[1]

The debate about the state's future absorbed much of its energy from private issues rooted within the changing material conditions that young people confronted in 1850s Virginia. The traditional routes to becoming a head of household through slave ownership and farming were closed to most young people as the state's economy endured a market revolution. As a result, the rules for achieving professional recognition, social respectability, and manhood were changing in the Old Dominion. Economic gyrations unleashed social consequences that left members of the last generation confused as to how they should establish their own households and gain recognition for themselves.[2] In searching for a sense of purpose in their lives, young Virginians came together as an age group by participating in a highly public debate over the meaning of progress in the Commonwealth. Their elders dismissed the political voice of these young people as a problem of youthful exuberance and immaturity. Undeterred, young Virginians furthered their cause by employing the language and ideas of Southern rights to prove Northern exploitation and to show that the Old Dominion's regional leadership would be at risk until economic reforms were enacted at home. In the race for progress, members of the last generation discovered a unifying mission that they believed would rejuvenate their native land while giving them the reputation of the state's saviors.

Young Virginians coalesced as a generation around a central issue: why had

Jubal Anderson Early (1816–94). Early was a quintessential "old fogy" who opposed many of the economic reforms that young Virginians embraced in the 1850s. After the Civil War, Early spearheaded the Lost Cause movement and sparred with members of the last generation over their easy acceptance of the New South creed. (From *Photographic History of the Civil War*, ed. Francis Trevelyan Miller, 1911)

Virginia declined materially and lost its influence in the Union since the Revolution? Instead of attributing the state's loss of stature to impersonal economic forces, as previous generations had done, young Virginians blamed the leaders of their parents' generation for failing to embrace the idea of progress and all of its trappings: railways, telegraphs, turnpikes, market relations, and limited manufacturing.[3] They reserved their harshest criticism for "old fogyism," an explanatory device that underscored the backward nature of Virginia's political class without identifying party affiliation or specific individuals.[4] In the eyes of the last generation, men of this intellectual persuasion had prevented the state from reaping the economic and intellectual improvements of the progressive age, which had resulted in a shameful loss of prestige in the Union. It should be noted that there were even plenty of older Virginians, such as Matthew Fontaine Maury, whose vision for the Old Dominion coincided with that of the last generation.[5]

To the old fogies, young Virginians appeared foolish and intellectually immature for entertaining such utopian dreams, but they refused to single out individual young people for their unqualified support of progress. The old fogies attacked the prophets of progress for their supposed unthinking endorsement of change. Jubal Anderson Early, a slaveholding Whig from southwest Virginia, was a quintessential old fogy who defended slaveholder interest at any cost, even if that meant turning back the clock in the Old Dominion and resisting any kind of progressive reform. "I am afraid that the spirit which is now evoked," Early wrote, "is an evil spirit, and that, if we follow its lead, we will rush upon our own destruction." He scoffed at the refrain that Virginia was "behind the times," reminding the voters of Franklin, Patrick, and Henry counties that "every innovation is not reform—every change is not improvement." James Massie made a similar argument when speaking to the Alumni Association of the Virginia Military Institute. He praised slavery for promoting conservatism in society and regarded people who indiscriminately lobbied for reform as dangerous fools. It "is a mistake to suppose that *progress* necessarily involves cardinal change. Change is the child of error, like Death or Sin; progress is development, enlargement, growth."[6]

Many young people saw in the words of Early and Massie a pernicious philosophy that had brought stagnation and embarrassment to Virginia. A quick comparison with the North revealed a relative scarcity of railroads, canals, and light industry in Virginia. Worst of all, the paltry sum devoted to education by the legislature attested to the state's backwardness. Members of the last generation could not tolerate such humiliation. They had been told from an early age that the Old Dominion possessed a natural right to lead the nation. These men refused to sit back and relinquish a privilege that had been earned by their Revolutionary forefathers, even if that meant a confrontation with their parents' generation for holding back the reins of development. Their condemnations of the old fogies upset generational relations, even though young Virginians, in their complaints, showed restraint and respect for age. They refused to name a specific person or political organization as responsible for

High Bridge, near Farmville, Virginia. This magnificent engineering feat was constructed in 1852, part of a railroad boom that consumed Virginia in the decade before the Civil War. Many members of the last generation seemed to downplay such impressive accomplishments and focused, instead, on the fact that Virginia lagged behind the rest of the nation when it came to economic development. (Courtesy of U.S. Army Military History Institute, Carlisle, Pa.)

the state's demise. Employing old fogyism as a rhetorical device thus camouflaged individual sin, making it possible for young people to contest adult authority without appearing to be brazen rebels. A Hampden-Sydney student expressed his grinding frustration in terms that could never be construed as slanderous or personal. He wrote in 1859 in the college's magazine: "There is an amount of old fogyism amongst us that is absolutely appalling." Why it took "a generation for a canal to get to Buchanan" and another "twenty-five or thirty years to construct a railroad from one end of the State to the other," he could not understand.[7] It should be remembered that not every father of the last generation was an old fogy, but virtually every old fogy was an elder Virginian. Men who fit into this category came from Democratic and Whig ranks and resided in all parts of the state, but they never organized formally or became a political force in the Old Dominion.

Despite the moderate approach of young people, their elders perceived them as being arrogant, rebellious, and disrespectful of authority. The charge was not entirely unfair. The most outspoken members of the last generation boldly proclaimed that their generation was more perceptive than past ones. To the Jefferson Society at the University of Virginia, William Roane Aylett announced that this is a "strange age in which we live—an age in which each succeeding generation is wiser than its predecessor." The message was clear: those waiting in the wings of power should assume leadership positions without delay, meeting Virginia's urgent need for an infusion of new talent. In his 1855 master's thesis on the effects of utilitarianism on literature, Gray Carroll boasted that his generation included "thousands of well educated men . . . in comparison with the hundreds, who [a] few years ago, were blessed with the merest rudiments of education." Considering this rise in intellectual power, Carroll proclaimed that "the indefinite development of man's powers is now no longer doubted." In their daily conversations, students often spoke of their readiness to take on the world. An editor for the *Virginia University Magazine* heard a number of his classmates, some as young as nineteen, complain "of being too old to be at college—they are too old to learn."[8]

Older Virginians, even those who were not quintessential old fogies, took offense at the intellectual arrogance of young people. In front of the Virginia State Agricultural Society in 1855, Franklin Minor questioned the aims of the last generation, even though he feared that he would be labeled anti-improvement for such a stand. The ranting of these young men in favor of advancement convinced him that Virginia might not be "progressing in the right way." While they relentlessly lobbied for innovation and change, Minor thought "it might be well to stop, if we could, and inquire, whither this mighty wave of physical progress is driving us—whether to the haven or the maelstrom." He wondered if the bridges to orderly progress had been burned by young Virginians. "The steam is up, the station house is passed, Young America is aboard," Minor exclaimed, "may heaven defend us from a smash." In this upheaval of generational power relations, he detected the beginnings of a dangerous trend. Minor predicted, rather sarcastically, that the future children of the last generation would refuse birth unless given the opportunity to vent their opinions inside the womb. "I pray you gentlemen," Minor concluded, "in this age of physical progress, look well to the early nurture of your sons and daughters, for it may come to be your last act of control over them."[9] Older Virginians like Minor mocked the intellectual capacity of young people and portrayed them as irreverent upstarts. They described the politicization of young people as an attack on adult authority and family values.[10]

The attempts to shame the last generation did not keep its members in their proper place. In response to their critics, young Virginians countered with the argument that the Commonwealth's declining fortunes could only be understood by looking to the past, where the decisions and actions of those who came before were decisively felt in the present. They pinpointed the origins of the decline to the passing of the Revolutionary generation. A new class of men assuming power in the 1830s had allowed the "mother ship" to fall into such disrepair that she was no longer seaworthy. The time had come, young Virginians believed, to confront the older generation, to make their elders see that Virginia had been left behind in port while other states in the Union explored uncharted waters, bringing fame and opportunities for people of all ages. Henry Smith Carter, while attending Emory and Henry College, savaged his elders in an 1854 article published in the *Southern Repertory and College Review*. Carter, a native of Russell County in southwest Virginia who would die in 1859, believed the situation demanded brutal honesty. He told his peers that shame had found a home in Virginia, that its prestige had been squandered by a pack of bloated aristocrats who cared more about appearance than achievement. "How instructive, yet painful, to compare the results of the collected wisdom of our multitudinous Legislature—in this age of progress, in the full meridian blaze of science both physical and political"—to the accomplishments of the Revolutionary generation. Such an inquiry, Carter hoped, would reveal that lesser men now commanded the state. With this indispensable knowledge, young people would awaken from their slumber to "unfurl the banner of revolt against our rulers."[11]

The rage that Carter and his contemporaries felt for the state's leaders can be traced to a general disillusionment with party politics. Although most of these young men identified strongly with their families' respective political traditions, they suffered a crisis in faith that transcended narrow party affiliation.[12] James DeWitt Hankins detested the demagogues who he believed had infested the system. He feared that they would satisfy their ambitions at the cost of the Union. A weary Hankins, tired of the wrangling over slavery, could take no more, and he informed a friend in 1860 that "I belong to no party because I think corruption and rottenness may be found in all now in existence."[13] Most young Virginians agreed with Hankins that a failure of leadership existed at all levels of government, but they generally would not take the extreme step of breaking with the political loyalties of their families. The uneven results of state-sponsored internal improvements in Virginia and scandals in President James Buchanan's administration confirmed fears of corruption among the public servants in their fathers' generation. The last generation perceived politicians as spoilsmen who were content to betray the interests of Virginia and the South for personal gain. When they formed their political identities in the 1850s, many young white Southerners had already shifted their loyalty to "the antiparty diatribes of the fire-eaters" and "stood largely outside the national political culture." George C. Rable argues that the demand to cleanse party politics "further weakened the bonds of Union" among Southerners whose "ultimate nightmare was that the corruption, which had so tainted the Northern states and the national capital, would overwhelm Southern liberty and honor."[14] Southern politicians and newspaper editors cast Northern politicians as heathens who recklessly abused their powers in Washington while Southern leaders carried the mantle of the noble statesmen. Virginia's Edmund Ruffin, for instance, declared in 1857 that "as a body, the majority of the northern members of congress are as corrupt, & destitute of private integrity as the majority of southern members are the reverse."[15]

Members of the last generation did not absolve their fathers' generation from responsibility for the highly partisan spirit of national politics, nor did they forgive them for the rise of professional politicians who groveled for votes from the white masses in their own state. Popular elections were essential to the democratic process, but true republicanism should neither cater to majority rule nor promote the interests of the majority at the expense of others. "It is this battling, this *warring*, this STORMING of parties," John L. Buchanan wrote bitterly, "that tends to work the masses of the people into a rabid multitude —an infuriated mob—in whose hands their own welfare cannot be trusted."[16] Buchanan, a resident of southwest Virginia and the son of a landowner with extensive holdings but no slaves, appears to have been an extreme advocate of social hierarchy. While he distrusted a political class that catered to the whims of the masses, he also loathed pompous Virginians filled with "self-love" and blinded by arrogance, who looked down "upon the common herd and their do-ings with inexpressible scorn and contempt."[17] No matter how much he feared the excesses of mass democracy, Buchanan was not a political or social reaction-ary. He resembled most of his peers in wanting a society open to talent and a political culture free from squabbling and interest-driven factions, one in which virtue and intelligence would earn a candidate public office. A purer form of republicanism appealed to the idealistic hopes of the last generation, for this idea neatly fit within their broader vision of Virginia as a more open society.

The belief that party politics was a corrupt failure in the Commonwealth reinforced the last generation's perception that Virginia's leadership had al-

lowed the state to fall behind in the race for progress. The technological innovations and economic advancements that had transformed Northern society
during the 1850s filled them with envy. Virginians were supposed to lead,
not follow, and the loss of prestige was seen as inexcusable. An editor for the
Virginia University Magazine wished "that some of the spirit of sister States
could be infused into Virginia to lead her to develop all her resources, and
become first in the march of progress and richest in material glory, as she is
richest in the glowing memories and reminiscences of the past."[18] The need
to develop Virginia's resources during the 1850s seemed even more urgent to
young men who visited the North and saw various modern improvements.

While a student at Dickinson College in Carlisle, Pennsylvania, William
Kinzer was struck by the differences between the two regions, confirming his
belief that the Old Dominion was materially deficient. During the election year
of 1856, he attended a number of political rallies where he heard Republican
diatribes against slavery that were so offensive to his sensibilities that he often
left the meetings in a rage. The antislavery message of the Republican party,
although appalling to Kinzer, did not lead him to an unthinking rejection of
everything Northern. A reflective and thoughtful young man, Kinzer enjoyed
the solitude of long walks to commune with nature. During these frequent
hikes, he sorted out the various personal and intellectual problems typically
faced by young college students. He confided in his diary that the landscape
had a magical effect on him, physically and spiritually, making him feel at
peace with God. Even when surrounded by some of the finest farmland in the
country, he found that the trappings of progress vied for his attention. During
one of his trips, Kinzer spotted for the first time a wire fence — something he
had "often read of . . . but had not seen any before." He was also struck by the
"durable houses," "substantial barns," and "finely cultivated farms." When he
returned to his dormitory room, he sat down with his diary and poured out
his feelings about Virginia's decrepit condition. He wished that "the people
of Va. would cultivate their farms more and better, and educate their sons and
daughters, like the people of Pa." Kinzer eventually left Dickinson and continued his education in his native Montgomery County, located in southwest
Virginia, where he studied law under James Francis Preston. Unable to secure
enough clients, he tried his luck in the Nebraska territory. The outbreak of
war brought Kinzer home, where he enlisted in the famous Stonewall Brigade
and served until he was captured at Spotsylvania on May 12, 1864. Less than
three months later, he died at Point Lookout Prison in Maryland.[19]

Those who never ventured above the Mason-Dixon Line often learned of the North's dramatic progress from newspapers, journals, and traveling friends and relatives. After seeing several exhibits at a mechanical fair in New York, Charles W. Turner's father wrote to his son that Americans "are a great people," and then confessed with much regret that Virginia had contributed little to the country's material advance. "*I am almost led to fear we are so far outstripped as never to recover,*" he admitted. Turner's father, a prosperous slaveholder in Goochland County, encouraged Charles and those of his generation to "cast behind the feeling of despondency" and infuse Virginia with a spirit of innovation and progress. "I would have all of you remember," he concluded, "that a part of this is your work and prepare for it."[20] Turner's message was also heard in the classroom. Matthew Fontaine Maury, the famous Virginia scientist and naval officer, pleaded with the young men at the University of Virginia to avoid simple answers to the seemingly insolvable problem of the state's decline. The popular notion among young people that the state's leaders lacked virtue and were badly out of step with the times disturbed Maury. Making reckless accusations drained mental energy from the issue at hand: how to transform the state into a progressive land where steam, the railroad, and the telegraph would enable Virginians to surpass the North.[21]

Admiration for Yankee ingenuity did not absolve the North for trying to suffocate Virginia's economic life. Young people did not believe that the state's leaders were entirely responsible for the Commonwealth's woes. They connected the state's defects to how outsiders had capitalized on them. In other words, self-critical commentaries on partisan politics and the old fogies intersected with the popular notion that Northerners had conspired against Virginia and the South. Many young Virginians charged that the state's rulers had allowed the Yankees to exploit the Old Dominion's economic resources and, in the process, had eliminated opportunities for the young. Henry Clay Pate was amazed that Virginia's leaders "have so long submitted to a foreign commercial monopoly." He touched on what his contemporaries considered the most damning evidence of misrule in Virginia: honorable, intelligent men would not allow Virginia to become helplessly dependent on the North. Pate estimated that the Old Dominion annually lost more than a million dollars to New York merchants in tobacco alone. "The longer we submit to the blasting monopoly of northern merchants," he sternly warned, "the more difficult will it be to cast off the yoke of oppression under which we live." To his mind, this issue epitomized the unfair trade practices committed against his people and accounted "for the little advancement made by the state of Virginia in those movements which have placed other states so much in advance of her."[22]

Pate's theory drew from an accepted assumption among all Virginians that the parasitic tactics of Northern merchants had created an exploitative, colonial relationship with the Old Dominion. The problem was simple: agricultural products grown in Virginia soil were being transported to Northern markets and manufacturing centers where they were converted into finished goods that Virginians bought at inflated prices. In the process, transportation costs drained money from the state, undermining investment and diversification. Writing in the college's magazine, a student at Hampden-Sydney concisely summed up the dependent nature of the South's relationship with the North: "In commerce, in finance, as well as in literature, the South, while possessing all the requisites to render her superior, has . . . occupied a position of comparative vassalage to the North."[23] As Virginia neared the sectional crisis of 1860, Republican and abolitionist tirades against slavery seemed to confirm the last generation's argument that the North intended to undermine the South's economy and dismantle its power base in the Union, keeping the region in a perpetual state of economic and political subordination.

Severing the colonial relationship with the North could not be achieved by young men who stood, for the most part, outside the state's circles of power. Such limitations, however, did not stop young people from forming a political voice. They informed Virginians of Yankee injustices without calling for secession or endorsing the extreme demands of Southern fire-eaters. In student university publications, speeches at literary societies, and other public addresses, the last generation called for the "home production" of textiles and other goods, a movement that was energized by John Brown's raid in 1859. In January 1860, an editor for the *Hampden Sydney Magazine* described "a high state of excitement with indignation towards our Northern people, for their perverse meddling with our domestic concerns." He also encouraged women to discard Northern dresses and wear only those made on Virginia looms. Another Hampden-Sydney student wrote a few months later that there was "an awakening of the people" to "develop our own resources" and "not expend a single dollar" for any article that cannot "be made at home." While young Virginians probably did little to alter the buying habits of their fellow citizens, the home production movement made these young men recognize that their agenda to develop Virginia could be furthered through the language of sectionalism and the framework of Southern interests. This vital intersection of state and regional interests paved the way for them to imagine Southerners as a distinctive people with their own agenda.[24]

The last generation may have been particularly sensitive to the state's economic struggles as they were encountering their own challenges in making the transition to adulthood. Paying for higher education stood as an almost insurmountable hurdle for most young Virginians. Even though many families of the last generation were socially prominent, they could not withstand the financial demands of college. At the University of Virginia, each class cost twenty-five dollars, and a student had to attend at least three. Additional money went to the library and infirmary, contingencies, boarding, washing, and fuel. In 1860, the total cost for the nine-month session amounted to $423.50.[25] If parents could not foot the bill, it was not uncommon for a young man to attend school for one or two years before taking a sabbatical to earn money elsewhere, typically by teaching at a private academy. Lancelot Blackford endured a number of unwelcome interruptions while studying at the University of Virginia in the late 1850s, and similar dilemmas disrupted the lives of many of his peers. "I am much obliged to you for your sympathy in my plans for College next session," he wrote to a cousin. "I anticipate a year there with much pleasure, and then suppose I shall be off again to make money to go back again and finish." Many young Virginians like Blackford worked their way through college or borrowed heavily from a local benefactor. Their connections to the state's planter class did not always result in a free ride. When the war forced W. F. Shepherd to pay off his student loans, he turned to a wealthy neighbor and slaveholder. "You are doubtless aware of the circumstances of my father . . . knowing that he had a large family to support, as well as educate, and being unwilling to permit him to furnish me with means any longer, . . . I resolved to attempt to borrow money, educate myself, and then work to repay it." "Therefore," Shepherd concluded, "knowing you to be a man of means, and well aware that you were always disposed to aid the needy, when you saw them endeavoring to aid themselves, I have determined to ask your assistance."[26] Young Virginians were resourceful, self-reliant, and committed to improving themselves through education.

Yet, some members of the last generation refused to make sacrifices for education and felt entitled to financial assistance. Complaints about the scarcity of tuition money could lead to confrontations between sons and fathers. When Richard Hobson Bagby, the son of a Powhatan farmer and teacher, insisted that he be allowed to attend college because his older brother had enjoyed the privilege with all expenses paid, his father called him "a *poor, niggardly, ungrateful, idle, do nothing*" son. The younger Bagby could not "refrain from tears" after reading his father's stinging rebuke, "just because I have found out my poverty and don't wish to be any poorer." Richard resented his father for saying that "it would take all my negroes to graduate me in medicine" when not a single slave was sold to send his brothers to college. As the youngest child, he always believed he should be "provided for" because he "had not the same advantages with the others, which you know Pa I have not had."[27]

Despite his angry tone, Bagby confined his response within the parameters of patriarchy. He never questioned his father's authority as head of the household and made it clear that "I know my age." His first duty rested with his family, not himself, wrote Bagby, who assured his father "that you shall not suffer for anything as long as I can work and can have God as my friend." He would continue to solicit his father's advice, as "I have always been thankful for it and ever will be." "Dear Father," he respectfully concluded, "I am willing at all times to do as you say." Bagby and his contemporaries stopped short of open generational conflict when it came to private matters. Parental expectations still steered the actions and goals of members of the last generation, who placed tremendous pressure on themselves to live up to their parents' hopes and ambitions.

At college, young Virginians were groomed to become the state's next generation of leaders. Prominent politicians, intellectuals, theologians, and scientists frequently spoke to student organizations about the last generation's unique responsibilities to Virginia. The flagship of the state's educational system, the University of Virginia, advertised itself as the training ground for the next Washington, Madison, or Henry. Lofty expectations reinforced the popular idea among members of the last generation that a higher mission awaited them.[28] They imagined themselves making a triumphant return home, running their own households, and becoming beloved and respected members of the community who would move Virginia forward. The image of the benevolent planter working for the common good and loved by all of his "dependents" was not empty of meaning for young Virginians. From their youngest days this ideal had shaped their understanding of what it meant to be a man. Yet, as they neared graduation, their dreams were punctured by the reality of adulthood. They discovered that the traditional path to slave ownership proved difficult. Quite simply, limited options and few opportunities existed for young people to buy property. A statistical survey of the sample group's occupations reinforces this observation. Among fathers of the last generation, 42 percent were identified as farmers, but only about 7 percent of the sample group of young Virginians followed in their fathers' footsteps. It should be noted that many of the men who were students could have engaged in agricultural pursuits once they left the university, but war interrupted their career plans. Nonetheless, it is striking that a vast majority of the last generation left the farm for other professional pursuits.[29]

Without control of a household, young Virginians found themselves in a subordinate position with seemingly no way out. This clashed with an upbringing that instructed Southern boys that men of their class must live on their own and command others. Even before James DeWitt Hankins completed his first year at the University of Virginia in 1860, he decided to leave the state for Helena, Arkansas, where he envisioned a thriving law practice and community acclaim. Any self-respecting young man who wanted honor, Hankins explained to his father, must depend solely on his own "resources" and "native talent." Hankins believed that his energy would be wasted at home. Many of his college friends had already established contacts in Arkansas, agreeing with Hankins that adult life in Virginia would only lead to debt and humiliation. Insurmountable obstacles, they understood, made it impossible to fulfill the "natural" role prescribed for young Southern men.[30]

For those who remained in the state, the frustrations of establishing a career coupled with youthful impatience took a psychological toll. While trying to sort out his options from the University of Virginia in 1854, Philip Cabell envisioned a triumphant return to his native Nelson County, where he would care for his loved ones and earn the respect of his community. "I want to come home & *work, work, work*," he wrote during his second year of school. From the time he was a boy, he had imagined a life as a farmer, and his academic courses were only getting in the way of his aspirations. Cabell recognized that if he suddenly left school he would not be able to get even "ten acres of land & one *nig* to work it." Without making some money first or marrying "a girl with a pocket full of rocks," he resigned himself to heading West. Returning home, Cabell realized, meant dependence on his father and the degradation of "working for him rather than myself." He hoped that his family would understand that he might leave for a distant land and try to make it as an engineer.[31]

When the ambitions of youth crashed against the rocky cliffs of adulthood, young men like Cabell could not reconcile their expectations with reality. To make matters worse, a confusing transition to adulthood caused emotional turmoil for these men that often lasted well into their mid-twenties. Without a recognizable age that marked the rite of passage to manhood, young Virginians needed independence to secure adult status.[32] Control of a household and power over dependents, the very badge of manhood, eluded most members of the last generation. Only fifty-one out of 121 men could be located on the 1860 census. This is a paltry number that would indicate that few young Virginians had become heads of household. Even more telling is the fact that nearly 24 percent of the sample was composed of professionals—lawyers, physicians, and teachers—who were still living at the family home even though they had established careers.[33] Public recognition also came through marriage, but before the war most of these men were unable to forge romantic relationships that led to the altar. Only 18 percent of the sample ($N = 44$) were married prior to 1861.[34] Without a wife, young Virginians would have had difficulty finding validation and the sense of mastery that they so badly craved.

Young Virginians nearing graduation wondered if they would inevitably follow previous generations into a humdrum life of obscurity. Hanover County's Charles Stringfellow sensed that many of his fellow students at the University of Virginia felt the inescapable "promptings of youthful ambition, and the desire to engage in the more real struggles of the great world." After the first encounter with the real world, Stringfellow knew that "this dream of youthful hope" will "be sadly dispelled." "Most of us must rest contented," he grimly concluded, to "discharge the duties in incident to the positions in which we may be placed."[35] Stringfellow's words became a self-fulfilling prophecy as soon as he left the University of Virginia in 1858. During the next three years, he followed a random pattern of employment as a teacher and lawyer that forced him to move, with great frequency, between Washington, D.C., Richmond, and Petersburg. He could not find that profitable career that would enable him to establish a household and begin a family. The Civil War finally brought an end to his vagabond existence.[36]

Without sufficient land or financial backing, an overwhelming majority of the last generation had no choice but to consider the professions of law, medicine, business, and teaching. Sixty percent of the sample, led by lawyers at 29 percent and followed by teachers at 27 percent, chose occupations in those fields. Students were tied with teachers as the second largest category, and upon graduation these young men would have discovered professional career paths, particularly the law, hopelessly clogged with older and more experienced men.[37] Members of the last generation endured extended periods of doubt and conflict in trying to discover their calling. They wondered if Virginia society afforded a suitable place for them. Simply following in the footsteps of their slaveholding fathers was no longer an option. In 1850, James E. B. Stuart entered West Point, hoping to find direction to his life. As a youth, he had witnessed his father's struggles as a farmer, even though the senior Stuart owned more than twenty slaves in the hills of Patrick County.

By the late 1840s, his father spent less time overseeing his fields and more time in politics and the law to support the family. While a student at Emory and Henry College, where Jeb once accidentally fell off a stage while trying to impress a young woman with his oratorical skills, he realized that he had arrived at a crossroads. Bewildered by the lack of options and having nowhere to turn, he summed up the dilemma facing most of his peers in the 1850s. Farming was not a realistic course, the future cavalry chief of the Army of Northern Virginia wrote, because "that always presupposes the possession of a *farm*," which was not "practicable" for a young man to purchase when he had not had time to accumulate capital. Stuart saw no choice but to "adopt one of the *hireling* professions as Law Medicine Engineering & Arms." He complained that a lawyer or physician "*seldom* receives his fees," and that an engineer "must first have a reputation before he can get desirable employment." Stuart concluded that the life of the "bold Dragoon" was for him, in part because there was "something in 'the pride and pomp and circumstance of glorious war.'" Few of Stuart's contemporaries had the luxury to follow romantic dreams in the military, but they did share his sense of generational martyrdom due to the lack of opportunity in the Old Dominion. Exclusion from positions of authority not only diminished the status of young people in the state; it also made members of the last generation feel trapped between adolescence and adulthood.[38]

College graduates possessed a classical education that made law one of the few viable options in an economy that needed more engineers and businessmen than slaveholders and gentlemen lawyers. Those who tried to establish a practice engaged in a fierce competition for cases offering meager financial compensation. Youthful hopes and idealism quickly gave way to cynicism. "I have been pretty well occupied but have no new business since I wrote," Robert Taylor Scott of Warrenton informed his fiancée in 1860, "[and] am of the opinion *the young lawyers* do not stand much chance of improving their practice." Even though Scott, who would survive Pickett's famous charge at Gettysburg, worked under his father, who was well established and respected in Warrenton, he still believed that younger men "must serve our apprenticeship longer and grow older in the profession ere we can obtain the confidence of the people, who dispense the patronage." After attending Hampden-Sydney and the University of Virginia, Lawrence S. Marye of Fredericksburg made a similarly gloomy assessment of the profession. He wrote in 1856 that "I expect to go to Richmond the first of January, to put my *brilliant* legal candle under a bushel, and bury myself in the clientless shades of a law office." "Young attornies [*sic*], by scores, go there & do nothing," he added, "but each thinks, at first, that he is to be an illustrious exception. And I, as a matter of course, am fanning this credulous hope in my *heathen* heart." In the *Virginia University Magazine*, Richmond's Hodijah Lincoln Meade sarcastically suggested that a young man should form a partnership with an eminent lawyer but be prepared to find that "he will seldom let you enter his thought, or trouble you with his society." "Be content," Meade concluded, "to wash his dirty linen and survey daily the workings of his gigantic mind."[39]

Virginians like Scott, Marye, and Meade, although deeply worried about the state of their own personal affairs, also realized that they perpetuated an employment pattern that mortgaged the state's economic future. In an 1852 commencement address at Randolph-Macon College, the speaker announced "that the supply of politicians, attornies and physicians, is greater than the demand." This imbalance, he argued, undermined the state's prosperity and caused young people to rejoice "in the words, 'Westward ho,'" instead of the "better sentiment of, 'Oh! carry us back to old Virginia.'"[40] In his senior address at the Virginia Military Institute, Alfred H. Jackson believed the "fashion of the day" was to go out West, a destructive trend that he wanted his fellow graduates to break. He suggested that "Virginia's sons ought to stay at home and take care of her interests." "In the dark days of the revolution," when Virginia's "misery could not as now be summed up in a beggarly account of dollars and cents, but was written in the blood of her children," Jackson concluded, the Founders did not "leave the land of their adoption." Jackson implored his fellow cadets to "let the history of our whole country answer the question, and bring the blush of shame to the cheek of him who would leave the old State in the hour of danger."[41]

Most members of the last generation sided with Jackson, but a small subgroup envisioned their future in the Southwest and acted upon those dreams. Only eleven out of a sample of 121 men elected to leave Virginia.[42] Thomas G. Pollock typified those who sought their fortunes outside the Old Dominion. Returning to his home in Warrenton after graduating from the University of Virginia in 1859, he practiced law under the shingle of his relative Robert E. Scott, whose son's career was also in its formative stages. Competition between the two young men forced Pollock to rent his own office, but he could only attract small cases that proved unprofitable. The county already had a number of established lawyers who "had the peoples' business in their hands."[43] Frustrated and impatient to fulfill his aspirations, Pollock removed himself to Shreveport, Louisiana, in the fall of 1860, where he reported to his mother that "it is the proper place for me I am satisfied—and as I always understood—the only difference between it & Warrenton is in the amount & nature of the legal business." The most striking difference, Pollock noted, was the preponderance of young men occupying the bar in Louisiana. Rather than being parvenus, they were "educated gentlemen—polished & refined in their manners & dress." He assured his mother that if his cousin moved to Pollock's new community, he would find "more substantial rewards for professional labor & success" than he could in Virginia. When the Old Dominion seceded, Pollock returned to his native state, served as a Confederate staff officer, and suffered a mortal head wound during Pickett's Charge. His body was never recovered.[44]

Westward migration increased resentment between young men and their elders. Hill Carter of the older generation understood why it was "a strong temptation to a young man living on a poor farm in Virginia" to leave for the fertile lands of the Mississippi Valley. But if "the same man," Carter predicted, had lived, saved, and worked "the same way in Virginia," he "might increase his wealth perhaps just as fast, and *die rich, too.*"[45] Before the literary societies at the Virginia Military Institute in 1854, B. J. Barbour told the cadets: "To all those who complain that within their own State they have no opportunity to rise, I am ever disposed to repeat the caustic reply once given to a young Virginian. He was asking an old gentleman just returned from the West, if he saw any opening for a young man of talent. 'Sir,' was the appropriate answer, 'there is an opening for a young man of talent *everywhere.*' "[46] Both Barbour and Carter spoke for many older Virginians who believed that what the Commonwealth needed most was for its best, brightest, and most talented young people to remain at home.

The young men who sought their fortunes elsewhere angered many older Virginians, who could not understand why members of the last generation demanded reform at home but fled west as soon as they met the slightest difficulty in establishing a career. Young people were blamed for contributing to Virginia's demise, the very charge that they tried to pin on the old fogies. The last generation must have bristled under attacks such as the one delivered in 1857 by the influential Robert Lewis Dabney of the Union Theological Seminary in Richmond. Dabney complained in the *Central Presbyterian* that a "melancholy state of affairs" in Virginia had benefited outsiders who "perpetually act upon the supposition that every efficient man among us must of course be anxious to get away." Dabney wanted to disabuse young people of the notion that "the way to be honored *in* Virginia is to go *out* of it." He reminded the last generation, as well as older Virginians, that when looking above the Mason-Dixon Line, "you found no flocks of New England youth migrating to Southern or Western schools." Every young Virginian who enrolled in Princeton or Yale, Dabney charged, was "practically asserting the worthlessness of similar schools at home."[47] While most young people agreed with Dabney that Virginians should receive an education at home and live in the state, they wanted older men to recognize that economic conditions would have to change in order for this to happen. Blaming young people for the flight of the state's young talent deflected attention away from the misrule of the old fogies. Members of the last generation wanted accountability from the state's leaders, not excuses made at their own expense. Older Virginians were understandably weary of the cry for reform from those who would not pursue a livelihood in the state. In their disgust, they overlooked the fact that most members of the last generation did remain in the Old Dominion during the 1850s, only to face slim prospects of earning a respectable living.

Dismal economic prospects intensified the last generation's sense of unity while increasing tension between young and old. Many parents, ministers, and editors showed little empathy for the last generation's plight, blaming unbridled ambition and the desire for fame for leading young men astray. Most young people, although at times enamored by the allure of fame, never seriously considered immortality a realistic goal, many felt they had no other option but the law or politics. A student at the University of Virginia agreed with his elders that "many young men are wasting the vigor and strength of their youth, in the profession of the Law," yet he resented the adult charge that young people flocked to the bar in order to spend their time "in inglorious ease." The idleness of young men stemmed from the simple fact that "they are *young*, and the world is unwilling to trust in youthful hands matters of moment, when there are older and wiser heads to do it."[48]

As this student suggested, accusations that the last generation only desired fame and notoriety actually revealed more about the sins of the old than it did about the defects of the young. Long before the arrival of the last generation, Virginians had acquired a national reputation of seeking fame at any cost. Older Virginians must have wondered if the young had inherited this debilitating trait, for they implored members of the last generation to exorcize it. The state's elders tried to maintain their position of moral authority over the young by reworking the last generation's calls for progress into problems of maturity. Matthew F. Maury, widely respected by the last generation for his advocacy of economic development, explained to an 1855 audience of University of Virginia students that young people were foolishly drawn into the vortex of politics, where they became "whirled and turned hither and thither to their great detriment."[49]

Youth cultivators and parents frequently reminded members of the last generation of their "spiritual" connection to Virginia's Revolutionary heroes and challenged them to prove that they were worthy heirs of this legacy. In the process, they sent a conflicting message to young Virginians. On the one hand, they wanted young people to achieve something of lasting value that would rival what the Founding Fathers had done. On the other, they did not want ambition to consume young people in a quest for fame. In the *Christian Intelligencer*, published in Charlottesville, an unnamed youth cultivator feared a "hidden potency" that he believed was concealed in young men. These "natural" tendencies, coupled with a desire to emulate the Founders, might lead them to lose their souls to an insatiable drive for individual accomplishment and accolades. This same writer pleaded with the last generation to exhibit the "patriotic virtues" of George Washington and the eloquence of Patrick Henry, and to shun the "polluted altar of passion" that would lead a young man away from God and cause him to "sink to degradation and death." "As I raise these great queries," the author concluded, "I at once do reverence to the high paternity of his nature, and tremble for his fate."[50]

Maury and the writer from the *Christian Intelligencer* agreed with many older Virginians that young people possessed a dangerous character flaw: an aversion to manual labor and practical pursuits. The possibilities of earning easy wealth and quick fame through law and politics seduced too many young men. In an 1853 issue of the *Southern Planter*, prominent Tidewater slaveholder Willoughby Newton complained that agriculture had failed to captivate "the imagination of youths" who left "the seminaries of learning . . . with a determination to carve their own way to fame and fortune." "They press into professions," he explained, "already crowded to suffocation, or try their fortunes in the precarious trade of the politician." Following "the progress of the army of aspirants that have left our colleges in Virginia during the last thirty years" would be "an instructive, though a melancholy lesson" for the state's young men, Newton believed. He wondered how many had "fainted by the way-side" or "turned their backs upon their native homes" to seek their fortunes elsewhere. In reprimanding young people for their poor work ethic, an adult speaker at the Virginia Military Institute acknowledged this long-standing flaw among Virginia men: "I hope and believe that the day of morbid thinking and miserable working is past—that the time is at hand when the youths of Virginia will deem it no degradation to earn an honorable independence in the cause of their State by the strength of their own good right arms—will believe that idleness is not meritorious, and labor not humiliating."[51]

Public criticism must have agitated members of the last generation as they tried to find their way in the adult world. Yet such harsh remarks did not turn them into unthinking hotheads. A few young men even concurred that too many of their peers had become recklessly confident because of the spirit of the times. Without seeking the advice of their elders, young people plunged into life not knowing the depth of the water. "Young America is afflicted with such an exceeding longing to begin the struggle of life that he is too impatient to prepare himself well for it," John H. Chamberlayne complained in his 1858 master's thesis at the University of Virginia. Instead of consulting the "old masters," he charged that "every boy of twenty fancies that he is able to solve the great problem of life, and he is eager to rush into the fray; neither knowing, nor caring for, the lessons which, if he would but take time, he might learn from the experience and the wisdom of the past." The promise of fame and the lure of money, Chamberlayne believed, had resulted in a dangerous lack of realism among many of his peers. These reckless and ill-prepared youths left college early, entering the world "blessed with the boldness which ignorance alone can give."[52] Chamberlayne stands as the most extreme critic of his generation, but his willingness to engage in self-evaluation was not uncommon among his contemporaries. Ironically, in the aftermath of Lincoln's election, Chamberlayne exclaimed that he would not trust the judgment of any man over twenty when it came to the question of secession.

Adult criticism of the last generation's work ethic drew from the stereotype of the lazy Southern youth who was depicted as an architect of grandiose schemes, lacking common sense and determined to squander the family's money. Some older people chastised their sons for vices viewed as defects in the Southern character since the American Revolution. This popular image was frequently used in the North to dismiss the South as a wasteland. Ironically, older Virginians also played upon this image to avoid responsibility for the state's woes.[53] Old fogies (as well as other Virginians who were more progressive minded) used the state's agricultural journal, the *Southern Planter*, to expose the sins of the young. Lewis Livingston (probably a pen name) dissected the concerns of elder Virginians in a mock letter to "Christopher Quandary," a prototype of the last generation who had recently graduated from college and was in the process of squandering the estate he inherited from his father. Pursuing Don Quixote–type dreams, living extravagantly, and lacking rigorous work habits had placed Quandary in a bad situation. Livingston reprimanded the young man's decision to destroy his father's home because it was "deficient in elegance and taste." Construction of a new building and the purchase of the finest New York furniture overloaded Quandary with debt. "The comfortable house in which your father died, might, you thought, do very well for an 'old fogey' like him, but was wholly unfit, as you believed, for 'Young America,'" Livingston disapprovingly wrote. "You have certainly made considerable 'progress,'" he added mockingly, "but whether or not in the right road is exceedingly questionable."[54]

Livingston's critique of the last generation reveals a series of interconnected points of conflict between young and old in 1850s Virginia; these generational tensions never erupted into open warfare but had important ramifications for how young men identified themselves as men, Virginians, and Southerners. In the eyes of their elders, members of the last generation were perceived as pampered, self-indulged children of privilege who cared only for style and appearance. The rush toward professional careers, particularly the law, signified to many older folks that young people were not practical minded, that they were too lazy to get their hands dirty, and that they cared only for fame and accolades. Members of the last generation, on the other hand, believed that they had no choice but to pursue careers away from the farm. With little or no capital to purchase land and slaves, their options were limited to jobs suited for Virginia's increasingly market-driven economy. On leaving college, however, many floundered in careers monopolized by older, more established professionals. Others turned to low-paying teaching jobs at private academies. Becoming the head of a household did not come easy, if at all, for most of these young men. Their personal frustrations and failures took an exaggerated form because they believed that they lived in a time of unlimited material progress. Everything they read attested to the fact that the rest of the world was scaling new heights at lightning speed and reaping the seemingly unlimited rewards of progress. Yet they encountered stagnation and limited opportunities at home. The last generation interpreted personal difficulties in establishing careers as a larger problem that could be traced to Virginia's political class. The leaders of their parents' generation responded by suggesting that the state's supposed decline stemmed from issues of morality tied to the temperamental emotions of young people.

Many young Virginians did not remain complacent in the face of such accusations. They took the offensive against the state's leaders, revealing in the process their own vision of the Old Dominion as a modern slave society, one that showed little concern for the future of the peculiar institution in a world that was moving toward free labor. The need to earn a reputation and to have full status as adults encouraged these young men to believe they could gain prominence within their own communities by transforming Virginia into a progressive land. Young Virginians refused to wait for others to induce this historical moment. If their stodgy fathers stood in the way, they would instigate change—even if it meant facing adult resistance at home.

Members of the last generation found it necessary to achieve honor for the Commonwealth if they wanted honor for themselves. In their minds, these goals were inseparable. Their crusade for progress at home, moreover, linked them to the broader cause of Southern interests, as many young Virginians called for development as part of the campaign to achieve regional economic independence. This desire to surpass the North in material and intellectual achievement also intensified their drive to stop Virginia's decline. Such a mission gave young Virginians cohesiveness as an age group while instilling in them a fierce loyalty to their native land. Devotion to their state and the dream of resurrecting Virginia made them more receptive to the idea that the Old Dominion's future resided within the collective efforts of her sister Southern states. It did not, however, lead to an extreme position on Southern rights. More than anything else, members of the last generation understood that reform at home depended on a change in character, that the state would only be remembered for what it had done during the Revolution unless young Virginians redefined what it meant to be a man.

Christian Gentlemen

· ·

Let the youth of our land be ambitious.
—Henry Clay Pate, *The American*
Vade Mecum

ONLY A FEW MONTHS SHY of his seventeenth
birthday in the summer of 1857, Alexander "Sandie" Pendleton worried about
Virginia's future. That July, he unburdened himself at Washington College's
commencement. Pendleton warned that the Commonwealth was losing its
reputation as the "choicest region of the globe." He located the problem not
among his peers but among established leaders, because they failed to live as
Christian gentlemen. Pendleton insisted that a loss of character had caused
Virginia's tailspin. Undoubtedly shocking the older folks in the audience, he
boldly commanded: "Witness the wasted energies and undeveloped resources
of our noble state, and the backward condition of her improvements, and let
warning be taken for the future."[1]

In addressing the problem of Virginia's decline, Pendleton framed the discussion of old fogydom within the context of Christianity, the cavalier tradition, and the historical memory of the Revolutionary era. Republicanism,
Christianity, and the "high-mindedness" of the Founders, he believed, had
created Virginia's unique "ancient character." It was this "inner spirit" of old
Virginia that had elevated the Commonwealth to greatness during the eighteenth century, but he feared that many of the state's leaders were no longer
in touch with this "ancient character." Pendleton suggested that this apostasy
had demoralized Virginia's political class and that the rest of the state had
subsequently succumbed to a debilitating lethargy of aristocratic ease. Many
citizens used traditional Virginia hospitality, Pendleton insisted, as a shameful
defense of "wastefulness, luxury, and indolence." These habits must change
if Virginians were to meet the challenges of the progressive age. He declared
that the moment had arrived for the Old Dominion to regain its title as the

"mother of Christian gentlemen." If "her sons of this and coming genera-tions" upheld "her ancient character," Pendleton assured his audience that they would remedy "the mistakes that have retarded her progress."[2]

Pendleton asked his contemporaries in the last generation to embark on a civic mission to simultaneously revive and revise Virginia character by reject-ing the cavalier for the Christian gentleman.[3] Pendleton was asking the im-possible. The cavalier tradition derived its form and substance as a model of manliness from a Christian slaveholding tradition and ethic that blossomed in eighteenth-century Virginia.[4] This cultural and intellectual heritage had shaped the thinking and behavior of their parents. Young Virginians, however, looked past their parents and found the "proper" representation of manliness in their grandfather's generation. Yet Pendleton realized that reconnecting to the "inner spirit" of Virginia's golden age would not in and of itself rescue the state's reputation. He knew that the Commonwealth needed a new personal-ity in order to compete in the world of progress. A disillusionment with party politics, limited career opportunities in Virginia, and Northern criticisms of Virginia character encouraged many young people to question inherited tradi-tions, particularly the model of the cavalier, which they considered a laughable symbol of the Old Dominion's irrelevance in the world. In a review of St. George Tucker's *A Tale of Bacon's Rebellion*, an editor for the *Virginia Uni-versity Magazine* thought he uncovered "the true reason" why authors from the Old Dominion languished in obscurity—they had glorified Virginians as cavaliers. "We have followed too long an old school, which the age is ceasing to relish; because we have imitated Sir Walter Scott too much."[5]

Members of the last generation developed their sense of self from Virginia's Revolutionary past, but they also looked outside the state's borders and tapped a more bourgeois style of manliness. This model took the form of the Chris-tian gentleman, an ideal that called for discipline, education, duty, and moral purity. Although such an ideal had guided the behavior of slaveholders for generations, young Virginians broke, to varying degrees, with the concept of obligation and reciprocal duties by insisting that a Christian gentleman must follow his personal ambitions. But no matter how hard they tried to invent a Virginia man who could meet the challenges of the progressive world, mem-bers of the last generation would always be pulled back to the traditional world of plantation slavery. Paternalism defined the master-slave relationship, and this concept also shaped the last generation's understanding of the Christian gentleman. It demanded reciprocal duties between master and slave while encouraging members of the ruling class to live their lives with a sense of duty, gentleness, and Christian civility. Many young men fell short of this ideal, but as Eugene Genovese correctly points out in regard to the idea of Southern chivalry: "That the practice of an ideal need not follow its preaching goes without saying, but only extraordinary naivete could dismiss the effect of the ideal on the lives of the men, high and low, who aspired to fame or simply to think of themselves as decent."[6]

Young Virginians confronted a practical predicament in their crusade to restore Virginia's ancient character. They were supposed to respect adult authority and follow the teachings of their youth, but at the same time they did not want to cast themselves in the same tired and worn-out mold of their fathers' generation. Young Virginians tried to escape this dilemma by turning the Revolutionary heroes into Christian gentlemen who had achieved the proper balance between individual ambition and religious duty. Washington, Jefferson, Henry, and others earned immortality for their high-mindedness and lasting contributions to the improvement of their state and country. Virginia's great men, the last generation believed, earned their reputations through action, drive, and intellectual creativity, rather than by pursuing a life of aristocratic ease. Through an imaginative revising of the values of Virginia's Revolutionary past, members of the last generation legitimated a version of masculinity that they believed had a decidedly more modern orientation than the cavalier outlook that they considered the hallmark of their parents' generation. Transforming Virginia's Founders into Christian gentlemen also made it possible for young Virginians to sincerely claim that they were loyal, dutiful sons who were simply following the models of their youth. Yet, even in their most reverent expressions of loyalty to Virginia's distinguished past, members of the last generation criticized their fathers' generation for a lack of ambition.[7]

They criticized their elders for a variety of sins, but the most serious crime was for a Virginian to misconstrue aristocratic ease as a sign of success.[8] Such thinking, many young people charged, accounted for the lack of enterprise in the Commonwealth. They traced this defect in Virginia character to the message of their youth. Members of the last generation were told as children that they, of all Americans, possessed the strongest link to the Founders. As much as young people were captivated by such an alluring idea, they also recognized that this notion legitimated the aristocratic belief that blood ties determined greatness. They objected strongly to the popular notion that reputation came from family connections alone. What about intellect, energy, and an individual's moral bearing? An obsession with bloodlines had incapacitated many old Virginia families, leaving them with memories of greatness while their farms fell into disrepair and their wealth melted away.

The rising generation imagined a society less concerned about bloodlines and more open to men of merit. Lynchburg's William Blackford articulated what many of his peers sensed — that Virginia had entered a new era, leaving behind the old world in which family prestige, social graces, and the appearance of refinement largely determined social status. From his observations of the economic life of southwest Virginia, a region bustling with activity in the 1850s, Blackford discovered that wealth defined the "aim of all," even if it meant sacrificing the "softer parts of our nature." In a letter to his mother, he praised those "young men of talent" who aspired to "thrift" above all other habits. Blackford also noticed in such a fluid community that "it makes not the *slightest* difference who a man is, what he is or where he came from so [long as] he has money." His mother challenged her son's perspective, decrying what she called "the worship of the golden calf." An age gap, Blackford perceived, accounted for their different perspectives. "Your tastes were formed in a community where wealth had long since been familiar and where it was not so eagerly sought after," he wrote on May 8, 1853. In his mother's generation, the "criteria of merit" depended on refined manners, a distinguished bloodline, and an intellectual bearing that could only come from classical training at private academies and universities. Now, Blackford suggested, the marketplace was the arena in which a young man, through sustained effort, practical knowledge, and hard work, could amass wealth and secure status.[9]

The image of the cavalier must have seemed a ridiculous anachronism to young men confronting an economy on the cusp between plantation agriculture and a mature market economy. Although there was a degree of unity on this point, there is no discernible pattern within the last generation as to what prompted particular men to criticize the cavalier model. Young people from all regions of the state and backgrounds spoke against the model while calling for reforms in Virginia's character. In the *Southern Repertory and College Review*, the literary publication of Emory and Henry College, Henry Smith Carter of southwest Virginia offered one of the most scathing attacks to come from the last generation. He simply considered the state's leaders a moral disgrace. Corrupted by "luxury" and "power," they had allowed "*Shame*" to find a home in Virginia, a state once "blessed of heaven, and . . . adorned with every virtue." When confronted with the tragic results of their misdeeds, Carter claimed that the politicians scurried for shelter under the "delusive mantle of vain-glory . . . that we are Virginians, emulous of extravagance and folly, servile to the mutations of taste and to fancy's fickle promptings." Carter, who despised mass democracy, was equally hostile to a decadent aristocracy whose parasitic rule, he believed, had sapped the moral and intellectual energy from the Old Dominion, making it possible for the proud state to be passed over in the march to modernity.[10]

The sons of Tidewater planters joined their western peers in denouncing anyone who sought a life of aristocratic ease. As the son of a prominent King William County planter, William Roane Aylett enjoyed all the privileges of the affluent life. He received the finest education available at local academies before graduating from the University of Virginia in 1854 with diplomas in French language and literature and in moral philosophy. Aylett was one of the few members of the last generation who became a farmer before the war, managing the family plantation, "Montville," and opening a successful legal practice as well. During the course of his academic training, Aylett borrowed heavily from Jeffersonian thought when he argued in his literary society that "the only true dignity and honor of life is in labor—that an idle man violates his own law and the law of nature." He knew of many lazy men in Virginia who squandered their lives by living off the reputations of their illustrious ancestors, never making an effort to build on the past deeds of family members or their accumulated wealth. The tendency among Virginians to tolerate a wasteful man as long as he possessed money or was of high birth particularly disturbed Aylett. He reminded his peers that many farms, once prosperous and a tribute to generations of hard-working family members, often ended up in the hands of strangers. Negligence forced the dissipated owners to sell their "broad acres." Not only had wealth disappeared because of aristocratic pretensions and dissolute habits, but in the process family honor had also been tarnished and lost forever.[11]

Those who believed that the First Families of Virginia had given birth to a special breed of grand cavaliers sent young people into convulsions of anger. Some members of the adult community sanctioned the last generation's hostility to the cavalier by admitting that Virginians had a "natural" tendency to see themselves as gallant cavaliers when in reality they were nothing more than indolent aristocrats. Addressing a group of William and Mary students in 1855, Richmonder Hugh Blair Grigsby demolished the cavalier model as a "miserable figment" that had deluded generations in the Old Dominion. An honest appraisal of the past, he explained, would reveal that Virginians had descended not from the "soft hands" of the cavalier but from England's wretched poor, the very "bone and sinew" of the Anglo-Saxon race. He bluntly told the young men that their ancestors "owed no obligations to the cavalier." In 1854, the students at Hampden-Sydney College invited a Petersburg resident, identified in the newspapers as Mr. Van Zant, to deliver the commencement address for the Union Society. Van Zant used this solemn occasion to roast Virginia's aristocrats. Some members of the audience must have grown restless when Van Zant made "a good deal of fun" of the First Families of Virginia for valuing bloodlines over achievement. Why Virginians believed "the blood" of this proud lineage coursed through their veins remained a mystery to him. Such pretensions had resulted in a loss of "higher virtues" and "restless energies." The Old Dominion needed a transfusion of new ideas and habits, and once this happened, Van Zant predicted that Virginians would be "relieved from our inferior position."[12] The message of Van Zant, Grigsby, and other youth cultivators must have encouraged young people to scrutinize adult behavior. Furthermore, both Van Zant and Grigsby spoke to the students as a distinct age group that faced its own challenges and duties. They pushed members of the last generation to interpret society's problems through the lens of age. Quite a few young people reached the obvious conclusion that the Commonwealth needed a revolution in behavior if the state were ever to enter the modern world.

Members of the last generation struggled to reconcile the cavalier tradition with the age of progress. Despite their disdain for the cavalier model, which glorified the Virginian as a pretentious oaf, they saw in the ancient knight—the original model for the cavalier—Christian values they would not sacrifice. The words of Van Zant and Grigsby prompted some young people to question why so many other older Virginians had claimed the cavalier as a distinct hallmark of the Old Dominion when it made the state appear ridiculous to outsiders. For many of these young men, the cavalier increasingly represented an anachronism of waywardness, extravagance, and slothfulness. No matter how loud they protested, however, members of the last generation remained tethered to the cavalier idea, for it originally stood for the virtues of Christian gentility—the very heart of the last generation's vision of the Christian gentleman. The last generation put a modern spin on the cavalier as an ideal. Only hard work, thrift, piety, and education promised to bring to the surface the "noble" qualities of Virginia chivalry. On those rare occasions when young people commented on the cavalier tradition, martial skills and bodily strength were significantly absent from their descriptions, further proof that members of the last generation did not delude themselves into believing that they were fierce warriors or gallant knights defending primal honor. In-stead, they emphasized how chivalry demanded that men respect women, protect the weak, and comfort strangers. In an 1851 article entitled "The Age of Chivalry," a University of Virginia student suggested that "love was as marked a feature in . . . [the cavalier] as valor." Another University of Virginia student conceded that chivalry could be "converted into extravagance and ridiculousness," turning men into embarrassing re-creations of Don Quixote. For the "gentleman of our day," however, he thought it offered the perfect blend of "tenderness and courage." Chivalry, in other words, humanized men. Truthfulness, generosity, and high-mindedness embodied a chivalrous man, qualities that this same writer admired as "the noblest qualities of [the] human heart."[13]

This commitment to the chivalric gentleman as a standard of behavior also shaped their historical memory of Virginia's Revolutionary heroes. They con-sidered these notable Virginians the pure embodiment of intelligence, nobility, and virtue. Significantly, young people did not see the Founders' greatness as originating within an idealized plantation setting. Members of the last gen-eration preferred to portray the Founders as men driven by ambition, guided by moral discipline, and born with a creative genius that enabled them to be visionaries. Surry County's James DeWitt Hankins captured his generation's perspective on the Revolutionary heroes. Like most mid-nineteenth-century Americans, he expressed a deep reverence for the Founders but also felt an intense pressure to surpass their achievements.[14] What draws notice about Hankins and many of his Virginia peers is the celebration of personal ambi-tion as the most admirable trait in Virginia's heroes, one deserving of emula-tion. Such a perspective clashed with that of the South's intellectual class, who wrote eloquently and sincerely about the need for reciprocal duties in a hierarchical slave society. Hankins, however, looked to the past to legitimate an individualism that could not be found in the chivalrous knight, who subor-dinated individual will to community duty and obligation. From his parents' plantation, just a few miles south of the James River, he contemplated his future on March 29, 1857. It was his sixteenth birthday, and Hankins felt rest-less. Stirring deep inside Hankins was a desire to strike out on his own, to earn fame as the Revolutionary heroes had done with an original contribution.

Living close to Virginia's colonial and Revolutionary heritage must have intensified Hankins's sense of connectedness with the state's heroic past while fueling an inner drive to make something of himself. The crumbling remains of Jamestown and the shallow trenches of Yorktown were nearby. Nathaniel

James DeWitt Hankins (1841–66). When he contemplated his future in Virginia,
Hankins faced the same professional concerns that burdened his peers. He realized
that there were more professional opportunities for young men in the Southwest,
but like most members of the last generation he decided to make his home in the Old
Dominion. Hankins survived the Civil War, only to be killed in an 1866 duel by a man
who had served in his artillery company. (Courtesy of APVA Preservation Virginia;
on display at Bacon's Castle)

Bacon's rebels occupied and pillaged his family's plantation in 1676, and their riotous behavior had become romantic lore by the nineteenth century. Locals started to refer to the Hankinses' residence as Bacon's Castle, even though the populist leader had never visited the house. Hankins used history as a yardstick to gauge the present, and he realized that the accomplishments of most civilizations, like those of individuals, were eventually swept away by the ravages of time. In his darker moments, he fantasized that the Union might be "buried in the dust" like Rome. Even if such a catastrophe occurred, Hankins knew that "the name[s] of the men who framed it will never die. Washington, Jefferson, Henry, and others will live until 'Time is no more.'" Reflecting about Virginia's statesmen caused Hankins to evaluate his own achievements, although he acknowledged that "the theater of my existence is just in its infancy." He found comfort in ambition because "it has stood for *ages*," and thus "it shall make me a name." By contrast, his father worried that James, with his impervious faith in ambition, had lost touch with reality and would become conceited about his abilities. With due respect, the younger Hankins replied that "vanity is the handmaid of Ambition. It is often the result of much good, & seldom the result of evil."[15]

More than any other quality except piety, young Virginians like Hankins prized ambition, and their blanket endorsement of ambition caused a great deal of tension between age groups. Older people considered ambition a rallying cry for a youthful insurgency that promoted individual action at the expense of social cohesion. The dispute over ambition paralleled the debate over progress between the old fogies and young Virginians. The former wanted a more contained and orderly version of ambition while the latter often dismissed or downplayed the potential social consequences of individualism. In a book written for college youth, Henry Clay Pate insisted that "ambition is not *necessarily* a dangerous sentiment." He pointed to the "illustrious examples" of Washington, Jefferson, and "hundreds of eminent statesmen of our country" as proof of the "loftiest results of ambitious desires." "*Let the youth of our land be* ambitious," Pate contended, "and emulate the example set before them by our great men!" He rebuked as "absurd" the notion expressed by some parents that "ambition is *dangerous*."[16] Private correspondence among members of the last generation attests to the popularity of Pate's public sentiments. In autograph books from the University of Virginia, students consistently wrote to their peers about the need to be ambitious, to have a sense of purpose, and to achieve professionally. Near the end of the 1852 session, a Virginia student offered his advice in a rather amusing poem: "In the world's broad field of battle / In the bivouac of Life / Be not like dumb, driven cattle / But be a hero in the strife." Another young Virginian instructed a friend of his on the importance of having lofty aspirations and taking action: "Go climb high up the hill of fame—Where thoughtless idlers are unknown—With ambition with a brilliant name—And claim earth's honors as your own."[17]

Ambition gave young people the belief that they could direct the course of their own lives. They did not want to aimlessly float down the stream of life like a fallen leaf. Having ambition also signified to the last generation that they possessed energy and those essential creative powers that inspired the Founders to achieve greatness. What drew young people to ambition was its power to arouse action. Many older people, on the other hand, believed that ambition turned young people into dreamy idealists, incapable of appreciating the sacrifices that greatness demanded. Culpeper's Henry Coons, a student at Richmond College, harbored no such illusions. In his essay "The Noble and Ambitious Youth," he contended that any youth who "looks back a moment upon the past" will see "that all those who have written their names upon the pages of time, did it by hard study and deep thought."[18]

Yet raw ambition was not the panacea for Virginia's woes. Ambition had to be tempered by Christian faith. An individual who ignored the teachings of Jesus Christ would recklessly pursue his own interests at the expense of others. The tension between individualism and community obligation surfaced among the most thoughtful men. Speaking to the young men at the Hampton Academy in 1857, Walter Monteiro, a twenty-three-year-old lawyer from Goochland County who had graduated from the University of Virginia, warned that ambition was "the daughter of vanity and the mother of a monster." He implored his youthful audience to pursue a purer form of ambition, free of selfishness and directed by Christian motives. "Without it," Monteiro concluded, "all our finer feelings and passions would sink into darkness of eternal night."[19] The religious education of Southern youth, grounded in a biblical defense of hierarchy, instructed young Virginians that a sweeping endorsement of ambition could lead to radical individualism.[20] The last generation wondered how a society, slave-based or not, could survive a spirit of individualism that resisted the moral authority of the church and family. Regardless of the contradictions in this position, young people made the important break, ever so slightly, away from the idea that they should always submit to the absolute authority of the household.

A youthful perspective that valued ambition over duty was a significant and undeniable shift toward the self in 1850s Virginia. Members of the last generation encouraged their fellow youth to follow their own dreams, to become more assertive in their calls for change, and to break with what they considered the dull thinking of the past. In the *Virginia University Magazine*, William Radford of Montgomery County wanted his University of Virginia classmates to remember that some men still "cling with the greatest obstinacy" to the notion that circumstances alone determine success. Such an outdated philosophy, he asserted, "would reduce the mind of man to a mere passive machine, to be driven about in every way by the influences of the external world." While Radford hoped that ambition would rescue Virginians from this paralyzing school of thought, he also recognized that ambition had a dangerous potential to lead to "selfishness," causing an individual to forget "that he is helping to carry out the general order of things; that he is a part of God's creation, and therefore bound by some tie to every portion of it." Radford, who would be killed in a savage Confederate attack at the 1862 battle of Williamsburg, understood that ambition could threaten a society devoted to inequality. Mutual dependence among all social classes—the basis of the organic vision that slaveholders idealized but never achieved in their society—could not survive in a world of radical individualism. Radford knew this, as did many in his age group, but he never found a satisfactory answer to the problem. He fumbled toward a solution, one filled with inconsistencies, but in the end he swallowed hard and endorsed ambition. Radford's decision reflected a growing belief among his peers that the pursuit of separate interests, even in the name of ambition, could have an uplifting effect on society. They were willing to take their chances. Despite his earlier claims that every individual must have a sense of mutual obligation, Radford's concluding argument spoke for many young men. A person "can best assist in this general progress by advancing his own best interest." Individual action, Radford proclaimed, would best serve society, for a person acting on his own initiative would actually be an assistant "in carrying out the great work of human advancement." Like his Revolutionary forebears, Radford confronted that classic humanist dilemma: pursuit of individual interest versus republican citizenship.[21]

Popular enthusiasm for ambition led some young Virginians to charge that their elders needed a stronger dose of the valued commodity. Although these young men grounded their defense of ambition in a historical and Christian framework, a number of youth cultivators thought they were a bunch of impudent scamps for critiquing Virginia's aristocratic and cavalier tradition. Petersburg's Rebecca Brodnax Hicks, editor of *The Kaleidoscope: A Family Journal Devoted to Literature, Temperance, and Education*, blasted the last generation for betraying the legacy of the "Old Virginia Gentleman." "Young Virginia is the inglorious son of a most glorious old father," she opined in 1855, and "he seems to take a wicked pride in shewing his pride and independence in every way but the right way." By focusing on the morals and manners of young Virginians, Hicks bypassed the substantial issues that animated the last generation's critique of the cavalier tradition. Blinded by evangelical fury, she denounced young people for smoking cigars, chewing tobacco, excessive drinking, loud talking, cussing, and boisterous laughing. "Dignity is wanting in Young Virginia's character," Hicks proclaimed. "If he had more real dignity, and less confidence in himself," she would have "more hope of him." Until members of the last generation reformed their manners, Hicks believed they should always be treated as "cubs." She found it amusing that they felt slighted by everyone, including those social groups that were supposed to recognize their authority as white men. For example, Hicks had heard a young Virginian "complain heavily that 'the gals kick him,' . . . and the 'niggers won't wait on him.'" Such an admission revealed to Hicks that the young man was "little thinking," for he had unwittingly acknowledged "that even 'gals' and 'niggers' know more than is dreamed of in *his* philosophy."[22]

More was at stake than just the moral condition of the last generation. Young people sought a political voice in the Commonwealth's future, but adults like Hicks saw an uprising at work that threatened power relations in the household.[23] Challenging adult authority in the antebellum South symbolized an assault against domestic patriarchy and, by implication, on the bulwark of slavery. Hicks believed that young adults attacked a system of beliefs that legitimated the hierarchy between young and old, men and women, and black and white. Although Hicks did not envision the immediate collapse of male or adult authority, she detected a disturbing shift in power. Young Virginia "thinks he knows all things, gives his views upon all subjects," she wrote, "and is already beginning to make and control public opinion."[24] Other writers and commentators on public affairs agreed with Hicks that, if unchecked, young people posed a dangerous threat to Southern society. The last generation needed to understand that youth represented a phase in the life cycle in which dangerous raw emotions clouded judgment. Thus Hicks and those of a like mind dismissed the last generation's attacks as a problem of young men growing up too quickly. An editor for the *Christian Intelligencer* claimed in 1858 that "children mature faster than ever before." "They come into womanhood and manhood about as soon as they pass into their teens," he added, "and here they demand attentions, and claim licenses, which, if permitted a quarter of a century since, would have brought derision if not severe discipline from parents."[25]

The perception wars between older and younger Virginians reveal how little they understood one another in the 1850s. Adults insisted that college was a dangerous period in which parental supervision was still needed. A single misstep could trigger a lifetime of self-destructive behavior. The *Southern Churchman* recommended that any young man attending the University of Virginia "who has not character sufficient to do his duty . . . , had better not be sent to the University."[26] Many parents and youth cultivators took such a position because they failed to appreciate that young men were devoted to the ideal of the Christian gentleman and thus were following the religious instruction of their youth.[27] Young Virginians resented adult attacks, for it was the fathers of the last generation who had earned a national reputation for hooliganism. Members of the last generation felt that they had to clean up after their fathers and overturn the perception of Southern youth as violent and anti-intellectual.[28] While attending the University of Virginia in the fall of 1860, Alexander Fleet received a disturbing note from his father. Although the elder Fleet was very proud of his son for attending college, he made it clear that he considered college a fantasy land that only prolonged his son's comfortable existence inside the womb of privilege. "I have long believed & known that the prevailing idea with young men generally is to go to college just to say they have been, spend all the money they can beg & borrow & come home far bigger fools than they were before they went, & with morals by no means improved."[29] Fleet's father expressed the common belief that adolescence and young adulthood marked an inescapable period of irrational behavior, and he tried to prevent the worst. Mr. Fleet's condemnation of young people seems extreme because his son appears to have lived a model existence at the University of Virginia. The younger Fleet joined a group of fellow students who taught Sunday school and reading to impoverished youth in Albemarle County. He also participated in a student-led campaign to build a chapel at the end of the Lawn. Mr. Fleet implicitly acknowledged that his attack against university life said more about his own moral shortcomings than about his son's behavior at school.

Members of the last generation saw through the contradiction of what their fathers preached and what they had practiced as impulsive young men. When Fleet's father and other adults lectured young Virginians about the sins of student life and the need for moderation, they made an implicit admission of guilt, confirming the last generation's suspicion that the problem of character in Virginia originated in their elders' misspent youth. John Minor admitted as much in an 1859 letter brimming with advice to his nephew at the University of Virginia. "But it is a mark of senility to be ever thrusting advice upon young people," he wrote. "Often they are worn out truisms—often the exploded doctrines of a past generation—and in most cases put forth not so much for the benefit of the patient as for the credit of the Doctor."[30]

In sum, young Virginians believed that they had inherited the stereotype of the grand cavalier and the caricature of the dissipated Southern youth from their fathers. They were embarrassed by such a legacy, but their resentment never boiled over into a rebellion against adult authority. Members of the last generation still followed in the intellectual wake of their fathers. Both age groups were informed by Scottish moral philosophy, eighteenth-century republicanism, and Protestant Christianity.[31] Although Virginians of all ages were the heirs of a similar religious and political tradition, young people nevertheless asserted a fresh identity. Their religious instruction played a key role in creating a unique sense of generational mission. Protestantism in Virginia, and probably the rest of the South, was a language of action that conveyed values stressing improvement of the individual and society as a whole. Religion told young Virginians to be pious, to get an education, to build character, and to achieve professionally. The last generation took this message to heart, and they set about to live each day as Christian gentlemen; but their personal struggle for moral perfection also pushed them to look at the world from a more critical perspective.

Religion gave purpose to their broader vision of Virginia as a place where scientific endeavors, religious inquiry, and material progress could coexist and flourish. They were so inspired that they engaged in a host of benevolent activities and lobbied for increased educational funding. If Virginians of all ages were the product of the same political culture and religious traditions, how did young people come together as a collective age group and pursue a civic mission that they considered uniquely their own? Student-controlled organizations provided the vehicle through which they forged personal relationships and identified the issues of their generation. Nearly every Virginia university had literary societies and secret fraternities that offered young people a unique opportunity to come together without adult interference. For the first time in their lives, these men controlled their own terrain. Students ran meetings, selected subjects for debate, researched and prepared their own papers, and administered fines and punishment against delinquent members. Rarely did a professor, administrator, or visiting lecturer violate their autonomy.[32]

Within these organizations a sense of duty and reciprocity bound the students together, imparting a moral purpose that encouraged young Virginians to identify themselves as a distinct generation. Young men displayed tremendous loyalty toward their respective literary societies. Richard McIlwaine, a student at Hampden-Sydney and resident of Petersburg, recalled that "I was attached with the most fervid affection" to the Philanthropic Society.[33]

Inside these organizations, members of the last generation refashioned male culture by turning away from aggressiveness and violence as the basis of friendship. Unfortunately, many scholars have failed to appreciate the softening of Southern manliness in the 1850s.[34] Young people desired relationships based on emotion, affection, and spiritual intimacy. The loneliness and isolation of a university setting provided the perfect backdrop for young men who longed for familial relationships and the emotional ties of the household.[35] Intense friendships developed in the student groups, where young men, in ritualized behavior, pledged their lifelong devotion to one another. When it came time to leave the university, it was extraordinarily difficult for many of these students to say good-bye. While such feelings are hardly surprising, what draws notice is the openness with which members of the last generation expressed their love for Christ in one another. Shortly after graduation, Albemarle's Hugh A. White wrote a former classmate: "College friendships are apt to be short lived. But they do much to give form and direction to our future lives, and should be cherished as great blessings, when they have been such as were formed between some of our class. Our friendship, I think, was based upon our love for the Saviour, and hence, if we are not false to our profession of faith in Him, we shall be friends forever." Similar expressions fill college autograph books, in which young men poured out feelings of deep personal loss and turmoil over a classmate's impending departure. "A feeling of sadness comes over me when I think that we, with all our College friends are about to part," wrote Robert W. Hunter in Cary Selden Alexander's autograph book in 1855. "The parting of friends is at all times distressing but with those who are *very* near & dear to us, it is peculiarly so."[36] Like many of his classmates, Hunter converted autograph books into manuals for living filled with pointed advice on spiritual and professional matters. Hunter, who would serve on the staff of the famous Confederate general John B. Gordon, hoped that his friend Cary Alexander would become an "ornament and honor to the profession which you have chosen & also the community in which you live." In the same sentence, Hunter prayed for his friend—who was to die unexpectedly in 1859—that "when called upon to throw off the frail shackles of mortality may your spirit ascend to your Father who gave it." Another associate, Thomas Elder of Lunenburg County, voiced a similar message to Alexander: "Then learn to live in this world . . . to prepare your soul for the other world in which it is to exist, after your dust has returned to dust."[37]

Members of the last generation served the vital function of spiritual counselors to their peers, constantly imploring classmates to prepare each day for the hereafter. Although life might separate them, young Virginians believed that if they were true to God, they would be reunited in the afterlife as Christian brothers. After deciding to leave the University of Virginia in March 1861, George Washington Nelson wrote a poignant letter to his cousin and fellow classmate Carter Nelson Minor. Both young men had grown up in Hanover County, attended the same private academy, and remained close at the university, where they joined the Delta Kappa Epsilon fraternity. Although Nelson treasured his time at school, he wanted to become a minister, marry, and settle down. In just three years he would be twenty-five years old, and by "taking the average, my life will be more than half gone." Believing that the sands of time were running out of the hourglass, Nelson suddenly felt the grinding pressures of adulthood, leading him to exclaim: "Oh! Age is a terrible thing, it brings with it so many cares and responsibilities. It causes the best of friends to part." He realized that in all likelihood his and Minor's "paths in life will hereafter be further and further apart." To illustrate this point, he drew their respective homes next to each other. Two lines emanated from the buildings, labeled "my path" and "your path." Both lines start side by side, virtually inseparable, but they gradually diverge until they abruptly come back together at a point marked "Heaven." Below the sketch, Nelson wrote: "The above explains itself. Side by side we have gone; now we part, but we shall meet again in Heaven."[38]

The emotional and spiritual intimacy that developed among young men fostered a public atmosphere that made it perfectly acceptable to proselytize. Not only did students convert many of their peers, but they also served as missionaries on campus and in their local communities, where they passed out tracts to the poor and taught them to read. These important efforts have often been overlooked in considering the religious awakening that took hold in 1850s Virginia. During this time of spiritual resurgence, new chapters of the Young Men's Christian Association sprang into existence across the state and student-led religious organizations flourished on Virginia campuses. No school was free of the revivals that routinely swept dormitories and student boarding houses. This religious awakening, in conjunction with the advice of moth-

George Washington Nelson to Carter Nelson Minor, March 27, 1861. Nelson's sketch of his and Minor's paths in life reveals the emotional and religious intimacy that many young men of the last generation shared while college students. (James Fontaine Minor Papers [#6769], Special Collections, University of Virginia Library)

ers and other youth cultivators, reshaped young Virginians' understanding of what it meant to be a man.[39] Even those who remained distant from their more religious peers were affected by the new ideas of manliness. Everyone at least recognized a standard of masculinity based on moral restraint, intellectual discipline, and professional drive. Young people governed by a fiery sense of honor who only talked of dueling and fighting or wasted time by playing cards and drinking were seen as an embarrassment, for many young Virginians associated such behavior with the dissipated and lethargic aristocrat—the very symbol of the Old Dominion's backwardness and decline. Thus members of the last generation were drawn to the model of the Christian gentleman, not just because it held out the possibility of moral greatness in this life and immortality in the next, but also for its modern appeal as a means of transforming young men into respectable citizens.[40]

The experience of Lancelot Blackford best represents how religion not only stimulated personal reform but also inspired young people to engage in benevolent activities. Although he came from a deeply religious home, where his mother closely monitored the family's spiritual development, Blackford struggled to become a true believer as a teenager. He was sixteen years old and teaching at a private academy in Powhatan County when an epiphany struck on May 4, 1854. Never again would he see the world the same way. On that day, Blackford received a letter from a University of Virginia student who expounded on the great "religious excitement" at the school and his own spiritual rebirth. When Blackford, who was baptized at birth in the Episcopal faith, reflected on his friend's conversion and the religious experience of his contemporaries at Charlottesville, he too felt the powers of the Holy Spirit. "From that day I date my own wakening to my state of sin & need of a Saviour," he confided to his diary. "My most earnest desire now," Blackford continued, "is to live this year 'as though it were my last' and to become each day more & more the child of God."[41] Two years elapsed before he received confirmation. During that time, he launched a full-scale assault against his imperfections, but they were so deeply entrenched that Blackford feared that he did not have the spiritual reserves needed to conquer himself. There were moments when he bordered on despondency, filling his diary with punishing diatribes against himself for failing to trust completely in God. "The lack of *faith* seems to be my difficulty," confided Lancelot Blackford to his diary. Disheartened and disgusted by his lack of piety, Blackford was "almost tempted to give up seeking Religion." He could never bring himself to take such a drastic step. Blackford endured a series of spiritual crises on the road to salvation, but his frustrations took him into the realm of religious skepticism.[42]

Blackford's search for spiritual enlightenment wrought a transformation in his daily habits that he deemed essential to becoming a Christian gentleman. Discipline, above all else, served as his watchword. He rigorously managed every aspect of his life with the idea that he could work, study, and pray more efficiently and effectively. Time mattered, and he would not waste it. He carried a little black book in which he carefully recorded his plans and activities for each day, listing every appointment and accounting for every hour used and every penny spent. A disciplined body and mind, Blackford believed, would bring moral purity. While he worked as a teacher in an attempt to earn tuition money so he could return to the University of Virginia, Blackford subjected himself to a demanding study regimen. Becoming educated, he knew, was a long and arduous process that demanded sacrifice, diligence, and energy. "I am trying to improve this winter, in an intellectual point of view, as the excellent opportunities afforded for study deserve to be," Blackford wrote to his mother on December 17, 1854, "and so . . . I may feel the benefit of it all my life." He acutely felt his ignorance, but he did not despair. "There is a sentence in Juvenal which applies well here, however, 'He who begins, has half done.' So there's no way so sure of accomplishing it all as by 'pitching right in it,' as the saying is."[43]

While teaching in Powhatan, Blackford lived a Spartan existence based on self-denial that allowed for little recreation. The monotony of this routine drove him to seek an occasional diversion. In November 1854, Blackford took a short leave from school and ventured into Richmond, where he socialized with friends at the Exchange Hotel, attended an agricultural meeting at the African Church, and toured the exhibits at a state mechanical fair. On his return home he managed a full night's sleep, but he did not feel refreshed in the morning when he returned to the academy. The thought of having to resume his predictable schedule of prayer, work, and study made him blanch, but he knew he had to push aside those tempting memories of "my late pleasuring" and renew a regime of character building. He confided to his diary that "my mind has also been much distracted from religious thoughts and feelings and my object now must be to show a well balanced mind in its fullest excellence by not allowing these distracting causes to have more than a momentary effect."[44]

Blackford could not shake off the residue of guilt from his Richmond adventure. These negative feelings intensified when a letter arrived from his older brother William, another member of the last generation, who chastised Lancelot for "'flying round'" to Richmond. Whether Lancelot could make up for the lost time was irrelevant. The elder Blackford wanted his sibling to understand that he had violated the cardinal principle of "steady application," which "to the business of life is what insures success." In the employment of a young man, William reminded Lancelot that "the first question is, is he steady? Has he business habits? Can he be relied on?" "A young Blood who flies off down to a Richmond Fair," William concluded, would always lose out to a "*business man*" who "is *steady*" while "our 'Blood' is prancing around."[45] William's advice seems rather harsh and unnecessary, for Lancelot clearly understood that professional success hinged on disciplined habits rooted in Christian faith. Throughout his diary, Lancelot wrote of his admiration of "*Practical* Religion" because it impressed upon the mind one of his favorite mottoes: "'Not slothful in business, fervent in Spirit, [and] serving the Lord.'"[46]

Lancelot's unrelenting drive for self-improvement spurred him to reform the immediate world around him. In his hometown of Lynchburg, he encouraged the creation of an athenaeum to promote scientific and literary learning. "The preachers, lawyers, doctors, and educated men in other professions," he insisted, "ought to be able to sustain something of this description." At the University of Virginia, Lancelot spread the gospel through a host of benevolent organizations that reached out to students, poor whites, and blacks in Albemarle County. In the fall of 1858, he helped form the first YMCA chapter on an American campus at the University of Virginia. As soon as the meeting concluded, he quickly returned to his room and reported the news to his mother. To Lancelot's delight, more than sixty young men enlisted, and he believed that "the students seem to take hold of it very readily."[47] The officers of the Christian association subsequently launched a recruiting campaign in the *Virginia University Magazine*: "*For the good of others*, your fellow students, and the ignorant poor in the neighborhood, we would urge you to join our Association."[48] Such pleas had the desired effect. In less than three years of existence, the organization's membership exceeded 150 students, many of whom "on every Sabbath, teach in Sunday Schools, or [are] otherwise engaged in works of active benevolence."[49] The rank and file energetically carried out this strategy through a methodical and professional approach to their missionary work. They divided the campus into seventeen districts, assigning a committee to each one to oversee weekly prayer meetings, to pass out tracts, and to encourage nonbelievers to attend church or join the association. The students also collected 300 religious volumes for a library that they made available to the public. Within an eight-mile radius of the university, the students formed eight "stations" where they held Sunday schools and Bible classes, primarily for the poor. They also reached out to the local boys attending private academies. On Sunday evenings, after an afternoon prayer meeting sponsored by university students, approximately twenty young men held a "Sabbath school" for black children and a separate meeting "for the instruction of adult negroes." Neither the status of these blacks nor their response to the white missionaries is known.[50]

Regardless of a potential convert's skin color, it is clear that members of the YMCA avoided camp revivals or stump speaking. Rather, they spread the gospel through a highly bureaucratic infrastructure in which they shifted the focus of missionary work to a classroom setting, even when they were operating outside the confines of the university. In the process, they demonstrated their overriding faith in education as the essential step to reforming morals. Reading rooms, libraries, mission schools, and Bible classes were the standard vehicles through which the YMCA's members tried to reach the minds as well as the spirits of the unconverted. Lectures were also popular, but the speakers were not always men of the cloth. Among others, Albert T. Bledsoe, the influential defender of slavery at the University of Virginia, addressed a Lynchburg audience of young men.[51] In fact, YMCAs were intended to facilitate intellectual activity by acquiring books on literary and scientific subjects, sponsoring lectures on scholarly topics, and holding public debates on a variety of secular issues. It is no wonder that the YMCA appealed to young Virginians who desired mental, moral, and material improvement in the Old Dominion. The organization encouraged a public discussion of current events while reinforcing the firm belief that benevolence, education, and salvation must go hand in hand.[52]

The last generation's efforts reflected the approach of most pastors in late antebellum Virginia. Most of these men, as Beth Barton Schweiger writes, "could hardly distinguish between schools and prayer meetings."[53] The activities of the University of Virginia's YMCA actually followed the course already taken by other state chapters. In 1856, for instance, the Lynchburg YMCA created a special committee to promote "scripture instruction" to "the coloured population of our city." Similar associations flourished in Richmond, Fredericksburg, Alexandria, and Leesburg, and were linked to an international movement based in England. In 1856, two members represented Richmond's chapter at the Confederation of Young Men's Christian Associations in Montreal.[54]

Though the YMCA drew a wide membership from across the state, it enjoyed the most success at the University of Virginia, where it received public acclaim for elevating student morals. A Charlottesville newspaper quoted an unidentified professor who was so impressed by the work of students that he claimed that "*a young man was safer at the University of Virginia than he was at home or somewhere in business.*"[55] While this academic might have overstated his case, it was true that identifiable changes had occurred in student behavior. In the spring of 1860, the district weekly prayer meetings averaged an attendance of two hundred students, including between sixty and seventy who did not profess a religion. Many of these young men soon joined their converted brethren and became church members. Attesting to the rise of "religious students" at Thomas Jefferson's university, the editors of the *Virginia University Magazine* released figures tracking those who received communion in Protestant churches during the 1855–56 session compared to those in the 1859–60 session. They found a significant increase from 17 percent of the student body in 1855 to 33 percent four years later. On one Sunday alone in 1860, twenty-seven young men joined the Episcopal Church. The pious had momentum, and they intensified their demands for the university to facilitate the practicing of the Christian faith. In 1859, a group of young men helped raise funds for a more spacious chapel on campus because the existing structure could not accommodate the ever-growing congregation. The war interrupted completion of the project.[56]

As part of this general religious awakening at the University of Virginia, a chapter of the Temperance Association sprang into existence in 1856, drawing an overwhelming response from students. Nearly five hundred students, according to Lancelot Blackford, filled the hall for the opening ceremony. In two days of speeches, during which time classes were canceled, ninety-seven men took the temperance oath, bringing total membership to more than 150. In the wake of this event, Blackford expected more recruits, for "those who cared nothing about the subject before are now enthusiastic friends of Temperance." "Still they come" was the cry heard around campus, and Blackford believed this was "truly melancholy to the ears of the devoted grog shop keepers about College whose trade is certainly languishing just now."[57] Their enthusiasm for temperance did not abate once they left the halls of the university. Shortly after William R. Aylett returned to his native King William County, he delivered a number of speeches for the crusade. He told his audience, composed of women and men, that their Temperance Association exhibited "so plainly the ever prevailing tendency of the human mind to rise from a lower to a higher state of mental, moral, and social improvement."[58]

The benevolent spirit that invigorated the University of Virginia also contributed to the beginnings of "muscular Christianity," a Protestant philosophy that would take off in the late 1800s when church leaders wanted to masculinize Christianity in order to thwart the enervating effects of Catholic immigration.[59] As a precursor to this phenomenon, many young Virginians became fixated on building their bodies, not out of some xenophobic fear, but as an important way of building Christian character. The tedium of school, young men feared, could lead to dissipation, and bored students would try anything to feel alive. Exercise presented an alternative for a young man to build his physical and spiritual strength by awakening his body to all the powers that God had bestowed on him. Taking time at the gymnasium did not compete with their religious obligations; it reinforced them. One University of Virginia student observed that developing one's physique would "give a strength, not otherwise to be obtained, to sincerity, cordiality, generosity and high-souled honor,— those emotions that raise man most nearly to the image of God; and they impart vigor to his whole being."[60]

The concept of becoming a better Christian through exercise originated in England and found a home among youth cultivators and adults in the United States and Virginia. University of Virginia professor John Minor instructed Lancelot Blackford to develop both mind and body while a student: "I hope that you are careful to mingle together body & mental exercise — the body as well as the mind, is the gift of God and he will not have his gifts neglected

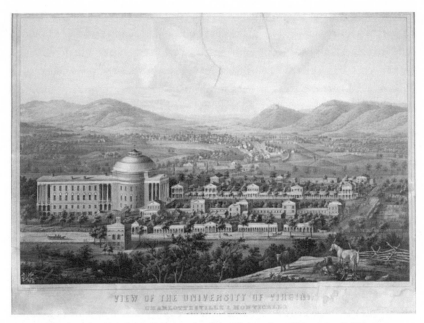

Edward Sachse produced this lithograph of the University of Virginia with the town of Charlottesville and Monticello in the distant background. This view of the campus, dating from 1856, focuses on the famous Rotunda and Lawn, which were the center of student intellectual and social life at the university. (Courtesy of Special Collections, University of Virginia Library)

with impurity." Ignoring the body would enfeeble the muscles, Minor warned. This, in turn, would lead to an inevitable and irreversible mental decline. "Such is the intimacy of the relations between the mind & the body," he added. Blackford followed Minor's advice, joining the university's gymnasium and working out regularly unless he walked to town, for this took "up all the time I have to dispose for exercise." Fellow student Alexander Frederick Fleet, who headed to the gym every evening at five o'clock, paid an extra fee to use the school's steam baths. "About the baths," he wrote to his younger brother, "it is thought that by coming into a room heated by steam, all the impurities will be drawn out through the pores, & by jumping in cold water it is all washed off."[61] It is crucial to note that those members of the last generation who wrote about their exercise routine did not see exercise as a way to offset the supposed feminizing effects of religion. Young Virginians used their time in the gym to improve their health and, more importantly, to harness and extinguish boyish energy. To bottle up such dangerous forces risked an explosion of illicit sexual behavior, including the "deadly habit" of masturbation. A Christian gentleman, the last generation believed, needed to work his body in order to cleanse his soul. Young Virginians were caught up in a national craze for calisthenics. Nineteenth-century Americans associated physical stature with power. Turning weak bodies into muscular ones might have fulfilled the longing for power that seemed out of reach for the last generation. One energetic student at the University of Virginia considered sports so essential to the physical and spiritual regenerative process that he called for the creation of cricket, baseball, archery, fencing, and boating clubs. One day, he hoped to see a "Regatta" on the Rivanna River to rival the festival that Oxford students put on the Isis. In 1860, twenty-four students organized the university's first cricket club with the help of the superintendent of the grounds, who secured a "suitable field" for use three times a week.[62]

Few could have anticipated the religious awakening and assorted benevolent activities that energized the students in Charlottesville. Before 1850, Virginians had long condemned the University of Virginia as a godless place where young men, free from the restraints of home, enjoyed the most popular vices of the adult world. A Charlottesville newspaperman writing in 1860 recalled that it was not long ago when Virginians had viewed the university as "a kind of infidel nursery" where "hot-blooded young gentlemen devoted themselves mainly to practising [sic] at a mark, or brandishing knives."[63] A number of destructive student riots, the most serious occurring in 1845, had caused Virginians to hold the University of Virginia in low regard. Many parents responded by keeping their sons away from Charlottesville, and admissions spiraled downward for the rest of the decade. The turning point for the University of Virginia came in the late 1840s with the appointment of five new professors—all Americans, including two from Virginia. The new hires calmed matters on campus. Europeans had previously dominated the faculty, resulting in a cultural gap with students who refused to submit to the authoritarian methods of foreign instructors. Relations between students and faculty clearly improved in the 1850s as new professors Henry St. George Tucker, John B. Minor, and William H. McGuffey created a sense of discipline without authoritarian tactics; they instilled a religious tone into student life without requiring church attendance, and permitted a degree of student self-regulation without enforcing petty rules that had caused ill-feeling in the past.[64] The student commotions seen in the 1820s, 1830s, and 1840s disappeared in the 1850s.

Though faculty changes helped, young people deserve most of the credit for improving the moral condition of the university. They took it upon themselves to form their own religious organizations and emulate the ideal of the Christian gentleman. A similar impulse inspired improvement in student behavior across the state. President George Junkin of Washington College applauded the work of the "Crusaders," a student-led temperance organization that had increased sobriety across the campus in the decade before the war. Junkin had complained about undergraduate profanity in 1850, but seven years later he noted that few students relied on vulgar language to express themselves. He was even more impressed that card playing had become an unpopular form of recreation.[65] In an address at the Virginia Military Institute in 1856, Superintendent Francis H. Smith judged the "religious tone" at West Point as "lamentably low" compared to that of the cadets in Lexington, who observed prayer daily and considered it a sacred duty. While the United States Military Academy limited chapel exercises to a single weekly service on the Sabbath and ignored Bible instruction in the curriculum, Smith boasted that his Virginia cadets had voluntarily organized themselves into prayer groups. At Randolph-Macon College, after a ten-day revival in 1852, a student wrote in his diary: "College is no longer what college has long been, a place of wickedness and sinfulness. The Devil's long held authority is fast declining."[66] None of this is to say that young men in Virginia suddenly turned into saints during the 1850s. They still engaged in mischief and rowdyism called frolics or "busts." They blackened their faces, dressed in outrageous clothing, and made hideous noises with horns and gongs to wake up sleeping professors, but these festivities did not turn into violent riots, nor did they result in the destruction of property.[67]

Religion, moreover, did not make young Virginians politically passive. If anything, they became more outspoken. This trend concerned adults like Rebecca Hicks, who charged that the last generation's critique of Virginia society was a sign that young people were becoming "fast," rebellious, and immoral when in fact the opposite seems to have been true. Most of these young men strongly identified with the masculine values of the Christian gentleman but rejected the more violent and aggressive behavior of Southern honor. They consequently saw themselves as more virtuous and progressive than their parents' generation. This perspective helped shape their view of the political system in the 1850s. Young Virginians charged that the state's ruling class suffered from arrested development as Christians. All age groups, members of the last generation believed, should grow closer to Christ. No one was exempt. Baptism, in fact, could serve as an age leveler. Young people suddenly felt superior to those who had turned away from God, regardless of how elderly they may have been. In the end, Christianity actually encouraged young people to question adult authority while at the same time instilling love and respect for parents.[68]

In trying to live as Christian gentlemen, members of the last generation developed a love affair with education, believing it to be the great panacea to Virginia's moral, intellectual, and material problems.[69] However, few were as enthusiastic about its redemptive powers as Charles M. Gibbons of Winchester, who envisioned a system of common schools throughout Virginia. Shining the light of education on those at the bottom of society, he believed, would show them the way out of their dens of iniquity to the pure air of virtuous living. A home without vices, more importantly, would foster a cultivated atmosphere for children to see "a new world opening before them."[70] Few members of the last generation joined Gibbons in his support for public education for the masses. Most showed the greatest concern for the quality of higher education because they perceived, fairly or not, that it did not receive adequate support from the state's political class. The insidious consequences of partisan politics, most argued, had prevented the state's leaders from acting out of principle to promote education. The Commonwealth's leaders had long devalued education, Henry Clay Pate averred. This state of affairs, he argued, "should create in the present generation of the youth, . . . a strong desire to redeem her from the condition of ignorance."[71] Such a charge was not particularly fair, considering that many politicians, religious leaders, and newspapermen successfully expanded educational opportunities at all levels in the 1850s. Governor Henry Wise, for instance, vigorously promoted the interests of state-supported schools, campaigned against illiteracy, and even floated the idea of a public school system for the poor. After assuming office in 1856, Wise softened his stance. He abandoned his proposal for common schools, no longer called for taxing the rich to pay for educational expenditures, and focused on trying to enlarge the patronage of the Virginia Military Institute, the University of Virginia, and other state colleges. Wise also persuaded the General Assembly to pass modest increases in appropriations for the military institute and the university during his tenure.[72]

Wise's compromised program reinforced the perception that the General Assembly had not been generous enough in its support of the state's institutions of higher education. This frustrated countless young men, particularly those who were struggling to pay for school. Instead of resorting to violence, young Virginians entered a dynamic and contentious public debate over the direction of education. In student periodicals they lobbied for increased public funding to reduce tuition fees, to expand the library, and to increase faculty salaries. When some groups of adults resisted their agenda, they perceived the same stagnant, antiprogressive thinking that had brought ruin to the Old Dominion. Governor Wise reinforced the negative perception of the state's public servants by exposing a misappropriation of $150,000 meant for the literary fund in order to service the state debt, an illegal activity that occurred between 1851 and 1857.[73] Another setback for the cause of education occurred in 1860 when the legislature defeated a proposal for an endowment fund for the University of Virginia by killing an appropriation bill of $25,000.[74] The students in Charlottesville denounced this action as a consequence of party politics. An editor for the *Virginia University Magazine* explained that a "portion of the Legislature known for their hostility to the University, who look upon its prosperity with a jealous eye and are willing to see it decline, have again triumphed in their cause and succeeded in keeping the institution in a state of financial embarrassment." The young man bitterly added: "When our legislators prostitute their positions and attempt to make them serve for party purposes, it is high time for the people to demand an examination of the matter and see if these suspicions are well founded." Most members of the last generation would have endorsed Charles S. Venable's 1858 condemnation of the General Assembly, in which the educator declared that "the heart of every patriotic son of the Old Dominion is sad and indignant to know that, in her legislative halls the rights of her youth are disregarded."[75]

The state's uneven commitment to education fueled the last generation's resentment against Virginia's political class. Once again, young men looked to the Revolutionary fathers' wise example as the proper course for the Old Dominion to follow. Alexander Pendleton reminded his fellow Virginians that George Washington had recognized the importance of higher education by donating personal stock to form Washington College. He implored the state's current leaders to make the refurbishment of Virginia's universities and colleges a priority. The last generation confidently believed that with the necessary funds the Old Dominion would again produce men of eminence and virtue.[76]

Pendleton, like most of his peers, pinned his hopes on the state's universities. Unless higher education became a priority, he affirmed, the state would fall farther behind the North. Furthermore, the University of Virginia's reputation as the finest school in the South would be at risk. While the politicians ignored the state's educational needs, Virginia parents shipped their sons to

Northern colleges well into the 1850s—a distressing admission of intellectual inferiority. Young Virginians, in fact, reacted defensively to any remark from a Northern educator. When the president of Brown University adopted a curriculum modeled after Jefferson's educational vision without acknowledging the University of Virginia, a student responded that "it is mortifying to our pride, to find that not even the slightest allusion is made to the fact, that such an institution as the University of Va. exists." Another student asked in 1860: *"Shall we be taunted with inferiority?* Shall it be said that Southern students are without the means of acquiring a *complete* education at home?" He and many of his contemporaries believed the University of Virginia would redeem not only Virginia but also the South. A superior educational institution in Virginia would show the world that intellect and creativity could flourish in a slave society. Members of the last generation felt a pressing need to convince adults that their universities offered society something useful.[77] "Before we can expect to become independent of the North in commerce and finance must we not make ourselves independent in education?" a Hampden-Sydney student rhetorically asked in the school's literary magazine. He argued that the vast flow of capital and young men to Northern schools over the years had prevented Virginia from achieving commercial, economic, and literary "independence." The young man could not think of a vassalage "more humiliating and disastrous than that of the mind."[78]

The dream of the University of Virginia serving as the intellectual center of the South reveals how young Virginians began to see an alliance with the South as a way to bring prosperity and prestige back to the Old Dominion. The cry of Southern rights and Southern distinctiveness had various meanings and purposes below the Mason-Dixon Line. Members of the last generation emphasized Southern unity to convince their elders that Virginia's leadership in the region would be at risk if they did not properly support higher education. In 1860, a University of Virginia student sent a list of demands to the *Richmond Enquirer*, ranging from boarding to academic issues. He wanted the Board of Visitors to address these problems in their annual meeting. There existed "disadvantages under which our noble institution is laboring," he wrote, and a public discussion would awaken his fellow citizens to these abuses. True Virginians, this student predicted, would demand justice for young people. To ignore the problems at the University of Virginia would threaten to derail the institution from reaching its final destiny: "to become the great fountain-head, from which not only the sons of Virginia, but of the whole South, will drink the waters of knowledge."[79]

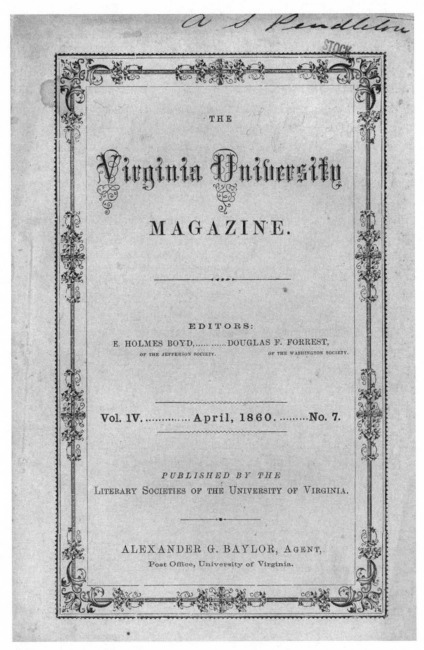

·THE·

Virginia University

MAGAZINE.

EDITORS:

E. HOLMES BOYD,............DOUGLAS F. FORREST,
OF THE JEFFERSON SOCIETY.   OF THE WASHINGTON SOCIETY.

Vol. IV............. April, 1860..........No. 7.

PUBLISHED BY THE
LITERARY SOCIETIES OF THE UNIVERSITY OF VIRGINIA.

ALEXANDER G. BAYLOR, AGENT,
Post Office, University of Virginia.

The *Virginia University Magazine* served as an invaluable forum for young people to engage the adult world about a wide range of intellectual and political matters. The last generation's Alexander "Sandie" Pendleton owned this particular issue. (In the possession of the author)

In lobbying for additional support for Virginia colleges and universities, the last generation participated in a powerful cultural trend that called for young people to stay in the region and receive a proper Southern education. Their protests, however, did not contribute to a fire-eater mentality or fuel a radical youth movement that demanded regional isolationism. While young Virginians staunchly defended shared Southern interests related to slavery and considered the Christian gentleman a unique product of their society, their social identities were also connected to a national style of social respectability and refinement. The large number of Southern students attending Princeton, Jefferson Medical College, and other Northern schools in the 1850s attests to a shared national vision among young people. Above all else, they wanted professional recognition and social achievement. They insisted that these should come through hard work, education, and good, clean living—thus foreshadowing the muscular Christianity of later decades. The rise of YMCAs in the Old Dominion underscored the desire of young Virginians to become members of a cosmopolitan community. They were well aware of the popular prescriptive literature of the day, including the influential *Tom Brown's School Days* by Englishman Thomas Hughes. Yet, in trying to gain acceptance from elsewhere, young people needed to purge their native land of an outdated, aristocratic character that made Virginians look foolish, violent, and backward in the "modern age." Nevertheless, no matter how badly the last generation longed for recognition in the bourgeois world, they refused to turn away from the unique political and economic interests of a slave society. Pursuing individual and societal improvement through the model of the Christian gentleman assured young Virginians that they would not sacrifice a way of life that, as they had been told throughout their formative years, stood as the last bastion of Christianity in a world swarming with infidels.[80]

Defenders of Virginia, Union, and the South

· ·

A union of equality and justice — the union
of our ancestors. — William R. Aylett,
untitled speech

IN HIS FINAL SPEECH at the University of Virginia,
graduating senior William Roane Aylett acknowledged that some of his "happiest and most instructive hours" occurred within the confines of his beloved
Jefferson Society. "I have learned here what one cannot acquire from the lips
of professors, nor gotten from the pages of books," he told his classmates in
1853. Aylett treasured the friendships formed over the years, but he looked
forward to the day when he and his peers would depart Charlottesville. The
occasion would bring them recognition as "*men*," not as "*youths*." "Many of
us, (and the rest of you are soon to follow) are about to launch our boats on
an untried sea," he exclaimed, "whose golden waves when viewed from afar
seem all bright and sparkling in the sunlight of the future." Beneath the placid
water, however, swirled dangerous political currents, and Aylett worried that
his nation would get pulled under, forever lost at the bottom of the ocean like
the great civilization of Atlantis. If the country's ship capsized in the rough
seas of sectionalism, he instructed his peers to cling to the "Union for our
anchor." Yet, even this stabilizing force posed its own dangers. Aylett insisted
that only "a union of equality and justice — the union of our ancestors" could
protect Virginia and, hence, preserve the Union. "Through no fault of our
own," he warned, equality of the states in the Union might be lost "in some
dark and gloomy night of misfortune." If this dreaded event occurred, Aylett
wanted his audience to understand that justice and liberty could only be found
in Southern honor — "our helm — our guide-star — Southern glory." Since
a reactionary European power or an abolitionist attack might threaten liberty

in the United States, he instructed his friends to be prepared because "the Union has claims upon us." In the same breath, he added, "so too, [does] Va. and the South."[1]

Duty to region, state, and nation pulled Aylett and his peers in conflicting directions. Aylett's deep love for the Union, his reverence for the Founders, and his belief that the United States stood as the world's great hope of republican liberty did not prevent him from imagining a Southern community as a protector of Virginia interests. He even backed his rhetoric with action by joining the University of Virginia's Southern Rights' Association in 1850.[2] How did Aylett reconcile his seemingly contradictory claims of allegiance to the Old Dominion, the Union, and the South? He ordered this bundle of conflicting ties by looking at loyalty as a fluid condition, always dependent on political events. Battles for power at the national level influenced how Aylett and other young Virginians perceived their interests and determined where they should place their loyalty. For most of the 1850s, members of the last generation envisioned the Union as a broad shield that protected local attachments. When political crises lowered the shield, they retreated from this nationalist position and called for Southern unity. Events like the Compromise of 1850, the Kansas-Nebraska Act of 1854, John C. Frémont's 1856 bid for the presidency, John Brown's 1859 raid on Harpers Ferry, and Lincoln's 1860 election awakened young Virginians to the possibility that a Southern alliance would be necessary to preserve a Union that accommodated slavery.

Although members of the last generation were the pupils of slavery's most passionate defenders and the products of a Southern education movement, they were not transformed into political radicals who envisioned or agitated for an independent Southern nation. They preached Union with the same fervor of previous generations, even though they came of age at a time of sectional unrest. They did, however, absorb the idea that Northern radicals intended to overthrow religious orthodoxy in the South and throughout the world. Young people sincerely believed that they lived in a unique Christian society trying to survive in a godless world. Such an ideological construct actually accommodated their loyalty to Virginia *and* the Union, while creating an imagined connection with the South. Those feelings of cultural unity with the South never inspired students to form a separatist political movement. National events, not a regional psyche, increasingly brought them to the realization that Southern unity offered Virginia the best protection of its institutions. Rarely did young people articulate regional differences within the framework of the Yankee Puritan and the Virginia cavalier.[3] Instead, they spoke in the broadest terms of a unique Virginia spirit that linked them to the state's Revolutionary past. From a decidedly cultural and environmental perspective, members of the last generation espoused the idea that Virginians constituted a separate people with their own history, morals, and manners.

As was the case for other mid-nineteenth-century Americans, kinship and loyalty to a specific locale anchored the last generation's cultural identity. Friction, resentment, and anger occasionally surfaced among family members, but — even with the inevitable tension — expressions of love, genuine concern, and mutual respect characterized the correspondence between parents and sons. No other facet of their lives attracted the affections and the loyalties of these young Virginians like family and home. They idealized the home as a haven from the corruption of the world, a place where they could purify their souls. "I think love for home is one of the tenderest feelings of our nature," reflected Matthew Page Andrews of the lower Shenandoah Valley. "Home must always be where the thoughts and affections are centered." When creditors threatened to confiscate Robert B. Davis's ancestral home, "Hickory Hill," he raised the necessary funds to save this "dear and hallowed spot." Indeed, obligation to family included all kin, living and dead. To show his devotion to those who once had lived "in wealth and opulence" at the family residence, Davis resolved not to "sell H. Hill, so long as I can live without that necessity. I can not part with it." The past clearly weighed heavily on the last generation. No one wanted to violate the sacred memory of departed relatives.[4]

Any disruption of family relations, whether from physical threat or insult, brought a fierce response from these young Virginians. Protection of family constituted the highest duty for antebellum men. "From the earliest times in Western history," Bertram Wyatt-Brown asserts in his study of Southern honor, "the cardinal principle of honor was family defense." Ignoring one's familial responsibility caused irreparable damage to a man's honor, marked by a decline in respect and reputation. A forceful response to any insult proved one's loyalty to loved ones past and present, but the stereotype of the hotheaded, slaveholding youth who dueled at the slightest provocation does not reflect the attitude of the last generation. Rather, these young men thought that conformity to the contentious image would make them look like animals. A Christian gentleman showed restraint. That cardinal virtue may have been absent from their parents' generation, they believed, but they would control such passions for the benefit of their families, their communities, and themselves.

William R. Aylett's reaction to a personal affront from his fiancée's family, the Brockenbroughs, reflects his generation's conception of honor and willingness to handle confrontations in a more diplomatic manner. Shortly before his scheduled marriage, the Brockenbroughs gave credence to a rumor that Aylett was mentally unstable. When the Brockenbroughs tried to convince their daughter to cancel the upcoming nuptials, Aylett learned of their intentions and rhetorically questioned his fiancée: "*If there was [a] probability or danger, even remotely, of what your family apprehended—don't you suppose, in such a case that my family would have been the first to have made the sad discovery, and to have opposed our union, and informed your family?*" In Aylett's mind, the accusations represented an attack against his entire family, "the *dead* and the *living.*" Aylett refused to forgive the Brockenbroughs for assuming that his relatives lacked the "intelligence, honor, justice and prudence" to prevent their daughter's union with a "madman." "I must be allowed to reply indignantly [to] such an imputation," he concluded, "and to request that your advisors cannot appreciate sufficiently the honor . . . of my family." The essence of Aylett's personal defense was a declaration of fidelity to his family. Like his contemporaries, Aylett defended his own principles within the broader context of family, home, community, and history.[5]

Members of the last generation entertained a highly personalized sense of history in which departed ancestors reappeared as mythical models of Victorian perfection. They tried to honor the memory of the dead by following a strict code of behavior. This concept of honor fostered great love and affection for family and community. It could also be intimidating, since young people felt they were forever being watched and judged by those in the grave. A famous ancestor who served in the Revolution could either inspire a young man with pride and ambition or haunt him into believing that he was inadequate and undeserving of the family name. Most did not feel the burdens of the past. In fact, they felt a burning desire to get closer to their family and state history. Once in touch with the spirit of the Old Dominion's greatness, young Virginians felt restored and ready to launch their own lives and possibly achieve everlasting fame.

Like many other Victorian-era Americans whose beliefs verged on pantheism, the members of the last generation felt connected to home and the state's famed past through their natural environment. Neighboring meadows, valleys, and hills were "the mystical chords of memory" that bound them to their ancestors and the famous men who had passed from this world. While serving as a cadet at the United States Military Academy, James Ewell Brown Stuart wrote that he considered West Point "a *magnificent spot*," but "I can not call it *home*, it can not, in my estimation, begin to compare with that humble spot—Drum Head." Every time he thought of the family homestead beneath the "dear old hills of Patrick [County]," his imagination was filled with "enchanting loveliness."[6]

One of Stuart's ancestors had been killed by a Tory at Drumhead, Virginia, not far from where his immediate family resided before the Civil War. Stuart's fascination with Drumhead reflected the prominent role that the living memory of forebears played in the self-definition of the last generation. Young Virginians were especially enthralled by the stories of ancestors who participated in the country's struggle against England. Displaying veneration for their Revolutionary heritage not only gave them a sense of place and tradition, but it also held out the promise that they too possessed the superior traits and manners that had once made Virginians the most respected and admired men in the country. Genetic links unquestionably mattered to Stuart, but place, more than anything else, shaped his expectations for the future and gave him hope that he too could excel in this world. By stressing the physical environment as the crucial factor in character formation, young people could uphold the popular belief that Virginia produced superior citizens without succumbing to the crippling notion that greatness depended entirely on genetics, which had been the old aristocratic creed.

Some members of the last generation thought a return to the countryside would awaken spirituality in young people and bring them in touch with Virginia's ancient spirit. Virginia students participated in a back-to-nature movement that became all the rage at colleges across the country. Members of the last generation made pilgrimages to Virginia's most spectacular natural attractions, such as the Peaks of Otter, Weyler's Cave, and the Natural Bridge.[7] Hiking through a forest of pines, listening to birds, or simply sitting on the banks of a river fulfilled a variety of psychological needs. Primarily, most young Virginians returned to nature to commune with God within a setting that could produce an intense emotional experience similar to conversion. This expression of Christianity fit within the last generation's overall reform efforts to improve morals, spirit, and body. Although many were led into the wilderness by the ideas of Romantics like Byron, it was more common for young Virginians to go to the countryside to find, as one student put it, "the temple of the living God."[8] The sight of towering mountains, cascading waterfalls, and luscious fields poignantly reminded them of God's infinite powers, making it impossible for the most determined atheist to deny the existence of a Supreme Being. Who, they wondered, would not be impressed by the harmony and interdependence of God's wild animals when compared to

A daguerreotype portrait of, in the center, James Ewell Brown Stuart (1833–64); George Washington Custis Lee (1832–1919), on the right; and Stephen D. Lee (1833–1908). This photograph was taken between 1850 and 1854, while the three young men were cadets at the U.S. Military Academy. In 1853, Stuart wrote that he considered West Point "a *magnificent spot*, but so long as it remains in Yankee land, . . . I can not call it *home*." (Courtesy of the Virginia Historical Society)

the fractious character of everyday human life? Appreciation of the Creator's most sublime works, they believed, would breathe a nobler spirit into man. "And as we accustom ourselves to derive our purest and most exquisite enjoyment from dwelling upon his goodness as manifested in nature," James McDowell Graham of Lexington suggested, "we will, by the invariable law of assimilation, become spiritualized and beautified in the inner man, and the soul will continue to approach in likeness nearer and nearer to the Divine Original."[9] If a fiery sermon or biblical tract failed to convert the unbelievers, young Virginians imagined that an Eden-like setting would draw people closer to God.

The last generation believed that anyone who discovered the sacredness of nature would not succumb to the growing tide of utilitarianism. The Shenandoah Valley's William F. Allen worried that the pursuit of the practical would turn people into dreary creatures—spiritually barren, morally spent, and ruled by the cash nexus. Communing with nature, Allen believed, elevated the mind and purified the soul. His 1860 thesis at the University of Virginia explored this popular topic, and he agreed with many of his peers that Americans had become too obsessed with practical pursuits, too interested in making money, and too distracted to improve their inner selves. Returning to nature would rescue the soulless by releasing pent-up emotions and imaginative powers.[10] Allen could sense God's presence in every stream, every grassy pasture, and every forest. He insisted that any man could liberate himself from the shackles of everyday life if he allowed nature to wash over him. Being surrounded by the pristine beauty of God's creations made personal rejuvenation possible through an emotional release. "Nature raises his soul above the arena on which are displayed the contentious, misfortunes, and triumphs of men," he wrote, "and filling it [with] noble and loftier contemplations, fits him to view from a higher stand-point the circumstances by which he is surrounded." Allen predicted that man would possess the most sublime of all human feelings—hope—when he came in touch with God's handiwork. On July 2, 1863, Allen found out whether there existed a higher power; he was killed at Gettysburg. His father, who was in the same unit, buried his son on the battlefield and inscribed the grave marker with a pocketknife.[11]

Members of the last generation worshiped nature to stir healthy emotions and eliminate baser instincts. They followed the cultural goals of Victorian Americans, who relentlessly strove for radical purity and enlightenment. While it is difficult to say whether character building actually occurred during these outdoor excursions, adults must have wondered whether young people should retire to the countryside without adult supervision. In the wilderness, students enjoyed a realm of youthful freedom, a place where they could congregate and feel apart from adult society. Stunning scenery often had the impact of uncorking "dangerous" feelings that parents and youth cultivators wanted to keep bottled up. The release of primitive emotions, students were told in their ethics courses, would awaken perilous passions and undermine self-control.[12] A number of young people disregarded this message when they communed with nature. The editorial staff of the *Virginia University Magazine* needed a break at the conclusion of the fall semester in 1856. Looking to escape the "tortures" of student life, they boarded the Central Virginia Railroad to travel to a mountain pass overlooking the Shenandoah Valley. As a panoramic view unfolded in front of these young men, they could feel "varied emotions" rising inside them. "One's thoughts and reflections mount upward," a member of the party wrote, "as he is elevated above man's accustomed dwelling." The same student was so overcome by the enchanting scenery that he felt the impulse to head west, where he could wander the prairies, hunt deer and buffalo, and live "wholly free from the invasion of man and his law." He knew that many of his peers entertained similar fantasies, for young Virginians longed to experience the "'fierce freedom of our forefathers.'" This writer was not afraid of the emotional liberation he felt while in natural surroundings, nor did he share his elders' fears of youthful imaginings released by such experiences. To the contrary, members of the last generation maintained that such an emotional release would recapture the creative powers that had lain dormant in the state since the Revolution. In an essay on the relationship between poetry and nature, Archibald M. Smith of the University of Virginia defended the value of imagination as the key to intellectual and moral development. He disagreed with anyone who thought it led to "folly" or compromised "dignity." Throughout history, imagination had produced great minds that helped the world grow "young again."[13] For the last generation, imagination promised to cure the dull thinking that had plagued Virginia leadership for decades.

The last generation's return to nature figured into their celebrations of Virginia's past. Visiting Mount Vernon, Jamestown, and even natural sites like the Natural Bridge provided a tangible link to Virginia's golden age. "Our great men are our idols," wrote Albemarle's Summerfield Smith in 1858, "and when they pass from us, their homes and burial places become shrines for pilgrimage. We love to linger around their tombs, and breathe into our souls the inspiring influences that ever dwell in the presence of the mighty dead."[14] College men engaged in ritual excursions designed to help them assimilate the spirits of the dead. Every spring, for example, the young men at Washington College organized a "tramp" to "Student's Rock" atop House Mountain. They elected a captain who wore the actual frock coat, chapeau, and sword of a Revolutionary officer, donated by the Cincinnati Society, a student literary organization. With great military formality, the students set out for their destination. Their "beardless captain" took on the airs of a great general, barking out commands and keeping straggling to a minimum until they reached "Student's Rock," a massive ledge of white sandstone where they established camp. The weary campers stayed up all night, telling stories, singing songs, and eating and drinking. Anyone caught napping received a blast in the ear from a tin horn. When the morning light filtered through the Blue Ridge Mountains and illuminated the Shenandoah Valley, one student remembered the moment as emotionally intense, far beyond his powers of description. Although it was only for a weekend, the young men at Washington College tried to create an atmosphere that would simultaneously bring them closer to Virginia's landscape and the state's famed past. They followed the military protocol of the Revolutionary army, endured the "rigors" of camp life, slept on the venerated soil of their state, and paid homage to the Founders through stories and tales told around the fire. Looking down on the valley floor, illuminated by the soft morning light, elevated the spirits of young Virginians. They felt as if they had reached the apogee of human existence, a heavenly spot from which to enjoy the special blessings that the Commonwealth had received from above.[15]

The correspondence and papers of the last generation further attest to the overriding belief that one could find in nature the ineffable spirit that made the Old Dominion a superior land. If this remarkable environment could nurture intellectual and moral greatness during the Revolution, members of the last generation thought that it could do the same for them. In an 1858 address to the Calliopean Society at Emory and Henry College, John Lee Buchanan told his peers that "along the wild banks of the wild rivers, amid the valleys, hills and mountains" would arise the next generation of great men who would lead the country. But the promise of Virginia's landscape could only be realized, men like Buchanan reasoned, if young people sufficiently honored the past. Returning to nature and studying history would together encourage love for homeland. In his 1855 senior speech at the Virginia Military Institute, Stapleton Crutchfield of Spotsylvania County explained that Virginia's landscape possessed magical powers that held its citizens enraptured, thus making it possible for them to attain one of "the true aims of life, . . . a devout and generous love of our own native state." The University of Virginia's William Cabell agreed that his fellow citizens needed to be versed in their heritage, or they would be lost in the future. He declared that "every man ought to know something of the History of his own native and beloved land." In an 1857 speech at Washington College, Alexander Pendleton reminded the audience that "to the past then we must recur in tracing the elements of Virginia character."[16]

In visiting the natural wonders and historical sites of the Commonwealth, some young Virginians recognized that the greatness of the state had been squandered. The most striking evidence of neglect could be found in the decrepit condition of Virginia's famous landmarks, indisputable proof that the leaders of their parents' generation were not carrying out their duty to the Founders. Widespread apathy in the state thwarted efforts to preserve George Washington's home until the Mount Vernon Ladies Association secured sufficient support in 1858.[17] Jamestown was also crumbling; only the ivy-choked remnants of the ancient church remained. Unless the people preserved the landmarks of past greatness, young Virginians worried that the virtues of the Founders—intellectual creativity, a strong work ethic, and a religious bearing—would also be lost to future generations. The general apathy of Virginians toward the past struck at the core of the last generation's sense of identity, particularly when they learned that Northerners devoted tremendous resources to the preservation and commemoration of their heritage. If Virginians did not preserve their own past with the same passion and devotion, the entire world would believe, according to the *Richmond Whig*, that the people of the United States all came from Plymouth Rock. A University of Virginia student concurred wholeheartedly. "Thousands annually flock to Plymouth, to commemorate the landing of the Pilgrim Fathers, whilst we, at long intervals and by spasmodic efforts, manage to get our patriotism to the 'sticking point,' and make some bungling attempt to have a Jamestown celebration." This same student thought it ironic that outsiders charged Virginians with living in the past when he knew that "our history is a sealed book" to many state residents.[18]

The wretched condition of Jefferson's Monticello particularly irked the students at the University of Virginia. Since Jefferson's death in 1826, the mansion had endured an ignominious decline. The editors of the *Virginia University Magazine* were embarrassed by Northern newspaper reports deprecating the sorry condition of the estate. They suggested in 1857 that the students raise funds for improvements at Jefferson's grave site, which had been defaced by curious visitors over the years. Any man who opposed the improvement of

This undated photograph of Thomas Jefferson's grave was probably taken in the mid-nineteenth century and shows the poor condition of the obelisk. It was the decaying state of this and other Virginia landmarks that caused such a furor among members of the last generation. (Courtesy of the Thomas Jefferson Foundation)

Jefferson's family cemetery, the editors wrote, "is little sensible to the spirit of patriotism and gratitude, and to the honor due, from all men, to the memory of the great Evangelist of Republican memory." Preserving Jefferson's grave site served a number of purposes for the students. Their efforts imparted a sense of spiritual closeness to the past, the link that might catapult them to personal success. Young Virginians also reprimanded the older generation for neglecting their adult duties. They believed that they, not their fathers, were the ones who honored the memory of their ancestors. Their planned re-memorialization of Jefferson would show the older generation that "the youth of America" was responsible and ready for the "mighty destinies that will soon be committed to their keeping."[19]

Virginians of all ages took pride in the state's celebrated history, but each generation articulated its own sense of identity based on its own reading of the past. Why the young men of the 1850s believed Virginians constituted a distinct people is difficult to sort out. Members of the last generation referred to a unique Virginia spirit, but they never agreed on a uniform set of characteristics or qualities that made someone a Virginian. Only hospitality and generosity consistently emerge in their descriptions of genuine Virginia traits. The cultural diversity of the state, which they fully acknowledged and praised, made it impossible to articulate one recipe that would produce the quintessential Virginian. Members of the last generation contradicted themselves when it came to Virginia identity. They often spoke of a common state character, but they also celebrated distinct regional differences within the Commonwealth. Why did the last generation glory in an exaggerated sense of provincialism? The physical geography of a specific locale played the decisive role in how young Virginians saw themselves. In their minds, place mattered above all else, and each particular area had its own peculiar sounds, smells, and sights. They likened specific communities to independent forges that hammered out a distinctive style. Henry Clay Pate, for instance, detected differences among Virginians that could be traced to the physical environment of individual communities. He grew up in Bedford County near the town of Liberty, which rested in the shadows of the famous Peaks of Otter, a part of the Blue Ridge chain. Living near the impressive mountain, Pate argued, turned the people into the "very princes of freemen; breathing, as they do, the pure breezes of their own blue mountains, and daily learning lessons of liberty and independence, from the wild bird that soars in unobstructed flight and proud defiance about the towering summit of the Peaks of Otter." Place also figured prominently in Lancelot Blackford's thinking about Virginia character, although he was not an extreme geographic determinist like Pate. "These people of Powhatan are the *finest*, the *kindest*, and *most lovable* in my knowledge," he wrote shortly after accepting a teaching position in the area. Blackford found the people to be so warm and inviting that he informed his mother that "my candid opinion is that there is not such another county in the state or out of it as Powhatan—and I don't think I shall ever cease to love it."[20]

The last generation boosted its morale by celebrating its state's unique "character." Virginians felt alienated from the intellectual trends and material prosperity that prevailed elsewhere. The world paid attention to the North, recognized its literature, sympathized with its antislavery movement, and admired its technological advancements. Virginia and the South, on the other hand, had been left behind. Provincialism appealed to those who felt like outsiders, for it enabled them to look inward and proclaim their collective self-worth, regardless of what others might say. In extolling the virtues of place, young Virginians did not take on a siege mentality or become uncritical of their own state. The last generation wanted the world to know that Virginia's local customs, natural landscape, and history contained a distinctive spirit that held out the promise of future greatness. This spirit stood as the first line of defense against Northern charges of backwardness and cultural depravity. The last generation glorified the wide variety of local Virginia expressions, traditions, and manners as a way to give dignity to their communities and their state. Henry Clay Pate may have grumbled about the lack of economic development in Virginia, but he could find nothing wrong in his hometown of Liberty. He considered it a fountainhead of virtue and grace. For those who had never heard of the place, Pate defiantly wrote: "So be it—yet they gain nothing by their ignorance of one of the most pleasant, as well as wealthy and intelligent regions in the world."[21]

The self-images of young people came largely from residing in specific Virginia locales, but this did not always overshadow their identities as Southerners and Americans. However, there is not a consistent, identifiable pattern in the way they expressed these seemingly conflicting loyalties and varied perceptions. The identity they showed to the world depended on the political circumstances. For example, in their speeches and published papers, young Virginians used both the rhetoric of Union and the language of Southern rights, but they clearly did not consider themselves among the fire-eating crusaders for a Southern nation. Until Lincoln's election, they flatly rejected any effort to break up the United States. At the same time, their commitment to the Union was circumscribed by the issues of slavery, political equality in Washington, and honor. No other Virginian generation, at least in its formative years, confronted such a contentious political scene in the decade of the "impending crisis." Although they were not radicalized by the ominous events of the 1850s, they were probably more inclined than their fathers to believe that the preservation of Virginia's distinctive culture rested with Southern political interests.

The last generation's sense of being Southern must be understood within the cultural context of the 1850s, when a Southern education became wildly popular. In that decade, the region's intellectual class pressured slaveholders to send their sons to Southern universities so that they could be taught "proper" values and ideas.[22] The last generation came of age just as this Southern educational movement blossomed, and most members of this age group obtained his education below the Mason-Dixon Line. They were quick to denounce any Southerner who preferred the halls of Princeton and Harvard to those of Southern institutions, but they said little else on this popular trend. Although they extolled the virtues of a Southern education, they almost never talked about what made Southern education unique. Neither did their professors.

Except in the case of Randolph-Macon, the curricula at Virginia's colleges and universities did not include specific courses on the South's social system. Members of the last generation probably felt more secure with teachers who came from the South. These men could defend the peculiar institution from a secular and a religious perspective. They also could discuss history, political economy, literature, and moral philosophy within the context of a slave society trying to survive in a world largely dominated by free-labor capitalism.

The last generation's Walter Monteiro was one of the few young men to analyze the purpose and meaning of a Southern education. At the Hampton Academy in 1857, he implored the young scholars to pursue their education in the Commonwealth while denouncing those Southern parents who "continue sending their children to these [northern] nurseries of abolitionism," which would inculcate them with principles "inimical to our laws and domestic institutions." This graduate of the University of Virginia did not want the defense of slavery to divert young people from redeeming Virginia's reputation. "We have been outstripped in nearly every department of knowledge by those very northern men whose Boetian dullness we are accustomed to deride," he proclaimed. Monteiro predicted that the feelings of inadequacy would disappear once Virginia and the South developed its native talent. If older Virginians kept their money and children in the state, native talent would be developed, and prestige and honor for the Old Dominion would follow. Surprisingly, Monteiro did not promote Southern education in order to foster uniform thinking across the region.[23]

The evidence of students engaged in dialogue with professors is limited, but it offers some insight into the impact of the Southern education movement. Members of the last generation wrote very little about classroom activity in their letters and diaries, and there seems to have been a modest amount of interaction with faculty outside standard recitation. "With the exception of Mr. [George F.] Holmes," recalled a University of Virginia student, "my relation to the teachers whose classes I attended was purely formal or mechanical." Informal gatherings did occur, but details about the frequency and content of these meetings are sketchy at best. In the spring of 1860, for instance, Professor McGuffey held Bible study classes with seventy to one hundred students every Sabbath.[24] What does exist in abundance are the speeches and published works of prominent Southern thinkers. With these sources, it is possible to extrapolate their ideas and compare them to those of the students. Young people were profoundly influenced by the return to orthodoxy among Virginia academics who extolled the Commonwealth and the South as Christian societies.

As Eugene Genovese has convincingly demonstrated, students responded to Southern educators because they successfully linked proslavery views to Christianity, republicanism, and time-honored social values.[25]

The return to orthodoxy was apparent not only in the thinking of faculty and students, but also in the ascendancy of state-supported institutions. Whether lecturing about the physical sciences or discussing political economy, Southern professors, although they often denied it, inserted theology into the classroom. They insisted that intellectual inquiry could not be divorced from religion. President George Junkin of Washington College reminded his students of this at the 1851 commencement: "The family, school, or College which does not base the principle of its moral discipline on the doctrine of a Deity and his perfections, will raise men capable of government only by brute force." In an 1859 address at the Virginia Military Institute, C. P. Gadsden bluntly told cadets that "the Bible should be a text book in all our schools. Our Colleges and institutes of Learning should honour it above every other volume, and place it in the forefront of their course of study."[26]

Behind the podiums at Virginia's universities and colleges stood some of the most influential proslavery thinkers of the time. Secular and religious leaders across the Old Dominion (and the rest of the South) such as James Holcombe, George Frederick Holmes, Albert Bledsoe, William Smith, Beverley Tucker, Edmund Ruffin, George Fitzhugh, George D. Armstrong, and Robert L. Dabney defended the South's way of life within a religious framework used to launch a full-scale attack against the North.[27] According to the last generation's Moncure Conway, these intellectuals captivated their younger audience. With some exaggeration, Conway recalled of the 1850s that "it was the time when a 'Young Virginia' was rising up to promulgate the philosophical, sociological, and ethical excellence of slavery." His father "was troubled by the efforts of the younger generation to capture me," but, despite parental reservations, Conway joined a Southern rights organization in his native town. He remembered that "in Virginia it was the most scholarly and philosophical young men who discarded old Virginia principles and advocated slavery *per se*."[28]

Although considerable diversity existed in proslavery thought, the message became more aggressive as sectional politics became more contentious. At the same time, Southern-bred teachers moved into Virginia classrooms in larger numbers during the decade before the Civil War. No longer content merely to defend their institutions, secular and religious thinkers took the offensive. They excoriated free-labor societies for their failure to preserve the dominant position of orthodox Christianity. In an argument typical of proslavery theorists in the 1850s, Edmund Ruffin suggested that the high level of "moral debasement and depravity" in the North conclusively proved the South's "superiority" in religion. "The greater number of the houseless families, of paupers, of criminals and of the insane [in the North]," Ruffin concluded, ". . . all show in their calamitous effects that there is much more suffering, of both body and mind, in the North than in the South."[29] Although Ruffin's sectional hostility exceeded that of his contemporaries, his colleagues hardly shied away from employing similar rhetoric. Their fiery denunciations of the North had a curious impact on young people. Most were so taken by the idea that the North had become a godless land that a deeper inquiry seemed unnecessary. Students rarely probed beyond the easy generalizations that equated free labor with evil and the slave-labor society with virtue.

The field of history could also discourage a closer examination of the South's social system. In studying the vicissitudes of the past, members of the last generation believed they could find indisputable "truths" regarding human behavior. These truths or laws, they believed, could explain the rise and fall of governments without ever taking into account the structure of a society. Ancient history, for instance, revealed to Southerners that debauchery and religious infidelity could topple the greatest of civilizations. At the University of Virginia, Don Peter Halsey of Lynchburg and David Watson of Louisa County both sat in the modern history class of Professor M. Schele de Vere. Halsey wrote in his notebook that Rome had collapsed from its "effeminacy, profligacy, & licentiousness," that its people "could sink no lower in degeneracy & degradation," and that its emperors were ruled by "wicked caprices." Watson's notes echo those of Halsey, who also understood that Romans had sacrificed liberty for worldly pursuits. Halsey concluded that "Rome rose by conquest & fell by conquest giving one of the best illustrations in the world of the Scriptural saying 'He that killeth with the sword shall fall by the sword.' " Both young men noted that their professors blamed the decline on the "great curse" of pagan religion, a Greek legacy that became a source of "unmitigated evil" to Romans. [30]

Although Halsey's and Watson's notes lack any reference to the North, the parallel would not have been lost on them. Southerners of all ages feared that any nation could regress like Rome. On the eve of the 1860 presidential election, the last generation's James DeWitt Hankins expressed a popular historical analogy between the two regimes: "In Republican Rome, men aspiring to high office neglected no means of gaining popularity, no matter how . . . immoral or illegal they might be. This hunting after power was, and remained one of the most fatal disorders of the Roman Republic." He wondered: "What better is the American Republic?"[31] Young men like Hankins, whose faith in the political system was shaky to begin with, became even less certain about the future after studying the past. The barbarian hordes, now in the form of the abolitionists, stood at the gates of power. Significantly, not a single member of the last generation mentioned Roman slavery; nor did they claim that the South was the heir of that "great tradition" of human servitude. It appears that they distanced themselves entirely from this controversial issue. They felt more comfortable with blanket descriptions of Yankee depravity that, intentionally or not, drew attention away from the central argument put forward by Southern social philosophers: that the social system of slavery stood as a bulwark against the modern excesses of the bourgeois world.

Thus Southern intellectuals proved most successful in their attempt to portray the South as a religious civilization struggling against an otherwise hostile, godless world. Their defense was not a pathological response to guilt over slavery or a feeling that the world had turned against them. The pro-slavery argument humanized white perceptions of the South's social system (while it dehumanized slaves) and, more importantly, reinforced the religious sensibilities of most young people. This influential message addressed their daily religious concerns while furthering their overriding goal to Christianize Virginia. A "nation without Religion," wrote a University of Virginia student in 1855, cannot "have civilization." He wanted the teachings of Jesus Christ to pervade every institution, to inspire every child, and to guide the actions of every politician. He adopted his generation's belief that Christianity made the people of the United States the most virtuous, intelligent, and prosperous in the world.[32] Identifying the South as a Christian community also satisfied the basic need of young people to see themselves as moral. In this, they were no different from ruling classes everywhere. Northerners might regard Southerners as brutish, stupid, and vulgar, but young Virginians repelled those insults by envisioning themselves as a truly Christian people. When a chapter of the Young Men's Christian Association came into existence at the University of Virginia, the students saw the rationale for the organization's presence in the "religious destitution and comparative spiritual, as well as mental, darkness prevailing in an adjoining section of the country."[33]

The belief that God had chosen Southerners to preserve orthodox Christianity must have appealed to members of the last generation. Such a mission promised them the respect and public recognition that they always craved and felt entitled to as Virginians. A few intellectuals even suggested to young people that the fate of Christianity and the nation were intertwined, with their future resting in the hands of the last generation. Professor William Andrew Smith warned his Randolph-Macon students that "the Southern States may be labored by the tempests that shall break upon them from other sources." He was confident that the people below the Mason-Dixon Line would "settle the great quarrel of the country between light and darkness, between religion and vile superstition!"[34] Professors and ministers set the stage for members of the last generation to show the world the moral superiority of their way of life. Young Virginians dutifully readied themselves for the possibility that their age group would become the leading actors in the climax of the Union's history.

Members of the last generation did not have to create a fantasy world to believe that Southerners represented a distinctly Christian people. A spirit of interdenominational cooperation and Christian fellowship flourished in the antebellum South. Bigotry and prejudice certainly existed, but these young Virginians displayed a remarkable degree of tolerance and acceptance of other faiths, including Catholicism and Judaism. "We had a good sermon, rather doctrinal to be generally popular," wrote John Samuel Apperson, an apprentice to a Blacksburg doctor. "However, this I allow all denominations. Each one has his belief and believes in his heart that the Bible sanctions and strengthens that belief. So I am for allowing Baptists, Methodists, Presbyterians and every other denomination [to] believe as they please." To prove that the South embraced a variety of religious practices, Lancelot Blackford pointed to Virginia's history: within "the borders [of] the Commonwealth of Virginia" originated "the Act for Religious Freedom" that granted equality among all denominations. As an indication of the state's tolerant and pluralistic mood, Blackford noted that in the colonial period Baptists had been "subjected to ignominious persecutions," but now they thrived in eastern Virginia. He thought it "remarkable and significant" that "there is now an overwhelming predominance of the very body of Christians who then and there suffered for their religion."[35] Men of various Protestant faiths affiliated with the University of Virginia encouraged students to think of themselves as part of a Christian brotherhood, and they wanted young people to learn about the different denominations through a series of lectures on Christianity. In 1850, the Presbyterians kicked off this lecture series, which was to be followed every year by ministers from a different church. The organizers of the project were adamant about avoiding any "appearance of sectarianism."[36]

Many young Virginians extended religious toleration to Catholicism. The rise of the anti-Catholic Know-Nothing Party disturbed some of these young men. Because the Know-Nothings had generated prejudice and resentment, some Americans doubted whether Catholics were loyal to republicanism and could properly fulfill their civic duties. James Boyd thought it a preposterous claim "that no Catholic can give . . . his allegiance to his government." The Pope, he wrote, "no longer lays claim to such direct authority." Moreover, he argued, it was a Catholic nation, France, that helped the United States secure its independence so that it could "proclaim to the world the great principles of religious toleration." To whom does America owe religious freedom? asked Boyd. "She owes it to her Catholics." In his 1860 master's thesis at the University of Virginia, Boyd extended his sympathetic eye to Islam. He admired the Koran for its beautiful prose, its elevating message, and its similarities to the Bible. "Prayer, earnest and incessant it [Koran] declares the great duty of man," Boyd wrote. "Benevolence and Charity, a broad, comprehensive Charity—it enforces as essential to eternal salvation." While he welcomed what he believed would be Islam's inevitable decline, he also acknowledged that Muhammad had given people spirituality in a place where the message of Christ fell flat. Islam prevented "ignorance and gross idolatry, and even from the most fearful Atheism." "All other remedy's [sic] had failed," he added. "The Christian religion itself had been tried. It but increased the evil. It was too pure, too holy, too undefiled to appeal to the gross natures with which it had to deal."[37] Although Boyd probably went further than most to understand other faiths, he shared with his peers a commitment to religious toleration. This powerful belief coincided with a sense of belonging to a Christian community. Even though Episcopalians, Presbyterians, Methodists, and Baptists disagreed on important theological questions, these young Virginians, like most slaveholders, articulated a coherent cultural ideology rooted in orthodox Christianity.

Claiming their region as the seat of Christian civilization brought the last generation closer to an idealized Southern community. This view of the South as a religious oasis also imparted sacred meaning and significance to the sectional struggles over slavery and territorial expansion. Young Virginians did not envision a religious war enveloping the nation, nor did they believe that mere economic and political power was at stake in the conflict with the North. They thought that nothing less than the fate of Christendom rested in their hands. In 1854, G. W. W. M. Simms of Albemarle County tapped into the almost universal white Southern belief that the region had minority status in the nation. He wrote in the *Southern Repertory Magazine and Review* that the South was a Christian community facing "a persecuting world" where Northern infidels "are counseled by him who is the 'King of Darkness in the abyss of night.'" Although he feared a "grim and awful specter" emanating from the North, he appealed "to the Immaculate God" because "justice dwelleth at his right hand."[38]

Most Virginia students seconded Simms's opinion that the South stood as a Christian bastion against an infidel North. It is tempting, as a result, to see young Southerners as pawns of slaveholder ideologues. Although public freedom of expression over slavery vanished after Nat Turner's failed insurrection in 1831, religious and secular thinkers did not exploit the last generation's idealism, political naïveté, and youthful energy to create unthinking zealots. Many young Virginians feared that religious skepticism might engulf the North, but as an age group they did not consider themselves crusaders in a religious war against Yankee abolitionists. They despised religious fanaticism in any form.[39] Historian John McCardell overstates his case when he argues that Southern educators wanted "to define, inculcate, and enforce orthodoxy, thus helping to prepare the Southern mind for separate nationhood."[40] The region's leading minds never intended to indoctrinate young people in secession or Southern cultural nationalism. The only exception was William A. Smith of Randolph-Macon College, who held "a deep conviction that the minds of young men" received "fatal direction" regarding the principles of slavery. This prompted Smith to organize a course devoted exclusively to human bondage that was a requirement of every senior at Randolph-Macon.[41] Those who did not study under Smith also received the standard racial, religious, and historical explanations of slavery. At the University of Virginia, for example, Professor William H. McGuffey gave his moral philosophy class a generic defense of the institution. "Slaves in this country [are] much better than native Africans," a student taking notes recorded in 1855. "Have we a right [to make] people better in spite of themselves? Parent does so with child. We have historical instances of people who had to be enslaved 400 years before fit to be free—Jews. We, however, [are] not in favor of the slave trade. Negroes [are] not fit to be free in this state of society. [They] can't attain proper appreciation of it."[42]

As members of the slaveholding class, Southern intellectuals understood the importance of fostering among all classes allegiance to the ruling elites. For this reason, they purposefully reached out to young people. George Fitzhugh, for example, spoke to the Young Men's Literary Society of Fredericksburg in 1860, imploring the audience to uphold their duties to family, county, and state. Although he briefly compared the relative merits of the North and the South, there is no record of Fitzhugh's trying to recruit young Virginians to the cause of secession.[43] Talk of revolution troubled Fitzhugh, as it did most of his fellow proslavery theorists who counseled against extremism. John Minor, a law professor at the University of Virginia and stalwart Unionist, tried to massage the Unionist tendencies in young people in the late 1850s. Patience, he advised his nephews at the University of Virginia, would deflate "the fanatical clamor" raised by John Brown's raid, and "give time for the more quiet & order loving people to make their voices heard."[44]

Despite the Unionist leanings of most Southern thinkers, they unintentionally primed the last generation to become secessionist gadflies. Virginia Unionists like Minor affirmed the dominant Southern rights view that Republicans and abolitionists would run roughshod over the South if given the chance. Agitating against slavery, Southern Unionists argued, provided the Republicans with a sluice to drive the waterwheel of federal power. Once Washington fell into Republican hands, the South would be pulverized. In the same letter to his nephews, Minor painted an ominous scenario that mirrored John C. Calhoun's dark prophecy in 1850. "The feeling however, which actuates the great body of that party [the Republicans]," he wrote, "is a desire by the extinction of slave labour to render the lands of the South, & South West comparatively valueless; so that it may be occupied by them at small cost."[45] Advising patience must have seemed incongruous to young people, for the political forecast warned of the South's humiliating downfall under a Republican regime. The last generation's response to Lincoln's election would demonstrate that young people saw no point in waiting for the noose to tighten around their necks. They would come to believe that only secession offered an honorable escape.

Virginia's intellectual and political classes also betrayed their conservative intentions by insisting that young people define themselves in opposition to the North. Even speeches intended solely to inspire youthful action in the Commonwealth contained reminders that Yankees ridiculed their way of life. Southern thinkers were not overreacting to Northern tirades against the South, which became after 1850 more hostile and demeaning. Historian Susan-Mary Grant insists that in the decade leading up to the Civil War, "much of the moderate sentiment in the North as a whole had given way to a far more hostile approach; consequently, a more negative image of the South began to dominate the northern mind."[46] Northern hostility elicited a furious counterattack by Southern leaders. In his 1856 address to the cadets at the Virginia Military

Institute, for instance, Unionist Francis H. Smith hailed the improvements in Virginia education as a triumph over Massachusetts. "*Virginia*—much abused *Virginia*," he declaimed, "with a white population which is less than that of the much lauded, but most disloyal state of *Massachusetts*, has actually, at *this* day, a greater number of young men who are students of college, than are afforded by the State of Massachusetts."[47] Smith reinforced the last generation's tendency to frame issues as part of a competition to surpass the North, and he was not alone in making this appeal. Many of his colleagues purposefully cultivated a spirit of sectional rivalry between young Virginians and the North. They bluntly told members of the last generation that the state's reputation depended on their future achievements and on keeping slavery alive.

Not all young Virginians accepted the idea that Northerners were a separate people so radically different in character, culture, and spirituality as to make them dangerous. At least one dissenter in the last generation, an editor for the *Virginia University Magazine*, perceived that this attitude of Southernism had been cultivated purposefully in the minds of the young. In 1860 he lamented that "the youth of the country" were inculcated with "bitter prejudices against the people of the opposite section." A young person's hostility blossomed in school, where he was "taught to believe that all the virtue and patriotism of the nation is, and ever has been confined to his own [section]." The editor suggested an exchange program and a "free interchange of educational patronage," but doubted its success as long as Northerners continued to taunt Virginians "*with inferiority*."[48] Even though the editor questioned the sensationalist depictions of Yankees, he ran into the insurmountable barrier of honor, making it impossible for him to stand on moderate ground. Popular outrage over Northern insults stopped young Virginians from raising a sensible voice at a time when mass culture and scholarly works were filled with exaggeration and distortion.

Even if it had been available, an exchange program probably would not have excited many young Virginians, who showed little inclination to venture North. Spending their entire youth in the South rendered it impossible to compare their preconceptions of Northerners with the actual living conditions above the Mason-Dixon Line. Jeb Stuart, however, is a valuable exception to this pattern. Through his experience, it is possible to understand how other members of the last generation interpreted the world around them from the vantage point of being a Virginian. This perspective joined their identities as Southerners and Americans. After attending Emory and Henry College, Stuart accepted an appointment to the United States Military Academy at

West Point in 1850. He expected the worst from a place so close to abolitionist New England, but upon his arrival he was surprised to find a "strong
Southern feeling" and equally relieved to know that "a majority of the officers
& Professors are from the South." In regard to the Northern cadets, he wrote
that "we are far from entertaining towards each other as marked antipathy as
the times would suggest," for "a sentiment of mutual forebearance" guided
behavior and, "in a word, with us all is harmony." "True," he added, "particular sects are more intimate than others for you know that 'birds of a feather
will roost together.'"[49]

Stuart quickly adjusted to the cultural and military environment at the
academy. In his free time, he delighted in taking moonlight strolls along the
Hudson River to tour the old trenches from the American Revolution or to
admire the enchanting landscape. But his admiration had its limits. Even
though West Point evoked strong national sentiments in Stuart, he assured
his cousin that "I . . . consider it a *magnificent spot*, but so long as it remains
in Yankee land, . . . I can not call it *home*." A few months later he wrote, "If it
were only inhabited by warm-hearted Virginians and moved to our mountains
I would never leave it."[50] In another letter to the same relative, he exclaimed:
"Virginia is the place after all, isn't it?" Stuart tried to soften the pain felt
by his self-imposed exile from the Old Dominion by decorating his room
with reminders from Virginia's countryside. Among his trinkets was a sprig
of *arbor vitae* picked from a Giles County mountaintop, and he was especially
fond of a gourd that came from his family's garden. Stuart felt his imagination taking over every time he looked at it "'on yonder hook.'" Several of his
classmates thought it curious that Stuart attached himself so fervently to a
dried vegetable, and they jokingly schemed to break it. "But," Stuart wrote,
"I do not anticipate such a calamity, the loss to them would be too *great*."[51]

Homesickness does not fully explain Stuart's deep longing for the Commonwealth, although it certainly contributed to his exaggerated sense of being
a Virginian. Yet even in his most nostalgic reflections on Virginia, he did
not become a hopeless romantic and he did not conjure up the image of the
cavalier when claiming Virginia's superiority. He never felt the need to invent
an identity, because he believed that a real cultural divide existed between
Virginians and Yankees. Stuart's contact with Northern women, more than
anything else, convinced him of these important differences. During his first
year of cadetship, he spotted a young woman ice skating on campus, a sight
that he considered one of the most shocking of his life. When Stuart collected himself, he was tempted to deliver a diatribe against "Yankee Customs."

"But my space is too precious," he injected, ". . . Let us go back to Dear old Virginia."[52] By his senior year, Stuart thought Northern women were irredeemable. "The more I see of these Yankee girls," he remarked, "the more thoroughly I am convinced of their inferiority in every respect to our Virginia ladies." He believed that most of the Northern women who visited West Point were "affected, fashionable, exquisite, flirts."[53]

Stuart's West Point letters rated women like a loved-starved adolescent, but his musings about the opposite sex say as much about his politics as they do about his taste in women. His notions of Virginia womanhood anchored his vision of a good society. Northern society must have lost its moral equilibrium, Stuart reasoned, or else Yankee women would not behave so brazenly. His writings further suggest that he understood the breakdown in gender roles within the context of slavery and abolition. Southern white men of all ages and classes believed that slavery preserved customary gender relations within the family, particularly the subordination of women. Not surprisingly, Stuart connected the "fastness" of Northern women to abolition. This connection reinforced his fears that such radicalism, if imposed on the South, would destroy not only slavery but also traditional gender roles and power relations within the family. [54]

One's first impression of Jeb Stuart at West Point is of a carefree youth, seemingly more interested in young women and riding horses than the issues of the day. But when he considered the abolitionist vision, Stuart lost his boyish outlook and became grave, reflective, and protective of Southern institutions. An attack against slavery forced him to put aside his Virginia provincialism and position the defense of his homeland within a broader Southern context. Although he described Virginians in opposition to the North, cultural differences did not spark a secessionist impulse. His sense of duty to the Founders and their gift of republicanism prevented him from seeing regional differences as a first step toward separation. He recognized that each region had its own provincial folkways and that such characteristics revealed much about a particular place and its people. When it came to the Commonwealth, Stuart celebrated his local community, its history, and its landscape, which in turn gave texture and meaning to his sacred regard for Virginia. The Old Dominion, furthermore, held together the vital elements of his loyalty, giving structure to those attachments that enlivened Stuart's sense of identity. In the deeper recesses of his psyche, however, slavery remained buried. He idealized Virginia society as a beloved community devoid of human bondage.

Although the last generation diminished slavery's role when constructing their identities as Virginians, Republican attacks against the institution forced young people to confront the fact that their existence, materially and ideologically, originated in a slave society. Political battles over slavery and the rise of the Republican Party brought the last generation's abstract sense of being Virginian and Southern into sharp focus. The Commonwealth's waning voice in national affairs long had troubled the men of the last generation. A further loss of power would destroy what little respect the Old Dominion still garnered in the Union. Under no circumstances were young Virginians willing to accept restrictions on the expansion of slavery. Abolitionist and Republican designs, which the last generation considered identical, would tarnish Virginia's honor and underscore its vassalage to the North. For young men trying to recover the Commonwealth's reputation and expand its influence, the Republican Party offered nothing except the end of their dream. However, they did not jump off the ship of Union when the political seas became turbulent in the 1850s, even though many of them could not overcome the fear that the election of a Republican president would lead to an inevitable collision of the two regions. Young and old Virginians alike spoke passionately in defense of the Union and the need for political moderation, and such flowery statements have led a number of historians to exaggerate the extent of the Old Dominion's conservatism.[55] These scholars are so taken in by Virginians who clamored for Union that they fail to appreciate the political requirements that conditioned pleas for national unity. The case of the last generation reveals that young people opposed a Union in which slavery did not have ironclad protection in the territories. Whether their personal futures depended on the expansion of slavery or not is irrelevant. Their sense of honor, their ideas about manifest destiny, their need for power, and their desire for Virginia to return to national leadership made compromise with the Republicans an impossibility. In the decade before Lincoln's election, these men consistently indicated that submission to antislavery forces would be akin to committing suicide.

As part of the state's ruling class, members of the last generation worried about their status at home, for if the Republicans gained control of Washington, a reshuffling of power relations in Virginia would certainly follow. A realignment probably seemed even more threatening to young people who were associated with the ruling class but did not exercise power. Young Virginians desired authority, and a political upheaval in the Old Dominion triggered by a Republican insurgency would make leadership positions unattainable. Yet such fears did not lead to a preemptive bid for a Southern Confederacy. For much of the decade, Unionism prevailed among the members of the last generation for reasons beyond a simple love for country. The Whig influence predominated in the Old Dominion throughout the 1850s, and the party's membership set a tone of moderation that permeated the state. Young Virginians also stood firm for Union because abolitionist and Republican demands were generally seen as the perverse consequence of party politics or fanaticism. Leaders of all political stripes impressed on the last generation that fanaticism endangered national existence, and they tried, with mixed results, to reassure young people that responsible leadership would ultimately win out. Before the Young Men's Christian Association of Richmond in 1856, William C. Rives, a prominent Whig politician and Unionist from Albemarle County, thought the "voices of Christian charity" would heal factionalism and defeat ambition before a fratricidal conflict erupted.[56]

James DeWitt Hankins of Tidewater Virginia who hailed from a prominent Whig family and Democrat John Lee Buchanan of southwest Virginia demonstrated the impressive degree of unity that existed among college-educated Virginians. When discussing the politics of slavery, both men revealed the interplay between state and national loyalty, slavery and power, and honor and manhood. Both men were committed Unionists who desired an American republic free of rancorous partisanship. They both blamed party politics and Northern and Southern demagogues for stirring sectional turmoil and for bringing the nation to the brink of disunion. While Hankins and Buchanan wanted to avoid a fratricidal conflict and clean up the rot in Washington, they both took a hard-line stand over slavery in the territories. National compromises over this issue violated their belief in political equality. With mad politicians and the "Black Republicans" gaining strength in the North, they turned fatalistic. Events, they believed, had assumed a life of their own. Without leaders who possessed the virtue and intelligence of the Revolutionary generation, the reins of power remained in the hands of reckless politicians. Hankins, Buchanan, and many other young men imagined these demagogues driving the nation to destruction.[57]

In an 1860 letter from the University of Virginia, Hankins excoriated Whigs, Democrats, and South Carolinians for their fractious behavior. If war erupted, he knew that the Commonwealth would become its great battlefield. Hankins hoped that "this agitation is but a bubble on the surface of our political sea which will soon disappear forever and we may never say: 'Mingled were our hearts together. Long time ago.' But rather, can we ever forget each other. No never no." What draws notice here is the fact that Hankins's belief in a perpetual Union rested on ideas that could never support a Republican administration. In his mind, the expansion of slavery must not be obstructed. Hankins condemned the Missouri Compromise, the Kansas-Nebraska Act, and the Lecompton Constitution for striking "a blow to the very heart of the South and the Union." With the rise of the Black Republicans, which he blamed on Southern Democrats and to a lesser degree the Whigs, Hankins could not see how the country could survive. "*Soon one morning*," he wrote, "we will hear a small *trumpet telling us* [to] *prepare to die*."[58]

John Lee Buchanan illustrates the dangers of imposing sharp ideological lines between slaveholders and nonslaveholders. Although he was the son of a nonslaveholder who lived in southwest Virginia, and even though he had limited access to the main centers of intellectual and political power, he subscribed to the dominant views of the master class. After receiving rudimentary training in a rude cabin that passed for a private academy, Buchanan began his professional career as a store clerk in the town of Marion. Conversations with passing customers aroused his intellectual curiosity. He read Shakespeare and ancient history in his spare time, but still hungered for more learning.

Buchanan eventually decided to quit his job and enter Emory and Henry College in the fall of 1851. By his third year, he published an article in the student literary magazine that argued in favor of Union as a noble cause but one that appeared doomed as long as demagogues played upon people's emotions. "Too long already has this fanatical spirit of the North been engaged in an unholy crusade upon Southern rights," he wrote. "For if the violence of party conflicts continues to increase and the remorseless spirit of Northern aggression continues to advance, the hot vapors that will rise up from the turbulent sea of human passion, will gather into a fiery storm-cloud of desolation." The following year he gave a highly charged address on the political ramifications of slavery, but not once did he investigate the institution as a social system. Buchanan lamented the constant battling of political parties, but, unlike Hankins, he placed the burden of guilt on the North's antislavery element. The Southern Democratic and Whig parties hardly entered into his speech. After tracing Northern aggression from the Missouri Compromise to the Kansas-Nebraska Act of 1854, Buchanan concluded that "the selfish domineering spirit of a cold hearted North" had infected Washington and posed an immediate danger to the Commonwealth. Denying Southerners the right to move their property violated Buchanan's sense of honor and his belief in regional equality in Washington. He wanted the world to know, moreover, that Northern designs to limit slavery were an attempt to blacklist the South as an uncivilized land. Buchanan saw few options for Virginia or for the region, as he could not imagine that Northern politicians would suddenly uphold the slaveholders' interpretation of the Constitution.[59]

Fears of a future cataclysm did not shake Buchanan's overriding faith in progress. He upheld his generation's position that a republican form of government and Christianity ensured the spread of freedom, intellectual advancement, and material improvement. He looked to the West as the region where the nation would realize its full potential. Thus Republican efforts to ban slavery from the territories threatened his generation's place in history. Just as many Free-Soilers staked their future beyond the Mississippi River, so did young Virginians like Buchanan. Even if they stayed in Virginia their entire lives, members of the last generation cared about the West as an outlet for the progressive spirit of the nation. If Western lands were blocked to slavery and Southern immigration, the South could regress, becoming stagnant and subordinate to the rest of the country. The promise of Manifest Destiny inspired the dreams and hopes of many young Virginians, and they deeply resented any attempt to cut the South off from the nation's divinely ordained purpose.

The issue of slavery and territorial expansion simultaneously built regional political consciousness and strengthened loyalty to the nation until Lincoln's election.[60] As was true of other young Virginians, Hankins and Buchanan's regional anxieties and sense of Southern consciousness rose and fell with the tide of political events. The Compromise of 1850, for instance, elicited a frenzied reaction in some parts of the South because it symbolized submission to the radical elements of the North.[61] A number of young Virginians joined the angry chorus, expressing support for regional unity by founding Southern rights organizations and literary magazines at schools across the state. At the University of Virginia, the students formed the Southern Rights' Association in 1851. The members alerted the "young men of the South" that "from the North, we have nothing to hope—everything to fear." Seventy-two Virginians signed their names to a proclamation that encouraged young people throughout the South to "bring about unanimity of sentiment, concert of action, and a fixedness of purpose on your part, to resist, 'to the last extremity, and at every hazard,' the wrongs and aggressions of the North." The group resolved "to form similar Associations throughout the South" where "Southern youths are educated." Just as their Revolutionary forefathers had kept themselves informed through "committees of correspondence," they desired an elaborate communication network among the various associations to keep a watchful eye on Northern activities.[62] Nothing ever came of their ambitious proposals, and Unionist sentiment prevailed. As soon as a political compromise was reached guaranteeing sectional political equality, the more radical students could not sustain the momentum for a Southern rights campaign. Interest faded, and it appears that the association disbanded for lack of members. Not a single student reference to the organization can be found for the rest of the decade except for an article in the *Richmond Whig* from 1853. An unidentified University of Virginia student, who had previously attended the Virginia Military Institute, recalled that while he was a cadet both literary societies voted down the motion to form a Southern rights association. He rejoiced over the collapse of the organization at the University of Virginia. "The utter failure . . . of the one formed at this University," he added, "shows the correct judgment of the Cadets, themselves, in rejecting the proposition."[63] Young people, it seems, preferred the YMCA, temperance organizations, athletic clubs, and secret fraternities to political organizations.

John Brown's raid in 1859 delivered a blow to the last generation's Unionism, and many young Virginians became receptive to the idea of a Southern nation. Unlike previous political events that inflamed sectional rhetoric and then cooled down with time, Brown's attempted insurrection permanently changed the tone at Virginia universities, militia organizations, and debating societies. Young people started to encourage any sign of Virginians' preparing themselves for what appeared to be an inevitable conflict with the "Black Republicans." The martial spirit that subsequently followed impressed Richmond's William R. J. Pegram. "You never saw anything like the military and patriotic feeling now existing at the South," he explained to his brother. "Before the Harpers Ferry outbreak this Regiment could not muster over three hundred and fifty men; now we have about seven hundred and fifty." When he looked at the First Regiment, he spotted men who "were never seen in any ranks" before.[64] Although a majority of the students frowned on the attempt to burn John Brown in effigy at the University of Virginia, the literary magazine congratulated those who went to Charlestown to witness the hanging. The editors of the *Virginia University Magazine* also reprinted what must have been the most shocking passage in an issue of the *Yale Literary Magazine*. The New England journal relayed a story of some University of Virginia students who fled Charlestown when they learned that men from Yale College "were coming to rescue John Brown." "It is said that they were so frightened that they *walked* right home," the Yale magazine added insultingly, "and have not been heard from since." The editors at the University of Virginia boldly responded that the students "who went to Charlestown,

As before, we have been compelled to italicize. Note the withering sarcasm of that last sentence ! !

 " The students of Virginia University having gone to Charlestown to prevent a rescue, this is a view of the manner in which they defended that city, when they heard that Yale College were coming to rescue " John Brown." It is said that they were so frightened that they *walked* right home, and have not been heard from since."

Here the wit being too profoundly obscured for even Yale penetration, the editors themselves kindly pointed it out. We hope their readers see it, and enjoy the fun, as also the very modest compliment to their valiant heroism.

In the wake of John Brown's raid, the editors of the *Virginia University Magazine* reprinted this inflammatory image and accompanying text from the *Yale Literary Magazine*. Despite this insult to the honor of the Virginia students and an abolitionist-led slave insurrection, cooler heads prevailed. No Southern rights associations or militia units were organized on the University of Virginia campus in response to the attack on Harpers Ferry. (In the possession of the author)

needed but an opportunity to prove that, though they may sometimes run, yet it is always with their faces towards the enemy." If the necessity should arise again, Virginia's young men promised to "march in a body to the defense of our border, whether against the raids of professional horse thieves and assassins, or the attacks of more reputable assailants."[65]

John Brown's failed insurrection also sectionalized nonmilitary youth organizations. The constitutional dimensions of slavery suddenly became a hot topic at YMCAs and debating clubs.[66] Limited evidence suggests that some young Virginians started to question even the conservative brand of Unionism. Inside the debating halls of Virginia's universities, students discussed contemporary problems away from faculty members and other adults. Here they experienced a form of education completely under their own control. Robert T. Barton of Winchester, Virginia, recalled that his father was "an old line Whig and a Unionist." "But in my society debates," Barton attested that he "learned a good deal of the story of the Constitution" and decided that the Whigs "offered no protection to the South from the oppressions of the Abolitionists." Because of his independent stand, Barton frequently heard his family members indignantly "cry that 'Papa' was a Whig and hence the Whigs must be right."[67]

Barton's experience was probably exceptional, for most debating societies were not bubbling cauldrons of Southern nationalism. Prior to John Brown's raid, young men did not leave their meetings in an emotional frenzy over perceived insults to Southern rights.[68] Most felt an aching sadness, a foreboding sense of doom that made them feel helpless in the face of abolitionists and Republicans who they believed were hell-bent on wrecking the country. For example, after the passage of the Kansas-Nebraska Act in 1854, John Buchanan told his fellow students that "the dissolution of this glorious and magnificent Union seems almost inevitable; & not only dissolution but the red eye of battle begins to stare us in the face and the bloody & ruin fraught scene of civil war begin to pass in review before our eye."[69]

Buchanan's opinions underscore a popular refrain found in the writings of these young Virginians: that their generation would inherit the reins of political leadership just as the inevitable conflict with the North erupted. In the prospectus for the University of Virginia's Southern Rights' Association, the founders stated: "We cannot forget that soon the destinies of the South must be entrusted to our keeping. The present occupants of the arena of action must soon pass away, and we [will] be called upon to fill their places, and to battle in their stead against impending dangers. It becomes therefore our sacred duty to prepare for the contest."[70]

Like most Southerners in the 1850s, young Virginians were conflicted and confused as to the proper course for their state and their region. They loved the Union and abhorred secession, but they could not give their allegiance to a national government that did not guarantee Southern rights and political equality. On the surface, it would seem that the last generation parroted the views of older Virginians. Similarities unquestionably existed, but each group looked at the future from a different perspective because they occupied a different quadrant in the life cycle. For the most part, young Virginians lacked political power, which was a source of inner tension because they were trained to command others yet had no one to command. The hostile political climate created the possibility that they would have an opportunity to become leaders like their Revolutionary heroes, returning Virginia to greatness, rescuing their families and friends from the clutches of abolition, and receiving public acclaim as the redeemers of the Old Dominion. Thus a generational consciousness came together around the prospect of exercising authority during an armed conflict against an aggressive, abolitionist North. This belief dovetailed with the notion that each generation would make a unique and lasting contribution to the world. On one level, the last generation planned to free

Virginia from the North's economic tentacles through progressive reforms, giving the state greater autonomy, material rewards, and prestige. On another level, these young men expressed a willingness to fight the fanatical abolitionists of the North if necessary. History might not have blessed their parents' generation with an opportunity to achieve greatness, but as the country moved through the 1850s it seemed to the men of the last generation that destiny and God were on their side.

 **Eager Confederates**

. . . .

Show me a white head & a boy of twenty, &
I will trust the boy.—John H. Chamberlayne
to George William Bagby, December 6, 1860

AS JOHN HAMPDEN CHAMBERLAYNE surveyed Virginia's political landscape in December 1860, the twenty-two-year-old from Hanover County sensed that his fellow Virginians desired secession. Chamberlayne, who had graduated two years earlier from the University of Virginia, wrote that "sentiment is changing . . . throughout the state with surprising rapidity" and disunion "soon will be acceptable to the people of Virginia." He worried about the "submissionists" who "change their position daily" in trying to appease the North. Such attempts at compromise reminded him that Virginia's politicians were "men of another generation." "Then in God's name let them go to their own place," Chamberlayne exclaimed. "They did very well in their generation." Chamberlayne believed "Grey heads" served better as "brakes" than as "a driving wheel" in a revolution. While living in Richmond, he asked men a variety of political questions regarding secession. "In every instance," he found "that the old men were wrong" and considered their "opinion to be foolish." "Show me a white head & a boy of twenty," Chamberlayne concluded, "& I will trust the boy."[1]

Chamberlayne was not the only young Virginian to condemn the state's leaders for seeking compromise with the Republicans during the secession crisis. Most of his contemporaries also rejected the Commonwealth's attempts to compromise with the newly elected Lincoln administration. These young people emerged as the most outspoken proponents of secession in Virginia, holding a position at odds with a vast majority of their elders.[2] The words and political actions of the last generation reveal much about their identities as young men, Virginians, and Southerners. Emotions were high during the secession winter of 1860–61, twisting perceptions, heightening the sense

John H. Chamberlayne (1838–82). While a student at the University of Virginia, Chamberlayne captured the generational tension over secession when he wrote an impassioned letter on December 6, 1860, in which he claimed that the older generation was wrong on every issue related to disunion. An exasperated Chamberlayne declared: "Show me a white head & a boy of twenty, & I will trust the boy." (From John Hampden Chamberlayne, *Ham Chamberlayne—Virginian*, ed. C. G. Chamberlayne,, 1932)

of injured honor, and ultimately pushing some to foolishly dream of martial glory. But the bloodletting of the last generation did not simply originate from a disastrous romanticism or a blind allegiance to the planter class. Most of these young men gave themselves physically to the Confederacy after calm deliberation and careful observation of the world around them. Not only did they believe that a Southern nation best guaranteed the Old Dominion's interests against a Republican regime, but they also advocated secession as a way to realize their generational mission to restore the Commonwealth to greatness. Honor did not always turn Southerners into unthinking warriors, deluded by a romantic sense of self that compelled them to fight. In the case of young Virginians, sober reflection trumped honor.

As secession was being debated, the last generation argued that leaving the Union would return Virginia to a position of leadership in a new Southern nation. During the 1850s, young Virginians had grown deeply troubled by the state's loss of prestige in the Union, and they blamed the leaders of their parents' generation for this embarrassing decline. The residue of this debate colored the last generation's secessionist protests, which often moved beyond an attack against the Republican Party to include an assault against their elders. Although not every cry for disunion sounded this note, Lincoln's election unleashed a long-brewing generational conflict. It is ironic that the secessionists among the last generation and the older Unionists alike believed they were acting to uphold Virginia's distinctive greatness.

Instead of passively submitting to the wisdom of their parents, the men of the last generation used militia units, debating societies, flag demonstrations, and various other forms of public protest to express their political views. Older Virginians were alarmed by these young upstarts who had seemingly forgotten their proper place in society. They responded to this youthful insurgency by dismissing the last generation's actions as childish pranks, often describing the young men as reckless and irresponsible.[3] Abolitionist and Republican rhetoric intensified young Virginians' need to prove their manliness.[4] Probably no other generation of males in the state's history had ever experienced such pressure to stand forth as Southern men. Secession, therefore, created an opportunity to reaffirm one's commitment to slavery and patriarchy while calling into question the leadership and manliness of the older generation. In the end, internal issues relating to antebellum Virginia, coupled with a devotion to the Christian defense of slavery and a deep hostility toward the Republican Party, explain why so many young Virginians challenged adult authority in promoting the secessionist cause.

Few could have predicted the eruption of generational warfare over the question of secession. Prior to Lincoln's election, fathers and sons, by all accounts, were devoted to Union.[5] Both age groups wanted to avoid a crisis at virtually any cost, and Tennessean John Bell of the Constitutional Union Party was attractive to Southern Unionists of all ages. James DeWitt Hankins, a twenty-year-old University of Virginia student from Surry County, spoke for his generation on the eve of the presidential election: "Let Virginia cast her vote for Jno. Bell. I believe her to be the brass pin that binds together the vestment of the Union." Hankins looked to Bell's Union Party as a shield against the "battle axe" of sectionalism.[6] While it is impossible to determine the exact voting patterns of the last generation, it appears that the majority supported Bell. Students at the University of Virginia held their own election at the Rotunda. Alexander Fleet reported the final tally by state: "After the result was read out there was a tremendous hurrah for Bell, & then cheers for Virginia, who had given him . . . [a] majority." The cadets at the Virginia Military Institute also favored Bell, casting 116 ballots for the Tennessean, 76 for John Breckinridge, and 12 for Stephen Douglas.[7] These sentiments mirrored those of their elders as Bell carried the entire Old Dominion in an extremely tight race.[8]

The vast majority of older Virginians wanted to preserve the Union unless the North declared war on the Deep South or Lincoln failed to make concessions to the Upper South. A South Carolinian who agitated for secession in Virginia captured the state's conservative outlook: "Virginia will not take sides until she is absolutely forced."[9] One careful student of the secession crisis in the Upper South has called conservative Virginians anti-coercionists. Virginians of this persuasion, the majority, did not adopt secession until Lincoln's call for seventy-five thousand troops on April 15, 1861.[10] Significantly, only a handful of men in the last generation sided with the anti-coercionists.

When Lincoln's election became a certainty at the beginning of November 1860, many young people broke with their elders and started to consider secession as a viable and necessary political alternative. It appears that party affiliation did not determine a young Virginian's stance on this question. They understood, perhaps with more clarity than their conservative elders, that power relations at the national level had radically changed with a Republican in the White House. No honorable way out of this political dilemma was possible, young Virginians concluded. Reluctantly, they embraced the idea of disunion and braced for the possibility of civil war. While sitting in his room at the University of Virginia, Richmonder William R. J. Pegram felt melancholy as he contemplated the nation's future with Lincoln at the helm. "On the one side we have a President, opposed to us in every way, and a vice-President, who is to preside over that August body, the Senate of the United States, a half-negro [body]; and the Germans for our *masters*; while on the other side, we have disunion, and the greatest of all evils, '*a civil war*' staring us in the face." "Isn't this perfectly dreadful," he added, in reference to the political situation. "This is not a mere Jno. Brown raid."[11] A foreboding sense of doom overwhelmed Pegram as it did many of his peers. These young men were not jubilant about the prospect of civil war, but resigned to what they considered to be an unavoidable reality. Pegram accepted disunion because he recognized that the Lincoln administration, despite its warm appeals to Union, represented antislavery interests. Although Pegram's family was not part of the planter class (his mother owned fewer than five slaves at their Richmond home), he still believed that he had a stake in the perpetuation of the institution. On this point Pegram enjoyed wide support from his peers, all of whom believed in the ethical, economic, and political arrangements of slavery, the very basis of their opposition to the Republican Party.

Although it would be a mistake to generalize too much from the words of Pegram, his response reveals how many students could accept secession as a necessary option without suddenly becoming Southern radicals. In fact, a number of young men hoped for reconciliation while condemning the extremists during November and early December 1860. Friction dramatically increased between Deep South students and Virginians at the University of Virginia. "A word or two about that great meeting of the '*Students*,'" William G. Ridley of Southampton County sarcastically wrote on December 5. He bitterly complained about a gathering of thirty "'fire-eating' Georgia and 'South-Carolina' students" who published a resolution favoring secession and signed the document "in the name of the 'Students of the University.'" Many "ridiculed" it "a great deal," and even the "'New-York Herald' gave it several [curses?]." In Ridley's opinion, the resolution had backfired and actually smothered the secessionist spirit at the university. "At one time," he noticed that "every man nearly that you could see about here had a 'blue cockade' stuck on his hat." But since the proclamation he did not believe that Henry Wise, Virginia's strongest backer of secession, would be welcomed to speak. Most of those wearing the blue cockade were from South Carolina and Alabama. A number of students from other states refused to follow this fashion trend when they discovered that the blue cockade had been made in the North.[12]

Even though Ridley probably overstated his case, his observations reveal the lack of unanimity among Virginia youth at the beginning of the secession debate. Acrimonious discussions filled the dining areas, classrooms, and residence halls at Virginia's schools. A University of Virginia student overheard supporters of Southern Democratic candidate John C. Breckinridge taunt admirers of Constitutional Unionist candidate John Bell: "You are a traitor to the South, and we'll hang every one of you old Whigs." Bell's advocates replied: "You are a traitor to the South, the North & the whole country. We'll hang every one [of] you disunionists." Shortly after the election, a student from Tennessee remarked that both disunionists and moderate Bell men frequently used the word "traitor" when describing each other. "All of which seems to be taken in good part," he added. Yet he could "tell . . . when not in each others' company that they are in earnest about it."[13]

Despite the fierce rhetoric, cooler heads prevailed among the members of the last generation. A challenge to their sense of honor did not elicit a visceral response. Instead they would first see how political events unfolded before taking decisive action, but their patience was short lived. By the end of December, young Virginians started to campaign as a collective body for secession through school organizations, militia companies, newspapers, and political gatherings. What occurred between Lincoln's election and the final month of 1860 is critical to understanding the seismic shift in the last generation's take on secession. Unfortunately, the evidence is limited, but it is possible that the antagonism between Virginians and Deep South students dissipated during those crucial three months, and that young people from the Deep South gained influence over their moderate peers. It also appears that Lincoln's failure to make immediate concessions to the South pushed many young Virginians into the secessionist camp. Since Lincoln had not officially assumed office, it is difficult to imagine what he could have possibly done to appease the last generation. Nonetheless, young Virginians had expected Republicans to demonstrate their good faith in relation to the South by repealing personal liberty laws, enacting a stronger fugitive slave law, and passing constitutional amendments protecting slavery in the states where it existed and in the federal territories. When Lincoln refused to meet every single one of the South's demands, these young men saw a wolf in sheep's clothing. Many felt betrayed and angry, including an eighteen-year-old University of Virginia student from Richmond, Hodijah Lincoln Meade, who gave up on the Republicans by the first of December. "Are you not for Secession now after Vermont refused to repeal those Personal Liberty laws, & the Republican congressman manifest such an unyielding disposition?" he asked. "I am for it now, without any further attempts at a reconciliation."[14]

The introduction of the Crittenden Compromise in December further alienated young Virginians, although many of the state's political leaders welcomed the effort as the most realistic chance to preserve the Union.[15] A substantial majority of the last generation condemned any concessions regarding slavery in the territories. Issues involving slavery, not rhetoric from Southern fire-eaters, spurred young Virginians to actively promote the disunionist cause. The Washington Society at the University of Virginia voted seventeen to three that the Crittenden resolution did not protect the South from Republican encroachments. Although he never attended a Virginia university, Winchester's Peter Kurtz blasted Virginia Unionists in a private letter for trying to appease the North by accepting proposals such as Crittenden's. "The Union party of the Border States are worse secessionists than the secessionists themselves, for they are holding their arms to the North, and inviting them to conquer or at least fight the South," Kurtz wrote to a local militia officer. "When fifteen Southern States cannot get their rights in the Union, I should like to know how they expect Virginia and one or two others to do so."[16] Without ironclad constitutional guarantees protecting Southern rights, young Virginians refused to submit to Republican rule.

While a genuine concern for slavery's future united these young men behind the banner of disunion, it would be a mistake to see the ideological and political dimensions of slavery as the only source of political motivation. The insatiable desire for honor also pushed members of the last generation to support secession. They saw their personal reputation as intimately connected to their state's. When South Carolina seceded on December 20, 1860, triggering the withdrawal of the Deep South, members of the last generation feared that Virginia was being left behind. Young Virginians wanted their state to assume a leadership position in a new Southern nation. To miss this opportunity, these young men believed, would be to surrender the Old Dominion's position as the "mother of all the states." Some of the young men had imagined the South's declaring its political sovereignty as one collective body. They wanted Virginia at the helm of the new nation in a role reminiscent of the state's illustrious history in the American Revolution. Although the chance to return Virginia to glory had finally presented itself, the state's older leaders kept the Old Dominion on the sidelines while the Deep South seized the initiative. George W. Grimm, a twenty-year-old from Winchester who never enrolled in a Virginia university, wrote on January 16, "I love the Union, I love the Constitution, but when the protection which the constitution guarantees to us is not enforced, then the union must go." More than anything, he wanted "to see the Old Dominion foremost in the Battle for the rise of the Southern Confederacy." A University of Virginia student from Goochland County, Charles W. Turner, also entertained high expectations for Virginia in a Southern nation. Once his native land entered into a compact with the other Southern states, he foresaw that the Commonwealth would become "the great manufacturing state of the South."[17]

Edwin Taliaferro of Gloucester County agreed but put his criticism of the state's inaction in a historical perspective. A member of the last generation, he had attended the University of Virginia and studied in Europe before accepting a professorship of modern languages at the College of William and Mary in 1858. There he had organized secessionist activity among his students, most of whom were only a few years younger than he and who shared his belief that Virginians possessed the God-given right to rule others. Although other states could have rightfully claimed the Revolutionary mantle, young Virginians believed they possessed the most direct link to the Revolutionary generation. During the secessionist winter, Taliaferro complained that "Poor old Virginia" had lost "her influence, and her caste." "It is a hard case for a State so long First in Councils of wisdom," he added, ". . . to be now in her old age [and] in the hands of . . . temporizing, submissive, Politicians."[18] Significantly, Taliaferro used the language of age and submissiveness to create a revealing metaphor. Virginia, in his mind, had become decrepit and impoverished. The old fogies had allowed the state to decline, and now they were keeping the Old Dominion from becoming the leader of a dynamic Southern nation. The implication was clear—a new class of leaders was needed, young, masculine, and forward thinking, who could throw off the yoke of Yankee domination and transform Virginia into a vibrant leader of a Confederate nation.

Many young Virginians shared Taliaferro's frustration with the state's politicians. Their moment in history had arrived, and they would not allow their elders to block this singular opportunity to earn immortal fame. Personal ambition and a chance to earn a high reputation for themselves and their state converged with their ideological commitment to slavery. To bypass their stodgy fathers, they engaged in their own form of political protest with the intention of pushing the state toward secession. On January 12, 1861, in one of the first symbolic acts against their fathers' generation, nearly two hundred University of Virginia students burned in effigy General Winfield Scott, one of the state's most famous sons, for suggesting coercion as a means of bringing the Lower South states back into the Union. At a rally on campus, the students offered repeated cheers for Georgian secessionist Robert Toombs and the states that had already left the Union. Before the crowd dispersed, a card that read "Winfield Scott, Would-be Dictator and Despot" was placed over the effigy. "Hurrah for the U.V.!" exclaimed one young man who believed that "the old rascal would have run from the boys" if he had been present. Once the effigy was fully consumed in flames, the students retired to their rooms, as one reported "without manifesting their excitement by rioting—be it said to their credit."[19] This description creates the impression that the members of the crowd were orderly gentlemen by diminishing the role of youthful exuberance. The demonstration against Scott clearly shows how ideology, political interest, and emotion inspired political acts in support of secession. At the most fundamental level, the University of Virginia students came together to defend what they believed was the Deep South's right to secede. Their sense of injustice took on an exaggerated form because of their antipathy toward the conservatism of the older generation. Scott became the symbolic old fogy standing in the way of young Virginians who sought authority and respect for themselves and their state in a new union of Southern states. Burning Scott in effigy was a symbolic burial of Virginia's old ruling class, pointing to a transfer of power to the younger men who would lead the state into a new Southern nation.

The students downplayed their emotional and vitriolic demonstration. Rather, they congratulated themselves for holding what they considered to be an orderly political demonstration. But the adult world viewed the act as a shameful display of irreverence and immaturity. The *Staunton Spectator* denounced the protest as "one of the most disrespectful and disgraceful proceedings which has ever occurred within this state." The editor of the paper also condemned the *Charlottesville Jeffersonian* for overlooking the *youths'* attacks on a native son who ranked second only to Washington in military fame. The *Staunton Spectator* demanded that the students involved be expelled immediately.[20]

The university never disciplined the students, perhaps encouraging members of the last generation to become more aggressive in their support of secession. By the time Texas left the Union on February 1, 1861, sentiment among the students at the University of Virginia had crystallized in favor of secession. Secessionist appeals were not confined to Charlottesville, however. On Washington's birthday, one of the literary societies at Washington College voted 43–8 in favor of secession. On the same day, cadets at the Virginia Military Institute reportedly offered strong disunion speeches.[21] Young men who no longer lived on campus also supported a Southern Confederacy in overwhelming numbers by February. Young Virginians imagined themselves as part of a Southern community for a variety of related reasons. Their political and ideological adherence to slavery formed the foundation of this shared sense of regional community. It would be a mistake to simply explain young Virginia's support for secession as an outgrowth of cultural nationalism. Not until the Civil War did they forcefully identify Southerners as a distinctive people with sensibilities, tastes, and habits of a particular nature. Their desire to forge a new nation originated within the political reality of a slave power that had suddenly lost its hold on the federal government. This triggered a unified political response among young men, but how they reached that conclusion depended on their sense of honor, their personal aspirations, and their vision for Virginia in a world embracing progress.[22]

The sudden growth in militia companies during January and February testified to the rising secessionist sentiment among young people. Members of the last generation rushed to organize companies on campus or join existing units throughout the state. By early January, the students at the University of Virginia secured faculty permission to raise two military companies. In honor of their Revolutionary heritage, one company was designated the "Sons of Liberty"; the other was called the "Southern Guard." Enlisting in a university company was not enough for many students, who also joined military organizations throughout the state. A Norfolk paper feared that the University of Virginia might have to close its doors because so many young men were preparing to leave school in early January. Students at Washington College also lobbied successfully to form a militia company, which they christened the "Southern Blues."[23] Significantly, Virginia's youth identified their militia organizations as "Southern" before their state seceded, as a sign of solidarity for the states that had already left the Union.

After intense student protests, the administration at the College of William and Mary lifted the ban on militia organizations. Late in the evening of January 14, during a pounding hailstorm, several William and Mary students inaugurated their military company with a series of rousing speeches. Although these young men were animated speakers, yelling over the roar of winter's fury, their rhetoric was surprisingly tame. In keeping with the last generation's long-standing desire to redeem the Old Dominion, the students at William and Mary defended their organization on the grounds that it would cultivate a new class of leaders. From the "old walls" of the college, they predicted that the next Thomas Jefferson or Patrick Henry would emerge and, if necessary, "draft a Declaration of Independence for the South, . . . in a still clearer and more logical manner, if possible, than it was done by the first."[24] The William and Mary proclamation underscores the importance of Virginia's Revolutionary heritage in shaping the secessionist impulses of young people. Young people insisted that disunion was a conservative act, allowing them to reconnect with a brilliant past that had been sacrificed in the Union.

The underlying conservatism of the last generation's call to arms, however, was lost on many older Virginians. The formation of militia units signified to many fathers that young men would no longer be obedient sons. Military organizations, not parents, would have the ultimate authority over them. Carter N. B. Minor's father scolded him for joining the Southern Guard at the University of Virginia, writing that "you have taken a very unwise step. Your native state does not need your military services. If she did, I would cheerfully counsel you to prompt action." He believed his son was like "thousands of young men who care not for an education, who would gladly avoid the labours of College & launch into the excitement of the occasion."[25] Minor's father voiced the common assumption that young Southerners stayed clear of

This image is a heretofore unpublished photograph of members of the University of Virginia's Southern Guard, a militia organization that the students organized in January 1861. Only Henry Clay Michie (1842–1925), who is standing to the left, has been identified. Michie was wounded three times during the war, including at the famous stone wall during Pickett's Charge on July 3, 1863. (Courtesy of Larry Williford)

serious labor and only desired fame, that they were childish and immature. He would not have scolded his son if he did not feel threatened by his action. Minor's father also revealed an important difference between young and old by demanding that his son adhere strictly to the future course pursued by the Old Dominion's politicians. The younger Minor, on the other hand, saw his loyalty to Virginia as dependent on a strong allegiance not just to Virginia but also to the newly formed Confederacy. John Newton Lyle of Botetourt County recalled that when his peers tried to organize a student military company at Washington College, a number of parents would not allow their sons to join unless some of the professors would serve as officers. "They were unwilling to risk their boys with officers who were mere youths," he added. The students made the concession to adult authority, and two faculty members agreed to command the unit.[26]

Professors at Richmond College and Hampden-Sydney also feared the consequences of military organizations governed exclusively by youths, and they succeeded in barring student militia companies at their institutions. Although the young men at Richmond College were permitted to organize and drill, the professors convinced the governor to reject their request for rifles. Lacking weaponry, the students at Richmond College eventually disbanded, but they would not go away quietly. In a public notice, they ridiculed the faculty for trying to crush their "spirit of patriotism" as a futile effort.[27] Faculty members at Hampden-Sydney also blocked students from organizing a military company with a series of "unpalatable restrictions." The students were probably not allowed to muster with weapons, and for having been subjected to such a regulation, the students at Hampden-Sydney publicly mocked their professors in the newspapers by referring to them as " 'noble and reverend senieurs.' " Although the young men were thwarted on campus, they scattered throughout the countryside, enlisting in various volunteer companies that were coming together in Prince Edward County.[28]

Militia activity also increased away from college campuses as young people in cities and towns formed companies reserved exclusively for their participation. Within these military organizations, the last generation identified youth as the prime defender of Virginia's honor. A young man of Lunenburg County, who went by the name "Mufti," wanted his peers to join a corps of minutemen. "Our parents, whose heads are blooming for the grave, are being foully insulted," declared "Mufti," "and their proud honor ranked among the lowest, vilest possessions on earth." To repel a possible invasion and protect the "virtue of our beloved sisters," "Mufti" proposed a meeting of the county's young men so they could form ranks and pledge their allegiance to the South. He also paid his respects to the county's elders, but ever so slightly, stating at the end of his letter that he would "be glad to see the old ones" enlist as well.[29]

In similar public statements throughout the state, young men advanced the cause of secession by appropriating the language of honor, which enabled them to claim that they, not their fathers, were the true protectors of their communities and state. This approach gave their cause legitimacy and deflected potential criticism that they were behaving like disrespectful youths. They took the offensive against Unionists by calling them "submissionists," a damaging and difficult label for the politically moderate and conservative to shake.[30] To these young men, Virginia Unionists seemed incapacitated, passively waiting for Lincoln to take action, while the young were on the offensive, organizing to defend hearth and home. The older men had no choice but to respond. Their honor was at stake. A few resisted this youthful insurgency by insisting that they were still capable of taking care of their families and communities. On January 30, there was an "Old Men's Meeting" in Westmoreland County that excluded anyone under the age of forty-five. The "grey heads" resolved that even though "many of us are bending under the weight of years, we are unwilling to rely on the younger men for protection while there is streng[t]h enough in our arms to strike a blow in defence of our homes and firesides."[31] The dialogue between young and old reveals the dynamic between emotion and political action. Tensions were high, and it is reasonable to believe that Virginia men of all ages were stirred to action by irrational fears and emotions. The pressure to appear manly and honorable limited the political options of Virginia men of all ages. Many probably thought they had no choice but to prepare for the coming onslaught of antislavery invaders.

While some members of the last generation expressed their loyalty to the South by joining militia companies, others locked horns with Unionists, such as the ones in Lexington whom the young men from Washington College and the Virginia Military Institute confronted. As a secessionist counterattack that rolled across Virginia in early February, the politicization of young people terrified Lexington's residents, who were accustomed to college student pranks, not to open challenges against adult authority. The fears of older Virginia suggests that the last generation exerted a modest degree of political influence even though younger people stood outside positions of power. A Lexington newspaperman overheard a fellow townsman say that the "fastness of Young America is the great sore of the Union." The counsel and experience of the old, the gentleman complained, no longer checked youthful ambition, and the nation risked disunion unless young people returned to their subordinate position. A writer for the *Valley Star* vigorously agreed with this bleak assessment of young people. "The colt has slipped the bridle," he declared; when that sort of thing has happened, it has "too often produced a *stampede* among quiet old hacks, whose age and experience should have saved them from such coltish pranks."[32]

The "rowdiness" of the last generation since Lincoln's election convinced this same writer that the political world had been turned upside down by young people. Students from Washington College and the Virginia Military Institute routinely disrupted political meetings intended to promote Unionism. Although these gatherings were for residents of Lexington and the surrounding Rockbridge County, students from both institutions seized control of the rallies. Whenever a local spoke in favor of Union, the students would yell and huzzah, demanding that one of their own take the podium. The *Valley Star*'s reporter was horrified by such disrespectful behavior and could not forgive the students for hissing at Rockbridge's older men when they pleaded for moderation. He was also outraged because the students had misrepresented popular opinion in a series of newspaper articles published throughout Virginia, claiming that Rockbridge, in reality a stronghold of Unionism, was rapidly moving toward secession. This false reporting, the *Valley Star* claimed, had converted the county's more pliable Unionist residents to secession. The student activists who succeeded in intimidating the "quiet men of the county" must have been thrilled, but it was a chilling development for the town's elder statesmen, who wanted to stop this youthful insurgency.[33]

The students at Washington College and the Virginia Military Institute had launched a secessionist campaign so aggressive and unrelenting that politically moderate Virginians were caught off guard, and adult authority was generally put on the defensive. The students' energetic and open support for a Southern Confederacy typified the last generation's response, reinforcing the perception among older Virginians that young people had forgotten their proper place, that they were immature, emotionally underdeveloped, and incapable of forming meaningful political ideas. Older Virginians in favor of Union hoped that the last generation would grow out of this rebellious stage and obey adult authority. "Young America is demoralized," the *Valley Star* concluded, and "is a *great sore* in the Union that requires medication. We hope the sore has not taken such deep roots as to defy all surgery."[34]

The students in Lexington, like most of their peers, had high expectations when elected representatives of Virginia's secession convention convened in

Richmond on February 19. Instead of quickly passing Virginia's secession ordinance, as young Virginians probably expected, the delegates engaged in lengthy debates, corresponded with the Deep South states, and tried to compromise with Republican officials. The convention's delegates, only one of whom was a member of the last generation, reflected the conservative mood of older Virginians, many of whom had participated in Unionist campaigns. Of the 152 delegates, fewer than forty were open secessionists.[35]

Infuriated by the convention's conservatism, young Virginians refused to sit back and allow their elders to dictate the course of events. They publicly denounced the convention as a symbol of the state's misguided political class—the very men who had allowed the Old Dominion's reputation and influence to decline since the Revolution. Once again, many young Virginians charged, politicians had sacrificed the Commonwealth's honor. In southwest Virginia John Samuel Apperson, who never attended a Virginia university, offered an assessment of the convention that typified the hostile reaction of his contemporaries. "The convention of Virginia has been in session a month without effecting anything except spending the peoples' money," Apperson wrote in his diary. "Consultation, consultation! is the perpetual cry, and I think people ought to put a stop to its monotous [sic] strains." Just a few short weeks after the debates opened in Richmond, the students at the University of Virginia applied the nickname "old fogie" to the convention's members.[36] Significantly, this was the same pejorative label young Virginians had used to chastise older people who resisted progressive reforms in the state during the 1850s. By advocating immediate secession, therefore, many young Virginians were calling for removal of the state's old guard. In response to the Unionism that prevailed in the state, a frustrated Robert Beale Davis, who would be killed in battle at Petersburg in 1864, declared that Virginia should "cast off the shackles, which the politicians have cast around her and once more think for herself and all will be well." He failed to understand why the convention could not see that unless Virginia seceded, she had only two choices: she had to either "'perish or submit'" to Republican demands. The ineptitude its members, matched only by their willingness to pacify the Lincoln administration, convinced Davis that if given the opportunity to attend the proceedings, "I would not be there for the world."[37]

The editors for the *Virginia University Magazine* were apoplectic over the convention's conservative ways. At the beginning of March, they sarcastically described the delegates as a "body of very great men." The students worried that the convention's passiveness would allow a Free-Soil Union Party to materialize in the Commonwealth. Then their leaders in Richmond, they imagined, would merely say in response: "'You shan't beat our Southern sisters, but if you will just rob and disgrace *us*, and do it quietly, we'll help you and thank you to boot.'" They finished the piece with a venomous conclusion: "The Sovereign Power of Virginia [is] shaping its action, not by what is in itself just, honourable and right, but by the insidious policy of a white-livered Demon, . . . as unworthy of trust as Satan himself. Virginians [are] confiding the honour and safety of their State to the keeping of WILLIAM H. SEWARD! . . . The once proud and noble Old Dominion [is] waiting for coercion, before it will do its duty. Monstrous!"[38] This editorial shows how difficult it is to categorize the political action of the last generation as either ideological in nature or simply a visceral response to a perceived violation of honor. The authors' sense of being disgraced animates their words, creating the impression that they have succumbed to a wild fit of anger so uncontrollable that they are unable to calmly look at the political landscape. However, they are careful to connect the loss of honor to the rise of a free-soil party and the antislavery leadership of William Seward. Their fears and anger were not irrational; they were well grounded in the political reality of Virginia, where nonslaveholding interests had been gaining strength and influence throughout the 1850s. Members of the last generation understood the high stakes of this game, and they also understood that the players at the table were not bluffing.

A number of young men believed the convention's intransigence had forever disgraced and dishonored the Old Dominion. In a fit of desperation, University of Virginia student George Woodville Latham observed on March 9: "I write with my heart full of tears for the old days that are gone. . . . There is no Virginia left in the world now. She was dead long since when you and I were proud to be her children." Latham, who grew up in Winchester, never realized that the Old Dominion "had gone down into her grave" until it was too late and he heard the "craven cries of submission" from the convention's delegates. If Virginia stayed in the Union, Latham and many other young men contemplated leaving the Commonwealth for the Deep South.[39] Feelings of humiliation must have motivated some members of the last generation to threaten such a radical course, as the state was increasingly subjected to the ridicule of other Southern papers. "Virginia [is] to be saved from degradation, not by the spirit of her sons, but by the blind folly of her enemies," the *Southern Literary Messenger* claimed in March.[40]

Frustration with Virginia's convention boiled over after Lincoln's inaugural address on March 4. The president's words, although intended to be conciliatory, extinguished what little Unionist feelings remained among young Virginians. Lincoln declared the right to control places and property belonging to the federal government. Because occupied garrisons in the Lower South could be returned only by force, many members of the last generation interpreted his message not as coercion, but as a virtual act of war. "How do you like Old Lincon's [sic] inaugural address?" Richard H. Bagby of Randolph-Macon College asked his father. "I think it is an open declaration of war against the South, and I think we ought to take it as such. I am for going *out* of the *Union* now." John Samuel Apperson also blasted Lincoln's speech as an "ill omen to our distracted country." "The conservative or union men are beginning to give way," he added, "Lincoln's course has struck them dumb. Memorials for secession are being sent to the delegates at Richmond demanding secession of our state." A student at the University of Virginia reported that Lincoln's inaugural produced a "tremendous sensation" on campus. "The Virginia students have had a meeting in wh[ich] were made strong Secession speeches; and strong resolutions to the same effect were adopted unanimously."[41]

One week after Lincoln's speech, Virginia students at the University of Virginia published a secessionist proclamation in newspapers across the state. This piece of evidence is extraordinarily important and a powerful testament to the last generation's organized support for secession. The Virginia students proclaimed that "we not only believe in the right of secession, but hold that the events of the last few months justify and demand the immediate exercise of this right." No attempt was made to soften the words out of deference to age or experience. The students, in fact, defended their position as a prerogative of youth. Unlike the older men who were currently deciding their fate in Richmond, they would have to contend with the long-term effects of the Old Dominion's staying in the Union. "We . . . have a right to be heard," the students concluded. Such a bold public statement, they hoped, would "invoke young men of the state to hold meetings and give similar expression to their views upon the questions now agitating our people." This published attack against Unionism also contained a powerful assault against adult authority as the Virginia students called for youth solidarity to bring the Commonwealth into the Confederacy. The article made it clear that young people across the state would raise their political voices without fear, as they had more at stake than their elders.[42]

Lincoln's inaugural address, coupled with the plodding conservatism of Virginia's secession convention, set off a wave of protests on Virginia's campuses during March and April. At each of these demonstrations, Virginia students raised secession flags to symbolize their bold and unequivocal stand for Southern independence. The highly politicized rituals also marked a declaration of independence from adult authority and influence. In mid-nineteenth-century America, flags evoked fierce expressions of patriotism that embodied the deepest and most sacred loyalties. Discarding the Stars and Stripes for secessionist banners, therefore, was not a careless gesture; it was a calculated political act that reflected a profound shift in allegiance from the United States to the South, as well as from adult authority to youth solidarity. Young Virginians, lacking access to the press, pulpit, or podium, had little choice but to resort to dramatic action. Most papers buried news of student demonstrations in brief articles that typically mocked their actions as the work of boys. By refusing to legitimate the political ideas of the last generation, the state's papers and adult society at large were denying to young people a sense of honor and, consequently, the status of manhood. By organizing their own political rituals, the young granted themselves the legitimacy refused by their elders.

Late in the evening on March 15, five students from Virginia and two from Maryland made a perilous night climb to the top of the University of Virginia's Rotunda and attached the banner of the rebellious states to the flagpole. When the morning sun revealed the deed, the students rushed out of their boarding houses and gathered on the Lawn. The cheering grew so loud that one bystander thought it "sounded as if the Lunatic Asylum" had been relocated to campus. Professor Albert Taylor Bledsoe, one of the South's leading intellectuals, stood in front of the young men and praised the symbolic meaning of the flag, but he suggested that they take it down. Bledsoe's colleagues were less empathetic and demanded immediate removal of the flag. "Dr. [Socrates] Maupin and the rest of the Union Profs made them take it down tho'," wrote one disgruntled student; "indeed all the Faculty disapproved of its being there."[43]

As the flag came down, the students let out "three groans" of disapproval. Some made secessionist speeches while a choir of young men began singing "Dixie." The banner disappeared with the young men who retrieved it, only to fly again on nearby Carr's Hill a few days later. By the end of March, smaller secessionist flags waved from all parts of the college, many on poles "50, 60, & 70 feet high." They purposefully hung from conspicuous places. The students wanted the Unionists from Charlottesville and surrounding Albemarle County to recognize the boundaries of their terrain. In their controlled space, far removed from adult authority, they could openly promote the cause of secession. The flags must have been visible for a considerable distance. Even if an indifferent press chose to ignore the young Virginians, they were still determined to confront their elders with the fact that young people no longer walked in lockstep with them in regard to the Commonwealth's place in the Union.[44]

In the month that preceded the firing on Fort Sumter on April 12, students raised secession flags at William and Mary, the Virginia Military Institute, Roanoke College, and Lynchburg College.[45] Evidence suggests that young people at Emory and Henry, Randolph-Macon, and Hampden-Sydney also agitated for disunion. The students at Washington College became the first to unfurl a secessionist flag in a surreptitious ceremony that occurred in late December 1860. Although far ahead of their peers, the actions of Washington College students reveal the generational dynamic of flag-raising ceremonies as declarations against both Unionism and adult authority. A participant in the flag incident at Washington College, Henry R. Morrison of Rockbridge County, explained to his sister that he and seven other young men had "put up a disunion flag on top of College. The flag was blue with one blood red star in the middle and DISUNION painted in large letters above it." A few students threatened to pull it down, but Morrison and his band intimidated the Unionists by threatening "war" on anyone who disturbed the banner.[46]

The president of Washington College, George Junkin, a committed Unionist, was infuriated by the act and demanded the flag's removal. Anticipating retaliation from Junkin, the prosecession students had concealed the only ladders on campus. Replacements did not arrive from Lexington until the next day, leaving the symbol of disunion above the college overnight. When the banner was finally retrieved, Junkin planned to burn it in a public ceremony, but Morrison and his energetic crew managed to steal the flag back. Outraged, Junkin conducted a thorough inspection of the college, charging unannounced into students' rooms and "squealing" for the flag that he never located. It seems that Morrison drew as much satisfaction in humiliating Junkin as he did in promoting the Southern cause.[47]

Numerous flag raisings revealed that Virginia campuses were the epicenter of secessionism, and the tremors that emanated from the ivory towers shook young people into action across the state. Members of the last generation who were outside the halls of academia expressed their political views in more conventional ways. They organized community meetings, wrote articles for local newspapers, and spoke at public gatherings to push Virginians down the secessionist road. George W. Grimm turned himself into a walking billboard

George Junkin (1790–1868). While president of Washington College, Junkin contested secessionist activity on campus. He tried to confiscate a secessionist flag but was unable to locate the banner. One student gleefully reported that Junkin charged into his room "squealing" for the flag. When Virginia seceded, Junkin promptly resigned his position and returned to Pennsylvania. (W&L Photograph Collection, Special Collections, Leyburn Library, Washington and Lee University, Lexington, Virginia)

for disunion in his hometown of Winchester. "I wear the badge of secession on my left collar and am dressed in a full suit of Blue home manufactured cloth," he boasted. "There are only two such suits in town," he added, "and I assure you they attract a great deal of attention."[48] The use of clothing to express political ideas (as well as flag raisings and disrupting Unionists' meetings) highlights how far removed members of the last generation were from the center of power. Their frustration of not having full adult status, of not being recognized as men, must have intensified during this time. Even though they operated on the periphery of state politics, their efforts helped bring focus to the political antitheses of secession and Union. The use of clothing and flag-raising celebrations allowed for the creation of an alliance among young people in Virginia. These local rites expressed a very specific political stance in favor of a Southern nation.

A few members of the last generation even tried to promote secessionist activity in Virginia's typically Unionist areas. "I did a considerable amount of electioneering," Matthew P. Andrews informed his fiancée from the mountains of Hardy County, "but as I am regarded as almost a secessionist I could not do much with the main body of the people who are in favor of the Union at all hazards." Edwin Harmon received a similarly cold greeting in his own

Tazewell County, located in southwest Virginia. Although still ambivalent about secession, he wrote on March 12 that "I have been enjoying myself for the last week trying to frighten the timid cowards of this section clear off the face of the earth." "Let them go to the caves and hide themselves," he added, "as they certainly would do, in the reality of my war talk to them."[49]

When the logic of their arguments and their alarmist rhetoric failed to convert Unionists to the Southern cause, members of the last generation exhibited little tolerance for dissent and sometimes resorted to violence. They labeled disunionists unmanly submissionists who sympathized with "Black Republicans." In Marion, the seat of Smyth County in deep southwest Virginia, John Samuel Apperson engaged some Unionists after he proclaimed "that any man that would not fight for the south . . . were not worthy of the name of a man." "Several took insult," Apperson reported, but calm heads prevailed and the contending parties were separated. The incident convinced Apperson to carry "a five shooter" in case Union sympathizers ambushed him.[50]

As members of the last generation became more vocal and agitated in their support for Southern unity in March and early April, they exerted intense pressure on the few young people who still clung to Union. Wayland F. Dunaway of the Northern Neck of Virginia acknowledged the influence of Professors James P. Holcombe and Bledsoe at the University of Virginia, but it took the "contagious example of my roommate, William H. Chapman," to convince Dunaway to accept secession. Eugene Blackford's resistance to secession alienated him from his fellow students. "It is a heresy of which very few indeed, of our young men are to be capable," Professor John Minor observed of Blackford's defiant stand. "The secession *feeling* is predominant amongst our youths as practically to have extinguished all Union *principle*. They hasten to 'follow a multitude' to *folly*."[51] Professor Minor, like so many older Virginians, saw youth solidarity on the issue of secession as a sign that young people were running out of control. Energized by raw, dangerous emotions, they were regarded as incapable of acting responsibly.

Minor was certainly correct in believing that members of the last generation exerted tremendous pressure on their peers. Albert Davidson, an anti-coercionist from Lexington, felt isolated at the University of Virginia among the overwhelming number of secessionists. "Almost everyone here is for immediate secession and if I venture to express an opinion on the other side," he wrote on March 11, "they throw out hints about Lexington being an abolition hole and think all that are not for immediate secession must be down right submissionists." Only a few of Davidson's contemporaries managed to endure such pressure and faithfully abide by their Union principles until Fort Sumter.[52]

Although some of the most prominent advocates of disunion were "grey heads" such as Edmund Ruffin and Henry Wise, most of the state's elders preached moderation. Instead of singling out the leaders of the antisecessionist cause such as Jubal Early and John Snyder Carlile, the last generation relied on a generalization that had served them well in explaining Virginia's decline: the state was in the hands of decrepit leaders who were out of touch. "Yesterday I went to see Prof. Minor and we had a long discussion about the politics of the day, he is a rabid Whig and favours me with a long tirade against secession, disunion and the slave trade," wrote James Keith, who, ironically, came from a prominent Whig family in Fauquier County. "He takes a very narrow view of things and relies entirely upon precedent and the authority of the people, he has about as little originality about him as any man I saw."[53] Keith's example reveals the dangers of simply equating a Whiggish political background with Unionism. When it came to the question of disunion, party loyalty among young Virginians probably receded. Furthermore, their disillusionment with the state's leadership and political parties in general fueled their secessionist crusade as they searched for ways to rid the Old Dominion of a political class that they considered out of touch and inept.

As the nation neared the climax of the sectional standoff that spring, tension between the last generation and Unionist forces almost erupted into violence. During the night of April 12, a handful of cadets at the Virginia Military Institute, unaware of the dramatic events unfolding in Charleston harbor, slipped into Lexington to foil a planned Unionist meeting. They proceeded to bore several holes into a "monster" flagpole, and when the Unionists tried to hoist their flag the following morning, it snapped into a number of pieces. The banner fell to the ground amid chunks of wood. The students were immediately suspected for sabotaging the event. An altercation ensued shortly thereafter when angry Unionists insulted Cadet John K. Thompson as he walked down the street. Rumor spread to the institute that some cadets were in danger of being killed. Immediately, the corps shouldered muskets, formed ranks, and marched in battle array to the crisis. It appears that some of the students from Washington College had followed the cadets into town, looking for a final showdown with local Unionists. There they met a hostile crowd that was growing in number by the minute, with reinforcements from the countryside. Before shots were fired, however, some anxious faculty members interceded and persuaded the young men to return to the barracks. With a great sense

This print of a Casimir Bohn engraving shows the main barracks of the Virginia Military Institute and other campus buildings as they looked in 1857. In the spring of 1861 the cadets from VMI joined forces with the students at neighboring Washington College to break up pro-Union meetings in the town of Lexington. (Courtesy of the Virginia Military Institute Archives).

of relief, the *Valley Star* of Lexington reported: "May civil strife always end thus."[54]

As the *Valley Star* and the rest of Virginia would soon discover, strife between young and old was easier to contain than the bitter political differences between North and South. The firing on Fort Sumter and Lincoln's subsequent call for troops convulsed the nation in civil war. The call to arms also brought unity between the last generation and their elders.[55] Sons and fathers suddenly stood together behind the Southern cause. In the *Richmond Daily Dispatch*, the student correspondent at the University of Virginia proclaimed that "Virginians, one and all . . . are determined that our rights shall be respected, or we will wipe the Black Republican Ape party from existence."[56] Although the men of the last generation rejoiced over Virginia's entry into the Confederacy, some remained bitter about the state's reluctant acceptance of secession. They believed that the passivity of Virginia's politicians had forever tarnished the state. Richard H. Bagby wrote with disgust that "Va the most powerful of the slave states, the mother of states," had been "kicked out" of the Union. In her slow and torturous road to disunion, the state, according to Bagby, had "utterly disgraced herself in the eyes of all civilized nations and brought s[h]ame & reproch [*sic*] upon her own beloved sons & daughters." He promised to redeem the "soil of our mother state" as should "every lover of liberty." In a tacit reference to the atonement of Christ, he declared that only "our blood" could "atone for the inactivity & cowardice of our rulers." In the "distressing times ahead," Bagby believed that the South would be "protected by Divine Providence and that she [would] come out conquerer [*sic*] in the end." Many of Bagby's peers had reached a similar conclusion.[57]

While young Virginians forever blamed the old fogies for delaying Virginia's grand entry into the Confederacy, elder Virginians could not forgive the last generation for attacking adult authority in the name of secession. Seven days after the firing on Fort Sumter, a writer for the *Richmond Whig* dismissed student political action as the "mischief" of boys, inspired by an "immature doctrine" and "false excitement." Political debates, flag raisings, speeches, militia companies, and Southern rights associations had kept young Virginians from studying, he charged. He went on to advise parents that a son who had attended the University of Virginia since Lincoln's election probably had "his mind poisoned, and will not acquire a knowledge of any of those subjects for the teaching of which colleges are instituted." Parents were sufficiently warned: they risked losing control of a son who had participated in the prosecessionist campaigns that had infected Virginia universities. The writer of the article must not have been aware of the fact that most Virginia professors preached conservatism to their students, because he blamed faculty members for allowing students to participate in such "follies."[58]

The *Whig* directed its message to the last generation as well as to their parents. The editor implored young people to understand that political activism at such a tender age was a passing phase of "foolery" when "lads of spirit" must "sew their wild oats of the mind." At the very least, the *Whig* hoped that these reckless ideas had been expelled so that the intellectual "chaff" would be "cleared away" before it was too late to plant "a real and practical crop" of ideas. In denouncing the political ideas of young Virginians, the paper was claiming that the members of the last generation lacked the mental capacity to form meaningful opinions, thereby denying them legitimacy. The extreme Southernism of Virginia's youth, elders believed, would pass in time like a bad childhood habit. The paper further insulted the last generation by labeling student protests as "boyish acts." For each man involved, the *Whig* suggested that "we are clear for instantly horsing and whipping him as a boy." Such inflammatory rhetoric was designed to discredit the politics of youth and force young people to return to their "proper place." The *Whig*, like most of the last generation's critics, portrayed young Virginians as being driven by emotion over intellect, arrogance over experience, and romanticism over reality—all of which created the perception that they were lacking in essential qualities of manliness.[59]

During the secession crisis, many adults had alleged that young Virginians were silly, emotional, and immature, all of which was a metaphor for effeminacy. Young Virginians, consequently, not only saw war as an opportunity to redeem their native state and the South, but also as a chance to prove themselves as men. In the wake of public attacks by their elders, young Virginians were, in part, motivated to join the Confederate war effort to prove that their generation possessed manly courage and self-discipline. Young men's wartime journals were filled with rhetoric about the war as an opportunity to grow up. On April 18, for instance, Cadet Andrew C. L. Gatewood wrote his parents from the Virginia Military Institute that he planned to enlist immediately. He promised them that "I will stand up and fight like a man for our rights." James H. Langhorne of southwest Virginia informed his mother shortly after enlisting that "I am truly in the full capacity of a man. I am treated as such & consequently expected to act as such."[60] Langhorne, like many of his peers, continued to ask for parental advice as Virginia embraced war. Nonetheless, the secession crisis had enabled young Virginians to declare their independence without rejecting the fundamental assumption of patriarchy. By relying on the language of honor and shame, words that slaveholders of all ages valued and understood, members of the last generation could assume a position at odds with their parents but still remain faithful to their social identity as Southern men. As a result, the last generation helped lead their state into the Confederacy.

Secession served as a rite of passage for young Virginians, but it would be a mistake to understand their advocacy of a Southern Confederacy as strictly an issue of manhood and honor. Their motives were also political. Secession, they believed, would resolve many of the internal conflicts that had plagued Virginia in the 1850s. During those critical years, when young Virginians had formed their political identities, they had pressured their fellow citizens to improve education, revamp the economy, reform party politics, and contribute to the arts and sciences. Entering the Confederacy, they believed, promised a way to achieve these lofty goals and return the state to a position of leadership, at the head of a new Southern nation. Young Virginians further argued that leaving the Union would induce a moral cleansing of the state because a new group of leaders would surely follow, displacing the men who had allowed the Old Dominion to decline. They never went into detail about who would take over from the established ruling class and how that change would be accomplished, but it is likely that young Virginians saw themselves stepping into positions of authority.

The last generation's strident support for secession drew from a number of related factors: a lack of faith in the state's leaders, a desire to be recognized as Southern men, a generational mission to redeem Virginia, and a refusal to recognize the Republican Party's antislavery agenda.[61] Antiparty ideology figured prominently in the last generation's decision to support secession. By ending the unholy alliance with the North, Virginians and other Southerners could liberate themselves from demagoguery and political sparring over slavery. Without the backdrop of parties, men would no longer promote their self-interest at society's expense. The last generation's vision of a Confederacy without parties reflected mainstream Southern opinion. Entering the Confederacy thus symbolized a "revolution against politics," a conservative act in the Burkean tradition that reaffirmed continuity with the Founders' vision of republicanism.[62]

Secession, war, and renewal of the Commonwealth thus dovetailed for young people. To understand the political action of young Virginians as simply a defective consequence of chivalric romanticism, a heightened sense of honor, or youthful idealism, would be to miss a rich opportunity to understand the ethical and intellectual world of young men coming of age in a slave society. The view of Southern youth as lazy, emotional, hotheaded, and anti-intellectual, which persists in the secondary scholarship, does not stand up to scrutiny. The last generation's sustained campaign for secession makes this clear. As soon as Lincoln was elected, young Virginians did not turn into "fire-eaters," nor did they take to the streets beating the drums of war. They were not drawn to the blue flame of secession like boys playing with fire. Their initial response was guarded, even moderate, although disunion was widely accepted as inevitable. Caution started to give way in January, and by February the last generation was unanimously and vocally in favor of secession. This consensus arose because of specific political acts committed by the Republican administration and the perceived passiveness of Virginia's secession convention.

When members of the last generation embraced secession, they protested in a measured and controlled manner. Ideologically, they framed their arguments within prevailing ideas about honor, patriarchy, and slavery. They worked within existing social forms of organization, such as militia companies and debating societies, or participated in accepted rituals such as flag raisings. The riots that nearly closed the University of Virginia during the 1830s—which were random and apolitical—were never duplicated on Virginia campuses during the secession crisis. Unlike their fathers' youthful rampages, the actions taken by the last generation had substance behind them. Moreover, young Virginians placed their critique of the state's leadership within a political and a historical context.

Many members of the last generation would emerge as some of the fiercest and most devoted Confederates. Their attachment to Southern nationhood must be traced to an antebellum vision of a good society, one that reflected the particular concerns of Virginia men coming of age in a slave society. The last generation's Southern identity rested on a complex foundation, but the ideological dimensions of that identity originated in the Old Dominion. "I am a Virginian and nothing else," Matthew Page Andrews explained to his fiancée during the secession crisis. At the same time, Andrews sensed that his loyalties merged into a new idea and entity as citizen in a Southern nation. "A Disunionist and a *True* Virginian," he concluded, "are synonimous [*sic*] terms."[63]

 # Paternalistic Officers

. . . .

Officers of all ranks, whose faces are not
known by the men, are equally exposed
to a volley of chaff. —Richard Corbin,
Letters of a Confederate Officer

SHORTLY AFTER FORT SUMTER, Richard Bagby
boasted to his father that a Mississippi slaveholder "offered a poor man $2000
to let him take his place [in the army], but the poor man refused to do it."[1]
Bagby had heard of similar patriotic demonstrations of nonslaveholders, leading him to conclude that all whites supported the master class's leadership.
Many young Virginians like Bagby arrogantly assumed that they presided over
a unified Confederacy. Not all lower-class whites strongly identified with the
Confederacy, and the last generation would soon discover that most did not
passively submit to slaveholder authority. Yet most nonslaveholders and small
farmers gave their allegiance to the Confederacy until the final six months of
the war. While it is understandable why young slaveholding Virginians fought
relentlessly in a war for class survival, it is more difficult to explain why nonslaveholders and members of the yeomanry overwhelmingly supported a nation that seemingly failed to represent their interests.[2]

This thorny issue cannot be explained by examining lower-class whites in
isolation. They recognized Confederate authority in part because of the men
in the last generation. Most young Virginians served as second-echelon officers in the army, the critical link between poorer white people and the Confederacy's intellectual and political leadership. Members of the last generation
were not the ideologues who fashioned Confederate nationalism; instead, they
served as negotiators in the practical battle to earn nonslaveholder allegiance
to the Confederate cause. Contrary to the popular depiction of a Confederacy
deeply fractured along class lines, young Virginians helped forge a remarkable

political and social consensus among lower-class whites through a reciprocal relationship, often based on military necessity, that required compromise and concession. The presence of an invading army also unified Virginians across class lines. Not only did 8,000 of the 12,000 deserters from Virginia eventually return to the army, but state officials also drew at least 80 percent of the Commonwealth's eligible men into the ranks.[3]

The last generation played a crucial role in the mobilization of the state's human resources. Although slaveholders have typically been seen as insensitive to the needs of their poorer neighbors, young Virginians subordinated narrow class interests to appease poor whites and keep them fighting. Their ability to compromise effectively with small farmers and members of the yeomanry improved the military efficiency of the Confederacy.[4] Even if the rich had pursued their interests with simple-minded determination, nonslaveholders would not have allowed aristocrats like these young Virginians to disregard their needs brazenly. Understanding how secondary officers gained the allegiance of the rank and file should not be interpreted as a tribute to their manipulative powers. Members of the last generation were repeatedly forced to compromise, to negotiate, and to enter into dialogue with enlisted men who realized that the Confederacy's success ultimately depended on their willingness to serve in the ranks. Many of these Virginia college boys were humbled by the ordinary man in the ranks who would not tolerate the aristocratic pretensions of an officer.

From the onset of the war, the men in the last generation attempted to create a sense of mutual obligation between officers and enlisted men. Their efforts naturally reflected the elitist view of the slaveholding class toward people whom they considered social inferiors. Young Virginians frequently described common soldiers as "children" or "naughty school boys" who lacked restraint and needed discipline. John Hampden Chamberlayne, for example, considered his company "of the peasant class." They were "ignorant" and "slovenly" in appearance and "docile" and "obedient" in action. In spite of their social inferiority, Chamberlayne admitted that he took special care to protect "their rights" and to ensure that "others . . . respect their rights."[5] Underlying Chamberlayne's arrogance was a recognition that nonslaveholders grasped their own class interests and, if provoked, would act on them. By acknowledging their rights, Chamberlayne gave his soldiers an important victory that they could not have achieved unless there had been a desperate shortage of manpower in the Confederacy. Nonslaveholders clearly understood that Southern independence depended on their support, and they compelled officers to accommodate the interests of common soldiers.

Young Virginians earned the consent of the rank and file by appealing to the religious sensibilities of their men. As soon as camps of instruction were opened, they took it upon themselves to provide for the religious as well as the military training of their men. Southern soldiers of all ages and backgrounds saw a link between courage and piety, insisting that godliness transformed ordinary men into superior fighters. Thomas Gordon Pollock opined in 1861 that "every army is stronger in [the] field which has [a] preacher in the camp and consequently the appointment of good chaplains should be no more neglected than the appointment of good colonels."[6] From the start of the war, Pollock and many of his contemporaries promoted revivals and prayer meetings, regardless of the military situation, taking great pride and satisfaction in the number of baptisms in their units.

Religion helped blur class distinctions between rich and poor as slaveholders of all ages conflated obedience to the supreme power with recognition of the master class's interests. At the same time, young Virginians were sincere when they proclaimed that all white men were bound together as Christian soldiers in the service of a higher authority. This appeal struck a cord with many privates whose lives also had been defined by evangelicalism before the war. Like the last generation, many poorer white Southerners believed their struggle for independence transcended narrow issues of power and politics. The idea that the Confederacy represented an integral part of God's plan did not have to be manufactured by young Virginians. Southerners of all classes had long recognized their region as the last bastion of Christian civilization.[7]

The religious worldview of nonslaveholders made them more receptive to the slaveholders' message that the Confederacy's interests were synonymous with God's word. But such an appeal did not turn them into passive agents who submitted to slaveholder demands. Common soldiers often compelled their officers to follow a rigorous Christian code while maintaining other religious activities in camp. The 45th Virginia, for example, held a revival from April to June 1863 at one of the high points in Confederate fortunes during the war. The religious example of the enlisted men, who came entirely from the mountainous region of southwest Virginia, forced their commander Edwin Harmon to attach "myself to the Church Members of our regt."[8] The same religious tone prevailed in most Confederate units throughout the war, including the Powhatan Artillery. A private in the company reported on July 21, 1861, that "we have prayers in our tent every night and services in church at six in the morning, the soldier[s] are not compelled to attend church but we have a law in our tent that any man who does not attend prayers in the morning shall go without his *butter* at breakfast."[9]

Contentment in the ranks, however, depended less on the religious tone of camp life and more on an officer's willingness to recognize the rights of subordinates. Young Virginians understood that nonslaveholders would not tolerate the slightest violation of their liberties. Most handled their men with sensitivity, restraint, and civility. Caroline County's Richard Corbin, who had spent most of his youth in France, captured the class tensions between lower-echelon officers and common soldiers while serving as a staff officer under General Charles W. Field. From the trenches of Petersburg in 1864, he observed that "in the Confederate army officers of all ranks, whose faces are not known by the men, are equally exposed to a volley of chaff, for the Southern soldiers is an inveterate *farceur*." "If you speak to them [privates] civilly," he added, "they will always give you an intelligent and ready reply; provided you are not arrogant or overbearing they will invariably try to oblige you with alacrity."[10] All officers faced an unruly rank and file unaccustomed to discipline, but young officers like Corbin faced the additional problem of not having age on their side. They had to walk a psychological tightrope when exercising authority over subordinates.

A firm enforcement of military regulations clashed with the independent nature of Southern soldiers. From an early age, all white males were taught to cherish their liberties, to defend against any perceived infringement of their rights, and to assert the freedoms that were entitled to them as Southern men. The restrictions of military life violated their code of honor at the most fundamental level. Southern soldiers, consequently, faced a difficult transition from civilian life. They often refused to follow orders that were not issued in a respectful manner or that they considered unnecessary. Tasks involving manual labor were sometimes ignored because such chores were only fit for slaves. The South's prewar militia tradition, in which the men enjoyed a degree of equality with their officers, reinforced this streak of rebelliousness in the ranks. Confederate enlisted men would not tolerate a domineering officer who ran roughshod over their freedoms. They demanded a voice in choosing officers and in deciding where they would serve and what branch of service they would join.[11]

A rebellion in the ranks awaited martinets. Greenlee Davidson, a twenty-eight-year-old lawyer from Lexington, Virginia, commanded a mutinous

Greenlee Davidson (1834–63).
Like many front-line officers,
Davidson discovered that com-
promise with his enlisted men
was essential to maintaining
order and discipline in the ranks.
He was killed on May 3, 1863,
at Chancellorsville. (Greenlee
Davidson Papers, Rockbridge
Historical Society Manuscripts,
Special Collections, Leyburn
Library, Washington and Lee
University, Lexington, Virginia)

crowd of lower-class whites from the city of Richmond. During a four-month
period in early 1862, his artillery battery lost a staggering 26 percent to desertion. His strong-arm tactics partially contributed to the mass exodus. Davidson frequently applied the lash to disobedient men and nearly killed one
impertinent soldier with a fence rail for refusing to go to the guardhouse.
Although Davidson, who was killed at the battle of Chancellorsville, considered force the surest way to keep his unruly men together, his subordinates
compelled him to compromise on occasion. Private John M. Travers, who left
camp without permission and headed to Richmond, became so inebriated that
he failed to report for roll call the following morning. He sent a letter to Davidson explaining that he happened to fall in "with some roving sons of Bacchus"
and expressing his apologies "for what I have done and am ready to return to
camp, as soon as I can ascertain whether any punishment is to be inflicted."
When he learned that Davidson would not " 'sweeten' me," he immediately
returned to camp for the less brutal punishment of the guardhouse.[12]

   This type of dialogue, while almost never allowed in professional armies,
mediated relations between officers and enlisted men who remained essentially

civilian in outlook. Davidson's treatment of Travers might be interpreted as a sign of weakness, but his soldiers appreciated such gestures as an acknowledgment of their rights as white men. Such concessions, however, frustrated army headquarters and Richmond officials. Compromise was viewed as softness by senior officials, who found a similar deficiency in military courts where leniency almost always prevailed. Unless a man had committed a heinous crime, such as murder or spying, soldiers almost always escaped with their lives, which encouraged others to misbehave. Subordinate officers inadvertently contributed to the problem. They routinely, but not always, treated deserters and stragglers with kid gloves. While such actions undermined Generals Robert E. Lee and Thomas J. Jackson's desire for swift and severe punishment, a more flexible handling of the rank and file enabled officers like Davidson to turn civilians into fairly reliable soldiers for the remainder of the war. At the grassroots level of the army, the subordinate officers of the last generation were caught in a crossfire of demands from above and below.

As soon as the first camps of instruction were formed, Davidson and many of his contemporaries discovered that desertion served as the most potent form of political protest among nonslaveholders, an effective weapon that kept the master class, military officers, and government officials on the defensive.[13] As the Confederacy grappled with a desperate manpower shortage in the final two years of the war, the bargaining power of the rich declined. Yet young Virginians did not interpret this shift in power relations as the first step toward class warfare. They astutely defused this issue by granting informal "French furloughs," a practice that allowed men to make brief trips home even though it violated military protocol at the most fundamental level. The constant presence of Lee's army in the Old Dominion contributed significantly to this phenomenon because the line between camp and home front was fluid throughout the war. During winter quarters or lulls between campaigns, enlisted men saw no reason why they should remain with the army when the urgent needs of their families required short trips home. Many subordinate officers and soldiers did not believe that such a policy undermined loyalty to the Confederacy. The available sources indicate that runaway soldiers did not desert because of class resentment or disillusionment with the war. Issues at home probably lured them away. Their pattern of behavior corresponds to what Kevin Conley Ruffner found in his superb study of the 44th Virginia Infantry. He discovered that the most important factors in desertion from the battalion were "age, physical condition, and family responsibilities rather than economic or class factors." Not until the fall of 1864 did an unofficial visit home represent a renunciation of the cause. If a wayward soldier returned to the ranks within a reasonable amount of time and offered a legitimate excuse for his truancy, lower-echelon officers generally looked the other way or inflicted a light punishment, such as a fine or a stint in the guardhouse.[14]

Higher military authorities usually refused to condone such behavior under any circumstances. In June 1862, for example, General James Longstreet believed that the military readiness of his command was jeopardized by Virginians who moved between camp and home without the slightest regard for official policy. He complained to Governor John Letcher that his command of twenty-three Virginia regiments and seventeen batteries was supposed to comprise 32,000 men, but 7,000 were absent from their posts without leave.[15] That sort of problem irritated Confederate officials and generals throughout the war. Their demands to tighten discipline, to turn civilians into professional soldiers, put secondary officers in a terrible predicament. The rank and file insisted on freedoms in the army that they understood as the universal rights of white men. The last generation's William Thomas Poague, a graduate of the Virginia Military Institute and captain of the famous Rockbridge Artillery, arrested several men for desertion in August 1862. The charged soldiers could not understand what had gotten into Poague. They said he was acting like a tyrant, a real martinet, even though Poague explained that he was merely carrying out instructions from above. "They became greatly incensed at me as if I had initiated the disciplinary action," Poague recalled, "and as if I ought to or could have prevented it." Poague's determination to tighten discipline in the Rockbridge Artillery nearly alienated him from his command. "I soon found myself getting unpopular with a certain class of men," Poague added. "This, of course, was not pleasant. My position was a trying one, and my ambition for promotion not sufficient to make me unwilling to exchange with a private in the ranks."[16]

Rather than give up a hard-earned commission, Poague, like many of his fellow officers, made concessions to enlisted men out of the practical need to earn the allegiance of the ordinary soldier. In the process, they contributed to the intractable problem of desertion and absence without leave by allowing their men to reaffirm local attachments as a means of reinforcing commitment to the nation. They appear to have been far more sensitive to meeting lower-class demands than previous studies have suggested, for such concessions strengthened army cohesiveness. In the face of tremendous pressure from the rank and file, they adeptly skirted Confederate policy without jeopardizing military efficiency or morale. Young Virginians implicitly understood the value of looking the other way while enlisted men took those short, but crucial trips home. In typical fashion, William Roane Aylett established his irregular furlough system by maintaining communication networks with his local community. He informed his wife that "Pat Fontaine has not yet reported for duty." "If he is in King Wm still," he stated, "tell him if he does not [report], he will get himself into difficulty & may forfeit his commission."[17] By personally exempting enlisted men from their duties, young Virginians maintained a personal involvement in their soldiers' lives. As the mediators between Confederate authority and local demands, they bargained with their men from a strong position. Ordinary privates realized that their immediate superiors could determine whether they enjoyed a short visit home or stayed in camp. Such power, if used judiciously, could forge a powerful bond between subordinate officers and the rank and file.

Young Virginians also recognized that providing material comforts was a basic requirement for earning the consent of the rank and file. The manner in which officers dispensed goods and equipment resembled forms of patronage between slaveholders and the yeomanry before the war. Sponsoring a commu- nity barbecue, allowing a neighbor to borrow some slaves for a day, or giving a poor farmer free use of a mill enabled prominent slaveholders to solidify their local power base, and the men of the last generation used similar techniques to maintain their authority in military organizations. Greenlee Davidson relied on his connections back home to acquire socks and woolen gloves from the Southern Crop Society of Rockbridge County. He also received a $500 check from his father to buy medicine, food, and other basic supplies for his men. John Hampden Chamberlayne opened a school for his company, even though he was "no advocate for education . . . for the masses." Chamberlayne ratio- nalized his decision on the grounds that "they are Virginians and near of kin to me."[18] Such displays of concern helped ease class tension in the ranks, but they were not enough to keep the army together, especially during the final six months of the war, when the Confederacy's resources were running out.

Throughout the war, however, young Virginians fiercely competed among themselves for the men's approval and support. Captains and lieutenants, the positions most often filled by the last generation, were elected by the rank and file. Those officers in turn selected the colonels, lieutenant colonels, and majors, even though the state government often issued commissions to regi- mental leaders. Campaigning for the men's vote often required lavish, expen- sive gestures.[19] Enlisted men were quick to exploit divisions among elites by raising the stakes of the game beyond the means of some members in the last generation. "The officers of our Battn also intend having a Tournament & Coronation Party some time next week," wrote Hodijah Lincoln Meade on November 4, 1863. Whenever the festivities started, he wanted "to get a sick furlough or be away" because "it will cost like Thunder." He complained that "it is getting to be much more expensive to be an Officer than to be a private." If Meade remained in his current post, he thought there would be "every prospect of my contracting a longer debt." He wondered if he should not resign and seek a rank below "petty officer."[20] A hint of indifference could also ruin an officer's career. A twenty-one-year-old captain in the 8th Virginia, Thomas Towson Smith, found his popularity sagging among his men. A comrade noticed that "he does not go amongst them and shows sufficient interest in them for his own good and they begin to notice it; they have succeeded in getting some right good jokes upon him and delight in teasing him."[21] Even John H. Chamberlayne wondered if his generous overtures had earned him the good will of his men. With some uncertainty, he wrote in the fall of 1864 that "I like them [his soldiers] & they obey me & seem to like me, as indeed they ought for I am hard at work for them in some way or another."[22]

As in the master-slave relationship, the tie between officers and men always contained the potential for brute force and raw coercion. Typically, stragglers and deserters received penalties in the form of humiliation. In the presence of their company, deserters might have their heads shaved, their left hips tattooed with the letter "D," or their bare backs flogged, sometimes as many as twenty times with the lash. Others were put to hard labor hobbled by a ball and chain, sent to solitary confinement on bread and water, or restricted to camp where they marked time on the head of a barrel. To be flogged was particularly degrading because this punishment had been reserved for slaves before the war. Even more disgraceful was the public shaming in front of their comrades, their community of peers. It forced not just the guilty party, but also the entire unit, to focus on the act committed. Appearing as less than a man stigmatized the convicted and discouraged observers from committing such acts in the future.[23] These disciplinary measures were not enough to deter countless men from reaffirming their local ties, particularly at a time when manpower shortages severely disrupted life along the home front. Young Virginia officers clearly understood that the source of their power was the military might of the Confederate government, but the vast majority employed physical punishment only as a final recourse. "One man of this Regt. was whipped 39 lashes on his bare back[,] branded on the hip, and is to work with a Ball and chain," reported Edwin Harmon on December 15, 1862. Although Harmon "was very sorry to see the fellow whipped, . . . it has had a good effect upon the men, and I think running away will not be so frequent hereafter."[24]

Humiliating punishments, rather than instilling discipline, frequently backfired and sparked uprisings in the ranks. During the Second Manassas Campaign, the Stonewall Brigade's commander, Charles Winder, ordered that any man who did not answer roll call in Gordonsville be bucked and gagged. This painful and humiliating punishment began by tying a soldier's hands together at the wrists before slipping them down over his knees. After he was bucked, a stick was then slid under the knees and over the arms. Gagging involved placing a bayonet in the mouth and tying it with a string behind the neck. This exceedingly harsh response shocked a number of officers who begged Winder to reconsider. He flatly refused. Nothing would prevent him from breaking up straggling in his Valley brigade.

The next day, about thirty men, including John Casler, were escorted to a nearby woods, placed under guard, and bucked from sunrise to sunset. Casler, who excelled at avoiding army regulations like few others, recalled that "it was a tiresome and painful situation, as we had to sit cramped up all day in one position, and if a fellow happened to fall over one of the guards would have to sit him up." "We were all as mad as fury about it," Casler bitterly wrote, "for it was a punishment that had never been inflicted in our brigade." The night after they were released, about one-half of those punished deserted. Others threatened to shoot the tyrannical Winder if he was "spotted" during the next battle. Casler told his captain that if bucked again for straggling he "would never shoulder my musket again for a cause that would treat soldiers in that manner."[25]

Members of the last generation learned that soldiers like Casler had a low threshold for humiliation. They would not tolerate such abuse. When it came to the death penalty, many secondary officers feared its indiscriminate use, for killing men who had the sympathy of their comrades would undermine discipline in the long run. After the battle of Gettysburg, when desertion skyrocketed in Lee's army, Thomas Elder hoped that President Davis's pardon and generous system of furloughs would "arrest the evil of desertion." If not, he feared that "many will have to be shot," although Elder insisted that "desertion must be stopped" by some other means.[26] Instead of relying on draconian measures, young Virginians distinguished between soldiers who deserved harsh punishment — usually criminals — and those who should be allowed to return to the army unmolested because they had left for family reasons. With this as a guiding philosophy, the last generation often defended soldiers who

The Barrel Shirt.
Is this soldier doing this for
fun? Not much, he ain't. He
was absent from camp without
leave and came back drunk.
The Colonel thinks this will
sober him.

Tied Up By the Thumbs.
The way of the transgressor
is hard.

Carrying the Rail.
Been absent without leave,
and sentenced to carry the rail
eight hours under guard.

Bucked and Gagged.

These drawings illustrate the various forms of punishment that officers might inflict on their enlisted men for being absent without permission. The men of the last generation preferred restraint and compromise rather than harsh measures such as these to instill discipline. (From John O. Casler, *Four Years in the Stonewall Brigade*, 1893)

were brought before military tribunals on charges of desertion. In May 1863, Thomas Elder confided to his wife that one of his friends had been "tried by a court martial for his long absence last summer and fully acquitted." The man had been absent from the army for nearly three months and returned without "a solitary certificate from any surgeon." Elder, who served on a general's staff, successfully spoke on behalf of his comrade, leading him to the conclusion that "a private stands but a bad chance before a court martial if he is unassisted by friends. The appearance of an officer of good rank and respectability as his counsel shows that the accused has friends who are not ashamed to help him and thus greatly aids his cause." Covering up the infractions of comrades and enlisted men, although it could lead to further abuse, actually served to maintain unit harmony and improve the strength of the fighting force in the long run. [27]

Only in the most extreme cases, when straggling and desertion increased to dangerous levels, did the men of the last generation favor executing deserters. During the first year of the war, there are few recorded instances of military executions in Virginia. Quite simply, the public would not have stood for the mass shooting of soldiers, and there is little evidence to suggest that secondary officers favored the death penalty. This political reality forced Generals Lee and Jackson to show restraint until the summer of 1862, when Confederate stragglers and deserters had exhausted the patience of civilians. The people welcomed a shift in Confederate policy toward what one historian has called "a new severity."[28] On August 19, 1862, in what might have been the first execution of deserters from Jackson's division, a firing squad killed three Shenandoah Valley soldiers. Before the orders were carried out, members of the 10th Virginia enacted their own form of justice. A fourth man from their unit, John Roadcap, was also to be shot that day. Unlike the other men, who were conscripts, he had enlisted and been a fairly reliable soldier. The rank and file, as well as most members of the last generation, differentiated between soldiers who temporarily left the ranks to care for those at home and deserters who used the uniform to engage in acts of lawlessness or to turn a profit by jumping bounty. Roadcap's actions, while a clear violation of military law, stayed within what the rank and file considered acceptable behavior. In the midnight darkness of August 19, Captain John Wesley Melhorn lined up the prisoners of the 10th Virginia, bluntly telling them that they would face a firing squad that afternoon. "I never saw such awful trembling as they manifested in my life," observed a member of the regiment who witnessed the reading of the sentences. Shortly after the men were dismissed, the guards, all from Company G, took matters into their own hands. Since Jackson had refused clemency, they would grant it. In an amazing display of military subversion, they allowed John Roadcap to disappear into the darkness. The same member of the regiment wrote: "His escape brought our company into great trouble, as we had charge of the prisoners, and five of the company are underground for letting [Roadcap] escape." "I don't know what will be done with them," he added, "but have no doubt they will be severely punished."[29]

While no member of the last generation spoke directly to Roadcap's escape, two young Virginians who witnessed the executions left revealing accounts. An important and consistent theme emerges from their conflicted reactions: force, no matter how measured it may be, must be applied only in extreme circumstances in order to instill national allegiance. When confronted with the hard choice between enforcing national loyalty or allowing the men to reaffirm their local attachments, members of the last generation came down in favor of a strong central authority and military order. After returning to his camp, artillerist William R. J. Pegram considered the event a "solemn and impressing sight," and he hoped that the executions would promote greater respect for military discipline. An officer in the 10th Virginia wrote to his hometown paper after the event: "We have just gone through one of the most painful scenes" the army has ever witnessed. Despite his deep sympathy for the victims, the officer thought "it is a fearful crime to desert the standard of their oppressed and bleeding country, in its time of trial, and the punishment of death ought to be a relief to the . . . shame they would be compelled to suffer if allowed to live." Although this officer thought that in this instance the death penalty was necessary, he never wanted his regiment to go through a similar ordeal again. "We hope in God," he concluded, "we may never again be called to record the execution of [another] deserter in the Confederate army."[30]

For officers and soldiers alike, the August 19 executions hardened them to the brutal realities of military life. Except during the fall of 1863, when clemency was widely granted to deserters, Lee and other Confederate officials consistently employed firing squads to dissuade soldiers from leaving the ranks without permission.[31] Executions demonstrated the fatal consequences of desertion to every soldier, but they did not turn enlisted men into obsequious, boot-licking subordinates who gave in to the random whims of officers. The fact that the guards of the 10th Virginia allowed John Roadcap to escape makes clear that the men had their own code of justice, and that if pushed too far, they would subvert military authority regardless of the risks. Such brazen violations of military law rarely happened, however. More often the discourse between officers and the rank and file was a subtle, ever-shifting power struggle that forced both sides into routine compromise. Only on rare occasions did the relationship between common soldiers and superior officers become contentious, even violent. Battlefield heroics and paternalistic overtures in camp create the impression that a spirit of comradeship sustained those in the ranks and that a sense of brotherhood bound them to their superiors. Although affection and mutual respect certainly kept men in the ranks, recent historical scholarship has properly shifted the emphasis to the roles of ideology, duty, and community in keeping soldiers together. Those factors provide valuable insights into soldier agency and move beyond one-dimensional images of happy-go-lucky privates or rowdy, disobedient country bumpkins.[32] Yet the role of force in promoting army cohesiveness cannot be overlooked. The soldiers who witnessed the August 19 executions understood better than most that the ultimate source of Stonewall Jackson's authority came from the end of a gun barrel.

Class animosity did surface in camp from time to time, but divisions between rich and poor disappeared on the battlefield, where the code of male honor united all men.[33] Fearlessness in front of the enemy earned the last generation the respect and admiration of the common soldier to the end of the war, and the young Virginians' bold courage inspired similar behavior from their own men. A tyrant in camp could redeem himself in battle by fighting with reckless abandon. Even a bloody, senseless attack like Pickett's Charge did not provoke the reaction that unbridled aggressiveness against rifled weapons was futile. William R. Aylett nearly lost his commission when he refused to participate in Lee's final attack at Gettysburg because of a questionable injury. Subordinates and superiors quickly dismissed men like Aylett who wavered even slightly in battle. General Jeb Stuart epitomized the ideal fighter of the last generation because he seemed oblivious to danger and contemptuous of the enemy's bullets.[34] By providing for the material comforts of their men and leading by example in battle, members of the last generation legitimated their authority. The common soldier valued superiors like Stuart because their bravery reflected well on the manliness of the entire unit—not only to the unit's satisfaction but also to that of the folks at home. Cowardly behavior under fire might jeopardize the regiment's standing with those on the home front. Subordinate officers of the last generation aggressively defended the reputation of their men against the slightest question of their courage. Lynchburg's George Woodville Latham wrote a lengthy article justifying his company's actions, but he instructed the editor not to publish it as a "vindication" for "it would be an admission that the courage of my boys had been questioned, or is questionable."[35]

Heroic action also satisfied the last generation's personal need for public acceptance as men. Once a young Virginian shouldered a musket in defense of his native land, how could his elders deny him adult status? After enlisting in the 4th Virginia Infantry, James Langhorne boasted to his family: "I am truly in the full capacity of a man. I am treated as such & consequently expected to act as such." Richard Bagby also felt he had reached full manhood once in the ranks. In response to his father's stinging remark that his son "was better at talking than doing," the younger Bagby asserted that he could not think of a time that "I have felt more serious." The war, he believed, had forced him to grow up, to become responsible, and to look at the world through the eyes of an adult.[36] Bagby and Langhorne soon discovered that there were many gradations of manhood. Although serving in the ranks brought public recognition, it often meant subordination to the will of others. Yet, few complained about their powerlessness, except for Langhorne who condemned his colonel for being too strict "for volunteers, and gentlemen.

He has been accustomed to manage old army regulars who were the scum of creation. He does not allow privates to speak to him on business."[37] It is likely that many more of Langhorne's peers resented the dictatorial authority that other men held over them, but they endured their inferior positions in silence.

Young Virginians were more vocal when it came to their desire for military honor. Romantic dreams of slaying Yankees and returning home as a conquering hero probably deluded a few young men. A member of the Stonewall Brigade observed in early 1861: "Some hearts, it may be, are now swelling with the desire for military distinction, and some heads [are] becoming dizzy with anticipations of earthly glory." Those visions of glory frequently vanished after seeing the lethal effects of a volley or holding a dying comrade in the final, spasmodic moments of life. Battlefield horrors might have sobered them to the realities of war, but they still craved power and responsibility in the army. Young Virginians looked to combat as the logical way to become leaders of men, not as a means of playing out male fantasies of aggression. John James Reeve of Richmond, like many of his peers, hungered for combat for a variety of interconnected reasons that came together around his overriding desire to exercise authority over other men. Missing First Manassas intensified Reeve's longing to "see the elephant." In January 1862, while separated from his command, he heard gunfire coming from the front. By the time he reached his company, the minor skirmish had ended, and Reeve bitterly lamented that he "never got a chance to interchange compliments with the yankees." The frustration continued to eat at him that winter, for he knew that promotion could only be secured by heroic action in battle, but the humdrum existence of winter quarters kept the armies safely apart. Reeve sought a staff officer position, knowing that this post would bring him under continuous fire as the brigadier general's right-hand man. If he received the position, he realized that the odds of getting killed would increase dramatically. The risks, although extreme, actually convinced Reeve that such a dangerous position would serve as a springboard to promotion. "Either for a bullet or a promotion," Reeve wrote. "Wouldn't it be gay if I could fight myself into a Commission?"[38] Not all young Virginians believed that bravery automatically earned a junior officer promotion, even if it were justly deserved. Popularity with the men in the ranks determined who would serve as captains and lieutenants, and the enemy's bullets made them majors, colonels, and generals. This practice frequently blocked the advancement of more qualified but lower-ranking officers, argued Lynchburg's John W. Daniel, for even if these men "performed prodigies of valor they could get it no sooner." "Thus selfishness and mediocrity were starred and wreathed," he concluded, "while patriotism and heroism bled and died in silence."[39]

William Pegram was of those young Virginians in the last generation who fought his way up the ranks. Through sheer bravery, Pegram earned the admiration of his superiors and subordinates. While under fire at Fredericksburg on December 13, 1862, he took the company's flag off the staff, wrapped the banner around his body, and walked among his abandoned guns until his cannoneers returned to their posts. Such personal recklessness typified his military career and complemented his aggressive artillery tactics of rushing his battery as close to the enemy as possible. Before Fort Sumter, few could have imagined that this shy, bespectacled youth would become a leader among men. His close associates described him as having the voice and manners of a schoolgirl. To some degree, Pegram probably felt the urge to prove his manhood, and combat gave him that opportunity. His letters fail to confirm that such an impulse stirred deep inside him, but they clearly reveal a man filled with a burning ambition to achieve the mutually reinforcing goals of power and reputation. Pegram shared his age group's conviction that ambition, if properly channeled through faith and courage, fueled action and created the possibility for greatness. They also believed that such a pursuit, regardless of the outcome, would result in improvement for the individual and society.

Pegram created his own opportunities in battle, and his eagerness to engage the enemy became legendary throughout the army. He sometimes elicited remarks from Lee's infantrymen such as "There's going to be a fight, for here comes that damn little man with the 'specs."[40] At Gettysburg, he requested that his batteries accompany an infantry expedition when intelligence indicated the presence of enemy troops. Pegram's superiors gave in to his demand, placed his battalion at the head of the column, and as a result he fired the first Confederate artillery shot of that famous battle. Such opportunities, however, were hard to come by for most of Pegram's peers. Some members of the last generation grew frustrated over the lack of opportunity to earn distinction. During the summer of 1864, Ham Chamberlayne longed for a chance to resuscitate his moribund career. He complained to his mother that he frittered away his days, riding along the lines, perfecting the trenches so that the men could fight "safely," even though he knew the enemy would never attack such a strong position. "For with me," Chamberlayne noted, "one day is very like the other." South of his position dramatic events were occurring below the city of Petersburg, including the stunning Confederate victory at Reams Station on August 25. The papers applauded the exploits of his friend Pegram, whose bold maneuvers paved the way for a successful infantry assault. Chamberlayne cheered his friend's achievements, but he could not help feeling a little jealous of Pegram's good fortune. "If I just could get a chance," Chamberlayne exclaimed. "But I rejoice with him, notwithstanding a natural envy at the luck which gives him all the hot places & chances for helping on the cause & making a name at the same time. But my time will come perhaps, and meanwhile I am now at least doing my duty in my less showy sphere."[41]

Members of the last generation put themselves at extreme physical risk to gain mastery over other men through battlefield promotions. Consequently, they sustained horrific losses on the battlefields of their native state. The human consequences were tragic for all young Southerners, regardless of their class position. Yet nonslaveholders and yeomen were infrequently remembered for making the ultimate sacrifice. Confederate ministers preferred to commemorate the lives of young slaveholding Virginians by turning them into the nation's great martyrs. Those slain members of the last generation, resting under the sod of their native state, embodied the perfect blend of Christianity, bravery, and patriotism for all to admire and emulate—Christian soldiers serving both God and country.

One such example was Captain Hugh White of Washington College, who gave his life to the Confederacy on August 30, 1862, while leading a charge at the battle of Second Manassas. Just before launching the attack, he unsheathed his sword with one hand and picked up the fallen regimental flag with the other. He advanced to the front, faced his men, and implored them to follow before disappearing into a cloud of smoke. No one stood next to him when he received the fatal bullet. He died before anyone could hear his final words. After the fighting had subsided, a comrade of White's found his lifeless captain, lying with his face to the ground, cradled in his hands, and his sword and pistol by his side. White, who studied at the Union Theological Seminary on the eve of the war and spent his summers selling religious tracts in Rockbridge County, possessed the necessary traits for Christian martyrdom. The war temporarily derailed his goal of becoming a Presbyterian minister, but he remained fixed on achieving moral purity for himself and others while in the army. Every night he held prayer meetings with his comrades, and in his free time he distributed religious tracts to soldiers in other units. "Why should not the army be a school for the reformation of the wicked?" Hugh asked his father. The glow of First Manassas did not blind him to the inhumanity that he witnessed on the battlefield, nor did he suddenly seek military honors over the pursuit of God's glory. "Yet the taste of victory," Hugh wrote shortly after the battle, "though bought by precious blood is sweet. But to preach would be far better."[42]

White's death proved emotionally devastating to his loved ones, and his loss raised a difficult question for those inside and outside the family circle — why had God taken such a devoted follower, a man so young and so full of promise, whose only desire in this world was to serve the Lord? Members of the White family, like many Confederates, were confused when trying to make sense of the physical destruction of the region's youth. William Spottswood White, Hugh's father, addressed this troubling issue in *Sketches of the Life of Captain Hugh A. White of the Stonewall Brigade.* This 1864 booklet contained a selection of Hugh's personal letters and various tributes from family members and friends, including an introduction by the influential Robert L. Dabney. Not only did this publication help ease the emotional distress of losing a son, but it also served a didactic purpose for soldiers and civilians on how to become good Confederates and Christians. The memory of Hugh White needed to be kept alive for his family and for the Confederacy, because, in celebrating his life, all Southerners could draw psychological comfort from knowing that men of nobility were giving their lives for the cause. The contributors to this booklet emphasized the ordinary position that White held in the army to show that love of fame or sordid ambition did not fuel his zeal. He had nothing at stake except his own principles. Only pure and noble sentiments, they insisted, motivated this young man. Dabney knew that the Southern people appreciated the sacrifices of their dead because they craved memorials that extolled "the christian courage and other graces of our young heroes." The time had come, however, for the rest of the world to acknowledge that White's military career paralleled the lives of countless other Confederates. In the face of such evidence, Dabney challenged the South's enemies to explain why so many good men supposedly espoused a bad cause.[43]

Dabney and William White may not have thought that Northerners would read their appeal, let alone be persuaded to believing that honorable men died for the Confederacy. Rather, they primarily aimed their message at a Southern audience with the purpose of instructing those in the ranks on how to become Christian soldiers. Both men identified White's entry into the military as the defining moment of passage into full adulthood. Inside the army, he acquired the traits that a man needed to exercise authority: he was disciplined, full of energy, moral, and courageous. Once he wore the Confederate gray, the wild emotionalism of youth abandoned him, replaced by the stern toughness and

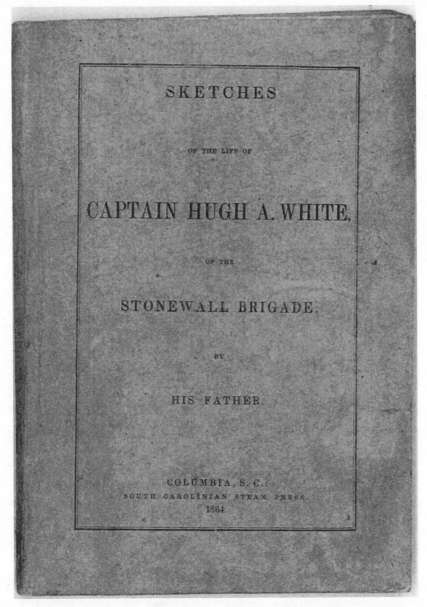

SKETCHES

OF THE LIFE OF

CAPTAIN HUGH A. WHITE,

OF THE

STONEWALL BRIGADE.

BY

HIS FATHER.

COLUMBIA, S. C.:
SOUTH CAROLINIAN STEAM PRESS.
1864.

Pamphlets such as *Sketches of the Life of Captain Hugh A. White* made martyrs of members of the last generation who fell in battle. In the introduction of this Confederate publication, the famous minister Robert L. Dabney hoped that other young Virginians would learn from White's life that the "ground of true courage . . . is the fear of God." (In the possession of the author) wisdom associated with maturity. Yet, living in the field, surrounded only by men and engaged in the business of killing, could turn the truest Christian into a brute. Dabney pointed to White as a sterling example of how the military could also preserve the innocence of youth and promote piety. This young Virginian displayed a sweet temperament, a gentle manner, a pure spirit, and a Christian character so strong that it gave him the fortitude to kill Yankees while extinguishing hateful emotions that could have annihilated his sense of humanity. "Yet in all the responsibilities of discipline and danger," Dabney wrote, "the sweet boy-man shone forth, full of nerve, energy, and heroism."[44] In death, White symbolically reconciled any conflict that might have existed between the duties of a soldier and the duties of a Christian. He also demonstrated to other young men that military service earned a soldier public esteem as a full member of the adult community. This honor came, not just from raw courage or aggressiveness in battle, but from a display of high character in camp and a Christian gentleness that inspired others to seek salvation.

Despite the impressive evidence that young Virginians were fulfilling their military and Christian duties beyond the highest civilian expectations, Dabney feared that the lure of military distinction was upsetting age relations, that ambition for promotion would lead to an insubordination of the young. He was wary lest the sudden rush of public acclaim might have gone to the heads of some young Virginians. He reminded his young readers that White never forgot his proper place, and that he never lost his respect for adult authority. "It is not rudeness, ingratitude, stubbornness against parental authority," Dabney suggested, "which makes the youth of spirit. On the contrary, we here see a filial love as tender and pure as that of a daughter, delighting to repose with childlike simplicity upon a mother's bosom, with perfect docility and reverence for parental authority."[45] Dabney could not deny members of the last generation the title of Southern men once they had experienced battle. Yet he was troubled that young Virginians might see themselves as superior since they now occupied important posts of authority in the army. This was a minor concern, however. More than anything else, Dabney wanted White and other young men to be remembered as Christian gentlemen and to learn "from such lives [that] the ground of true courage, . . . is the fear of God."[46]

At the most fundamental level, White's memorial booklet served the emotional needs of his immediate family and other civilians who had lost a loved one to the Confederate cause. Hugh's father explained to the reader that it did not matter that his son died alone. No one needed to hear his final confession or a plea for divine forgiveness. From his earliest days, Hugh had prepared himself for death, and his participation in a virtuous cause secured his entry into God's kingdom. "His parents have no recollection of the period when—according to their best judgment—his life was not that of a child of God. From the time he could read, he loved to read of Christ, and long before that he loved to hear of him."[47] Although White's piety was striking, even by the high standards of the last generation, his attainment of de facto sainthood does not ring true in places. He comes across as a man not born in sin but saintly from his conception. The self-doubts, the internal conflicts that plague every person, that give texture to an individual's experience, were lost in his martyrdom.

Understandably, White's parents wanted to reassure themselves that their son was going to heaven, that he had followed the Christian instruction of his youth, and that he had brought honor to the family. Final confirmation of White's stainless character came from his comrades, many of whom sent sympathy letters to the family, letters that his father included in the memorial booklet. While these soldiers expressed their sincere condolences, they also had a specific social purpose in mind. They enshrined White as a Christian martyr who would forever be a shining example to those in the field. "We loved him not only as a soldier, but also and especially as a Christian gentleman," wrote a member of the 4th Virginia. "As a soldier and officer he was a model; to his company he was exceedingly kind, but his kindness never assumed the form of partiality. . . . In action he was perfectly fearless, yet his courage was controlled by sound discretion." This soldier never heard White utter the command "Go *on*." Rather, White would always lead men into the face of the enemy while crying out, "Come on." Stonewall Jackson also wrote of White's death, expressing his sorrow over the loss of his friend, but he found solace in the fact that the young Virginian would be immortalized as a Confederate patriot. "In the army he adorned the doctrine of Christ, his Saviour," Jackson penned. "When Testaments or other religious works were to be distributed, I found him ready for the work. Though his loss must be mourned, yet it is gratifying to know that he has left us a bright example."[48]

The letters of White's comrades played a crucial role in transforming Hugh's lonely, isolated death at Second Manassas into a transcendent moment for the collective benefit of all Southerners. His family could draw comfort and satisfaction in knowing that their son had performed his Christian and military duties while members of the rank and file would have nothing to fear on the battlefield if they lived up to White's example. A heavenly reward awaited any man who took a Yankee bullet. The concept of Christian martyrdom eased doubt about why God would allow the Yankees to destroy the flower of the South's youth. The slaughter of so many young men, filled with promise and the love of Christ, caused many Southerners to question the ways of Providence. "Well may the old ask," White's father wrote, "why are we feeble withered, fruitless branches spared, and they, so young, so fresh, so fruitful, taken away?" He knew that "God's ways are not our ways." Such a belief enabled him to glorify his son's life and endure his death. He believed that his son's "life was beautiful, and his death safe, honorable, and useful."[49]

Many of White's soldiers found his example to be an inspiring model of behavior that would bring recognition in this world and salvation in the next. Legions of young men lost their lives trying to attain this impossible goal of moral purity, believing that extreme bravery brought them public recognition as Christian soldiers. When a Union shell killed the University of Virginia's Randolph Fairfax, Robert E. Lee praised the young man for his piety. After reading Lee's letter, a comrade of Fairfax's exclaimed: "Such an honor were indeed worth dying for."[50] The martyrdom of slain young Virginians also assured members of the rank and file, even those who were not pious, that they followed honorable men, that their cause was just, and that becoming a Christian guaranteed an honorable Confederate death. White's stainless image did not delude all his men into believing that he was beyond fault while alive. White had served on the court-martial of a Virginia soldier convicted of desertion. This man was the first in Jackson's Division to be sentenced to face a firing squad. Not long after the execution, White and two other officers involved in the court-martial died at Second Manassas. It was reported after the battle that many veterans of the Stonewall Brigade looked upon the death of White and his fellow officers as a form of divine retribution for their comrade's brutal execution.[51]

Despite an occasional backlash from disgruntled subordinates, White and other members of the last generation still managed to gain public recognition through armed conflict. Yet they could not live up to one important aspect of the masculine ideal. They could not provide for the material needs of their loved ones, nor could they control the daily activities of the household. With sons and husbands serving in the ranks, women suddenly exercised more authority, handled responsibilities typically reserved for men, and contended with the constant danger of invading, marauding Union armies.[52] This upheaval in gender roles frustrated the members of the last generation, at times even led to angry outbursts and fits of despondency, but it did not undermine morale or weaken their commitment to the Confederacy. Young Virginians and the women who were part of their lives understood the blurring of gen-der distinctions as a temporary consequence of the war. Accommodation was necessary if the South was to secure its independence.[53]

The war's disruption of traditional gendered patterns of authority made religion critical to maintaining a sense of family and community. Prayer, the last generation believed, could assure one of divine grace and protection and preserve a spiritual connection between soldiers and loved ones. Norfolk's Walter Taylor, who had attended the Virginia Military Institute and served on Robert E. Lee's staff, felt a sense of security and hope about his own moral state and the Confederate cause when he asked his fiancée to "join your prayers with mine . . . that together we may pass thro life's scenes a mutual support & comfort."[54] Taylor and his contemporaries in the last generation drew comfort and confidence from their entreaties to God. Even though Northern depreda-tions might have left wives and children in a half-starving condition, they still believed Providence's hand governed their lives as a chosen people. The Bible demonstrated that God recognized as His chosen people those who suffered the most. Enduring hardship was a test of faith. Although young Virginians could not personally aid their loved ones, they considered their prayers a con-tribution to the household's welfare. Asking God to watch over the people back home became an important responsibility that helped alleviate feelings of helplessness while away in camp. A young Virginian, in other words, could become a man through prayer as well as in battle. After learning that some Union soldiers had murdered his father at the family home in Warrenton, Robert Taylor Scott wrote to his wife: "Oh! how my heart bleeds when I think of them all; of mother, dear old Grandma, my sisters and the poor little ones. Alone and without a protector, tho' I humbly trust not unprotected. God has promised succour to the needy, support to the afflicted. I've prayed to him earnestly [and] asked him to direct and guide me in the path of duty and sup-port me in all my trials."[55]

No matter how earnest or sincere, prayer could not ease all burdens or solve all problems. Neither could it fill empty stomachs nor scare away Union soldiers. It spurred the last generation to assume an active role in ameliorat-ing conditions on the home front. As lower-grade officers, young Virginians organized benevolent activities for the areas from which their regiments were drawn, especially after 1863, when basic resources became increasingly scarce. Richard W. Corbin observed from the trenches of Richmond during the sum-mer of 1864 that "some of the brigades are so abundantly provided for that they have frequently given their rations to the poor of the city, amongst whom there is really a great deal of suffering owing to the exorbitant prices of food."[56] Soldiers also made regular financial contributions to relief organizations that eased public discontent over the war while renewing ties between men in uniform and their local communities.[57] As members of the South's ruling class, young Virginians did not blindly ignore the pain and hardship on the home front.[58] They listened and responded to the charge that the war had become a poor man's fight.

The women associated with the last generation were also of the slaveholding class, and they were probably more supportive of the war and more willing to endure hardships than the average Southern woman. Like many of their men, a paralysis of will reflected a crisis of faith in God and in the Confederacy. "I have determined to try & fight against gloom & despondency, & to discharge all my duties faithfully," Fanny Scott informed her husband in 1861. "Altho' it is a hard struggle, I believe help will be given me from above, almost every breath I draw, is a prayer for your safety, & for perfect resignation to God's will."[59] Knowing that Providence directed affairs from above inspired women to endure tremendous hardship. Just as the last generation claimed that divine rewards befell soldiers who showed fortitude in the ranks, Virginia's women also hoped for eternal glory by fulfilling their new duties as heads of household. They expressed pessimism and anger over the war's hardships and disruptive effects, but weariness should not be interpreted as a rejection of the Confederate cause. No matter how tired slaveholding women were of the war, the immediate threat of an invading Union army inextricably bound them to the men in the field.[60]

Confederate women in Virginia quickly proved to themselves and to the last generation that they could cope with the burdens of war. As the conflict brought civilians within its destructive sphere, most women became more assertive and confident in their new roles. In a hardening process similar to the one that soldiers experienced on the battlefield, women grew accustomed to the privations and the constant danger posed by an invading army. In March 1865, Matthew P. Andrews observed that Southern women could withstand brutal living conditions because they "have become callous to dangers." The sight of Union troops in Surry County became so routine that James DeWitt Hankins's sister mocked some enemy soldiers who terrorized the locals during the summer of 1864. "Last Wednesday Morning, we were surprised by the clanking of sabres in the lane, & looking up saw the Yankee Cavalry in *full charge* coming up to the house, it was the first intimation we had of their proximity to us," she informed her brother. "Their sabres were drawn, and their pistols cocked! Ah! these were *brave* men, charging so valorously on women & little children, how proud and undaunted they looked."[61]

There were times, however, when slaveholding and nonslaveholding women bitterly complained about their plight and expressed weariness over the war, especially when battlefield defeats became routine after the fall of 1864. Even during moments of severe trial, most Virginia women wanted their men to stay in the army regardless of the situation at home. The presence of a hostile enemy largely explains their resilience. William Pegram believed that his mother and sisters would have preferred to see him return home in a casket than visit Richmond without permission. When black soldiers occupied the downstairs of her family's plantation house, Virginia Wilson Hankins could not understand why God inflicted on her such a trial, but she instructed her son: "*Do not think of coming home.*" All she wanted was a "100 good men" to "protect us from these marauding parties."[62] Mrs. Hankins recognized that only the expulsion of Union forces from Virginia would restore a degree of normalcy and order to their lives. Encouraging soldiers to leave their posts to care for those at home, most women realized, would leave their families even more vulnerable to a ruthless Union army.

Members of the last generation unanimously admired the determination and courage of Southern women during the war. Their heroic example forged a powerful bond with those in the ranks. A common spirit of sacrifice united men and women in a collective effort against the North. Young Virginians extolled the contributions women made for the Confederate war effort, although words of praise were still framed within the parameters of patriarchy. After learning that his plantation had been pillaged by a party of Union cavalrymen in the summer of 1863, William R. Aylett did not know how "my darling . . . managed to get through such a day, and yet you must have [handled] yourself admirably." Aylett felt proud of his wife "for the courage and heroism you evinced. You are a woman and what you did was harder for *you*, than facing bullets and bayonets is to me—because I am a man and it is expected of me."[63]

Acts of sacrifice on the home front increased the last generation's devotion to the localities they came from and also reinforced their Confederate loyalties. The sight of women tending to a dilapidated farm or a band of refugees leaving their homes outraged these young men, many of whom demanded vengeance against the enemy.[64] Only a noble, divinely ordained cause, young Virginians maintained, could incite the fierce devotion of Southern women. In the winter of 1863, Walter Taylor complimented his fiancée and the other women who worked in the Treasury Department. "It must be some consolation to you girls

Walter Taylor (1838–1916). As was the case with many of his peers, Taylor recognized the important contributions that women made to the cause, and he drew inspiration from their sacrifices. He wrote to his fiancée in 1863 that he expected "to see the women of our land relieve the men of all character of work except the actual fighting. It will be convincing evidence of the earnestness of the people." This 1864 image has not been published before. (Courtesy of Sargeant Memorial Room, Kim Memorial Library, Norfolk, Virginia)

to think that each of you, by occupying your present positions, relieves an able-bodied, strong man and adds one soldier to the Army in the field." If the war continued much longer, Taylor expected "to see the women of our land relieve the men of all character of work except the actual fighting. It will be convincing evidence of the earnestness of the people."[65] Young Virginians accepted the breakdown of traditional gender roles as a necessary war measure, stressing the need for collaboration and encouragement from those at home if the Confederacy were to succeed. "Indeed in this war more truly than in any other," wrote Jeb Stuart to his wife in the fall of 1863, "the spirit of lovely woman points the dart, hurls the javelin, ignites the mine, pulls the trigger, draws the lanyard and gives a fiercer truer temper to the blade in a far more literal sense than the mere muscular aggressions of man."[66]

The last generation's outspoken support for Confederate legislation that violated community autonomy and conscripted slaveholders also helped ease class tension. This supports William Blair's conclusion that the citizens of the Old Dominion generally favored the centralizing tendencies of the national government and tended not to invoke states' rights principles. Citizens even asked for increased government intervention to relieve problems on the home front, although they might later complain about the enforcement of those policies. Young Virginians were outspoken proponents of stronger federal

Elizabeth S. "Bettie" Saunders served in the Treasury Department for much of the war, and her fiancée, Walter Taylor, complimented Saunders and her peers for their devoted work. "It must be of some consolation to you girls," he wrote in late 1863, "to think that each of you, by occupying your present positions, relieves an able-bodied, strong man and adds one soldier to the Army in the field." (Courtesy of Sargeant Memorial Room, Kim Memorial Library, Norfolk, Va.)

power. While serving in the army, they became sensitive to the importance of maximizing the South's resources, even if it forced their fellow slaveholders to shoulder a musket or accept the impressment of their slaves and crops. Loopholes that enabled slaveholders to escape military duty infuriated most young Virginians, although some used family connections to obtain comfortable staff positions. When nonslaveholders began to condemn the war as a poor man's fight in the fall of 1863, the state's authorities wisely responded by eliminating class-based privileges that allowed the wealthy to escape service. The third year of the war witnessed a dramatic shift in Confederate policy. In 1864, lawmakers focused on the needs of small slaveowners and nonslaveowning farmers. On January 5, 1864, President Jefferson Davis signed a bill that forced all men into the ranks who had avoided military duty by purchasing substitutes. The following month Congress passed legislation that essentially required all men to join the army. Congress's elimination of substitutes restored the Stonewall Brigade's John Henry Stover Funk's confidence in Confederate officials. "All we shall need is a congress equal to the times—bold and energetic—and that I think we have—The addition we will receive, at the repeal of the substitute law, and the conscription of those, furnishing substitutes will be over one hundred thousand men."[67]

Funk and his contemporaries desired a stronger central government in Richmond because they had lost their civilian perspective. On the front lines, they witnessed how shortages in matériel and manpower routinely threatened the military efficiency of Lee's army. Their perspective as soldiers created a state of mind that made them more open to the enlargement of Confederate powers. They advocated a stronger central government until the end of the war. William Pegram, for example, welcomed the end of substitution in 1864 but later desired even stronger measures to force men in noncombatant positions to bear arms. On September 24, he complained that the army did not have "more than half of our strength in the field," while "every city & county is filled with clerks, petty state officers, & details for this or that business." Angered by these bureaucratic exemptions, he insisted that all men should serve in the field.[68] Strengthening the South's military capacity might alienate some slaveholders, the last generation conceded, but government intervention in the lives of its citizens was necessary to prosecute the war. The last generation did not see this viewpoint as an abandonment of antebellum notions of government. Once Southern independence had been established, limited government and local prerogative could be restored.[69]

In order to bolster the ranks of Confederate armies and lessen the burdens on poorer whites, some young Virginians advocated the arming of slaves, a policy that violently clashed with the interests of the master class. Fragmentary evidence suggests that the last generation generally approved of the incorporation of blacks into the army by the spring of 1865. William Pegram believed the enlistment of slaves met "with general approbation" among his fellow soldiers. Some of the best Confederate officers, he reported, "are trying to get commands in the Corps D'Afrique." In late December 1864, Richard Corbin favored arming the slaves as a wartime necessity in "this dark hour in the history of our revolution." Because Lincoln's plan of "subjugation involves the manumission of our slaves," Corbin reasoned that it would "be better for us to say to the negroes, 'Fight for us, and you will not only be free, but you will retain your homes.'" Although he knew this admission would startle his mother, Corbin assured her that "the necessities of the case have forced me to adopt" such an extreme position and "I still say and think that the negro's happiest condition is slavery."[70]

Like many of their contemporaries, Pegram and Corbin understood the enlistment of slaves in the army as a temporary war measure, one that implied no final rejection of the peculiar institution. The last generation's willingness to consolidate national authority and to arm slaves reflected their uncompromising commitment to Southern independence. Although young Virginians were not rejecting slavery, they were tampering with the very institution that defined their power and status in the South. This strongly suggests that young Virginians may have been some of the most extreme nationalists in the Confederacy. It is also possible that young Virginians were willing to relinquish an institution that offered them few personal opportunities of advancement during the 1850s.

In 1911, the last generation's Berkeley Minor believed that pride had sunk the Confederate ship. Rather than saving themselves by tossing slavery overboard, Minor argued that "we, the people of the States of the Confederacy were to blame" for resisting the only course to independence. Even in his golden years, Minor still regretted this mistake, caused by the blinding arrogance of the people. "We should have been willing to give it up," he asserted, "to save ourselves from a union in which we could have no rights, except what our conquerors should allow us." In Reconstruction, Minor believed that God had allowed "so cruel a mode of emancipation, only because those who could and should have done away with slavery . . . missed their opportunity, like the Israelites at Kadesh," who met with disastrous defeat, and then spent "more than forty years wandering in the wilderness."[71] Minor should have been thankful that Virginians only had to wait four years until home rule was returned to white conservatives.

 **Christian Martyrs**

· ·

Conquer them we must and will, for God
cannot intend that such wickedness should
succeed.—William R. Aylett to Alice Roane
(Brockenbrough) Aylett, July 20 and 21, 1863

A TWENTY-THREE-YEAR-OLD captain from Hamp-
ton, Virginia, William Gordon McCabe, watched in disbelief as Lee's soldiers deserted during the retreat to Appomattox. Writing two days before the
surrender, McCabe refused to "give up this beloved Virginia because of the
faint-heartedness & cowardice of these men, who have deserted their colours."
"If the men will only remain at their posts & trust in God," he asserted,
"every thing would go right. . . . If we lose our country, it is our own fault." A
friend of McCabe's, John Hampden Chamberlayne, also refused to abandon
the Confederate cause "to attend the funeral at Appomattox C.H." Instead of
surrendering with the rest of his comrades, he rode to Joseph E. Johnston's
army in North Carolina, informing his family along the way that "I am not
conquered by any means & shall not be while alive—My life is of no further
value—Farewell to my beloved Virginia."[1]

McCabe's and Chamberlayne's commitment to the Confederacy was extreme in 1865, when most white Southerners had either abandoned the cause
or admitted to the inevitability of defeat. As an age group, the last generation
stood out for its impressive display of loyalty to the Confederacy that only
intensified as the war became more physically grueling and emotionally demanding. This should come as no surprise, for members of the last generation,
with their strong ties to the South's ruling class, had everything to lose—their
material and ideological interest in slavery, their ambition for public recognition, their honor, and, most of all, their sense of national identity. Their letters
and diaries overwhelmingly attest to an unshakeable faith in nation that could
not be equivocated. During the final seven months of the war, when most

Southern civilians acknowledged the inevitability of defeat, the last generation remained resolute, determined, and defiant. The question of whether or not young Virginians articulated an authentic and durable expression of Confederate nationalism can be easily answered. The words and battlefield actions of the last generation make abundantly clear that the political and ideological mission of the Confederacy resonated with them, sustained their morale, and kept them in uniform long past the point of endurance of most Southerners. A more useful line of inquiry focuses on the ways in which young Virginians identified with Southern nationhood and how the basis of that loyalty changed over the course of the war.

The last generation's understanding of the Confederate experiment is rooted in the intellectual and religious milieu of the 1850s. These young people became convinced that the South defended Christian orthodoxy against Northern Unitarianism and Universalism, evil forces that were seen as allies of the abolitionists and Republicans. Together, these radical powers crusaded against the conservative traditions of a slave society. When war finally came, young Virginians had little trouble envisioning themselves as Christian and Confederate soldiers, fighting for both religious *and* political liberty. To them, the Confederacy was the realization of the abstract notion of a Southern Christian community. Within this framework, their commitment to Christ flowed into their commitment to the Confederacy. Neither cause could be easily compromised.

Confederate civil religious patriotism did have its risks. As long as the Southern nation stayed true to the principles of Christianity and upheld the virtues of the Founders, young Virginians confidently predicted the divinely sanctioned reward of independence. Though most Southerners generally lived up to the patriotic expectations of the last generation, dissent, war weariness, immorality, profiteering, and military setbacks raised troubling questions about the Confederacy's status as God's favored nation. Many scholars argue that white Southerners lost the will to fight because they thought God had abandoned the Confederacy, that He was displeased about slavery, speculation, or some other national sin. Yet the experience of young Virginians does not fit this historiographical trend.[2] In adjusting to the revolutionary consequences of the war, the last generation demonstrated an amazing ability to interpret social upheaval within established patterns of cultural continuity. Too many historians perceive and sometimes even exaggerate contradictions in Southern society regarding slavery, religion, gender relations, and lower-class dissent. Many of these dilemmas either remained hidden to the people at the time or were rationalized away with minimal psychological discomfort. In the case of the last generation, the collapse of slavery, civilian profiteering, and the breakdown of traditional gender roles did not raise permanent doubts about the moral condition of the South. Indisputable proof that God favored the Confederacy came from the hands of the enemy, whose depredations in Virginia reinforced claims that North and South differed in morals and character.

Identifying the Confederacy as a Christian nation was not a cynical ploy by slaveholders to earn lower-class support, but a belief consistent with the antebellum message that the South embodied a Christian community in a hostile godless world.[3] The formation of the Confederacy conformed to well-established notions that Providence had chosen Southerners to preserve the nation's historical and cultural past. Claiming God as a Southern nationalist imparted a transcendent purpose to the Confederacy while keeping the new nation within the religious framework of the antebellum South. For most Southerners, the war represented a second contest for American liberty, a defense of the Revolutionary heritage and Christianity. Such a mission resonated deeply with young Virginians. Defending the Confederacy satisfied their need for a higher calling that echoed the Founders' noble exploits in the first War for Independence.

Like most Confederates, the last generation proclaimed their nation to be the keeper of America's Revolutionary heritage. They argued that secession did not represent a radical break with the past; it was a return to those cherished principles of pure republicanism.[4] This was not a movement in the tradition of the French Revolution, they insisted, but rather a conservative effort to liberate the republic from the decadent North. The historical parallels between the Confederacy and the American colonies inspired Southerners of all ages to believe they could overcome overwhelming odds through shared sacrifice and faith, just as their ancestors had persevered against the British. "The Hessians may run us back for two years—even five years, but still they will ultimately be driven out of our land as wild geese are driven south in the fall by chilling winds of the North Pole," wrote the Valley's George W. Koontz in 1861. Because he believed that an "All Wise being directs, things" and that "we are only battling for what our forefathers did in the Revolution," Koontz was "confident of Success."[5]

Simply following the example of the Revolutionary heroes, however, could not guarantee success. Koontz confidently submitted the Confederacy's future to Providence, believing that a just God would empower the righteous over the mighty. As soon as he was mustered into service, Koontz connected the Confederacy to higher ends. What stands out is how quickly he and his peers in the last generation fastened Southern nationhood to the designs of God. They also sought salvation in camp as a way to prepare for their duties in battle. Drew Gilpin Faust, among others, has argued that Confederate soldiers at the beginning of the war criticized evangelicals for undermining military effectiveness with a spiritual message promoting womanly virtues.[6] While ministers might have met some resistance among callous unbelievers, members of the last generation did not reject the word of God; they welcomed it. In fact, young Virginians promoted religion as a way to turn civilians into superior soldiers. Christianity instilled a sense of duty, demanded discipline, and inspired courage. A saved man did not fear the dangers of battle. The last generation's prewar belief in chivalry accommodated the conflicting demands of Confederate military life, enabling a young man to simultaneously endorse aggressiveness and tenderness, killing and piety. At an early age, men were instructed that a purity of heart softened the South's code of honor without sacrificing violence as a legitimate option if their homes came under attack or their women were insulted. Confederate ministers successfully reconciled such contradictions, making it clear that a manly soldier loved Jesus. Robert L. Dabney, for instance, wrote in 1863: "Let the young man learn here how consistent manliness is with purity and tenderness." In a published tribute to a fallen member of the last generation, the Reverend Philip Slaughter concluded that "a conscientious Christian" makes "the best soldier."[7] Young Virginians agreed with both ministers, for they looked upon a soldier with a gentle soul as having the potential to become a warrior in battle.

As discussed in the previous chapter, members of the last generation considered courage intimately connected to godliness. Young Virginians, consequently, scrutinized their behavior in battle. Bold, aggressive actions signified faith in the Confederacy and in God. Such displays in battle convinced many young Virginians that Providence would consider Southerners His most devoted followers. "God helps those who help themselves" was a phrase that the last generation took to heart. These young men did not ridicule chaplains or discourage religious activity among the troops. They did not fear that religious faith would make the rank and file too effeminate to fight. Young Virginians, in fact, felt a bolt of courage from their spiritual relationship with God. "Don't be uneasy Mother," James Keith wrote in May 1864, "God has spared me so far for some wise purpose[.] if it be his will all the bullets of the Yankees can't hurt me[.] if he has decreed otherwise I could not die in a better cause." After receiving four bullet holes through his coat at the battle of Cedar Mountain in 1862, William R. J. Pegram gratefully acknowledged that "an ever merciful God again took me under His protection and brought me safely through the fight." He exclaimed: "What have I to fear from Yankee bullets and shells, as long as I am under His protection?" And the Stonewall Brigade's Hugh A. White informed his brother that "if I am killed, I have a good hope, that I should at once enter Heaven, and be happy forever. The hope cheers and animates me at all times, so that while death walks on every side, no tormenting fears arise." At First Manassas, White had heard the terror in the voices of nonbelievers, mortally wounded men appealing for God's mercy during their final moments on earth. Their cries "seemed louder than the roar of the cannon," piercing his "heart with keener anguish."[8]

For White, Pegram, and Keith, personal faith was deeply embedded in both their identity as Confederate soldiers and their political allegiance to Southern nationhood. Yet these young Virginians did not equate their struggle against the Yankees with a holy war until the final year of the conflict. They scrupulously avoided anything that smacked of religious fanaticism, but at the same time they did acknowledge that religious issues were at stake for the Southern people, individually and collectively. Shortly after he enlisted in the 4th Virginia Infantry, Hugh White assured his family that if he did not survive the "great effusion of blood" that would surely come, "I am of the Lord's." Giving his life for political independence motivated White to a degree, but what truly animated him was knowing that great religious questions were at issue. "If we are conquered," he explained, "farewell forever to the bright visions of philanthropists and christians as to the civil and religious freedom America was to maintain at home and scatter abroad. But if we conquer, as I think we shall eventually, these visions and hopes may again be cherished." Identifying the war with religious issues set the stage for the last generation to identify Southern independence as a religious crusade. Just one year later White considered death on the battlefield a sacred act, an offering made on the altar of the Confederacy. In 1862, he described the loss of cavalryman Turner Ashby as "a most noble sacrifice to our holy cause."[9]

Although White embraced the religious significance attached to the conflict, he was concerned, like many Southern clergymen, about the popular idea that wearing the Confederate gray was an act of salvation that could replace conversion. Fighting was not, he believed, synonymous with being saved. Accepting Christ and living a moral life, these men argued, determined one's spiritual fate. Just as they had preached personal reform when they were students in the 1850s, members of the last generation demanded moral purity from themselves, civilians, and other Confederate soldiers. War created new spiritual circumstances that made Southerners feel a sense of urgency about finding salvation. Young Virginians used that historical moment to convert others or to gain salvation themselves. They obediently followed Confederate spokesmen, clerical and lay, who frightened Southerners into believing that unholiness might send God reeling away from the Confederacy and into the waiting arms of the North. Nonbelievers needed to find God now and atone for their sins, religious leaders maintained, for Christian living would secure the Confederacy divine favor. Members of the last generation heeded this warning until the very end of the war. They scrutinized their own behavior with the understanding that an individual's personal relationship with God was inseparable from the public life of the Confederacy and the fate of the nation.

Robert Taylor Scott of Warrenton followed a pattern of religious and political beliefs common to the last generation. Scott graduated from the University of Virginia in 1854 and was admitted to the Warrenton bar three years later. He came from a prominent Whig family—his father was a stubborn advocate of Union at the Richmond secession convention—and the younger Scott assumed a similar conservative position. But he switched allegiances quickly at the outbreak of the war and organized a military company for service in the 8th Virginia Infantry. From the beginning, duty to God and to the Confederacy merged in his mind, but Scott never imagined himself slaughtering Yankees for the glory of God. The idea of becoming a Christian martyr seemed even more ludicrous to him. At least during the first two years of the war, religion soothed the passions of young men like Scott. Scott prayed for the God of peace to triumph, holding out the hope that Northerners would have a sudden epiphany in which they would see their evil ways, seek forgiveness, and evacuate the South.

Fellow University of Virginia alumnus Thomas Elder also sought the God of peace when he first encountered the inhumanity of war. While walking along the "shell strewn beach" of the James River on April, 6, 1862, Elder admired the placid water glistening in the bright sunshine. This sight almost deceived him into believing that all was right with the world. As he breathed in the serenity of a "beautiful Sabbath" morning, he heard the peals of "thundering artillery" in the background, jolting him back to the brutal reality of war, death, destruction, and the "wickedness of man." "Perhaps hundreds of manly forms created by God . . . and designed by him to live together in brotherly love," Elder predicted, ". . . will be laid on the bloody field stiff in the cold embrace of death, slain by the hands of each other." Yet he did not blame the South for taking arms. "What else can men do than defend their wives and children and parents, homes and firesides, all that is dear on earth when invaded by a cruel and unrelenting foe." Elder wished that Northerners and Southerners would study their Bibles, read chapter 13 of Genesis, and emulate the story of the peaceful separation of Abraham and Lot. "These men of God did separate and there was peace between them," he reasoned. "Would that the two sections of this unhappy land follow this example!"[10]

Elder and Scott wanted peace not out of war weariness or disillusionment with the Confederacy, but out of a desire to stop the sin of killing and to restore cherished family relations disrupted by war. Leaving his wife and children proved particularly difficult for Scott, who felt lost without the stability and support of home. The daily possibility of sudden death added to his personal confusion and intensified his need to find meaning in a war that he did not want. On August 15, 1861, he poured out his conflicted feelings about enlisting in the army to his wife: "God knows it is the hardest trial and saddest duty I was ever called upon to execute . . . My heart yearns for my darling wife," he added, "I feel desolate without her. Oh! that this horrid war was at an end and peace, thrice blessed peace again restored." During this severe trial, he imagined a scourge of fire and blood trailing across his native land. Faith rescued Scott from giving in to these dark visions. He placed his personal safety, his family's well-being, and the political hopes of his nation in the hands of God. Believing that a higher power protected the weak, punished the wicked, and awarded the righteous gave Scott and many other Southerners the resolve to keep fighting. Young Virginians were united in the belief that God might test His people but would never abandon them. Scott drew solace from the words of a local minister: "'All things work for good to them that love God.'" "I believe it," he assured his wife, "and placing my hope in His mercy and fatherly protection I am ready to make the sacrifice required at my hands."[11] By the spring of 1862, he had compressed his duties as soldier and Christian into a refrain typical of his generation: "I shall try to do *my duty, my whole duty to God and to my country. My trust is in Him, may it never be confounded.*"[12]

For Scott and many other like-minded Virginians, Confederate nationalism did not subsume religious beliefs. Each body of thought sustained the other until they merged.[13] From the war's inception, Southern ministers conflated religious and political duties. In May 1862, the last generation's Randolph Fairfax was among the many enlisted men who heard a sermon by Stonewall Jackson's chaplain, Robert Dabney. As the minister spoke, the sounds of the enemy's guns rang in the background—powerful reverberations that impressed Fairfax almost as much as the minister's words did. With evangelical fury, Dabney told the soldiers that God had visited war upon the nation for America's collective sins. Unless Southerners repented, he expected that "more terrible punishments may come upon us." Dabney also braced his congregation for the possibility of setbacks and suffering, for "God sometimes uses a more wicked instrument to punish a more innocent one." Even if this was to occur, he predicted that the North, a veritable modern Babylon in his estimation, would be destroyed by a wrathful God as long as Southerners sought His merciful salvation. At the conclusion of this inspiring sermon, Fairfax made the crucial link between faith, Confederate duty, and final victory. He wrote: "I think the fate of the country is now in the hands of the praying people, and though I cannot see how or when, I believe God will certainly answer the prayers of His faithful people in the land."[14] Fairfax embraced what his age group and many other Southerners considered the key to personal salvation and national independence: simple faith and trust in God and an assurance that they were, as Dabney had said, the "more innocent" ones.

The blurring of sacred and secular purposes narrowed the parameters of acceptable political dissent. Even the slightest criticism of the Confederacy could be interpreted as a loss of will and a violation of divine authority. In the wake of Fort Sumter, members of the last generation were influenced by clergymen and politicians whose sermons and speeches equated duty to God with duty to nation. A similar message came from the home front, where wives and mothers felt compassion for soldiers caught in a tug-of-war between national and local demands. They wanted men to understand that serving in the ranks fulfilled one's obligations to country, God, and family, no matter how difficult the sacrifices and suffering might become for those left behind. Failing to do civic duty, many women argued, violated divine will and exposed the family, community, and nation to God's wrath. Just a month before Robert Taylor Scott left for active service, his wife Fanny refused to stand in his way. "I feel that you must leave me, & I fear the time is not distant when your duty (whose will you will *ever* heed) will call you from me, to encounter all the danger & perils of war, & to battle for your rights, & even the safety of your own wife & children, I would not ask, could not desire you to stay one day longer than you thought right." The thought of losing Scott, of his dying away from home, filled her with a sickening agony. "But then Taylor," she added, "the thought strikes me are we both prepared to die, to be happy with God & with each other in heaven." Fanny knew that she must strive to surrender to God's will and that her example would prepare Scott for the trials to come. Two months after he left for the army, she wrote that "I have determined to try to fight against gloom & despondency, & to discharge all my duties faithfully, altho' it is a hard struggle, I believe help will be given me from above, almost every breath I draw, is a prayer for your safety, & for perfect resignation to God's will."[15] Robert Scott tried to follow his wife's example, affirming a week later that "I'm determined with God's aid to make a good fight and trust all to Him, who does all things for the best. In Him is our only hope my own dear wife, if He wills it I will return in safety to the bosom of my own family, otherwise and you must look to Him for support in the time of trouble and affliction." Every day in the army Scott felt a stronger urge to join the church, to proclaim publicly that "He is my Saviour, My Protection and my God."[16]

The uncertainty of military life encouraged Scott and many of his peers either to embrace religion for the first time or to reaffirm existing beliefs. Some members of the last generation undoubtedly turned to religion as a bomb-proof from the brutality of armed conflict. Seeking religion during a time of duress should not raise doubts about the sincerity of their beliefs. Religion has always served people who try to make emotional, intellectual, and moral sense of their lives during chaotic and confusing times. After surviving a disastrous charge at the battle of Williamsburg on May 5, 1862, William Weldon Bentley of the Virginia Military Institute could not explain the unexplainable — why he had survived when so many of his comrades had fallen. Bentley nearly suffered an emotional collapse after the battle when he thought about the men he would never see again. "Oh! My Dear Mother you do not know how my *heart aches & how sad* I feel when I think that I may never see you all again . . . & that my body may not rest under the sod of my own dear home but may be left to moulder on the field probably with the bodies of the wicked invaders." More than ever before, Bentley was amazed by the mysterious powers of Providence and the need to trust "His infinite goodness." Faith, he believed, would get him through the horrors of combat and enable him to perform his duty to the Confederacy. "I will endeavor to do my duty," he explained to his mother, "& may it be the will of Almighty God to spare me to see the independence of my country achieved. I derive great comfort from the precious promises of Our Lord & Saviour. May God give me faith to sustain me under every trial & to feel full assurance of His Favor in this life & in the world to come."[17]

The religious world of the last generation withstood the hammer blows of frontal assaults, the slaughter of comrades, and the invisible enemy of disease.

Providence gave meaning and order to the macabre scenes of war for young Virginians. This does not mean, however, that they suffered no doubts or psychological trauma. Combat shattered their belief that the side with the most courage would always win. Rifled weaponry behind earthworks obliterated the brave, while the cowards always managed to escape. Yet only rarely did the horrors of combat spur a tirade against God. Only one example could be found of a young Virginian questioning the ways of Providence. It comes from Richmonder John Reeve, who was overwhelmed by rage after the costly Seven Days' campaign of 1862. The Union army had been defeated, but not destroyed, in a campaign that cost the Confederacy more than twenty thousand men. "I think it is high time for the God of Battles to show himself the God of Justice too," he demanded, "& not allow the battle which has cost us so much noble blood to result as all our others have in 'sound & fury signifying nothing.'"[18] Though these bloodlettings early in the war forced officers and soldiers to modify their fighting style, they did little to alter their belief system. The evidence does not indicate that young Virginians questioned the existence of God, the virtue of the cause, or whether the Confederacy would be successful. The men might have become hardened and insensitive to the ravages of war, and on occasion they grew frustrated with the Confederate people for lacking faith, but they never succumbed to disillusionment or cynicism. Inside their camps, these young men encouraged others to read the Bible daily, attend services every Sunday, and pray regularly, a continuation of the work begun at Virginia universities during the 1850s.

A number of men in the last generation, however, thought it impossible to live as Christians in the sinful environment of the military. The monotony of camp life encouraged every conceivable vice, ranging from harmless offenses such as playing cards and using profanity to the more serious crimes of drinking and consorting with prostitutes. Without the presence of women in the army, soldiers of all ages complained that they lacked moral guidance. As the romanticism of soldiering gradually faded, the ravages of disease and the physical destruction of war delivered the most serious blow against basic notions of humanity and moral decency.[19] "Every day I now pass disgusts me more and more with military life," bemoaned Robert Scott in early 1862. He believed the constant exposure "to danger and disease" had encouraged "the men and (I blush to say it) very many of the officers to give way to excess and dissipation, drinking and gambling are carried on to a dreadful extent in the army."[20]

Significantly, though, Scott's faith prevented him from damning the Con-

An extraordinarily candid shot of Confederate soldiers after a night of drinking. Many men of the last generation considered the army a sinkhole of dissipation. Robert Taylor Scott of the 8th Virginia Infantry complained in 1862: "Every day I now pass disgusts me more and more with military life." It appears that all of these men were cadets at the Virginia Military Institute, probably serving as drillmasters in Richmond. Alfred W. Clopton (? – 1864), the soldier standing on the far right with the bottle, is the only soldier who is identified. Clopton was reprimanded for playing cards at VMI before entering Confederate service in the 4th Virginia Cavalry. During the winter of 1863 he contracted syphilis and died in the summer of 1864 of "fever."

federate cause because of his own shortcomings or the immorality of fellow soldiers. He drew confidence from what the last generation considered a truism throughout the war: "Our cause is just, holy and sacred so we must be contented to take it as human nature, depraved as it makes it, and pray that God will order all things for the best and out of this evil produce good."[21] Failure to create a truly Christian army left members of the last generation frustrated at times, but for every drunken soldier there were others who organized a prayer group or helped construct a regimental chapel. Most men in the last generation performed an intellectual juggling act. They played down reasons for Providential wrath while finding hope for divine grace. Although the wicked behavior of some men shocked the sensibilities of young Virginians, such immorality conformed to antebellum notions of man's inherent sinfulness. The theme of man's depraved nature was central to evangelical thought and had prepared the last generation to understand corruption as part of human behavior, rather than as a defect in the moral fabric in the Confederacy or a reason for God to condemn the Southern cause.[22]

Earnest prayers and pure faith, however, failed to eradicate the sins of the Confederacy. Members of the last generation joined the chorus of indignant Confederates who bemoaned the immorality of their fellow citizens. They focused their moral outrage on two issues: excessive pride and speculation.[23] Members of the last generation decried, more than any other sin, the lack of humility among Confederate soldiers and civilians. Excessive pride, a trait that many young people had denounced before the war, seemed to be on the rise in the Confederacy, proving conclusively that there was too much reliance on man and his armies. The Union debacle at First Manassas convinced many Southerners that God was on their side and that the Confederacy was free of sin. The last generation's Philip Cabell rejoiced over the war's first major victory after discussions with veterans of the battle who confirmed the presence of divine favor. "From all I can learn," he wrote his wife, "the result is as signally one to the interposition of Divine Providence as any Philistine or Syrian rout in Holy Writ. . . . And when I see the result, I can with renewed confidence, throw myself into the arms of that Good Heavenly Father without one shade of anxiety or one fear for the future."[24] Southern ministers worried about men like Cabell. They did not want their congregations to believe that God's grace was a permanent condition, but rather a blessing that must always be earned. Military disasters, on the other hand, awakened Southerners to the possibility of their own moral declension, and young Virginians responded to these crises by renewing their faith. They interpreted defeat as an opportunity for repentance and a chance to examine the moral condition of the army and the nation.

After the death of Stonewall Jackson on May 10, 1863, Richmonder William Pegram expressed his deep sadness over the general's passing—a tragic event, but one that could teach the Confederacy an important lesson about humility. Despite his plea for complete faith in God, Pegram could not avoid undue confidence in human agency. "We never knew how much we all loved him until he died," he wrote to his sister. The young artillerist had trouble understanding why God would take Jackson from the Confederacy when his career appeared so promising and his life was so holy. He suspected that his comrades might be partially responsible for this tragedy because they held up Jackson as their deliverer. "Some of our troops made too much of an Idol of him," he explained, "and lost sight of God's mercies"; even he was guilty of placing too much faith in his superior officers. In the same paragraph, Pegram elevated Lee as the army's new savior. "His [Jackson's] death will not have the effect of making our troops fight any worse. Besides being the bravest troops in the world, they have the most unbounded confidence in their *great leader*, Genl. Lee." He violated his own plea for humility by assuring his family that the valor of the ordinary private would ultimately sustain the army. "Our troops will fight well under any body," he confidently wrote. "Fortunately with us, the soldiers make the officers, & not the officers the soldiers." The contradictions in Pegram's thought, so apparent to modern observers, did not paralyze the young artillerist. He smoothed over these inconsistencies by acknowledging that God would have the final say. Although Pegram knew that Lee and the men in the field would continue to do their duty after Jackson's death, he drew more comfort in knowing that God ordered the world for the benefit of His people. "I have no doubt however," he concluded, "but that 'all things are for the best.'" [25]

Military disasters such as the Confederate loss at Gettysburg also reminded Southerners that God's relationship with the Confederacy was a tenuous one. Richard H. Bagby's impressions after Gettysburg were widely shared among his contemporaries. "We as a people & as a nation have been too Wicked and Proud heretofore and were not thankful enough for the great blessings that we have been enjoying," Bagby wrote his father. "If we all would rely entirely on the arm of God and not put so much confidence in our Generals we would do much better." George Koontz also believed that the defeat at Gettysburg revealed that "our people have put too much confidence in our army." Only God, he added, "could deliver us from the oppression of our enemies [*sic*]."[26] It would seem that interpreting military defeat as divine punishment created an internal strain and psychological turmoil among Confederates that could have only resulted in a loss of will.

In reality, this interpretive framework prevented young Virginians, and probably most Southerners, from seeing an ineluctable decline in Confederate fortunes after Gettysburg. Their jeremiads expressed the hope that God's favor was not permanently lost but could be earned again through simple faith. Such a conviction made it impossible for members of the last generation to countenance the idea of inevitable defeat.[27]

The conviction that battlefield success depended on faith drew attention away from the real causes of Confederate military defeat: superior Federal generalship, Northern will, and a dearth of troops and supplies. In other words, young Virginians closed themselves off to the possibility that the enemy could dictate the war's outcome. This helps to explain why members of the last generation were oblivious to the ridiculous odds facing the Confederacy during the final stages of the conflict and why they continued to resist after Northern armies had exhausted the South's logistical base. The last generation also refused to give up because they did not blame battlefield defeat on an entrenched defect in the Southern character. Whereas Yankees were described as a race of people with fixed traits, irredeemable in God's eyes, young Virginians shared the common belief that for the morally superior South regeneration was always possible, no matter how grim the news from the front lines.

The last generation's greatest fears for the Confederacy came not from immorality in the ranks but from waywardness on the home front. To some it seemed that unscrupulous profiteers, doomsayers, and deserters were destroying the moral fabric of the Confederacy, thereby undermining the war effort. If these perfidious elements became dominant, the last generation feared that the South might fall into disfavor with God. Young Virginians complained most about the rise in financial speculation. "How rare it is to meet with a generous heart in this day of speculation and vile extortion," James DeWitt Hankins wrote on February 12, 1863. "There is nothing so low-born as this detestable spirit that lives and grows fat upon the life blood of the country."[28] Although Hankins and others considered speculation a national sin, they did not indict all Southerners, nor did they passively accept the sermons of ministers who questioned the Confederacy's standing with God. John Samuel Apperson, for example, rejected a sermon that condemned all Southerners as sinners. He countered the minister's argument by insisting that profiteering actually brought attention to loyal Confederates. When he thought of the "speculating gentlemen at home" in comparison to the "men who have boldly stood the fiery storm of lead" and were "now shivering and shaking without shoes around the camp," he grew angry. Yet when he considered "that all this suffering [in the army] is without a murmur—without a dissenting voice," he could not help but "admire southern valour and fortitude more than ever before."[29]

Although members of the last generation denounced the seemingly intractable sin of speculation as unpatriotic, they perceived, for the most part, a degree of harmony among all classes for most of the war. Even organized dissent on the home front did not alter their perception of a united Confederacy. They interpreted civilian unrest according to their own class assumptions, condemning political protest as criminal deviance. After the Richmond bread riots on April 2, 1863, for example, Thomas Elder complained to his wife that "they were the most disgraceful outrages upon law and order; and it is manifest from all the accounts I have seen that the women engaged in it were much more intent on stealing dry goods for which they were in most cases able to pay." John Samuel Apperson reached a similar conclusion, informing his diary that "a gang of prostitutes, hag Irish and dutch Irish had a considerable disturbance in Richmond yesterday." Apperson agreed with a friend that "it is no bread riot as jewelers and dry goods stores were broken into more frequently than any others."[30] As defenders of the Confederacy, they looked at the conflict from the perspective of the nation's ruling class. Through their blinders, social protest could only resemble criminal acts committed by aliens in their midst.

Just as the last generation had proclaimed the South a society blessed by social harmony before the war, these young men badly wanted to believe that all Southerners were united behind the Confederate cause. It is significant that Apperson and Elder blamed the riots on people whom they considered, before the war, inherently immoral and inferior: foreigners and prostitutes. The behavior of working women in Richmond was not a reflection on the South, young Virginians asserted, but consistent with that specific class of people. The last generation located the source of corruption in the Confederacy among people who by their "nature" were not Southern. They were Yankees in disguise. One member of the last generation, Eugene Blackford, observed of Wilmington, North Carolina, that "three fourths of the society . . . are Yankees, one half of the remainder are Jews, and the remaining and only respectable eight are genuine old N.C. families."[31] Blackford refused to believe that the finer slaveholding families could become greedy and trade with the enemy. From the class perspective of the last generation, the problem originated with newcomers and parvenus, not with Confederate institutions or principles.

Within the army, the last generation not only retained their class perspective, but also assumed a new identity as Confederate soldiers. The military experience, while reinforcing loyalty to the ruling class, also imparted a feeling of dissociation from the rest of society. Young Virginians considered themselves to be in the best position to judge the condition of the Confederacy and the progress of the war. Having been denied authority by their elders in the 1850s, they set themselves up as moral arbiters of the Confederacy. Repulsed by what they perceived as the frivolity and corruption of civilian life, they increasingly turned to the army for examples of patriotism and virtue. In the

1850s they had searched for men who would selflessly serve their state. They found these men in the ranks of Lee's army. The sacrifices of their comrades convinced members of the last generation that the Confederacy and Virginia would never suffer a moral collapse like Rome. Despite ample evidence of sin in the army, there were just as many examples of collective piety, of Southern soldiers coming together in prayer meetings, revivals, and scripture lessons to create a wholesome environment where men of all faiths could beseech the mercies of God.

Relations between civilians and young Virginians frayed over time and reached the point of disintegration during the last year of the conflict. Yet resentment and hostility toward civilians did not automatically cause soldier disillusionment. In fact, alienation from the home front could intensify nationalist sentiments. This occurred with many young men, including artillerist William Pegram. His mother and two sisters remained in Richmond during the war, where they ran a boardinghouse and a girls' school. Pegram confided his deepest thoughts and warmest affections to his family throughout the war. While his heart never hardened toward the Pegram women, by the summer of 1864 he grew frustrated with their rather limited and unrealistic view of the conflict. Pegram detected a disturbing apathy among his family members. He sensed a debilitating malaise that he believed prevented civilians from fully appreciating the sacrifices of the Army of Northern Virginia. His oldest sister, Mary, must have questioned why Lee's troops failed to match the daring victories of earlier campaigns. A defensive Pegram was quick to justify the army's reputation. On October 5, 1864, he wrote: "The reason why the men do not charge the enemy out of their works as they did in 1862 is not from the want of courage, but from the want of physical strength." Pegram did not want his family to think he was complaining. "I merely mention these facts in justice to this noble army, to shew you the reason why it does not achieve the brilliant feats that characterized it in '62." Whenever he looked back on the Petersburg campaign, Pegram beamed with pride and looked to the future without fear. "It would be impossible for the best writer in the world to do justice to this noble army," he declared.[32]

Tragedy struck the Pegram family on February 6, 1865, when the oldest son, Confederate general John Pegram, was killed south of Petersburg. His brother's death nearly plunged William into depression, for there was not another man on the earth whom he admired more. He managed to put aside his personal feelings, and returned to the army in early March. Shortly after his arrival, he sent a long letter home to comfort his mother and sisters, who

William R. J. Pegram (1841–65). Many men in the last generation like Pegram grew frustrated with civilians who seemingly did not understand or fully appreciate the restraints of army life or the reality of combat against rifled weaponry. In the fall of 1864 he defended Lee's army against his sister's charge that it had lost its aggressive spirit: "The reason why the men do not charge the enemy out of their works as they did in 1862 is not from the want of courage, but from the want of physical strength." Pegram was mortally wounded at Five Forks eight days before the end of the war. (From John Hampden Chamberlayne, *Ham Chamberlayne — Virginian*, ed. C. G. Chamberlayne, 1932)

were deep in mourning. He hoped that they could look beyond their personal grief to see the promising military prospects of the Confederacy. "I thank God that this is growing brighter each day. I hope you are able to see this as clearly as I, and every one in this army, do." But Pegram feared that this was not the case, that the people of Richmond were demoralized, and that his family failed to rank the opinion of military men as supreme. He captured the disgust of most soldiers when he bluntly informed his sister that "you are so completely surrounded by croakers & cowards that it was not surprising the mind is so excited with rumours, conceived in their craven hearts, and spread by every idle tongue." Because of disloyal people, Pegram warned "you cannot look coolly or dispassionately on anything," and he judged that the "spirit & opinion of the army is worth more than that of the people of Richmond, or of people out of it."[33] Indeed, Pegram had lost all faith in Southerners outside the military, including his own family. Only a veteran, in his view, could evaluate the progress of the war.

Fellow soldier Jeb Stuart also lost all patience with Richmonders. In the spring of 1864, he told his wife: "Richmond is a queer place with a *few* queer people in it. If anyone speaks to you of subjugation, tell them it shows a total ignorance of what constitutes *our armies*." While many young Virginians like Stuart and Pegram entertained a harsh view of the people back home, they never wavered in their conviction that Southerners as a whole remained God's chosen people. Animosity toward civilians often fired the resolve of the soldiers. That same spring Stuart sensed that civilians were prepared to capitulate just when he knew that "our armies will tread with the triumph of victorious freemen over the dead bodies of the vainglorious foes."[34]

Rampant speculation, excessive pride, and indifferent civilians tried the patience of young Virginians for much of the war, but the severest test did not come until the fall of 1864, when Union victories in the Shenandoah Valley and the capture of Atlanta and Mobile sealed Lincoln's reelection. Morale collapsed across the state with the prospect of four more years of fighting. To make matters worse, networks of subsistence had been destroyed by Northern armies; lines of communication were fragmented; and manpower reserves were depleted. Common soldiers and most civilians believed that the Old Dominion no longer possessed the ability to wage war. Desertion soared throughout the winter of 1864 and into the spring of the following year. Unlike the men who had escaped on French furlough earlier in the conflict, these soldiers left because they had lost hope in the Confederacy. Their departure contributed significantly to the collapse of Lee's army.[35]

As the Confederacy crumbled around the men of the last generation during the final seven months of the war, many of them seemed oblivious or refused to acknowledge its imminent demise. In their view, military reversals were temporary, a moment for individual redemption rather than a final judgment against the South's way of life. Defeat on the battlefield resembled a passing storm, tumultuous in nature but short in duration and always followed by clear skies. They perceived a fluid situation that fluctuated in relation to events on the battlefield. John Chamberlayne captured this dynamic on October 9, 1864: "These crises, if you notice, all bear a marked family likeness, in every one we . . . go down, down, down, till the times grow despondent & even the brave shake their head." "Always just then some skirmish gives us a slight advantage," he added, "then another slight & favourable battle, then some pitched battle, & then the full tide of prosperity comes up, lasts for a few months & ebbs away again in adversity to be succeeded by another & still another flux & reflux."[36]

Although the fall of 1864 marked the breaking point for most Confederates, the available records of the last generation's views attest to an unwavering spirit. Their determination can only be explained by looking at the entirety of their military experience. The last generation's defiant stand during the final eight months of the war must be seen as rooted within the gradual experience of their becoming veterans in a war that turned revolutionary in its methods and consequences. Several factors shed light on their tenacity. First of all, the men in the last generation fought with such desperation because the Army of Northern Virginia's theater of operations was centered in the Old Dominion. Unlike Southerners who fought away from their native states, young Virginians defended the soil of their birth. They made up the only line of defense between the enemy and their families. Fighting in defense of their home solidified the last generation's local, state, and national attachments into unqualified support for the Confederacy. The dilemma of fighting in a distant land while an invading enemy threatened home and hearth never presented itself to young Virginians in the soul-wrenching way it did to a Georgian, Mississippian, or Texan.

The extreme nationalism of young Virginians can also be explained by looking at the varied but interrelated reasons that led them to believe that God would never forsake the Confederacy. The sins of Union soldiers, which appeared so heinous in the eyes of Southerners, could only result in Northern damnation. Enemy depredations against civilians provided an inexhaustible source of ammunition for the claim that the last generation was engaged in a righteous crusade.[37] Young Virginians could not imagine why God would favor a country that preyed on helpless women and children. This encouraged members of the last generation to become predators themselves, but they never recognized that they were moving toward a hard-war policy that they had condemned the Yankees for practicing. During the Army of Northern Virginia's raid on the North in 1863, William Roane Aylett commanded a regiment in Pickett's division. Lee's veterans took freely from Pennsylvania farmers and seized public property, which Aylett initially supported. He even ordered "several boxes of matches" for his regiment with the idea of turning Pennsylvania into a smoking inferno. "Genl. Lee may order private property to be respected, but I don't mean to obey & the Army will not," he promised his wife. "My men should take & destroy just what they please—so it become according to my orders in a systematic regular way." But a few days later, after seeing a Confederate column trample a wheat field, Aylett confessed to his wife that "[we are] not taking more than the army needs, but this is bad enough treatment. Really I can't help feeling sorry for the people, bad as they have done us."[38]

The bloody failure of Pickett's Charge at Gettysburg and the decisive repulse of Lee's forces put Aylett in a violent mood during the army's retreat to Virginia. He admitted to his wife that "we hear of nothing but trouble & distress on every side, truly God [has] afflicted us as a people, but he has some good & wise purpose for so doing. Our recent disasters have made us sad, together . . . [with] the loss of so many of our noble soldiers." A letter from his wife darkened his mood as he read that Yankee raiders had invaded his plantation and terrorized his family. "Your letter my dearest was long and painfully interesting," he wrote, "and never in my life have I been more moved and filled with deeper and more lasting indignation." After he folded the letter and put it aside, an enraged Aylett took the eighty Union prisoners under his care and determined, "by way of retaliation," to have twelve "shot on the spot." He issued the necessary orders and was prepared to carry out the executions when a staff officer interceded, convincing Aylett of "the impropriety of such a course, & that their killing would have been *murder.*" Even after he had "cooled down," Aylett wanted the "civilized world . . . to know how these villains are waging war." "For myself," he vowed, "I'll fight them as long as I have a leg to stand on or an arm to strike. Conquer them we must and will, for God cannot intend that such wickedness should succeed."[39]

For many Southerners, the idea that Providence would allow them to be subjugated was beyond their understanding of a moral and just God. Robert

Scott, who prayed for a compassionate God earlier in the war, quickly lost his sense of Christian charity. Yankee marauders had killed his father in 1862, and the total devastation of Virginia filled Scott with vengeance. Above all else, he desired retribution for the North's inhumane mode of warfare. "No set of miscreants, barbarians, thieves and scoundrels, disgraces of humanity, as the *Yankees*, can ever succeed," he wrote on December 31, 1862. "I some times think the avenging angel of a righteous and just God will ultimately bolt them out of existence."[40] Union attacks against helpless civilians and the pointless destruction of Southern property extinguished the possibility of Union victory in Scott's mind, a conviction that resisted the overwhelming evidence that God was a turncoat.

The North's hard-war strategy unwittingly reinforced the last generation's allegiance to the Confederacy. Federal "atrocities" also validated prewar cultural perceptions of the Yankees as a villainous people, radicals who wanted to destroy the South's social system and start a race war. The war erased any doubt as to whether or not Northerners and Southerners constituted two distinct races. In the opinion of Confederates of all ages, Northern soldiers trampled on property rights and liberty to achieve their materialistic ends. Cultural perceptions of the North readily explained the abuses committed against the Southern populace. In the ranks of the Union army, the last generation asserted, stood foreign mercenaries, men of questionable motives and morals who served for lucrative bounties or were tricked into service by Northern politicians. In October 1864, Carter Nelson Minor met some Union deserters, "mostly Irish & French," and conversed with one who "had been in service 3 weeks, had been a Pennsylvania Miner, & had enlisted while drunk." Minor predicted that the same man "will probably go North & enlist again for the bounty & try his old trick." "What a chapter of rascality!" he exclaimed. "I suppose his story with few alterations will suit them all."[41]

The experience of the last generation during the Gettysburg campaign might have reoriented their cultural explanation of Northern character as a problem of biology. This shift in thinking cemented the loyalties of young Virginians to the Confederacy. While some civilians interpreted the Union victory as an irreversible turning point, Lee's veterans remained confident. Although the memories of fallen comrades and poor generalship faded with time, young Virginians did not easily forget the morals and manners of Pennsylvania civilians. Lee's veterans campaigned in a section of Pennsylvania dominated by German immigrants, so the soldiers found support for the popular Southern view that foreigners with radical ideas and strange social habits had overwhelmed the North. Through the dusty haze of a marching column, Confederate staff officer Alexander "Sandie" Pendleton admired the magnificent scenery unfolding before him as he entered Pennsylvania's Cumberland Valley. The picturesque landscape appealed to Pendleton's deep love of nature, but the physical contrast to his native Virginia struck him forcibly. Images of ruined Southern towns, burned-out fields, and helpless civilians raced through his mind. The striking difference between war-ravaged Virginia and the pristine Pennsylvania landscape led him to reflect on the differences between the character of the North and that of the South.[42] Pendleton's faith in the Confederate rank and file stemmed from his prewar conviction that Northerners and Southerners constituted two separate peoples. While a student at Washington College and the University of Virginia, he became convinced that an "innate difference" existed between the "Yankee & a Southerner." His observations of Confederate troops during the Gettysburg campaign supported his long-standing belief in the "exalted superiority" of the Southern race. Just a few days before fighting erupted at Gettysburg, he had followed Robert E. Rodes's division on an eighteen-mile march, noticing only one broken tree limb. The Army of the Potomac, he ventured, would have laid waste to the land if it had been Virginia.

Pennsylvania's lethargic response to Lee's invasion further underscored the differences between Northerners and Southerners. Instead of rushing to the colors, Pendleton thought Pennsylvanians preferred "staying at home & saving property." "The only way to touch them is to burn their property, and [as] much as I deplore the horror of war, I am ready to begin it." The shocking news that Union troops had destroyed Darien, Georgia, reached Lee's men in Pennsylvania. An angry Pendleton confronted a Northern professor at Dickinson College over the matter. Instead of backing down at Pendleton's challenge, the bold academic "had the face" to defend the burning of the town. "I'll pay him for that sentiment," Pendleton grimly promised. Later that afternoon Pendleton and a fellow officer "confiscated" chemicals and other supplies from Dickinson as a "reprisal" for the enemy's molestation of the College of William and Mary in 1862.[43]

A spirit of revenge hardened Pendleton toward the enemy, caused him to violate his principles of civilized war, and forced him to reexamine whether or not Northerners and Southerners truly were different. Americans on both sides of the Mason-Dixon Line had addressed the question of regional identity before Fort Sumter. The last generation acknowledged perceived regional differences, but they never articulated a powerful Southern nationalism dur-

Alexander "Sandie" Pendleton (1840–64). The failed 1863 Gettysburg campaign did not shatter Pendleton's faith in the Confederacy. Like many young Virginians who served in Lee's army, Pendleton found that what he observed of Pennsylvanians reaffirmed his belief in the South's ultimate victory, even if that entailed waging a "hard war" against the North. He bitterly concluded that "the only way to touch them [Pennsylvanians] is to burn their property, and [as] much as I deplore the horror of war, I am ready to begin it." Pendleton was mortally wounded at Fisher's Hill on September 22, 1864. (Courtesy of Tony Marion)

ing the 1850s. During the war, however, young soldiers needed to make sense of the death and killing that surrounded them. Demonizing the enemy served this vital purpose. A few young Virginians broke new ground in their portraits of godless, brutish Yankees. They explained perceived differences between Northerners and Southerners by conflating biological and environmental factors — nature and nurture. In the 1850s, regional identity was largely discussed in terms of culture, but, in wartime, members of the last generation described Northern traits as "natural," "fixed," and rooted in physiology. Pendleton's observations of Pennsylvanians during the Gettysburg campaign convinced him that Northerners and Southerners were inherently dissimilar. Science, as well as environment, explained the differences in habits and morals. "What a race of people!" Pendleton exclaimed with disgust. Physical attributes, as he perceived them, anchored his theory of two separate races. He used the language of what would become in the late nineteenth century the theory of scientific racism to prove his point that Yankees were an inferior people. He categorized Pennsylvanians as "real specimens of the Dutch Boor," with their "heavy brutish lips, [and] thick drooping eyelids." Such a peculiar appearance, Pendleton asserted, revealed "plainly the stupidity of the people," their vile nature, and hopelessly degraded condition.[44]

Robert Scott also returned from Pennsylvania convinced that Northerners and Southerners were biologically two different people. "Our men are more than ever disgusted with the Yankees and their nature," he wrote on July 16, 1863. "We can't live together, oil and water will not mix, between our respective natures the same dissimilarity exists. Before this campaign I imagined I hated the Yankee race with a perfect hatred. I find I was mistaken, they are too mean spirited, too low and cringing to *hate*. I *despise* them thoroughly, my contempt for them knows no bounds."[45] The demonization of the enemy occurs in all wars, but for members of the last generation and many other Confederates, this construction did more than ease their consciences over killing Yankees. It fastened the political loyalty of young Virginians to the Confederate nation. Surrender to such an evil force conjured up a nightmarish scenario that included submission to black soldiers, Union troops' terrorizing the countryside, and the extinction of liberty.

As the conflict entered its final two years, young Virginians drew from these earlier experiences and gradually started to see the contest for political independence as a holy war. They believed they were fighting a depraved Yankee race of rapists and plunderers. This image became widely accepted in the South because President Lincoln had abandoned conciliation for a harsher Southern strategy. To most Confederates, his new approach reinforced prewar images of Republicans as the radical agents of abolition who would subjugate the South by freeing the slaves and overthrowing constitutional liberties. Although Lincoln was slow to embrace emancipation as a weapon of war, his official proclamation, issued in 1863, enraged Southerners despite its limited application. Northern soldiers were suddenly viewed as champions of black equality, not restorers of the old Union. Employing black soldiers supported Confederate charges that Northerners would resort to the most radical measures to win the war. Jefferson Davis bluntly told Southerners at the beginning of 1863 that their very existence was at stake in this war. "It is in keeping however, with the character of the people that seeks dominion over you, [they will] . . . try to reduce you to subjection" and "incite servile insurrection." The aim of the Union armies, Davis warned, was the extermination of the Southern people.[46]

Lincoln's Emancipation Proclamation peeled back the cultural layers of Confederate identity to reveal the unifying interest at stake for the last generation: the preservation of slavery and white superiority. Although some young Virginians expressed a willingness to secure independence without slavery, they were not as open minded when it came to the treatment of United States Colored Troops. At the battle of the Crater on July 30, 1864, a division of black Union soldiers met a furious Confederate counterattack. Enraged that the enemy had exploded a mine filled with black powder, many of these Southern soldiers refused to give quarter. Trapped in a massive pit left by the explosion of a Union mine, white and black Northern soldiers were pinned down under a hellish fire. Escape was impossible. The Federal employment of black troops turned Confederate soldiers into bloodthirsty warriors. William Pegram watched the ensuing massacre unfold. The men became "exasperated" if they were wounded by the "negroes" and refused to leave the front lines. Pegram was in a reflective mood after the battle, writing to his sister Jennie that he always had desired that "the enemy would bring some negroes against this army" because "it has a splendid effect on our men." In every bombproof, Pegram counted "one or two dead negroes . . . who had skulked out of the fight, & been found & killed by our men." Fewer than half of the blacks who put down their arms, he estimated, "ever reached the rear." Pegram considered it "perfectly" correct to slaughter captured black soldiers "as a matter of policy." Imagining, though, that Jennie might think it was "cruel to murder them in cold blood," he explained that the men who committed these acts "had very good cause for doing so."[47] The slow, but steady destruction of slavery during the war did not create an ideological crisis for men like Pegram. They would murder, if necessary, to preserve a social order that kept blacks at the bottom. The *Richmond Enquirer* sanctioned the Confederate atrocities at the Crater with the recommendation to Southern officers to "let the work, which God has entrusted to you and your brave men, go forward to its full completion that is, until every negro has been slaughtered."[48]

The presence of black troops at a wholesale defeat like the Crater boosted morale in both the short and the long term. But even in times of national duress, members of the last generation found reason for hope by exaggerating the slightest hint of dissatisfaction among the Federals. They scoured Northern newspapers for examples of dissent, especially after a Confederate defeat.[49] Although the North remained virtually untouched by enemy armies, organized antiwar protests occurred more frequently and with greater intensity above the Mason-Dixon Line than they did in the South. In the last generation's estimation, draft riots, labor strikes, and the Copperhead movement attested to the lack of moral purpose in the Union cause.[50]

In the fall of 1864, shortly after Abraham Lincoln was reelected, the last generation's James Keith denounced Northerners for taking "immense bounties" to enlist. Men financially induced to fight for their country were barren of patriotic virtue, he argued, and he welcomed the next batch of a million men that Lincoln promised to send South. "If he [Lincoln] gets them," Keith wrote, "God help the poor fools." The young Virginian hoped the new recruits would "take a last look at all they love, if love they can, for Lee is an insatiable monster & would gobble up a few more hundred thousand Yanks & lick his chops for more."[51]

When Union soldiers fought gallantly during the war—creating the distinct possibility that God might choose the other side as the most committed—the last generation ascribed their acts of patriotism to the influences of alcohol, money, or political gain. After the massive Union assaults at Cold Harbor on June 3, 1864, Richard W. Corbin reported that "I have not spoken to a single soldier here who was not convinced that the Yankee courage in the recent battles has been screwed up by means of the strongest whisky." "In some cases," he added, "they were so mad with liquor that they would throw away their muskets and run into the cannon's mouth."[52] It never dawned on Corbin that a similar misperception could apply to Lee's men at Gettysburg. Like most of his contemporaries, Corbin molded the war to fit his preconceptions, tossing aside conflicting evidence like irrelevant scraps of paper.

Military victories, rather than cultural perceptions, played a greater role in determining soldier and civilian morale. Fortunately for these young Virginians, they fought under the South's best general. Robert E. Lee's repeated success on the battlefield earned him the unyielding confidence of soldiers and civilians. John H. Chamberlayne claimed as early as 1862 that Lee would "rank at the side of the Great Captains, Hannibal, Caesar, Eugene, Napoleon."[53] From the Seven Days' battles of 1862 to the fall of Richmond in 1865, the Army of Northern Virginia sustained only one decisive defeat at Gettysburg. Even the disaster in Pennsylvania failed to shake the last generation's confidence in their commanding general. In 1864, when facing overwhelming odds, the Confederate chieftain not only stymied Ulysses S. Grant's offensive designs but also achieved impressive victories at the Wilderness (May 5–6), Cold Harbor (June 3), the opening attacks against Petersburg (June 15–18), the Crater (July 30), Reams Station (August 25), and the Boydton Plank Road

(October 27). Although military affairs turned ugly in other areas of the South late in the war, the Army of Northern Virginia continued to rack up victories, offering tangible proof that Lee's generalship reigned supreme. A young Virginian serving in the Army of Tennessee, John James Reeve, succinctly captured what Lee's presence meant to Southern armies. He wrote in the summer of 1864 that western Confederates differed from their counterparts in Virginia in one crucial aspect: "One has Genl. Lee and the other hasn't."[54]

By 1864, Lee had become synonymous with the Confederacy in the minds of the last generation. He was the nation, a model of the supposed virtues and values of the Old South, the George Washington of the Confederacy. In the commanding general, the last generation found the virtuous leader for whom they had searched so desperately before the war, a man who truly embodied the Virginia spirit of revolutionary times. William Pegram expressed the sentiments of his generation and the entire army when he wrote in the summer of 1864 that Lee ranked as "one of the few great men who ever lived, who could be trusted." Pegram confessed that he "should like to see him King or Dictator."[55] Men such as Pegram pointed to Lee as irrefutable proof of why God would never abandon the South. While the last generation saw in Lee and other senior officers of the Confederacy an undoubted nobility, they maintained that the Union's generals and politicians had duped the Northern people for their personal gain. Lee's religious bearing particularly impressed his subordinates, including Walter Taylor, who wrote in 1864 that the general "attends the meetings of the chaplains and in many ways tries by example and orders to inculcate lessons of morality and piety among the troops." His "noble example," Taylor believed, contributed to "the decided interest that men and officers throughout the army appear to take in spiritual matters." Lee did more than offer public gestures of faith. He was one of the first to respond to the call for financial assistance from the Evangelical Tract Society, contributing $100 to the association.[56] Faith in Robert E. Lee largely explains why members of the last generation remained devoted to Confederate institutions during the final year of the war. They fiercely clung to the hope that their beloved general could accomplish the impossible under the guiding hand of Providence.

Of the various classes that made up the Army of Northern Virginia, Lee's second-echelon leaders, many of whom belonged to the last generation, stand out as the most zealous nationalists when compared to the enlisted men. Youth played a role in fostering such intense loyalty, for these men came of age believing that Southerners had created a unique Christian community that defended orthodoxy against Northern apostasy. Placing Northern and

A highly romanticized postwar sketch of Robert E. Lee attending a soldiers' prayer meeting. The general is the focal point of this drawing even though he is clearly not leading the devotional service. The campfire also illuminates his figure while most of the soldiers are huddled around him in the darkness. This piece effectively captures Lee's involvement in the religious affairs of his troops. The last generation's Walter Taylor wrote that the commanding general "attends the meetings of the chaplains and in many ways tries by example and orders to inculcate lessons of morality and piety among the troops." (From William W. Bennett, *A Narrative of the Great Revival Which Prevailed in the Southern Armies*, 1876)

Southern differences within a religious framework prepared young Virginians to meet the call for nationhood. Political allegiance to the nation, as the war progressed, increasingly became a religious duty in their minds. War also provided young Virginians with an opportunity to prove themselves worthy of the title "Christian gentleman." Frustrated in their attempts to become heads of household, they obtained from the army the sense of responsibility and duty that earned them community respect. They could show the adult world that they were men, virtuous and selfless, fighting for the reputation of their native land in a mission that could bring them immortality. Thus ambitions that drove them before the war gave shape and form to their wartime experiences. It is possible, however, to take the generational approach too far. Robert E. Lee and Jefferson Davis, both of whom abhorred political extremism prior to Fort Sumter and both men of faith, were as devoted to the Confederacy as the army's young officers. Both men were unflagging patriots who pledged themselves to final victory, even when military affairs and public discontent overwhelmingly suggested defeat.

The evidence of this shared sense of purpose between generations does not call into question the exceptionalism of the young Virginian experience. Unlike the older men who occupied relatively safe positions as high-ranking officers or petty bureaucrats, most young Virginians operated on the front lines, where they were renowned for their reckless aggression. The bravest ones, as they well knew, were often the first to die. Survival meant facing death in its most sudden and hideous forms. Seeing mutilated bodies and lifeless comrades became all too familiar, but, in accepting death as commonplace, these men risked losing the sense that life was sacred.

The promise of Christian martyrdom rescued young Virginians from the brutal dehumanization of war while instilling in them a religious devotion to the political goal of Southern independence. Ministers reinforced this message by promising heaven to any soldier of Christ who died in battle. In early 1863, the Reverend Philip Slaughter proclaimed that "the soldier who fights and falls in such a cause, not only obeys instincts which are a law of nature, but is a martyr to [Christian] principle." Dying for religious beliefs, the minister suggested, elevated death to a sacred moment, surpassing in poignancy and spiritual meaning the fate of the man who fights out of a loyalty to comrades.[57] By the second half of the war, it became increasingly difficult for men like Alexander Pendleton to differentiate between the Confederate cause and the cause of Christ. Secular acts of patriotism became indistinguishable from the divine. Young Virginians viewed death in battle as a sacrament received on the altar of the Confederacy. "Of one thing only I am sure," wrote Pendleton after Gettysburg, "that to the war shall my powers be devoted until it or I am finished by act of God. And if the latter which I do not anticipate I hope to be ready to go."[58] A little more than a year later, Pendleton gave his life at the battle of Fisher's Hill, just weeks before his wife gave birth to their only child.

The literary traces of the last generation are appallingly scarce from October 1864 to Lee's surrender on April 9, 1865. What does survive reveals a group of young men so driven by hatred, so infused with religious zeal, and so fearful of enduring the humiliation of defeat, that they lost touch with the military situation facing the Confederacy. Although no one can deny the sincerity of the last generation's beliefs, it is apparent that any promise of final victory after Lincoln's reelection was an illusion to most sensible people.[59] Thousands of disaffected civilians and enlisted men made it abundantly clear that the flame of resistance only flickered in the hearts of a few. Fauquier County's James Keith, a graduate of the University of Virginia and member of the 4th Virginia Cavalry, was like many of his peers during the final stages of the war. He suffered a dislocation of the mind, a loss of focus caused by an extreme sense of faith and honor and the need for revenge. Keith spun the most wretched military news into a ridiculously hopeful prognosis for Southern victory. On December 2, 1864, for instance, he conjured up a wild scenario that resulted in the destruction of William T. Sherman's army during its March to the Sea. Keith knew that Sherman faced minimal Confederate resistance, but he thought the Union general would fall into a trap once he reached the coast. Scattered Confederate forces would suddenly appear on Sherman's flanks, and Keith predicted that "he will fall an easy prey." Where the Confederacy could find additional Southern troops was curiously absent from his hypothetical situation. Additional proof of Sherman's inevitable demise came from David Hunter's 1864 raid into the Shenandoah Valley. "Hunter last spring undertook & executed an equally magnificent raid . . . yet what has come of it[?] A great reputation at first but so disastrous was it in its effects that without a fight his army milled away & Hunter had entirely disappeared from [our] vulgar gaze." To suggest that Sherman would magically disappear was fantasy. Nonetheless, Keith thought his analogy between the two Union generals should encourage his mother. "So be not cast," he told her, and stop listening to "croakers."[60] Keith felt uncomfortable with his family's war weariness because such expressions of disaffection equaled disloyalty in his mind. He looked upon sacrifice for the Southern nation as proof of piety as well as an expression of national loyalty. Furthermore, he believed surrendering the Confederacy would disgrace the memory of the Revolutionary heroes and all those who had given their lives in the Southern crusade. A violation of this magnitude guaranteed a lifetime of shame.

Though honor did not make young Virginians crazed fighters incapable of anything but bloody revenge, it did heighten their already extreme commitment to liberty and severely limited what they were able to perceive as acceptable courses of wartime action. Surrender equaled public humiliation, an unequivocal announcement to the world that Southerners were not manly enough to defend their own homes and freedom. Subjugation, a word frequently employed by Confederates, was interpreted as an admission of inferiority and loss of rank that placed them dangerously close to enslavement. In the 1850s, furthermore, Virginia students had associated military victory with judgment against the defeated society. One member of the last generation, after discussing Native Americans at the University of Virginia, had scribbled in his notebook that a conquered people were an inferior people, desperately in need of civilizing. Keith entertained a similar perspective and was unwilling to give up because surrender meant emasculation. He wanted everyone back home to know that he possessed an uncompromising sense of duty to Southern nationhood. Keith custom-printed his code of honor on his stationery. It grimly promised: "Far better to perish with honor. Far better to go to the grave. And better to die a freeman, Than to live as a Northerner's slave."[61] In less than a month before Appomattox, artillerist William Poague explained to his mother why he could not give up. "The question with me is what is my duty," he wrote on March 17, 1865. "It is not a difficult one to answer. My duty is plain. It is to defend my country, and what does this word country embrace in its meaning." Significantly, defense of home was not a vague abstraction, but it included the basic building blocks of identity, including the reputations of his family members, living and dead. Fighting for his homeland, Poague added, "means the government of my choice, the religion of my choice, the graves of my fathers, property, friends, relatives, my mother and my little brother. It means all that I love or value on earth."[62]

Honor also insulated the last generation from the military reality facing the Confederacy. Keith's mother offered a blunt assessment of the military situation after Lincoln's 1864 reelection: the Confederacy was doomed. Such an utterance was a heretical opinion that her son regarded as an insult to fallen comrades and God. "Shall we who four years ago called heaven itself and all the people of the earth to witness our solemn declaration of determination to be free & independent" now give up? asked Keith. Surrender meant retracing "our steps to Sodom," he added, and why "turn back" when the Army of Northern Virginia had repulsed "McClellan, Burnside Hooker Grant & others in all the pride of unexhausted reserves armed & equipped with every appliance that science and a demoniac energy & more than devilish hatred could suggest or invent." He finished this letter with an emotionally charged appeal: "It seems to me that every man woman & child ought in the face of God this day [and] in the language of our forefathers to pledge their lives, their future . . . & their sacred honor to the prosecution of this war[.] If this generation could do it bequeath it on [our] death beds to the next & summoning all our energy, our resolution, & our resources to that one object make the prosecution of this war the business of our lives."[63]

Members of the last generation such as Keith uniformly believed that God would not forsake those who believed in Him. Their religious background instructed them that God chastised the ones he loves. Southerners of all ages saw a striking parallel between their struggle for independence and that of the children of Israel. Just as God had forced the Jews to endure persecution to prove their faith, so, in the minds of many Confederates in the last generation, they would have to suffer a similar fate.[64] In the final eights months of the war, young Virginians looked to these dark times as an opportunity to prove the sincerity of their faith. "Good people do very well [illegible] as the tide favors them but don't like swimming against the current," wrote Keith on December 29, 1864. He thought Southerners "ought to nerve ourselves to breast the current though it does roar & boil around us & though many stout swimmers may go down before we reach the shore but sure they ought still to struggle on when the blessed haven is almost in sight." Even if the Confederacy were overrun with Federal armies, Keith would hold to the refrain that gave so many of his peers just comfort and cause to die: "We may be chastised for our sins for when he loveth he chastiseth." "My faith in final & entire success," he wrote, was ". . . as perfect as it was four years ago."[65] William Pegram uttered similar words of encouragement to his sister a month before Appomattox. "We must fight against every thing like despondency," he wrote. "If all things were ordered by our enemy, and the present state of affairs was placed upon us by human agency," Pegram knew that "there would indeed be cause to despond." Because "this is not the case," he trusted that " 'God reigneth,' and 'all things work together for good, to those that love God.' "[66]

Resignation to defeat made the tremendous loss of life, the vast destruction of property, and the Herculean sacrifices of Southerners virtually meaningless. Talk of peace in 1864 angered James Hankins because it "seems a mockery at the sufferings of tens of thousands." He believed "there is but little to fear . . . with a firm reliance upon the sword of Almighty-God who disposes all things justly we will succeed."[67] The evangelical training of the last generation reminded them that God's mysterious ways, though seemingly irrational, would be revealed to his people in due course. Young Virginians warned that submission to the North would end a way of life that they cherished, respected, and, most of all, believed God had ordained. In other words, losing made no sense if God had blessed the South's way of life. Indeed, Northern aggressions during the war did not bode well for a future under Union rule. James Hankins predicted early in 1865 that if the South should capitulate, "iron despotism . . . will be established over us," making Virginia similar to Ireland, "kept down by . . . bayonets."[68] It is not surprising, then, that Hankins and so many of his contemporaries in the last generation viewed surrender as a fate worse than death.

In the Confederate experience of these young Virginians rests the foundation on which Southern ideologues would build their Lost Cause dogma. According to this postwar interpretation, white Southerners were a truly Christian people who defended a noble way of life against an enemy who ruthlessly waged war on property and civilians. The writings of Keith, Pegram, Hankins, and others suggest that they might have been looking ahead, bracing themselves for the trauma of defeat and the inevitable challenges of a political world turned upside down. On May 7, 1865, the Virginia Military Institute's Abraham Fulkerson sent a letter from a Northern prison camp to prepare his wife for life after Appomattox. Final justice still awaited the South, he insisted, and neither incarceration nor military collapse swayed him from this belief. The Confederacy, Fulkerson admitted, "is broken," but "the spirit is not." "The ball has been put in motion by the people of the South," he proclaimed, "an impetus has been given it, which will eventually result in the destruction of the U.S." Even if God failed to do so now, He would eventually reward the right rather than the might of conquering Union armies. The distant promise of retribution did not ease the degradation of defeat or the shame of having to return home subjugated. "I expect to meet you soon," he wrote, "not crowned with the laurels of victory but with the oath crammed down my throat, a quiescent citizen of the United States." All that was left in a land vanquished by war and occupied in defeat were the memories of serving in a noble cause. Despite a future that appeared hopelessly dark and fraught with danger, Fulkerson found the "sweet consolation . . . of having served the cause faithfully. I sacrificed everything but life, and hazarded that, many times & in many ways, in behalf of my country." Yet the knowledge of having done his duty would not make it any easier to accept Union military rule. "I have performed my duty and now abandon the cause as (at present) hopeless, without in the least having changed my opinion as to the justness of that cause. I go now to share with the people of the south the deep humiliation which will be dictated by yankee vindictiveness."[69] The purpose and meaning of Reconstruction remained to be seen, but even in the immediate aftermath of defeat, Fulkerson steeled himself for a more severe test than war: the terms of a Northern-imposed reunion.

 **From Conservative Unionism to Old Fogydom**

· ·

Let us learn MODERATION. — "Editors'
Drawer," *Virginia University Magazine*,
May and June 1868

JOHN HAMPDEN CHAMBERLAYNE refused to attend
the "funeral" at Appomattox. He believed that there was too much life left in
the Confederacy. As Robert E. Lee surrendered in Wilmer McLean's front
parlor to Ulysses S. Grant, Chamberlayne slipped through the enemy's picket
line with the intention of joining Joseph E. Johnston's army in North Carolina.
The subsequent news of Johnston's armistice on April 18 only strengthened
his resolve to keep fighting. He promised to continue the struggle in Mississippi, where he imagined himself leading newly raised Confederate regiments. Somewhere between Charlotte, North Carolina, and Athens, Georgia,
Chamberlayne had an epiphany. He realized that his Southern nation no longer existed, that military defeat and subjugation constituted the new reality,
and that further resistance was hopeless. On May 5, Chamberlayne took the
oath of allegiance before continuing his journey west, away from his beloved
Virginia.

Chamberlayne stayed with some Mississippi relatives for the remainder of
the summer, spending his days trying not to think about the past, the present,
or the future. Chamberlayne equated the dreariness of his existence with an
"enforced idleness." With so much time on his hands, he could not help but to
reflect on the meaning of the war for himself and for the South. "The war and
its objects, its causes, & the causes of its failure, are not subjects of thought
with me as are other things," he wrote on August 1, "but are become thought
itself, parts of my mind, burned into my heart as with a branding iron." Defeat

enshrouded Chamberlayne's world, defining his every perception and coloring his every thought, but it did not incapacitate him. Vindication would come, he predicted, for he refused to believe that the Southern people would patiently endure Northern enslavement. "Every drop of blood of ours that was spilled is," he wrote, ". . . a seed in the ground, whence will spring wrath and armed men."[1] If this day of retribution did not come in Chamberlayne's life, he drew solace from the prospect of moving the South closer to the moment of resurrection, when a new rebellion inspired by the spirits of his martyred comrades would rise.

Ten years later, in an address given at Randolph-Macon College, John Hampden Chamberlayne no longer hoped for the second coming of the Confederacy. He accepted Northern victory, even welcomed it, because it had liberated Virginia of slavery. Although his family had owned African Americans before the war, Chamberlayne did not lament the passing of the "peculiar institution." The religious defense of slavery, he argued, had closed Southern minds, while freedom of thought had flourished in the North, encouraging creativity and innovation. "Now, you cannot limit the mind without dwarfing it, nor shut off all light without weakening the eye," Chamberlayne concluded. "So, when we left our faculties unused we began to lose them, and digging for ourselves a mammoth cave of darkness, we went near to be blind as its fish."[2] Material progress, as a result, took off in free societies while Virginia languished economically and intellectually.

A writer for the *Cincinnati Commercial* thought Chamberlayne's speech signified a new beginning in the South. He believed that Chamberlayne represented the class of young men who had grown up during the war and, since Appomattox, had "emancipated themselves from the prejudices, traditions and authority of the[ir] elders." Chamberlayne's strong words further demonstrated, according to the *Cincinnati Commercial*, that "Young Virginia . . . now boldly asserts itself in a way that proclaims Virginia henceforth another field, where free inquiry can range at will." "The old fogies," the newspaper article concluded, would probably denounce "the new generation" for exercising and enjoying its freedom to its fullest.[3]

The *Cincinnati Commercial* located in Chamberlayne's message an important generational difference in postwar philosophy between the Virginians of the last generation and older and more prominent Lost Cause spokesmen such as Jubal A. Early and William Nelson Pendleton. Although there were scores of older Virginians who were New South boosters, Early and Pendleton led an influential Virginia contingent of ex-Confederates who renounced Northern ideas of free labor and industrial capitalism, hoping that Southerners would turn back the clock and re-create a golden age of the Confederacy where aristocratic values ruled over a pastoral landscape.[4] The experiences of the last generation suggest that a significant number of Virginians were not embittered ex-Confederates who desired a restoration of the Confederate tradition or sought refuge in the "moonlight and magnolias" view of the Old South.[5] The moderation of these men during Reconstruction is striking. Not only did they avoid fighting the old battles of the Civil War, but they also advocated a plan of economic diversification, internal improvements, and industrial growth that resembled the North's vision of Reconstruction. A typical pronouncement of the last generation can be found in an 1868 issue of the *Virginia University Magazine*. The student editors reminded their fellow classmates, virtually all of whom had military experience, that they were best suited for the challenges ahead: "It lies with the young men of the South to build up our fallen heritage. And how are they to do it? Not by war—that has failed them. How then? *We must stay here, in our old homes, and work.*" "Let us go to work like men," the editors concluded, "just as faithfully as we fought. . . . And over all and above all, let us learn MODERATION."[6] Why did these ex-soldiers, many of whom were fanatical in their devotion to the Confederacy, construct a bridge between their antebellum and postwar worlds that followed the blueprint of the New South architects and Northern capitalists?

Quite simply, military occupation demanded that these Virginians accept the new order. They understood, as do most people who lose a war, that power resides with those who have the most guns.[7] Resuming the struggle was not a viable option when the Confederacy was in ruins and white Southerners appeared demoralized. Only cooperation with Northern Republicans would bring an end to military occupation. There could be no future for white Virginians until Federal troops left the state. Pragmatism and a quest for home rule, however, do not entirely explain why members of the last generation accepted New South orthodoxy and the death of slavery with relative ease. The intellectual impact of the Civil War on these men must be explored in order to fully understand the transition to free labor and industrial capitalism.

Excluding the issues of slavery and emancipation, this group of veterans largely reconstructed their lives without having to reconstruct their intellectual worlds. A generational critique of antebellum Virginia society, which included a call for sweeping economic reforms and new development, provided the framework for their New South vision. The industrial might of Northern armies did not awaken the last generation to a vision of economic innovation and development; they had advocated such a course before Fort Sumter.[8] Their campaign, however, had produced uneven results, leaving them frustrated and bitter in the 1850s. Reconstruction provided a second chance to reform Virginia character and instill the state with a spirit of innovation and prosperity.

In the immediate wake of Appomattox, members of the last generation did not concern themselves with rebuilding a war-ravaged Virginia. Union victory numbed Confederate soldiers of all ages, and they struggled to comprehend the enormity of military defeat and its consequences for themselves and for their region. How they would be treated as a conquered people was the burning question of the day, and the possible responses conjured up the most horrific images of "Black Republican" rule. Young Virginians struggled to regain their sense of self-worth as men. Defending their homes and loved ones from Yankee invaders during the war earned them acceptance as men. Defeat canceled their newfound status, and they returned to their families feeling emasculated and useless. John H. Chamberlayne doubted if he could even be of service to his widowed mother. These feelings of powerlessness spawned emotions that ranged from depression to unadulterated hatred of the North. A fit of desperation could easily trigger a tirade against the Yankees.

Members of the last generation spoke of seeking revenge against the North, but it is significant that those who promised retribution never acted on their bold promises of renewed violence. John Dooley of Pickett's division kept a detailed diary as he traveled across Southside Virginia after Johnston's surrender. Along the way, he encountered ex-slaves "deserting" their masters and flaunting their new freedom, and considered their behavior one of several reasons why the fight should be continued. When he saw the ruins of his native Richmond and the demoralized condition of its people, his feelings grew so strong that he refused to describe them in his diary. Dooley could only hope that "the triumphant army of our malignant foes" would animate every Southern heart with a desire for revenge. Peace came at the unbearable price of humiliation, Dooley wrote, and he promised never to reconcile himself to a dishonorable surrender. This young man, who would enter the priesthood after the war, included an important caveat in his diatribes against the North. He acknowledged that the South lay prostrate before the Federal army, that Virginia's spiritual and material arsenals were spent, and that submission to the enemy's terms was the only option. "Bow down, now, crushed Southern hearts," Dooley wrote on April 30, 1865, "bow down the head to receive the servile yoke which the money making puritan [sic] has so long yearned to place upon thy neck. They have the power now."[9] Like so many of his comrades from the last generation, Dooley had witnessed the demise of the most powerful army in the Confederacy, had encountered widespread civilian resistance against the war, and knew the terror that Union armies could easily inflict on a vanquished land. In the end, young Virginians like Dooley preferred to lay down their arms for good and endure the humiliating posture of submission rather than embark on a future filled with senseless bloodshed.

Once Dooley and his fellow soldiers of the last generation returned home, they faced a desperate struggle for survival. The demands of rebuilding their wrecked farms and businesses often exceeded human endurance. Most of these men, at least initially, tried to scratch out a living as farmers. Robert E. Lee Jr. and several other young officers took residence in a "shanty" next to the ruins of the family's old manor house on the Pamunkey River. They used their "old war chargers" to plow the fields for corn, bought a few hogs, and raised some chickens for "'bread and meat,'" because sustenance was, according to one observer, the "'burning question' to these aristocratic 'field hands.'"[10] Very few members of the last generation had engaged in agricultural pursuits before the war. Their limited experience, combined with tough economic conditions, forced many to return to their antebellum occupations of law and education. Both fields attracted an overwhelming percentage of my sample group after the war, though it is impossible to determine how long the men persisted in their efforts to revive old family farms. John H. Chamberlayne, for example, tirelessly worked on his mother's Hanover property for two years until he suffered a breakdown in 1867. For an entire year he refused to leave his bedroom or receive visitors. When he emerged from the darkest period of his life, he changed careers and became a telegraph operator and then a journalist.[11]

The economic and social forces of Reconstruction did not set a common career trajectory for these Virginians as they entered full adulthood. Their professional lives, as might be expected, followed a variety of courses. Lawyers and educators made up more than 65 percent of the sample.[12] Whichever career they ultimately selected is not particularly important, nor even revealing, as the idea that a certain occupation would predispose an individual to either accept or reject New South dogma is highly questionable. What stands out about the 1865–70 period is the paucity of first-hand documentation from the last generation. A lack of financial resources must have prevented these men from publishing pamphlets or speeches as they had done before the war. In the 1850s, most of these men were students, schoolmasters, or lawyers who resided with their parents. After Appomattox, living patterns and relationships changed, and, for the first time, most of these men became heads of household. The marital status of forty-four members of the last generation has been determined. Of those, nearly 82 percent were married after the war.[13] The heavy responsibilities that followed consumed the time they might have devoted to writing about current issues. It is possible that members of the last generation were also politically apathetic, but the surviving sources neither support nor contradict such a theory.

Only one member of the last generation, Lynchburg's John Warwick Daniel, left a significant body of published work from the 1865–70 period. Daniel typifies the men of the last generation who survived the war. He served in Lee's army, stayed in Virginia after Appomattox, and became a Democrat and staunch supporter of home rule while preaching reconciliation and the gospel of the New South. In three speeches delivered between 1866 and 1868, Daniel evoked the 1850s message of Young Virginia, expressing the belief that material and moral progress would continue as long as Southerners helped themselves and trusted in God. In the fall of 1865, a twenty-three-year-old Daniel literally hobbled into the University of Virginia. He had received a grievous war wound at the battle of the Wilderness that nearly crippled him. When the spring term was over, Daniel spoke to members of the Jefferson Literary Society—as veterans, not as students—and reminded his peers that God had chosen them to survive while "thousands of our comrades rest among the 'unreturning brave' on distant fields of honor . . . [and] while thousands more still languish on the beds of agony, or totter through life in a premature old age."[14] Throughout his speech Daniel employed metaphorical imagery that drew almost exclusively from the last generation's shared military experience. The Spartan discipline, the comradeship, and the devotion to duty that Daniel and his peers acquired in the army would serve them well in Virginia's Reconstruction. They would need these skills for a new campaign, he announced, to "raise the drooping and torn, though not dishonored, standards of your country, and advance them in the nobler battle fields of thought."[15]

Daniel's optimistic view of the future drew from a key prewar assumption of the last generation. While God remained the moral steward of the Universe, young Virginians believed that an individual possessed the power to develop the earth's resources, to spread Christianity and republicanism, to contribute to the arts, and to build material wealth. The carnage of war, the profiteering of civilians, the collapse of slavery, and military defeat did not shake Daniel or his peers in the belief that society would move onward and upward be-

John Warwick Daniel (1842–1910). This photograph of Daniel was probably taken near the turn of the century after he had distanced himself from his Reconstruction message of reconciliation. In 1868 he told a Confederate memorial association: "It becomes us not to weep that the Confederacy is not. 'Thy will be done!'" It is worth noting that Daniel posed for this photograph sporting Confederate battle flag cuff links. (From *Speeches and Orations of John Warwick Daniel*, comp. Edward M. Daniel, 1911)

cause human destiny ultimately rested with God.[16] Defeat would not deter progress. Although Confederates like Daniel had insisted to the very end that God would never forsake the Confederacy, Union victory did not produce a spiritual crisis in him or other members of the last generation. Unfortunately, the available sources do not permit an inquiry into how they reconciled themselves to the loss of their Christian slave society. They were ex-soldiers, not ministers or intellectuals, and they did not fully explain how they reoriented their religious thinking as they made the transition to a free-labor society. However, one fundamental wartime assumption is conspicuously absent in their post-1865 writings: the idea that Southerners were God's chosen people. For obvious reasons, young men could no longer cling to this belief. Ironically, the surrendering of this notion proved liberating for members of the last generation, because it gave them more freedom to critique their own society during Reconstruction.

Daniel followed in the intellectual wake of many Southerners who steadied themselves in the turbulent postwar waters by insisting that even in a time of duress Christians have an opportunity to advance the cause of God and progress. He admitted that evil forces currently ruled over Virginia, but he maintained that those malignant powers could never prevent his native land from fulfilling its higher mission. The Radical Republicans, he argued, "may throw themselves in the path and detain, but they can not overthrow the Car of Progress as with Divine Providence holding the reins, and the human races pulling in the traces, it moves sublimely on to accomplish the destinies of mankind."[17] It is amazing how easily Daniel accepted the vicissitudes of history, for when he looked at the past, he neither became disillusioned with the world nor called for Virginia to turn back the clock. Daniel, like so many in his age group, looked to Reconstruction as an opportunity for Virginia to unfurl the flag of civilization — not by conquering cities or battlefields as the North had done, but through progressive achievements in the arts and sciences. He was not fatalistic about the future.[18]

Daniel recognized the risks of a heroic interpretation of the Confederacy in the midst of Reconstruction and refused to romanticize the Confederate experience. He wanted Virginians to remember the sacrifices of his comrades, but he feared that hero worship could lead to apathy if the people thought that the golden age of the Commonwealth had passed with the Confederacy. A similar problem had presented itself to the last generation before the war, when many of their fellow citizens seemed incapacitated by the fading glories of the American Revolution. Daniel feared that his fellow Virginians would simply wait for a group of great men to rescue them. According to Daniel and other members of the last generation, this self-inflicted paralysis had occurred in 1850s Virginia when the state's citizens, rather than confronting the ills of their society, simply waited for the second coming of George Washington, Patrick Henry, and Thomas Jefferson. Daniel made it clear after the war that only the people could restore the Old Dominion to greatness. There were no noble men to rescue the Commonwealth. They were gone, the fallen heroes of the Confederacy.

Daniel risked sacrificing the public's memory of the Confederacy with this declaration, but he fought his way out of the problem by trying to transform Southern martyrs into American heroes. In an 1868 speech to a Confederate memorial association, he stated that a restoration of the Confederacy was not only impossible but also undesirable. He further argued, although rather disingenuously, that Southern soldiers fought and died so that the American republic could fulfill its democratic promise. "It becomes us not to weep that the Confederacy is not," he explained. "'Thy will be done!' . . . Be ours [the] living." He wanted Virginians to appreciate that Southern blood was spilled as an act of contrition for the nation's sins. Daniel thought this noble sacrifice would enable his fellow citizens to reclaim their citizenship without any loss of honor. "A Government of the People lives," Daniel exclaimed, "and that we are in it, and with it, and of it, to do our part to make it great and glorious and to make it endure forever."[19] Daniel's words of reconciliation and his emphatic plea for industrial capitalism confused the older generation. Jefferson Davis could not understand why the young Virginian conceded so much to the Yankees. Was not the South's cause just, the ex-president asked? Brushing aside Confederate traditions in the name of progress also troubled the editors of the *Norfolk Virginian*, who condemned Daniel's last generation for dismissing their elders as "recalcitrant," "reactionary," "fogies," "obsolete," and "dead."[20] The generational tensions of the 1850s resurfaced, shaping once again Virginia's political discourse over the meaning of progress.

Daniel's valuable speeches between 1866 and 1870 outline the intellectual contours of the last generation's postwar message until the late 1890s. They were focused on reviving their 1850s crusade of bringing Christianity and material progress to the Commonwealth. At the center of the antebellum campaign stood the model of the Christian gentleman.[21] Not until the turn of the century did young Virginians stop rejecting aspects of the cavalier tradition. But for most of the Reconstruction period they denounced the cavalier model for its celebration of luxury, aristocratic ease, and violence—debilitating traits that they believed too many Virginians wanted to emulate. In an 1867 edition of the *Southern Opinion*, Edward Pollard of the last generation worried that his fellow citizens would seek a carefree existence by claiming that they were simply living as their aristocratic forebears had done. The adversity of the times, Pollard wrote, demanded that a man "must earn his bread by some more solid service than petting the children and mending the whips." "We want men of thought and action," he wrote, because "Virginia has been rudely wakened from her long dream of Utopian ease to find herself in a sternly work-day world."[22]

Virginia's partisan press, conservative and independent, reiterated Pollard's words throughout the 1870s. A close look at the newspapers of this time indicates that members of the last generation were not intellectually isolated; they were engaged and influential in a public debate over the proper role of the male citizenry and the state's future. An editor of the *Richmond Enquirer* ridiculed the "good old easy days of Virginia" for producing men whose self-worth depended on "thousands of acres and hundreds of slaves." The editor was thankful that they had passed away, taking to the grave their lazy habits and anachronistic ideas about progress. The depressed and distressed condition of the state could only be reversed, the editor concluded, if members of the rising generation disassociated themselves from the "grand old country gentlemen of Virginia." In 1879, a *Richmond Dispatch* editor proclaimed: "The rising generations must be educated to economy and industry. . . . The young cannot fall into the possession of the ability of their fathers to lead lives of leisure and abundance."[23]

This widespread call for a progressive way of life in the Old Dominion originated within the last generation's antebellum critique of Virginia and its male citizenry. This message not only survived the Civil War, but also blossomed during Reconstruction in part because age relations decisively shifted in favor of young Virginians who were then entering middle age. Before 1861, these men stood outside the state's political circles because of their youthful status, but, after Appomattox, the veterans of the last generation returned home as men who had endured horrible privation in defense of their communities. Recognition for their service and sacrifice naturally followed, and with this sudden attention came opportunities to enter state politics. A few men turned to the Republican Party, and even fewer turned to the Readjusters, but most participated in a conservative movement that gained control of the Old Dominion in 1869. The Conservative Party stood for the establishment of home rule, the subordination of African Americans, the return to power of the state's elite, and internal economic development and diversification.[24] The story of Virginia's Conservative Party and the political history of the state from 1867 to 1879 has been brilliantly recounted by Jack P. Maddex Jr. A discussion of the internal political struggles that shaped the Old Dominion in the decade after Appomattox—such as the assumption of the state debt and the emergence of the Readjuster movement—is outside the scope of this book.

The paucity of sources makes it difficult to discern in detail how members of the last generation reacted to these debates, but their support of Conservative Party principles does signify a broader commitment to an agenda of economic development that dovetailed with the plans of their Northern conquerors. Maddex argues that "the very essence of the adaptation the Conservative leaders promoted was the economic regeneration of Virginia on Northern capitalist lines."[25] What can be learned about members of the last generation during the late 1860s and the 1870s validates Maddex's assertion. With an unimpeachable war record, they could easily fend off any charge of selling out to the Yankees. In fact, they touted their battlefield exploits to gain the trust and, more importantly, the votes of the electorate. This strategy paved the way for an important generational shift in power relations. Influential antebellum political actors, like Henry A. Wise, William Smith, and John Letcher, lost their clout after the war. In 1874, Democrat Frank Ruffin lamented the passing of the old guard and the rise of the Confederacy's young bloods. "To me the most melancholy thing of all is that *Young Virginia* did the work," he wrote, "& stamps this election, as it has done all its previous work, with the seal of mediocrity. Henceforth, the test of patriotism & ability is to be the number of wounds received in battle, & the highest statesman is the bravest color bearer." In another instance of Young Virginia's driving ambitions, a combination of veterans and former Whigs blocked the candidacy of Virginia's last wartime governor, William Smith. Smith had wryly told his young opponents that he would probably die in a few years, thus creating an opening, and that the younger aspirants could use the intervening years to advance their own competitive positions.[26]

Although Confederate military service sparked the political careers of the last generation, combat experience did not have a great impact on Young Virginia's postwar vision. It was not war that alerted members of the last generation to the Commonwealth's need to modernize its economy and to transform the character of its citizenry; they had learned this lesson long before the industrial might of Union armies laid waste to the Southern countryside.

What they did discover between 1861 and 1865, however, was the temporary realization of their antebellum dream of progress. The demands of war, some argued, awakened the state from its deep slumber, brought the listless to life, and invigorated the Virginia economy. John Hampden Chamberlayne admitted that the state "was weak" before the war. Armed conflict, however, "awoke that public spirit which had seemed dead, but was only sleeping." "The slothful became energetic," he added, "the luxurious hardy, the arrogant submitted to discipline, the selfish subdued self to the common good, and the four years began of sacrifice, devotion, endurance and achievement." John Warwick Daniel also endorsed this interpretation of the war. "The whole country was converted into an arsenal and a hospital," he observed in 1877, "and under trial and hardship which would have broken a feeble race, her genius burst forth in exploits of mechanical invention and economical skill not less splendid than her feats of arms." With an eye toward the future, Daniel wanted Virginians to duplicate their wartime achievements. If Southerners could plow fields, harvest trees, build roads, and develop industries in the face of Federal armies, they should achieve even greater feats during peacetime. Daniel reminded his audience that "the first gun of Sumter broke the stagnant, dreamy langor [sic] of our Southern lotus-land."[27] Men of Daniel's generation believed the war had extinguished any notion that Southern talents rested exclusively on agricultural pursuits. The Confederacy's successful conversion to war production demonstrated that Southerners possessed the ability and genius to make lasting achievements in the mechanical arts.

Examples of Southern innovation and reform during the Civil War led some members of the last generation to believe that the Commonwealth's citizens now possessed the habits necessary for a modern economy, but not all Virginians were as optimistic about the state's future or their ability to adjust to the demands of the new order. One year after Appomattox, William Gordon McCabe of Hampton, Virginia, observed that "things are bad enough here, and we must tear down 'Sic Semper', and write 'Ichabod' on our shield." "There is an apathy," he concluded, "beyond anything you can imagine."[28] These feelings of hopelessness persisted well into the 1870s, and it seemed as if nothing could shake the people out of their lethargy. Some members of the last generation returned to their antebellum jeremiads about Virginia's decline with the hope that a historical perspective might turn people away from despondency. They wanted to show that the period of economic stagnation between the Era of Good Feeling and the Civil War paralleled the "dark days" of Reconstruction. The last generation hoped that the juxtaposition of the mistakes of their elders and the current crisis would spur Virginians to shed their reputation as irrelevant cavaliers and prove to the world that they were an industrious, intelligent, and moral people.

The perception that Virginia had declined since the Revolution served as the intellectual rallying point for young Virginians in the 1850s and, for the same men, again in the 1870s. Rather than explore the complex forces behind the state's economic malaise, the last generation blamed the leaders of their parents' generation by creating a straw man with the "old fogy" who symbolized the backward thinking of Virginia's leaders. Generational resentment lingered after Appomattox, and the residue of the contentious antebellum debate can be found in Chamberlayne's 1875 address, "Public Spirit." "With the year 1825," Chamberlayne asserted, "the heroic period of Virginia may be said to end, and a decadence followed which we are apt enough to forget, but which to study is our highest duty, since the lessons it teaches are needful." He denounced his parents' generation because it "produced no leader of thought, no model of style, no discoverer of truth, but fell to one dead level of mediocrity and ignorant content." Allegiance to slavery had closed their minds, although Chamberlayne did notice promising "signs of reaction" among his generation in the 1850s.[29] Nonetheless, he did not want Virginians to repeat the sins of the past by cutting themselves off to new ideas. The road to prosperity, he realized, could only be traveled by people who were open to discovery and innovation. With slavery dead, Chamberlayne wanted Virginians to fully appreciate their intellectual freedom, for he believed that they were now in a position to revive the campaign of the 1850s that had been derailed by the Civil War.

Richmond's Archer Anderson, the son of Tredegar's Joseph Reid Anderson and a graduate of the University of Virginia, agreed with Chamberlayne that Virginians would find valuable lessons by studying the state's decline since the Revolution. "But let me read you one more lesson out of your own annals," he stated, "Virginia has, within the memory of living men, recovered from a painful condition of ruin and bankruptcy, only to furnish an arena for the long pent up passions of sectional strife." He wanted Virginians to "compare the depression of all her material interests" following the "peace of 1815" with the energy and determination of the war years.[30] Anderson bluntly presented the options facing his fellow Virginians: they could either lead the state down the road of progress or return to the lethargic days of the old fogies who kept the Old Dominion in the backwaters of the world. Anderson and Chamberlayne did not invent a mythical Old South that idealized the rural over the city, the farm over the factory, or slavery over free labor. Rather, they incorporated a progressive agenda into their Lost Cause appeal, an approach followed by many ex-Confederates.[31]

It is crucial to remember that members of the last generation did not break completely with their antebellum past to create a New South future. Even continuity with past traditions, however, did not protect them from Southern critics. Anderson, Chamberlayne, and the rest of the war generation had to tread lightly because of Jubal Early, the intellectual caretaker of the *Southern Historical Society Papers*. Early savaged anyone who disagreed with his rabid pro-Confederate views. As a slaveholder and old-line Whig before the war, Early was the quintessential old fogy who enraged the younger generation. Confederate defeat intensified his political and social conservatism to such a point that he can easily be seen as a violent reactionary. Early gloried in the charge that he was one of those "who deprecate the new theories, are said to be behind the age, and called fossils, fogies, and Bourbons." His critics, however, realized that Early lived in the past so that he could shape the future. Early's attempts to control the public memory of the Civil War were part of a larger effort to stop the advance of industrial capitalism and Northern ideas of progress. In his 1872 address at the Lee Chapel in Lexington, Early warned his audience that there were traitors in their midst who were trying to seduce Southerners into sacrificing their Confederate traditions for the promise of material riches. "We are told that our ideas are all obsolete," Early proclaimed, "and asked to adopt the spirit of progress from our enemies, in order to restore the prosperity of our country, and start it on a new career of material development and physical power."[32]

Early and his followers offered an enduring interpretation of Confederate military defeat and the generalship of Robert E. Lee. Northern industrial might and superior numbers, ran the argument, enabled the bloodthirsty Ulysses S. Grant to overwhelm but not outgeneral the brilliant Lee.[33] Members of the last generation enthusiastically endorsed this explanation, and for the remainder of their lives they seized every opportunity to speak about the nobility of the Southern soldier who fought manfully against impossible odds. They also backed Early's emphasis on Virginia as the most important theater of the war, because it drew attention to their own military exploits.[34] Yet there was a jarring difference between Early's characterization of Marse Robert and the symbolic qualities that the last generation found in Lee. Both sides portrayed the general as the model Christian gentleman, but for strikingly different purposes. Early thought Lee's purity and moral perfectibility attested to the superiority of an aristocratic slave society. Younger Virginians argued that Christianity instilled in Lee a controlled ambition and a focused energy that propelled him to professional success. The way in which he managed the Army of Northern Virginia demonstrated that Lee was not mired in the past and wedded to values unfit for the rising New South. Members of the last generation focused on Lee's Christian virtues and military prowess without using the general as a symbol to defend the Old South or Virginia's aristocratic traditions.

During the last week of May 1890, more than one hundred thousand Southerners congregated in Richmond for the unveiling of a statue of Robert E. Lee. Archer Anderson delivered the keynote address in which he spoke of the commanding general's rare combination of Christian virtues and sublime bravery. But he was not content to focus on the heroic nature of Lee and the Confederacy. Anderson moved beyond a narrow justification of the South's actions during the war by portraying Lee as a man of action, intelligence, and vigor. He praised Lee for his abilities as an administrator, who demonstrated "energy, forecast, and watchfulness . . . in the prosaic work of providing the means of subsistence for his army!" Anderson considered these "the necessary elements" of his "great character," the individual skills that Southerners needed in order to thrive in an emerging world of industrial capitalism.[35]

In keeping with the last generation's celebration of individualism, Anderson pointed to ambition as the key to self-improvement and the betterment of society. The hard-driving careers of senior military men made Confederate generals—especially those who were aggressive on the battlefield—the exemplars for the New South campaign. Other members of the last generation had promoted such an idea before. In an 1868 speech at Manassas, Virginia, John Warwick Daniel applauded Stonewall Jackson's overpowering ambition and his ceaseless drive to improve himself for the benefit of others. "Jackson was a man of the highest ambition. He aspired to eminence in whatever he undertook," Daniel proclaimed. "He had that thirst for glory which is the almost invariable quality of elevated minds. By severe discipline he has acquired the power of concentrating or relaxing his energies at will. His punctuality became a proverb. He slept, ate, studied, and did every duty by clockwork; and his associates kept the time of day by the movements of Major Jackson."[36] Daniel carefully emphasized the aspects of Jackson's behavior that Virginians would need to emulate in order to succeed in the mechanized world of the New South. Stonewall represented the ideal Confederate hero not only because he was deeply religious, but also because, as a western Virginian, he was not a descendant of the cavalier tradition. Humble origins, Daniel believed, had instilled in Jackson a relentless energy that rarely could be found in a Virginia aristocrat. A comparison between Jackson and Lee revealed this point. "Of one class Lee is a type, of the other Jackson," Daniel wrote, "and Jackson's was the type we needed. Jackson was ambitious — Lee was not. Jackson sprung from poverty and obscurity, had to hew his way upward." Lee was "the scion of an influential, and aristocratic house," and this privileged environment imparted a suffocating conservatism that hemmed in his thinking during the war. Daniel wanted his fellow citizens to appreciate in Jackson the value of prayer and action, even if it came at the expense of the aristocratic Lee.

The last generation's New South vision was not cut off from the ideological moorings of its antebellum world, and these veterans did not turn their backs on the Confederate past as Jubal Early had charged. They drew from both traditions as part of a broader campaign to promote sectional healing. But in the end Early's charge of apostasy was not a reckless one. These young Virginians refused to revive Confederate traditions. Their eagerness to move forward with the process of reunion is somewhat surprising, given that they had condemned the North during the war for inflicting unimaginable horrors on the South. The moderation of Federal policies, probably more than anything else, allowed these veterans to switch allegiances without feeling like a craven pack of Judases. Richmond's Edward Pollard, a fiery pro-Confederate writer of Early's ilk, initially rejected reintegration into the Union on any terms. Within five years of Appomattox, he had been reconstructed. When Pollard discovered that the Republicans were not out for vengeance and that their policies would not annihilate the white South, he recognized that cooperation was the surest way to achieve home rule. In an 1870 issue of *Lippincott's Magazine*, Pollard admitted that there was much to be disgusted by in postwar Virginia. He resented military occupation, opposed black suffrage, and regretted the expansion of the federal government's authority. However, these developments did not bring the reign of terror that most Southerners had predicted would befall a defeated Confederate nation. Self-critical Virginians, Pollard believed, would admit that, contrary to their initial fears, Northern subjugation had proven not to be "'a fate worse than death.'" "Measured by their own declared anticipations," he added, "'reconstruction' has been a miracle of generosity."[37]

Pollard correctly perceived the uniqueness of Virginia's Reconstruction experience. The Old Dominion returned to the Union in 1869, long before military rule came to an end in most Southern states. This occurred in part because white Virginians of all ages focused on achieving voting rights for ex-Confederates rather than campaigning for black disfranchisement. The Grant administration responded by pushing for the Commonwealth's readmittance. The president simultaneously called for a popular vote on Virginia's new constitution and the election of state officials. Members of the last generation worked within a relatively benign political environment, and, as Eric Foner has observed, Virginia was the only Confederate state to avoid a period of Radical Reconstruction.[38] Washington's olive-branch approach probably made it easier for Virginians to entertain the idea that the Civil War had forged a stronger sense of Americanism between Northerners and Southerners. Privately, however, many of these young men were not so quick to forgive the Yankees. The last generation's Fitzhugh Lee, for example, spoke at the 1875 centennial observance at Bunker Hill and celebrated the common heritage of Northerners and Southerners. When he returned to Virginia, he found a letter from an ex-comrade chiding him for speaking above the Mason-Dixon Line. A defensive Fitz Lee wrote back that he was "no *repentant rebel*," that he considered the trip a necessity in order to foster good will between the sections.[39] Only when favorable relations were restored would the Democratic Party unite all sections of the country and deliver the Radical Republicans their deathblow. Every public plea of national loyalty, Fitz Lee realized, was designed to hurt the cause of the Radical Republicans and give white Southerners more authority to control their own affairs. Northern politicians on either side of the aisle responded as the last generation had hoped. They increasingly became convinced that Virginia was back in the fold and that its people had been rehabilitated.

By the 1880s, when the veterans of the last generation were middle aged, Reconstruction had ended, home rule had been established, and the memory of Confederate defeat did not seem as traumatic. Men on both sides were ready to return to the battlefields to show that former enemies could meet as American brothers on the old killing grounds. In 1887, veterans from the last generation helped organize the first reunion at Gettysburg. This was not only a Confederate event; the men of Pickett's famous division would join forces with the Philadelphia Brigade, the very unit that the Virginians had battled on July 3, 1863. Once they had been granted permission to erect a monument near the high water mark, the Virginians left for two days of festivities in Gettysburg, which included plenty of flag waving, handshaking, and patriotic speeches. At the height of this American lovefest, William Roane Aylett—an 1854 graduate of the University of Virginia, a founder of the school's Southern Rights' Association, and the former colonel of the 53rd Virginia Infantry—delivered the keynote address for the Virginia contingent. Aylett made no attempt to justify secession, slavery, or the "cause" in general. The spirit that had compelled his comrades to charge Cemetery Ridge, he assured the audience, no longer animated Southerners. For this, he thanked God. "From the baptism of blood and fire in which we were consumed," Aylett asserted, emerged a new class of Southerners filled with filial love.[40] War had turned Northerners and Southerners into a united people, and Aylett saw the reunion as an opportunity to "worship" the Star-Spangled Banner on the sacred ground of Gettysburg.

When Aylett served in the Army of Northern Virginia during the summer of 1863, he had endorsed and executed a policy of hard war against Pennsylvania's civilians. He tried to shoot Union prisoners as an act of retaliation, and, at the end of the failed campaign, he promised his wife that "I'll fight them as long as I have a leg to stand on or an arm to strike . . . for God cannot intend that such wickedness should succeed."[41] At the first "Blue & Gray" reunion, Aylett was selective in what he recalled; he never mentioned his controversial acts or his true feelings about the enemy in 1863. The 1887 reunion culminated with the recording of a powerful symbolic act. Aylett and his fellow comrades once again met their former enemies at the stone wall along Cemetery Ridge—the high water mark of Pickett's assault—but this time they shook hands as photographers captured the enduring image of brotherly reconciliation.

Aylett and his comrades falsified Confederate history with reckless impunity at Gettysburg. The Virginians succeeded in overlooking the past in part because Northerners desired a more sanitized version of the Civil War in the mid-1880s. Instead of condemning the Confederacy as a traitorous cause, middle- and upper-class Northerners idealized the Southern crusade as a struggle to preserve a hierarchical world of benevolent paternalism. As part of this romantic view, Union veterans paid homage to Southern bravery as a pure expression of American manhood.[42] This gesture fully restored Southern honor and, therefore, made it psychologically possible for young Virginians to reach across the divide of war and embrace their Northern enemies without feeling as if they had committed a horrendous apostasy. The restoration of their manly reputations also gave them the political room to join the reconciliation crusade. No self-respecting Southerner could possibly recognize a government that deemed him inferior, but as long as honor was publicly acknowledged, one could join the orgy of American patriotism without humiliation. When the Philadelphia Brigade visited Richmond in 1888 for the unveiling

Veterans of Pickett's division and members of the Philadelphia Brigade posed along the famous stone wall at Gettysburg's Angle in a powerfully symbolic act of sectional reconciliation. It was at this 1877 reunion that the last generation's William Roane Aylett proclaimed: "Southern men don't care who keeps the flags. The past went down in war, and we recognize now the banners of our fathers." (From Anthony W. McDermott, *A Brief History of the 69th Regiment Pennsylvania Veteran Volunteers*, 1889)

of the George Pickett monument, Robert Taylor Scott of the last generation told the Northern veterans that "we meet as citizens, co-equal citizens, of our common country." Having insisted that Northerners and Southerners had entered a brotherhood of equals, Scott felt free to simultaneously claim that the Confederate cause was just and that Southerners no longer harbored rebellious thoughts. Both sides had behaved as true men during the war, he said in conclusion. Scott proclaimed that "to-day, in 'Our Father's House,' Virginia and 'The Old South,' pledge with you allegiance to this Union—an indissoluble union of sovereign and indestructible States."[43]

Just as the reconciliation movement reached its zenith during the Spanish-American War, some members of the last generation started to question the benefits of Northern victory.[44] Their answers mark a philosophical shift to a more militant Confederate perspective, one more in keeping with the "moonlight and magnolias" tradition than with the conservative Unionism they had espoused during most of the postwar years. This ideological transformation must be rooted within the last generation's changing life cycle, their disillusionment with America's Gilded Age, and their belief that only disfranchisement and segregation could legitimate their political authority.[45] In her important book on the reconstruction of white Southern womanhood, Jane Turner Censer also found that women at this same time—particularly female novelists—became more critical of the North, more romantic about the South's pastoral tradition, and more defensive about Southern manhood. She astutely points out that this response is attributable to the fact that "members of the old elite found themselves faced with the problem of demarcating class while simultaneously downplaying the prominence of the marker of wealth." As young Virginians attained old fogy status, they clung more tenaciously to the memories of the war as they worried about their own class status. They refused to surrender what they considered to be the most dramatic event of their lives. In 1906, Virginia cavalryman James Keith explained that "for the men of the generation which is rapidly passing away, the war is and must be the one great over-shadowing fact. It looms up on the memory in such vast proportions that all else which happened before and since seems trivial and of little worth."[46]

With the passing of every comrade, the last generation felt a renewed sense of urgency to protect their historical reputations. Their sons seemed uninterested in becoming the guardians of Confederate traditions.[47] Moreover, the enthusiasm younger Southerners expressed for the Spanish-American War in 1895 must have concerned older Confederate veterans, who worried that their military exploits were being forgotten. At least one son of a Virginia Confederate, however, saw the Spanish-American conflict as an opportunity to pay homage to his Southern ancestry: "We of the young generation owe you of '61 a debt of untold gratitude and admiration for the noble examples & high ideals set for us to follow."[48] Such statements must have been gratifying to the last generation because they vindicated their own manliness during the Civil War. In turn, the men of the last generation were effusive in their support for this imperialistic war. But in the lovefest of Americanism that followed the conflict, some of them worried that they had conceded too much to the North. They feared that the rising generation might actually believe that the morally just side had won the war. Two years before he died in 1918, conservative Unionist Archer Anderson, who had long championed reconciliation, captured his generation's concerns about the future of Confederate memory. He bluntly stated: "I can never cease to regret our defeat after such a glorious struggle." Anderson worried that too many historical writers celebrated the destruction of slavery and Reconstruction at the expense of the Confederate cause and the suffering of the Southern people. "The South was irretrievably injured by the defeat of our Armies," Anderson stated unequivocally. He compared the Confederacy's destruction to a shipwreck, and Anderson wanted Southerners to know that in the postwar years "we saved as much of the wreck" as was possible. The salvaging was done for the benefit of future generations.[49]

In a 1902 edition of the *Baltimore Sun*, the last generation's Charles L. C. Minor uncovered the basic contradiction of the reconciliation movement—one that had been avoided since Appomattox. If Confederate veterans paid homage to Grant and Lincoln as true American heroes, then how could future Southern generations believe that their ancestors were just in fighting for independence? This jarring contradiction revealed itself to Minor at a Confederate memorial service where he heard a former comrade announce that no Southerner would have wanted the Civil War to end differently. If one agreed with this sentiment and remained intellectually consistent, Minor reasoned that one would also have to believe the following: "'I am glad that we failed in our efforts in 1861–1865 to establish a government separate from and independent of the Government of the United States, because if we had succeeded and won the political independence we were fighting for our conditions as a people would have been worse than it is now.'"[50] Minor knew that any logical man who worked from such an assumption could only conclude that Southerners were morally wrong and that the men "on the other side" should be honored and imitated. When he considered the sacrifices of his fellow Confederate soldiers, he could not bring himself to say that "'we made a grave mistake in 1861, and it was best for the Confederacy to fail. Forgive us the mistake, costly and ruinous as it was, for the sake of our good and honest intentions. Bring up your children to love those who risked their lives or died to preserve the Union.'" Minor wanted his former comrades to recognize that every time they praised their former enemies, they were also ensuring that future generations, including their own children, would damn the Southern cause as an unholy crusade to destroy the Union. At the end of the article, Minor recalled an incident in Richmond when he spotted a poster of Lincoln that read, "'If Davis was a patriot, what was I?'" "This picture sets forth a great truth," Minor asserted. "One of two things is true; there is no middle ground. If Davis was a patriot, Lincoln was a tyrant. . . . Lincoln conquered the South and built up a powerful nation, in which true lovers of liberty cannot rejoice, for it cost the lives of two noble republics, the old United States of America and the Confederate States of America."[51]

Although Minor recognized what few of his peers were willing to admit — that they were destroying their own historical reputations — members of the last generation did agree with the unreconstructed Minor that Southerners were losing the historical memory of the Civil War to the Yankees. Their desire to pass on the true legacy of the war, however, does not completely explain why the last generation began to contest the "brother versus brother" version of the Civil War. This age group reoriented its thinking about the Confederate past out of a deep concern for Virginia's future in a modern world. Ironically, the arrival of progress that young Virginians had sought since the 1850s triggered their second rebellion against the North. As New South capital transformed the Virginian landscape, they saw the jarring difference between the promise of progress and its reality. Economic changes in the late nineteenth century produced amazing wealth and impressive technological achievements — just as these Virginians had predicted — but they were not prepared for the monsterlike economy that consumed lives, chewed up the environment, and corrupted humanist values. The wave of political unrest that plagued urban and rural America horrified the last generation, for its members feared that foreigners and political extremists threatened the "natural order" of society. In the last decade of the nineteenth century, Virginia witnessed a mass exodus of its rural citizens. African Americans led this movement from field to factory.

The social upheaval produced by industrial capitalism forced young Virginians to question their identities as Americans, Southerners, and Virginians. Faced with a multitude of cultural divisions in industrial America, members of the last generation worried that the citizens of their region were losing their distinctiveness as a people. The pursuit of Mammon was leading them astray from Southern values. It is difficult to gauge what these men truly meant by Southern values, but the core of them was generally understood as a respect for hierarchy. Although the members of the last generation had spent much of their adult lives denouncing the cavalier ideal as anachronistic and harmful to the Commonwealth, the myth was resilient and proved to be especially seductive to a people searching for public vindication and social cohesion. The cavalier image cast a shadow of Victorian purity that obscured the deep problems of the New South — intense poverty, racial violence, segregation, and demagogic politics — by creating an artificial history of the Old South, where content slaves, women in hoop skirts, and courtly squires lived in a rural utopia.[52]

As members of the last generation neared the end of their lives and worried about their legacy, the cavalier myth supported their claim of fighting as Christian soldiers for a noble way of life. The cavalier myth also held out the possibility of Victorian perfectibility, of order, and of stability in a mechanized, market-driven world that subordinated all moral questions to the cash nexus. In the end, members of the last generation used the cavalier tradition to resist modernism while elevating themselves as the perfect Southerners.[53] If Virginians were the finest example of Confederate manhood, some members of the last generation reasoned, then military defeat could only be explained by the moral shortcomings of other Southerners and the treachery of the enemy. Winchester's Holmes Conrad voiced this strident opinion at the unveiling of the "Virginia Mourning Her Dead" monument in 1910. Among other denigrating remarks, he called the Yankees "irresponsible marauders" for their destruction of the Shenandoah Valley. But the thrust of his address centered on the unique character of the Virginia cadets, which Conrad carefully juxtaposed to a valueless modern world gone wild. "It may be, indeed, that in this age of shams and mockeries, . . . [that] the acquisition and possession of wealth is accounted the highest evidence of human merit," Conrad argued. He thought it abhorrent "when the standards and maxims of our former civilization are perverted and distorted to dignify the vulgarity of a gross materialism." People had forgotten in this age of progress that a successful life depended on a firm sense of duty and an unswerving obedience. Such a model could be found in the Virginia soldier. Conrad idealized the Virginia Military Institute cadets as the embodiment of the South's "loftiest ideals of human excellence" because they show that "spirit of self-sacrifice — of 'proud submission, [and] of dignified obedience.'"[54]

As members of the last generation neared the end of their lives, they created a mythical world of perfect Confederate heroes fighting in defense of a noble land against a materialistic, godless foe. Throughout the 1850s, young Virginians had charged that their elders had lived off the fading glories of the Old Dominion's Revolutionary past. These old veterans, in the end, repeated the sins of their fathers as they lost themselves in a golden age of history that never existed in the Commonwealth. This retreat into a Confederate make-believe-land signified a break with the idea that progress was inevitable and always resulted in the improvement of society. They had surrendered the very principle that had guided their thinking from 1850 to the 1880s. Although members of the last generation, to varying degrees, came to question the New South creed, they remained committed to a new Americanism based on romantic sentimentalism, scientific racism, laissez-faire economics, and imperialism.

While this was an unmistakable betrayal of inherited antebellum traditions, the last generation's conservative Unionism must be understood as a product of their antebellum world. There was no cynical capitulation to New South propaganda. Since the 1850s, members of the last generation had held to a progressive vision. As often is the case, the reality of the dream never quite fulfilled its glorious promise. At the turn of the century, members of the last generation found themselves trapped in a materialistic marketplace that they did not understand or desire, leaving them cynical and depressed in their old age and longing for the return of a world that was a terrible fiction.

Appendix

Table 1. Birth Dates of the Last Generation ($N = 110$)

Year	N	Percent
1830	1	0.91
1831	3	2.73
1832	4	3.64
1833	6	5.45
1834	10	9.09
1835	13	11.82
1836	9	8.18
1837	14	12.73
1838	10	9.09
1839	12	10.91
1840	8	7.27
1841	9	8.18
1842	7	6.36
1843	4	3.64

Table 2. Occupations of Fathers of the Last Generation ($N = 66$)

Occupation	N	Percent
Boardinghouse keeper	1	1.52
Bricklayer	1	1.52
Civil engineer	1	1.52
Domestic	1	1.52
Farmer	28	42.42
Industrialist	1	1.52
Lawyer	6	9.09
Merchant	3	4.55
Minister	6	9.09
Newspaper editor	3	4.55
Physician	4	6.06
Politician	1	1.52
Senior sergeant	1	1.52
Stage conductor	1	1.52
Teacher	2	3.03
Tobacconist	2	3.03
U.S. military personnel	3	4.55
Widow	1	1.52

Note: Four farmers also practiced law, and one lawyer was also a mill owner. "Widow" was listed as an occupational category in the 1860 census.

Table 3. Religious Affiliations of the Last Generation ($N = 35$)

Religion	N	Percent
Baptist	2	5.71
Catholic	1	2.86
Episcopal	21	60
Methodist	3	8.57
Methodist/Episcopal	1	2.86
Presbyterian	7	20

Table 4. Prewar Occupations of the Last Generation ($N = 103$)

Occupation	N	Percent
Banker	1	0.97
Clerk	1	0.97
Doctor	1	0.97
Engineer	1	0.97
Farmer	7	6.8
Lawyer	30	29.13
Minister	1	0.97
Paymaster in U.S. Army	1	0.97
Student	28	27.18
Student and Teacher	2	1.94
Teacher	28	27.18
U.S. military personnel	2	1.94

Note: Of the lawyers, one also farmed, six also taught, two were also editors, and one was also a businessman.

Table 5. Marital Status of the Last Generation ($N = 44$)

Married	N	Percent
Before 1861	8	18.18
After 1861	36	81.92

Table 6. Political Affiliations of the Last Generation ($N = 11$)

Party	N	Percent
Whigs	10	90.90
Whigs/Know-Nothings	1	9.10

Table 7. Military Survival Rate of the Last Generation ($N = 93$)

Survived	N	Percent
Yes	67	72.04
No	26	27.96

Table 8. Postwar Occupations of the Last Generation ($N = 66$)

Occupation	N	Percent
Banker	2	3.03
Educator	21	31.82
Educator and Minister	2	3.03
Farmer	5	7.58
Industrialist	1	1.52
Lawyer	23	34.85
Minister	5	7.58
Newspaper editor	2	3.03
Physician	2	3.03
Politician and farmer	2	3.03
U.S. military personnel	1	1.52

Note: Seven lawyers were also politicians; two were also editors; and there was one lawyer that also worked in each of the following occupations: education, the ministry, and farming.

Table 9. Emigration from Virginia among the Last Generation ($N = 66$)

Emigrated from Virginia	N	Percent
Yes	11	19.70
No	53	80.30

Table 10. College and University Affiliations of the Last Generation ($N = 113$)

University	N	Percent
College of New Jersey (Princeton)	1	0.88
Dickinson College	1	0.88
Emory and Henry College	5	4.42
Georgetown College	1	0.88
Harvard Divinity School	1	0.88
Harvard College and VMI	1	0.88
Lynchburg College	2	1.77
No university training	6	5.31
Overseas university	2	1.77
Private academy	1	0.88
Randolph–Macon College	1	0.88
Union Theological Seminary (Richmond)	1	0.88
United States Military Academy	2	1.77
University of Virginia	77	68.13
Virginia Military Institute	7	6.19
Washington College	3	2.65
Winchester Medical College	1	0.88

Table 11. Slaveholder Representation in the Last Generation ($N = 34$)

Slaveholder	N	Percent
Yes	32	94.12
No	2	5.88

Table 12. 1860 Census Listing in the Last Generation ($N = 51$)

Listing	N	Percent
Head of household	20	39.22
Lawyer living at home	7	13.73
Physician living at home	1	1.96
Student	1	1.96
Student living at home	16	31.37
Teacher	1	1.96
Teacher living at home	4	7.84
U.S. Army clerk	1	1.96

Notes

ABBREVIATIONS

AL   Albert and Shirley Small Special Collections Library, Alderman
          Library, University of Virginia, Charlottesville, Va.
DU   Rare Book, Manuscript, and Special Collections Library, Duke
          University, Durham, N.C.
EU   Special Collections, Emory University General Library, Atlanta, Ga.
FSNMP   Fredericksburg and Spotsylvania National Military Park Library,
          Fredericksburg, Va.
SHC   Southern Historical Collection, Wilson Library, University of North
          Carolina at Chapel Hill, Chapel Hill, N.C.
VHS   Virginia Historical Society, Richmond, Va.
VMI   Virginia Military Institute Archives, Preston Library, Virginia Military
          Institute, Lexington, Va.
VT   Special Collections, Virginia Polytechnic Institute and State University,
          Blacksburg, Va.
W&L   Special Collections, James Graham Leyburn Library, Washington and
          Lee University, Lexington, Va.

PROLOGUE

1. William R. Aylett to Alice Roane (Brockenbrough) Aylett, July 20 and July 21, 1863, Aylett Family Papers, VHS.

2. "North and South at Gettysburg," *Army and Navy Journal*, July 1887, 1001.

3. Ibid.

INTRODUCTION

1. Generations originate within specific historical experiences through which people who live at the same time and in the same place are able to forge social groups. Economic conditions, state and national politics, class relations, youth organizations, adult initiatives, and various networks of institutions present the reality in which young people try to make sense of their world and, in some cases, ultimately come together as a collective body. It is within a specific historical context that they can experience

a mystic feeling of oneness within their own age group. Youth solidarity arises when young people believe that they share a common destiny, a driving, overriding purpose that infuses them with the capacity to believe they are at odds with the dominant opinion of their elders. Once they discover a common destiny and begin to act on it, young people typically emerge as a distinct political force in society with their own agenda and interests. In conceptualizing what a generation is, I have been aided by the work of Karl Mannheim, Marvin Rintala, and Alan B. Spitzer, who argue that between the ages of seventeen and twenty-five, a political outlook is basically formed and a group consciousness established. Generational consciousness must demonstrate a relationship between the historical-social process and the cohort's formative years. I consider Southern men born between 1830 and 1843 to be part of the same generation because they became "political beings" during the 1850s. See the following works: Karl Mannheim, "The Problem of the Generations," in Mannheim, *Essays on the Sociology of Knowledge*, ed. Paul Kecskemeti (New York: Oxford University Press, 1952), 300–303; Marvin Rintala, "Generations: Political Generations," in *International Encyclopedia of the Social Sciences*, ed. David L. Sills (New York: Macmillan, 1973), 5:92–95; Alan B. Spitzer, "The Historical Problem of Generations," *American Historical Review* 78 (December 1973): 1353–85. See also Norman B. Ryder, "The Cohort as a Concept in the Study of Social Change," *American Sociological Review* 30 (August 1965): 843–61.

2. Mannheim, "The Problem of the Generations," 308–9.

3. Although his study of Southern manhood focuses on the postwar period, Ted Ownby upholds a common perspective on manhood in the antebellum South. He writes: "And Southern men did not feel the same impulse toward upright behavior that drove middle-class men in the North. The lessons of economic morality—sobriety, thrift, and self-denial—that accompanied the development of a commercially minded Northern middle class in the nineteenth century were slow to gain acceptance in the rural South." Although this statement does not accurately describe the experience of the last generation, Ownby deserves credit for recognizing that religion moderated male behavior. See his *Subduing Satan: Religion, Recreation, and Manhood in the Rural South* (Chapel Hill: University of North Carolina Press, 1990), 11. Southern historians who echo Ownby's idea operate from a static view of what it meant to be a man in the Old South. Ideas about Southern manhood were not frozen over time. Many historians have not fully appreciated the evolution of Southern manliness because they have underestimated the softening influences of religion in the 1850s. As a result, they subscribe to the stereotype of Southern youth as lazy, irresponsible, anti-intellectual, and hotheaded. The authors cited below accept the image of the violent, hypersensitive, dissipated Southern youth at the expense of a more complex reading of male identity. Their explorations into Southern manhood, however, do not go so far as to support the caricature of Southern men that nineteenth-century Northerners invented. My criticisms do not undermine the core arguments of these scholars or take away from their important contributions. Orville Vernon Burton, *In My Father's House Are Many Mansions: Family and Community in Edgefield, South Carolina* (Chapel Hill: University of North Carolina Press, 1985), 90–99, 114–15; Dickson D. Bruce Jr., *Violence and Culture in the Antebellum South* (Austin: University of Texas Press, 1979), 62–65; Bertram Wyatt-Brown, *South-*

ern Honor: Ethics and Behavior in the Old South (New York: Oxford University Press, 1982), 149–74; Christine Leigh Heyrman, *Southern Cross: The Beginnings of the Bible Belt* (New York: Alfred A. Knopf, 1997), 211–12; Lisa C. Tolbert, *Constructing Townscapes: Space and Society in Antebellum Tennessee* (Chapel Hill: University of North Carolina Press, 1999), 120, 165, 170, 181, 184; John Hope Franklin, *The Militant South, 1800–1861* (Cambridge, Mass.: Belknap Press of Harvard University Press, 1956); W. J. Cash, *The Mind of the South* (1941; reprint, New York: Vintage Books, 1991); Grady McWhiney and Perry D. Jamieson, *Attack and Die: Civil War Military Tactics and the Southern Heritage* (University, Ala.: University of Alabama Press, 1982), 170–72.

4. See the appendix for a statistical survey of the last generation.

5. Some of the finest scholarship on Virginia's attitude toward secession has unfortunately overlooked the role of young people. See Daniel W. Crofts, *Reluctant Confederates: Upper South Unionists in the Secession Crisis* (Chapel Hill: University of North Carolina Press, 1989), 53–54, 277–83, 308–23; Henry T. Shanks, *The Secession Movement in Virginia* (Richmond: Garrett and Massie, 1934), 103–213; Charles B. Dew, *Apostles of Disunion: Southern Secession Commissioners and the Causes of the Civil War* (Charlottesville: University Press of Virginia, 2001).

6. William T. Sherman to Henry W. Halleck, September 17, 1863, *Sherman's Civil War: Selected Correspondence of William T. Sherman, 1860–1865*, ed. Brooks D. Simpson and Jean V. Berlin (Chapel Hill: University of North Carolina Press, 1999), 545–46.

7. By 1830, the word "fogy" had become a disrespectful nickname for men advanced in age. According to David Hackett Fischer, the term gained popularity during the 1850s with the rise of the "Young America Movement." See Fischer, *Growing Old in America* (New York: Oxford University Press, 1977), 90–92. For a more precise historical explanation of the word "fogy" and its evolution over time, see "fogy" in *A Dictionary of American English on Historical Principles*, ed. Sir William A. Craigie and James R. Hulbert (Chicago: University of Chicago Press, 1940), 2:1027; "fogy or fogey" in *Random House Historical Dictionary of American Slang*, ed. J. E. Lighter (New York: Random House, 1994), 1:796.

8. Although he looks exclusively at New England men, E. Anthony Rotundo has offered a valuable framework in which to understand the evolution of manliness in nineteenth-century America. This approach does not take into account regional differences, but Rotundo is sensitive to change over time; for this reason his work is useful. See his *American Manhood: Transformations in Masculinity from the Revolution to the Modern Era* (New York: Basic Books, 1993), 2–7.

9. On the place of universities in nineteenth-century American society, see Frederick Rudolph, *The American College and University* (New York: Alfred A. Knopf, 1965); Helen Lefkowitz Horowitz, *Campus Life: Undergraduate Cultures from the End of the Eighteenth Century to the Present* (New York: Alfred A. Knopf, 1987); Oscar Handlin and Mary F. Handlin, *The American College and American Culture: Socialization as a Function of Higher Education* (New York: McGraw-Hill, 1970); John S. Brubacher and Willis Rudy, *Higher Education in Transition: A History of American Colleges and Universities, 1636–1976* (New York: Harper and Row, 1976). For the most complete history

of the University of Virginia, see Philip Alexander Bruce, *History of the University of Virginia, 1819–1919*, 5 vols. (New York: Macmillan, 1920–21). Other secondary works include Ervin L. Jordan Jr., *Charlottesville and the University of Virginia in the Civil War* (Lynchburg, Va.: H. E. Howard, 1988); John S. Patton, *Jefferson, Cabell and the University of Virginia* (New York: Neale Publishing Co., 1906); Charles Coleman Wall Jr., "Students and Student Life at the University of Virginia, 1825–1861" (Ph.D. diss., University of Virginia, 1978). Secondary studies of Virginia's other prominent universities abound. See George J. Stevenson, *Increase in Excellence: A History of Emory and Henry College* (New York: Appleton-Century-Crofts, 1963); Herbert C. Bradshaw, *History of Hampden-Sydney College*, 2 vols. (Durham, N.C.: Fisher-Harrison, 1976); John Luster Brinkley, *On This Hill: A Narrative History of Hampden-Sydney College, 1774–1994* (Farmville, Va.: Hampden-Sydney, 1994); Richard Irby, *History of Randolph-Macon College, Virginia: The Oldest Incorporated Methodist College in America* (Richmond: Whittet and Shepperson, n.d.); James Edward Scanlon, *Randolph-Macon College: A Southern History, 1825–1967* (Charlottesville: University Press of Virginia, 1983); Reuben E. Alley, *History of the University of Richmond, 1830–1971* (Charlottesville: University Press of Virginia, 1977); W. Harrison Daniel, *History of the University of Richmond* (Richmond: Print Shop, 1991); Francis H. Smith, *History of the Virginia Military Institute* (Lynchburg: J. P. Bell, 1912); Jennings C. Wise, *The Military History of the Virginia Military Institute from 1839 to 1865* (Lynchburg: J. P. Bell, 1915); Richard M. McMurry, *Virginia Military Institute Alumni in the Civil War* (Lynchburg: H. E. Howard, 1999); Ollinger Crenshaw, "General Lee's College: Rise and Growth of Washington and Lee," 2 vols. (typescript, Washington and Lee University, 1973), W&L; Susan H. Godson, Ludwell H. Johnson, Richard B. Sherman, Thad W. Tate, and Helen C. Walker, *The College of William and Mary: A History*, 2 vols. (Williamsburg: King and Queen Press, 1993).

10. My understanding of Victorian culture draws heavily from the following authors, who agree that radical innocence, moral discipline, and social refinement characterized the Victorian man. See Daniel Joseph Singal, *The War Within: From Victorian to Modernist Thought in the South, 1919 to 1945* (Chapel Hill: University of North Carolina Press, 1982), 5, 6, 7; Anne C. Rose, *Victorian America and the Civil War* (New York: Cambridge University Press, 1992), 4–5, 7–9; Gail Bederman, *Manliness and Civilization: A Cultural History of Gender and Race in the United States, 1880–1917* (Chicago: University of Chicago Press, 1995), 10–12.

11. Eric Foner and Michael O'Brien have encouraged historians to examine the secession crisis within the context of modernization. See Foner, *Politics and Ideology* (New York: Oxford University Press, 1980), 33; O'Brien, *Rethinking the South: Essays in Intellectual History* (Athens: University of Georgia Press, 1993), 112–28. I have tried to follow their suggestion and the example of other scholars who insist that secession forced white Southerners not only to come to terms with a sectional Republican Party but also to resolve internal issues and questions of power. Studies on Georgia and Alabama have demonstrated that slaveholders used secession to consolidate their power and to turn back the democratic advances in the previous decade. See Michael P. Johnson, *Toward a Patriarchal Republic: The Secession of Georgia* (Baton Rouge: Louisiana State

University Press, 1977); J. Mills Thornton III, *Politics and Power in a Slave Society: Alabama, 1800–1860* (Baton Rouge: Louisiana State University Press, 1978); William L. Barney, *The Secessionist Impulse: Alabama and Mississippi in 1860* (Princeton: Princeton University Press, 1974).

12. For works that attribute Confederate defeat to the insensitivity of the Confederacy's ruling class, see Paul D. Escott, *After Secession: Jefferson Davis and the Failure of Confederate Nationalism* (Baton Rouge: Louisiana State University, 1978); Steven Hahn, *The Roots of Southern Populism: Yeoman Farmers and the Transformation of the Georgia Upcountry, 1850–1890* (New York: Oxford University Press, 1983); J. William Harris, *Plain Folk and Gentry in a Slave Society: White Liberty and Black Slavery in Augusta's Hinterlands* (Middletown, Conn.: Wesleyan University Press, 1985); Wayne K. Durrill, *War of Another Kind: A Southern Community in the Great Rebellion* (New York: Oxford University Press, 1990); William C. Davis, *Look Away! A History of the Confederate States of America* (New York: Free Press, 2002).

13. Gary W. Gallagher, *The Confederate War: How Popular Will, Nationalism, and Military Strategy Could Not Stave Off Defeat* (Cambridge, Mass.: Harvard University Press, 1997); William Blair, *Virginia's Private War: Feeding Body and Soul in the Confederacy, 1861–1865* (New York: Oxford University Press, 1998).

14. Historians who argue that the Southern impulse to industrialize originated during the Civil War include Jack P. Maddex Jr., *The Virginia Conservatives, 1867–1879: A Study in Reconstruction Politics* (Chapel Hill: University of North Carolina Press, 1970); Paul M. Gaston, *The New South Creed: A Study in Southern Myth-Making* (New York: Alfred A. Knopf, 1970).

15. Generational relations in Virginia grew tense during a time of economic revitalization. Prosperous days returned in the 1850s as the Old Dominion experienced a remarkable market and transportation revolution. Prices for tobacco and foodstuffs steadily increased for weary farmers who had grown accustomed to paltry returns. A railroad boom spurred economic growth while connecting Virginia to distant markets. In the decade before the Civil War, existing track in Virginia increased from 350 to 1,673 miles. By 1861, the state had contributed nearly $45 million toward railroad construction. Additional improvements in bridge building, canals, roads, and turnpikes also modernized the state's infrastructure. These transportation developments facilitated the rise of commercial agriculture, particularly along major rivers such as the James, York, Rappahannock, and Potomac, and in the Shenandoah Valley. Farmers everywhere started growing more wheat, vegetables, and corn, although it appears that tobacco enticed the richest and the poorest farmers to take a chance on this cash crop with its promise of lucrative profits. New trade routes enabled Virginia farmers to sell their goods to Northern and international markets. This increased commercial activity energized towns and cities, particularly Richmond, Petersburg, Lynchburg, and Norfolk, which became buzzing hubs of economic activity. Light manufacturing led the way as iron foundries and tobacco factories occupied a conspicuous place in the urban landscape. In the 1850s, Virginia was becoming a diversified economy, merging the worlds of slave and free labor.

"Flush times" had returned to the Old Dominion, and this "new economy" altered power relations within the household. Many hired-out slaves came into contact with free blacks—and an ever-expanding working class of immigrants and poor whites—clustered around cities and towns. Mechanics and laborers also congregated around railroads, such as the Virginia and Tennessee Railroad in southwest Virginia. A roving proletariat, by all accounts, had emerged in 1850s Virginia, a consequence of a growing market economy that placed many working-class whites outside long-accepted patterns of work and authority. On Virginia's move toward a market economy in the 1850s, see Shanks, *The Secession Movement in Virginia*, 1–17; Avery Craven, *Soil Exhaustion as a Factor in the Agricultural History of Virginia and Maryland, 1606–1860* (1926; reprint, Gloucester, Mass.: Peter Smith, 1965), 122–62; Kenneth W. Noe, *Southwest Virginia's Railroad: Modernization and the Sectional Crisis* (Urbana: University of Illinois Press, 1994), 4–9; Steven Elliott Tripp, *Yankee Town, Southern City: Race and Class Relations in Civil War Lynchburg* (New York: New York University Press, 1997), 6–12; Gregg D. Kimball, *American City, Southern Place: A Cultural History of Antebellum Richmond* (Athens: University of Georgia Press, 2000), 15–36; John Majewski, *A House Dividing: Economic Development in Pennsylvania and Virginia before the Civil War* (Cambridge: Cambridge University Press, 2000), 12–14. William Link explores the breakdown of the master-slave relationship in 1850s Virginia. See his *Roots of Secession: Slavery and Politics in Antebellum Virginia* (Chapel Hill: University of North Carolina Press, 2003).

16. David M. Potter, "The Historian's Use of Nationalism and Vice Versa," in Potter, *The South and the Sectional Conflict* (Baton Rouge: Louisiana State University Press, 1968), 34–83.

17. For a critical analysis of identity and whiteness studies, see Barbara J. Fields, *"Origins of the New South* and the Negro Question," in *"Origins of the New South" Fifty Years Later: The Continuing Influence of a Historical Classic*, ed. John B. Boles and Bethany L. Johnson (Baton Rouge: Louisiana State University Press, 2003), 261–77.

CHAPTER ONE

1. William R. Aylett, "Temperance Speech," [1853], Aylett Family Papers, AL.

2. For the best treatment of the South's intellectual class and the issue of progress, see Eugene D. Genovese, *The Slaveholders' Dilemma: Freedom and Progress in Southern Conservative Thought, 1820–1860* (Columbia: University of South Carolina Press, 1992). My argument takes issue with Dan R. Frost who sees antebellum Southerners, particularly those in higher education, firmly opposed to progress because of slavery. See his *Thinking Confederates: Academia and the Idea of Progress in the New South* (Knoxville: University of Tennessee Press, 2000), 1–17.

3. Moncure Daniel Conway, *Autobiography, Memories and Experiences of Moncure Daniel Conway* (Boston: Houghton, Mifflin, 1904), 1:113. Conway's contemporaries in the last generation drew on the traditional arguments of the time, ranging from the racial inferiority of African Americans to the idea that slavery enabled a class of educated men to rule. Only a few young men openly debated the merits of the institution, confining their criticism to slavery's effects on whites and its economic backwardness.

An overwhelming majority considered any objection to the institution beyond the pale. Yet they surprisingly distanced themselves from the South's intellectual class by excluding slavery from their idealized portrait of the South. Even Edward Pollard, the last generation's most aggressive and thoughtful proponent of the institution, broadly defended the South as a "civilized" land without suggesting that a dependent form of labor created harmonious social relations. He portrayed the North as a dangerous land of "radical" philosophies that scorned the word of God. In his "Hints on Southern Civilization," Pollard challenged the heathenish North: "Come to us of the South, and we will show you 'the mistress of the virtues!'" On his proslavery views, see [Edward Pollard], "Hints on Southern Civilization," *Southern Literary Messenger* 32 (March 1861): 310. A masterful treatment of Pollard's antebellum views can be found in Jack P. Maddex Jr., *The Reconstruction of Edward A. Pollard: A Rebel's Conversion to Postbellum Unionism* (Chapel Hill: University of North Carolina Press, 1974), 24–42.

Young Virginians tended to gloss over the deeper philosophical issues of proslavery thought that attracted the energy of the region's intellectual class. If young Virginians broached the topic, they found little wrong with the institution. Harmony, interdependence, and obligation, they believed, mediated relations between whites and blacks. "The town has been filled with our colored population today being Easter Monday," wrote Robert T. Scott in 1858. "I think their happy faces, & contented enjoyment would have been a severe rebuke to that Philanthropic Abolitionists, who by severing their fetters would condemn theirs to absolute poverty, penury, want and destitution." See Robert T. Scott to Fanny (Carter) Scott, April 5, 1858, Keith Family Papers, VHS. Like so many of his fellow slaveholders, Scott conveniently forgot about the abuses of their system, including the role of the lash. Scott and his peers envisioned their communities as Christian utopias in which blacks and whites were bound together through a paternalistic ethic that the last generation aspired to uphold. The last generation shared the sentiments of most Southerners when it came to slavery. See William R. Aylett, "Essay on Slavery," [n.d.], Aylett Family Papers, VHS; Alexander S. Pendleton, "Cincinnati Oration," July 2, 1857, Ellinor Porcher Gadsden Papers, W&L; "Slavery," *Hampden Sydney Magazine* 2 (June 1860): 241–51. For examples of young Virginians raising questions about the economic viability of slavery, see Lancelot Blackford Diary, May 25, 1849, Blackford Family Papers, SHC; "Our Only Hope," *Hampden Sydney Magazine* 2 (June 1860): 268–69.

4. On Virginia's constitutional reforms during the 1850–51 convention, see Alison Goodyear Freehling, *Drift toward Dissolution: The Virginia Slavery Debate of 1831–32* (Baton Rouge: Louisiana State University Press, 1982), 235–41; William W. Freehling, *The Road to Disunion: Secessionists at Bay, 1776–1854* (New York: Oxford University Press, 1990), 513–15. In front of the Jefferson Society at the University of Virginia, William R. Aylett of the last generation railed against the new democratic reforms, arguing that "this new Constitution is going to convert this, our good old state, into one vast bar room." See his "Speech against New Constitution," [October 19, 1851?], Aylett Family Papers, AL.

5. Daniel W. Crofts, *Old Southampton: Politics and Society in a Virginia County, 1834–1869* (Charlottesville: University Press of Virginia, 1992), 134–35; Link, *Roots of*

Secession: Slavery and Politics in Antebellum Virginia (Chapel Hill: University of North Carolina Press, 2003), 170, 175–76.

6. [Richard M. Venable], "Principles—Their Growth," *Virginia University Magazine* 4 (April 1860): 219.

7. Ibid., 218. For those members of the last generation who insisted that material progress must accompany moral progress and remain faithful to the law of Christianity, see Douglas Gannon, "A Discourse on the Soul" (master's thesis, University of Virginia, 1859), in Student and Alumni Papers, UVA Master's Theses, AL; William G. Strange, "The Study of Man, in the Formation of his Character" (master's thesis, University of Virginia, [1850–1860?]), in Student and Alumni Papers, UVA Master's Theses, AL; James M. Garnett, [No title] (master's thesis, University of Virginia, 1859), in Student and Alumni Papers, UVA Master's Theses, AL; Summerfield Smith, "The Development of Society" (master's thesis, University of Virginia, 1858), in Student and Alumni Papers, UVA Master's Theses, AL. See also Henry Clay Pate, "Patriotic Discourse on Local and General History," *Southern Repertory and College Review* 2 (December 1852): 137; Aylett, "Temperance Speech," [1853], Aylett Family Papers, AL.

8. J. A. Latane, "The Value of Grecian History to the American Student" (master's thesis, University of Virginia, 1851), in Student and Alumni Papers, UVA Master's Theses, AL. Among the last generation, there was a consensus about the inevitability of progress and its widespread benefits. For some of the best examples, see Blackford Diary, March 23, 1855, Blackford Family Papers, SHC; E. T. Fristoe, "The Wonders and Tendencies of Modern Science" (master's thesis, University of Virginia, [1854–1861?]), in Student and Alumni Papers, UVA Master's Theses, AL. [Robert M. T. Hunter Jr.], "Novels and Novel Reading," *Virginia University Magazine* 4 (October 1859): 19; [Carter M. Louthan], "Progress," *Virginia University Magazine* 3 (May 1859): 450–53; [Venable], "Principles—Their Growth," *Virginia University Magazine*, 219; Aylett, "Temperance Speech," [1853], Aylett Family Papers, AL; Joseph M. Logan, "Young America," *Southern Repertory and College Review* 4 (December 1855): 146–47; Albert G. Pendleton, "The Aspirations of the American Youth," *Southern Repertory and College Review* 4 (January 1855): 30–31; [James M. Boyd], "Roman Catholicism and Free Institutions," *Virginia University Magazine* 4 (April 1860): 340.

9. [Boyd], "Roman Catholicism and Free Institutions," 343–44; "Slavery," *Hampden Sydney Magazine*, 243; Henry Wilkins Coons to [?], April 14, 1850, Coons Family Papers, VHS. John Lee Buchanan agonized over how to reconcile liberty and progress with his belief in the fall of man. See his "Is Slavery Right Per Se: A Speech to Be Delivered in the Hermesian Hall," April [?], 1857, in John B. May, "The Life of John Lee Buchanan," (Ph.D diss., University of Virginia, 1937), 38–39. On the hierarchical view of Southern theologians, see Eugene D. Genovese and Elizabeth Fox-Genovese, "The Social Thought of Antebellum Southern Theologians," in *Looking South: Chapters in the Story of an American Region*, ed. Winfred B. Moore Jr. and Joseph F. Tripp (New York: Greenwood Press, 1989), 37, 39.

10. Robert T. Scott to Fanny (Carter) Scott, November 23, 1857, Keith Family Papers, VHS. James DeWitt Hankins believed that God bestowed ambition on humans

as the mechanism that would drive individual and societal improvement. See his letter to Virginia Wilson Hankins, April 21, 1858, Hankins Family Papers, VHS.

11. "The Fourth of July," *Lexington Gazette and General Advertiser*, July 9, 1857, p. 2.

12. Henry Wilkins Coons, [untitled essay], [1859?], and "Position in Life," November 12, 1859, Coons Family Papers, VHS. Coons expressed similar concerns about the potential of youthful depravity in his essay "Reading," January 8, 1859, Coons Family Papers, VHS. As did many young Virginians, he paid attention to his father's advice. On November 15, 1857, Robertson Coons wrote to his son: "You have now arrived to an age to form habits and associations which will be apt to go with you through life. Try if possible to rise in the company you keep, rather than lower yourself." See Robertson Coons to Henry Wilkins Coons, November 15, 1857, Coons Family Papers, VHS. In his study of antebellum New York City and "Young America," Edward L. Widmer discovered that young people gravitated toward the Democratic Party because it retained a commitment to the radical message of the Revolution while rejecting the Whigs' model citizenship of restraint and regulation. With the sources available on the last generation, I was unable to detect any such pattern among Virginians. While the scope of my work does not allow for a fair comparison to Widmer's study group, one must question his assumption that young people are restless by nature and thus automatically drawn to the party that promises to satisfy that irrepressible longing. See his *Young America: The Flowering of Democracy in New York City* (New York: Oxford University Press, 1999), 5–6.

13. H. W. Coons, [untitled essay], [1859?], and "Position in Life," November 12, 1859, Coons Family Papers, VHS.

14. Henry W. Coons to [?], [n.d.], Coons Family Papers, VHS. It should be remembered that "Young America" was used more as a rhetorical device, often connected to westward expansion, and had less to do with formal party politics. On the "Young America Movement," see Charles H. Brown, *Agents of Manifest Destiny: The Lives and Times of the Filibusters* (Chapel Hill: University of North Carolina Press, 1980), 95; Widmer, *Young America*.

15. Logan, "Young America," 146.

16. William P. Louthan, "The Influence of Moral Principles on the Prosperity of Nations" (master's thesis, University of Virginia, 1859), in Student and Alumni Papers, UVA Master's Theses, AL. For other members of the last generation who believed that man had control of his own destiny, see Strange, "The Study of Man, in the Formation of His Character" (master's thesis, University of Virginia, [1854?]), in Student and Alumni Papers, UVA Master's Theses, AL; Pate, "Patriotic Discourse on Local and General History," *Southern Repertory and College Review*, 136. Enthusiasm for man's capabilities to control his environment did not ease the concerns of some young men who insisted that every society must submit to the will of God, not man. Questioning God's authority was an unthinkable act. For the best examples of this perspective, see [Charles S. Stringfellow], "The Christ of History," *Virginia University Magazine* 3 (November 1858): 68–77; [Camm Patterson], "Ideal Perfection," *Virginia University Magazine* 5 (February 1860): 261–63.

17. R. Rives, "Crusades—Some of Their Causes and Effects" (master's thesis, University of Virginia, [1859]), in Student and Alumni Papers, UVA Master's Theses, AL. After reading English history, Lancelot Blackford could not understand how anyone could argue against the inevitability of progress. See Blackford Diary, March 23, 1855, Blackford Family Papers, SHC. Like many Southern intellectuals, young Virginians pointed to the Reformation as the key to unlocking the door of progress. See Robert Beale Davis Diary, March 27, 1868, Beale and Davis Family Papers, SHC.

18. Powell Harrison, "A Few Remarks on 'The Perpetuity of the Union'" (master's thesis, University of Virginia, 1855), in Student and Alumni Papers, UVA Master's Theses, AL. For a similar view of Greek history, see Edwin Taliaferro, "The Poetry of Greece" (master's thesis, University of Virginia, 1855), in Student and Alumni Papers, UVA Master's Theses, AL; John Brown Magruder, "The Greek Myths—Their Origins and Development" (master's thesis, University of Virginia, 1860), in Student and Alumni Papers, UVA Master's Theses, AL. Other members of the last generation found reason to hope for the future after looking at the past, including R. M. T. Hunter Jr. in "On the Advantages of Historical Study" (master's thesis, University of Virginia, [1860?]), in Student and Alumni Papers, UVA Master's Theses, AL.

19. David Hunter Strother, *A Virginia Yankee in the Civil War: The Diaries of David Hunter Strother*, ed. Cecil D. Eby Jr. (Chapel Hill: University of North Carolina Press, 1961), 22. "Religion in the University of VA.," *The Review* (Charlottesville), May 8, 1860, p. 2.

20. [James McDowell Graham], "The Worship of Nature," *Virginia University Magazine* 3 (June 1859): 515–16.

21. Ibid. For a more forceful argument against utilitarianism, see John Hampden Chamberlayne, "Essay on American Literature" (master's thesis, University of Virginia, 1858), in Student and Alumni Papers, UVA Master's Theses, AL; S. Smith, "The Development of Society," (master's thesis, University of Virginia, 1858), in Student and Alumni Papers, UVA Master's Theses, AL. Young Virginians saw an intimate connection between aesthetics and morality. For their general observations on this relationship, see R. Herbert Harris, "Essay" (master's thesis, University of Virginia, 1860), in Student and Alumni Papers, UVA Master's Theses, AL; Strange, "The Study of Man, in the Formation of His Character," (master's thesis, University of Virginia, [1854?]) in Student and Alumni Papers, UVA Master's Theses, AL.

22. Henry M. Mathews, "Poetry in America" (master's thesis, University of Virginia, 1854), in Student and Alumni Papers, UVA Master's Theses, AL.

23. It is striking that so few members of the last generation wrote or debated about the institution of slavery in their literary societies or student publications. Those who delved into the subject offered generic defenses of the institution, insisting that the South was a morally and intellectually superior land while Northern workers were brutalized by Yankee capitalists who only cared about the almighty dollar. In his debating society at the University of Virginia, William Roane Aylett, the son of a prominent King William County slaveholder, claimed that Ohio, without slavery as a check to foreign immigration, had become a "stagnant pool whose green and slimy surface was never disturbed, save by the contortions of the reptiles beneath." Throughout his compara-

tive speech on the North and the South, Aylett, like most Southerners, was obsessed with rank and reputation, always careful, because of the dictates of honor, to demonstrate the superiority of life in Dixie. Opinion in the last generation mirrored Aylett's ideas, for very few young men idealized life in the Old Dominion as an organic social system. Moreover, they did not see themselves struggling against the modern world. They wanted to become leaders of it. The best representations of the last generation's views on slavery include Aylett, "Essay on Slavery," [n.d.], Aylett Family Papers, VHS; and Buchanan, "Is Slavery Right Per Se." The last generation's view of the South as a distinctly Christian civilization receives a more detailed treatment in chapter 3.

24. In confronting the issue of Southern distinctiveness, Lewis P. Simpson has made an invaluable contribution by showing how the South existed as a modern slave society within a capitalist world. He refuses to describe the South as feudalistic or middle class, terms that have largely defined the two opposing camps in this debate. He offers, instead, a different approach that focuses on what he calls the concept of the Mind of Man over the Mind of God. Simpson argues that Northern intellectuals embraced the Mind of Man, a reflection of their commitment to the self that caused them to experience a feeling of alienation from their own communities. Their Southern counterparts, because of their commitment to the master-slave relationship and its attendant hierarchical relations, refused to take a position that placed them in opposition to their community. As proslavery thought matured, they increasingly supported a view of society that was organic in nature. The best elaboration of this point can be found in Simpson's *The Dispossessed Garden: Pastoral and History in Southern Literature* (Athens: University of Georgia Press, 1975). For a sensitive and useful discussion of Simpson's views, see Elizabeth Fox-Genovese and Eugene D. Genovese, "The Cultural History of Southern Slave Society: Reflections on the Work of Lewis P. Simpson," in *American Letters and the Historical Consciousness: Essays in Honor of Lewis P. Simpson*, ed. J. Gerald Kennedy and Daniel Mark Fogel (Baton Rouge: Louisiana State University Press, 1987), 15–41. While I adhere to the basic contours of Simpson's argument, I find a subtle difference in how the last generation approached the issue of the Mind of Man and the Mind of God. Young Virginians believed that man must not see himself as the arbiter of moral truth. At the same time, they insisted that man was the master of his own intellectual world and that he had been empowered by God to discover the mysteries of the universe. This crucial distinction helps explains how the last generation could be enthusiastic boosters of progress and could at the same time believe that the South, unlike the North, remained fixed to its Christian moorings.

25. [Louthan], "Progress," *Virginia University Magazine*, 451.

26. Blackford Diary, March 23, 1855, Blackford Family Papers, SHC.

27. Blackford Diary, November 2, 1854, Blackford Family Papers, SHC. On Blackford's ideas about literature, see Lancelot Blackford, "Advantages of Fictitious Reading" (master's thesis, University of Virginia, 1860), and his "Importance of Classical Education" (master's thesis, University of Virginia, 1860), both in Student and Alumni Papers, UVA Master's Theses, AL.

28. For a masterful treatment of the ethic of honor, see Bertram Wyatt-Brown, *Southern Honor: Ethics and Behavior in the Old South* (New York: Oxford University Press,

1982). Significantly, the connection between progress and honor is not explored by Wyatt-Brown in this invaluable study. He is more concerned with how honor shaped private behavior, but he also offers a persuasive explanation regarding honor's role in shaping the South's sectional battles with the North leading up to the Civil War.

CHAPTER TWO

1. Henry Clay Pate, *The American Vade Mecum; or, The Companion of Youth, and Guide to College* (Cincinnati: Morgan, 1852), 68–76. For a survey of Pate's life, see "H. Clay Pate," in John Lipscomb Johnson, *The University Memorial: Biographical Sketches of Alumni of the University of Virginia Who Fell in the Confederate War* (Baltimore: Turnbull Brothers, 1871), 578–90.

2. An individual's place in the social order played an important role in shaping personal self-esteem in the South. See Steven M. Stowe, *Intimacy and Power in the Old South: Ritual in the Lives of the Planters* (Baltimore: Johns Hopkins University Press, 1987), 252. Oscar and Mary F. Handlin have found that the colleges in nineteenth-century America turned young boys into "gentlemen," but they did not prepare them for a career suitable to their social position. The jarring gap between reality and expectations caused a great deal of frustration among young people throughout the country. They wanted universities to become vehicles of social mobility. See the Handlins' *The American College and American Culture: Socialization as a Function of Higher Education* (New York: McGraw-Hill, 1970), 22, 24. On the tension between age groups when the elders hold a disproportionate amount of power, see E. Anthony Rotundo, *American Manhood: Transformations in Masculinity from the Revolution to the Modern Era* (New York: Basic Books, 1993), 38; F. Musgrove, *Youth and the Social Order* (Bloomington: Indiana University Press, 1965), 125–26.

3. Robert P. Sutton makes a strong case that slaveholders in late–Jeffersonian Virginia, the parents of the last generation, blamed their personal struggles and the state's general decline on outside economic forces. To attack the state's ruling class would be an assault on many of the men who were idolized for their participation in the American Revolution. That was an unthinkable step for most Virginians. See Sutton's "Nostalgia, Pessimism, and Malaise: The Doomed Aristocrat in Late–Jeffersonian Virginia," *Virginia Magazine of History and Biography* 76 (January 1986): 46–47. The last generation, on the other hand, held the leaders of their parents' age group to the standard set by the Revolutionary heroes and found them accountable for the state's demise. The question of Virginia's decline also took on new relevance and urgency during the political sectionalism of the 1850s for young Virginians who wanted a better reputation for the Commonwealth to counter claims of Southern backwardness.

4. See n. 7 of the introduction.

5. Matthew F. Maury, *Address Delivered before the Literary Societies of the University of Virginia, on the 28th June, 1855* (Richmond: H. K. Ellyson, 1855), 11–13.

6. "The Fourth of July," *Lexington Gazette and General Advertiser,* July 9, 1857, p. 2; Jubal A. Early, "To the Voters of the Counties of Franklin, Henry, and Patrick," July 20, 1850, Scrapbook, Jubal A. Early Papers, Library of Congress, Washington D.C.; James

W. Massie, *An Address Delivered before the Society of Alumni of the Virginia Military Institute, July 3rd, 1857* (Richmond: MacFarlane and Fergusson, 1857), 34. Old Fogies also worried that young people, in their enthusiasm for change, might lead Virginia down the road of radical individualism. See B. J. Barbour, "Address: Delivered before the Literary Societies of the Virginia Military Institute" (July 4, 1854), *Southern Literary Messenger* 20 (September 1854): 515.

7. "The Education System of Prussia," *Hampden Sydney Magazine* 1 (June 1859): 227.

8. Gray Carroll, "Essay on the Utilitarian Spirit of the Present Day as Affecting Our Literature" (master's thesis, University of Virginia, 1859), in Student and Alumni Papers, UVA Master's Theses, AL; William R. Aylett, [Speech to Jefferson Society], [1850–52], Aylett Family Papers, AL; "A Common Mistake," *Virginia University Magazine* 2 (April 1858): 180. For a similar opinion, see R. M. T. Hunter Jr., "On the Advantages of Historical Study" (master's thesis, University of Virginia, [1860?]), in Student and Alumni Papers, UVA Master's Theses, AL.

9. Franklin Minor, "Address to the Virginia State Agriculture Society," *Southern Planter* 15 (December 1855): 371–72. In a similar message from the adult community, Matthew F. Maury reminded the students at the University of Virginia not to embark on the "sea of life" without relying on the advice of the "old mariner." See his *Address Delivered before the Literary Societies of the University of Virginia*, 6, 7.

10. The editor of the *Southern Churchman* worried that young people were too outspoken and had forgotten their proper place. "It is sinful to say of any man 'he is old' — obsolete. The proper inquiry is: is he active, cheerful, benevolent, kind-hearted, contented, diligent in his labors, waiting for the coming of the Lord?" See "Growing Old," *Southern Churchman*, March 29, 1861, p. 1. The "fastness of Young America" put mothers, fathers, and professors on alert, for many adults worried about the stability of the household and the security of parental authority. Irreverence toward adults did occasionally surface, usually in the form of a satire, thus giving substance to adult claims that young people were impudent scamps. In the *Hampden Sydney Magazine*, a student using the name "Nigidius" mocked his elders when he wrote in 1859: "The old folks, who have been distanced in the march now and then call out to us about young men and women. But these good people are behind the times in more respects than one, and we pardon them for using the language of by-gone days." "Nigidius's" lack of decorum must have contributed to the perception that the family was in crisis in the 1850s. See "Nigidius," "The Rising Generation," *Hampden Sydney Magazine* 1 (March 1859): 128. Also on the fastness of Virginia youth, see "A Word to the Boys," *Charlottesville Advocate*, March 16, 1860, p. 1; "Old Age," *Southern Churchman*, March 29, 1861, p. 4.

11. Henry Smith Carter, "Glory and Shame of Virginia," *Southern Repertory and College Review* 3 (June 1854): 204. For additional critiques of Virginia's political class by the last generation, see Alexander S. Pendleton, "Cincinnati Oration," July 2, 1857, Ellinor Porcher Gadsden Papers, W&L; J. H. Halley, "Proscription of the Clergy," *Southern Repertory and College Review* 4 (January 1855): 34.

12. Glenn C. Altshuler and Stuart M. Blumin remind us that the political engagement of Americans varied over time during the nineteenth century and that skepticism over

partisan electoral politics sometimes prevailed. Their observations, while overstated in places, help explain the last generation's schizophrenic relationship with politics. Those Americans with deep religious sensibilities and those trying to obtain middle-class respectability, like young Virginians, were often the first to become disillusioned with party politics. See Altshuler and Blumin's *Rude Republic: Americans and Their Politics in the Nineteenth Century* (Princeton: Princeton University Press, 2000). On the ugly and inept politics of railroad building in Virginia, see John Majewski, *A House Dividing: Economic Development in Pennsylvania and Virginia before the Civil War* (Cambridge: Cambridge University Press, 2000). There are countless examples of the last generation's laments about a system that only promoted second-class politicians, whose rise to power depended less on virtue and intelligence and more on patronage and partisanship. For some of the best, see Alexander S. Pendleton, "Cincinnati Oration," July 2, 1857, Ellinor Porcher Gadsden Papers, W&L; Sam Davis to Peachy Breckinridge, May 8, 1858, Breckinridge Family Papers, AL; Robert T. Scott to Fanny (Carter) Scott, February 23, 1857, Keith Family Papers, VHS; John L. Buchanan, "The Conflicts of Parties," *Southern Repertory and College Review*, 140–44; Editors' Table, "The University and Its Politics," *Virginia University Magazine* 4 (May 1860): 461–62; James E. B. Stuart to Bettie Hairston, March 7, [1853], in "J. E. B. Stuart's Letters to His Hairston Kin, 1850–1855," ed. Peter W. Hairston, *North Carolina Historical Review* 6 (July 1974): 294.

13. James DeWitt Hankins to George Duffield, January 24, 1860, Hankins Family Papers, VHS. Disillusionment with mass politics turned a few young Virginians to the Know-Nothing Party. William Cabell explained to his diary how the Know-Nothing Party would purify the political system. See his diary entry for March 22, 1855, Cabell Family Papers, AL.

14. Scholars who have detected the rise of an antiparty spirit in the 1850s South include Christopher J. Olsen, *Political Culture and Secession in Mississippi: Masculinity, Honor, and the Antiparty Tradition, 1830–1860* (New York: Oxford University Press, 2000); George Rable, *The Confederate Republic: A Revolution against Politics* (Chapel Hill: University of North Carolina Press, 1994). On the slaveholders' critique of Jacksonian politics and their distinct view of republicanism, see Lacy K. Ford Jr., *Origins of Southern Radicalism: The South Carolina Upcountry, 1800–1860* (New York: Oxford University Press, 1988), 288–89.

15. Edmund Ruffin quoted in Rable, *The Confederate Republic*, 17.

16. Buchanan, "The Conflict of Parties," *Southern Repertory and College Review*, 142; Rable, *The Confederate Republic*, 300.

17. John Lee Buchanan, "Speech before Calliopean and Hermesian Societies at Emory and Henry College," January 10, 1855, in John B. May, "The Life of John Lee Buchanan" (Ph.D. diss., University of Virginia, 1937), 11.

18. "Editors' Table," *Virginia University Magazine* 4 (March 1860): 336.

19. William T. Kinzer Diary, January 11, 1856, William T. Kinzer Papers, VHS.

20. George W. Turner to Charles W. Turner, May 10, 1856, George W. Turner Papers, DU.

21. Maury, *Address Delivered before the Literary Societies of the University of Virginia*, 10–11.

22. Pate, *American Vade Mecum*, 170–73.

23. "Southern Education for Southern Youth," *Hampden Sydney Magazine* 1 (March 1859): 81.

24. "State Aid to Our College," *Hampden Sydney Magazine* 2 (January 1860): 41; "The Future of the South," *Hampden Sydney Magazine* 2 (April 1860): 182.

25. *Catalogue of the University of Virginia, Session of 1860–61* (Richmond: Chas. H. Wynne, 1861), 36–37, 42–43.

26. Lancelot Blackford to his cousin, February 10, 1855, Blackford Family Papers, SHC; W. F. Shepherd to Genl. Cocke, May 1, 1861, in *Bulletin of Fluvanna County Historical Society* 38 (October 1984): 15. For more examples of the last generation's experiencing financial hardship while attending school, see Kinzer Diary, September 19, 1857, William T. Kinzer Papers, VHS; Greenlee Davidson to his father, October 11, 1855, and December 10, 1855, in *Captain Greenlee Davidson, C.S.A.: Diary and Letters, 1851–1863*, ed. Charles W. Turner (Verona, Va.: McClure Press, 1975), 20–22; James E. B. Stuart to his father, July 22, 1851, in *The Letters of Major General James E. B. Stuart*, ed. Adele H. Mitchell (n.p.: Mosby Historical Society, 1990), 36–37; Henry Wilkins Coons to Andrew Jackson Coons, May 31, 1860, Coons Family Papers, VHS.

27. Richard H. Bagby to Bennette M. Bagby, [ca. 1859], Bennette M. Bagby Papers, DU. Parents frequently reminded members of the last generation that God dictated that children respect and honor their mothers and fathers. This message undermined any capacity to rebel against domestic patriarchy. See J. H. Davis to "My Dear Boy," July 27, 1855, Beale and Davis Family Papers, SHC.

28. [Henry Herbert Harris], "New Preachment from an Old Text," *Virginia University Magazine* 3 (May 1859): 445; [Carter M. Louthan], "The Present and the Past," *Virginia University Magazine* 4 (January 1860): 170.

29. See tables 2 and 4 in the appendix.

30. James DeWitt Hankins to John H. Hankins, February 5, 1860, Hankins Family Papers, VHS.

31. Philip Cabell to William Cabell, November 19, 1854, and March 11, 1855, Cabell Family Papers, AL. In her study of Virginia's planter class from 1790 to 1860, Lorraine Eva Holland discovered that opportunities for wealth and status were in "nontraditional occupations." An aspiring youth would "have to direct banks, finance internal improvements, run merchant mills and snuff factories." In fact, many fathers realized that their sons faced a grim future in the Old Dominion as tobacco farmers. See Holland's "Rise and Fall of the Ante-bellum Virginia Aristocracy: A Generational Analysis," (Ph.D diss., University of California Irvine, 1980), 379, 398.

32. Confusion existed as to what constituted adulthood since it was not immediately conferred at a certain age. Age-differentiated stages of life remained elastic until the twentieth century in the United States. Before the Civil War, the term "youth" could apply to anyone between the ages of sixteen and thirty. Admittance to the adult community did not come automatically when one turned eighteen or twenty-one, thus creating a fuzzy situation for young men in their twenties who felt they were in limbo. After graduating from the University of Virginia in 1854, for instance, twenty-one-year-old William R. Aylett still did not consider himself a man. To the local temperance

organization he admitted "that unlike most of you, I am not yet physically or mentally a man, and have not had my mind yet influenced and matured by the observations and experience of age, and the calm reflection of manhood." See William R. Aylett, "Temperance Speech," 1853, Aylett Family Papers, AL. On the blurred age distinctions in nineteenth-century America, see Winthrop D. Jordan, "Searching for Adulthood in America," in *Adulthood*, ed. Erik H. Erikson (New York: W. W. Norton, 1976), 192; Howard P. Chudacoff, *How Old Are You? Age Consciousness in American Culture* (Princeton: Princeton University Press, 1989), 9–28.

33. See table 13 in the appendix.

34. See table 5 in the appendix.

35. [Charles S. Stringfellow], "Fixed Purpose, and Fixed Principles of Action," *Virginia University Magazine* 3 (November 1858): 172. For other members of the last generation who found the transition to adulthood emotionally difficult, see Robert Beale Davis Diary, February 18, 1856, Beale and Davis Family Papers, SHC; Carter Nelson Minor letter book, March 27, 1861, James Fontaine Minor Collection, AL; Henry W. Coons, "Passing Away," December 4, 1858, Coons Family Papers, VHS; [Walter G. Jones], "Woman vs. Success," *Virginia University Magazine* 3 (November 1858): 61–62; James DeWitt Hankins to Virginia Wilson Hankins, April 28, 1858, Hankins Family Papers, VHS.

36. The inability to find suitable employment in Virginia created overwhelming financial pressures for many of these young men, some of whom drowned in debt when they graduated from college. Too many members of the last generation could sympathize with George Woodville Latham's plight after one year at the University of Virginia. Only twenty-three years old and living in his native Lynchburg, he wished "I were dead — *to my creditors* — I think I could do something if people at every corner would quit poking their d—nable 'little bills' in my face." He planned "to turn knave and marry a fortune in self-defence — instead of making one like an honest gentleman." While residing in southwest Virginia, William Kinzer reported a similar situation to his diary in 1858, exclaiming that "life looks dreary, dark, forsaken! I am in debt three or four hundred dollars and know not how the sum may be canceled." To earn the necessary funds, he decided to move to "some of the Western States or Territories" within the next six months. Kinzer followed through on his promise and went to Kansas shortly thereafter, only to return to Virginia in less than a year without a significant improvement in his finances. On Latham and Kinzer, see George Woodville Latham to George William Bagby, October 7, 1853, Bagby Family Papers, VHS; Kinzer Diary, December 15, 1858, William T. Kinzer Papers, VHS. For other members of the last generation who faced financial difficulties after college, see Davis Diary, April 29, 1856, Beale and Davis Papers, SHC.

37. See table 4 in the appendix.

38. J. E. B. Stuart to Bettie Hairston, October 28, [1853], in "J. E. B. Stuart's Letters to His Hairston Kin," *North Carolina Historical Review*, 304.

39. Robert T. Scott to Fanny (Carter) Scott, March 1, 1860, Keith Family Papers, VHS; Lawrence Slaughter Marye to William R. Aylett, December 9, 1856, Aylett Fam-

ily Papers, VHS. [Hodijah Lincoln Meade], "Legal Ethics," *Virginia University Magazine* 4 (November 1859): 88.

40. "Address," *Randolph-Macon Magazine* 2 (June 1852): 255, 259.

41. Alfred H. Jackson, "Valedictorian Speech," *Lexington Gazette and General Advertiser*, July 9, 1857, p. 2.

42. See table 9 in the appendix.

43. Abram David Pollock, "Thomas Gordon Pollock, a Biography, 1830–1860," 4:205–6, Abram David Pollock Papers, SHC.

44. Thomas Gordon Pollock to his mother, October 27, 1860, Abram David Pollock Papers, SHC. James DeWitt Hankins offers an insightful commentary on why young Virginians left for the Southwest. See his letter to his father, February 5, 1860, Hankins Family Papers, VHS. For additional examples of men of the last generation who fled Virginia for opportunity in the West, see Andrew Jackson Coons to Henry Wilkins Coons, November 8, 1860, Coons Family Papers, VHS; Henry Clay Pate to his mother, April 8, 1856, John L. Johnson Papers, SHC; Richard Hobson Bagby to Bennette M. Bagby, March 8, 1861, Bennette M. Bagby Papers, DU; Kinzer Diary, December 15, 1858, William T. Kinzer Papers, VHS.

45. Hill Carter, "Address of Hill Carter, Esq.," *Southern Planter* 20 (May 1860): 272.

46. Barbour, "Address," *Southern Literary Messenger*, 518. Some older Virginians recognized that young people faced a difficult future in Virginia. A writer for the *Southern Literary Messenger* sympathetically wrote: "Although her sons are just as capable now as their fathers were, they have not the same field for labour which they had; the country has outgrown her, and she no longer occupies, either really or comparatively, her former position or influence. Her sons have migrated to other states, and many have risen to honours, which it may fairly be asserted they would never have obtained at home." See "History of Richmond," *Southern Literary Messenger* 18 (February 1852): 98.

47. Robert L. Dabney, "Co-operation: Something for Virginians to Read," *Central Presbyterian*, October 31, 1857, in *Discussions: Evangelical and Theological* (London: Banner of Truth Trust, 1967), 171, 174.

48. "A Common Mistake," *Virginia University Magazine* 2 (April 1858): 178. Parental pressure sometimes encouraged young men to desire public acclaim as proof of familial loyalty and pride. See James DeWitt Hankins to John H. Hankins, July [?], 1858, Hankins Family Papers, VHS.

49. Maury, "Address Delivered before the Literary Societies of the University of Virginia," 10. A concerned alumnus of Emory and Henry College, writing in the university's literary magazine, chastised young people for choosing professional careers, particularly the law, over manual pursuits. "Frequently," he said, ". . . young men when permitted to grow up to the age of discretion without any undue bias towards a professional life, greatly misguide in selecting the Law." He thought most young people resorted to the law as a "speedy and easy way to get rich." See "Alumnus," "The Law," *Southern Repertory and College Review* 2 (December 1852): 168–71. For a similar warning to the students of Emory and Henry, see "D.," "Agricultural Resources of S.W. Virginia," *Southern Repertory and College Review* 2 (October 1852): 69–70.

50. "Young Men," *Christian Intelligencer*, July 19, 1858, p. 3.

51. Willoughby Newton, "Address," *Southern Planter* 13 (March 1853): 6; Barbour, "Address," *Southern Literary Messenger*, 517. For a similar opinion, see Minor, "Address to the Virginia State Agricultural Society," 377.

52. John H. Chamberlayne, "Essay on American Literature" (master's thesis, University of Virginia, 1858), in Student and Alumni Papers, UVA Master's Theses, AL. For a similar opinion, see John Lee Buchanan, "Oration Delivered before the Calliopean Society of Emory and Henry College," June 9, 1858, in May, "The Life of John Lee Buchanan," 46–47. Young Virginians were careful to distinguish between a desire for fame, which they considered to be a defect in the Virginian character, and youthful ambition, which they almost always praised. A discussion of ambition can be found in chapter 3.

53. For a discussion of the South's work ethic, or lack thereof, see David Bertelson, *The Lazy South* (New York: Oxford University Press, 1967).

54. Lewis Livingston, "To Christopher Quandary," *Southern Planter* 16 (August 1856): 230–31.

CHAPTER THREE

1. Alexander S. Pendleton, "The Cincinnati Oration," July 2, 1857, Ellinor Porcher Gadsden Papers, W&L.

2. Ibid. I disagree with Pendleton's biographer, W. G. Bean, who believes the young man was infatuated with the cavalier tradition. Despite our interpretive differences, I consider Bean's study to be first rate. See his *Stonewall's Man: Sandie Pendleton* (Chapel Hill: University of North Carolina Press, 1959), 12.

3. The traits that young Virginians assigned to the Christian gentleman correspond to Gail Bederman's description of antebellum middle-class identity. See her *Manliness and Civilization: A Cultural History of Gender and Race in the United States, 1880–1917* (Chicago: University of Chicago Press, 1995), 11, 12. Robert B. Bonner unravels the complex attitudes toward the cavalier ideal and concludes that the cavaliers of Southern literature "were more often than not objects of humor, not subjects to emulate." For his discussion of the decline of the cavalier image in Virginia during the 1850s, see "Roundheaded Cavaliers? The Context and Limits of a Confederate Racial Project," *Civil War History* 48 (March 2002): 38. As early as the 1830s, a few Virginia novelists, most notably John Pendleton Kennedy, mocked Virginia's aristocrats for their pretentious manners and quixotic outlook. Most novelists continued to idealize the Commonwealth as the land of the chivalrous aristocrat. Young Virginians wrote very little about writers from their native state, except to complain about the lack of important novelists. Popular literature, with its emphasis on the romantic cavalier, must not have offered an authentic rendition of their society. For a survey of Virginia novelists and their work, see Ritchie Devon Watson Jr., *The Cavalier in Virginia Fiction* (Baton Rouge: Louisiana State University Press, 1985); on Kennedy and William A. Caruthers specifically, see 177–224.

4. The best discussion of the cavalier tradition as an expression of Christian virtue

can be found in Eugene D. Genovese, "The Chivalric Tradition in the Old South," *Sewanee Review* 108 (Spring 2000): 180–98.

5. "Hansford," *Virginia University Magazine* 1 (June 1857): 282.

6. Genovese, "The Chivalric Tradition in the Old South," 180–98 (from unpaginated online version).

7. Tension over ambition is explored by Stephen M. Stowe. See his *Intimacy and Power in the Old South: Ritual in the Lives of the Planters* (Baltimore: Johns Hopkins University Press, 1987), 155–56.

8. Ibid. For an example of a last-generation critique of the aristocratic character of Virginia calling for reform, see [Lancelot Minor Blackford], "The Past and the Present," *Virginia University Magazine* 4 (February 1860): 257–58. Blackford was among the members of the last generation who implored their fellow youths to attack life, to achieve through sustained effort, and to avoid extravagance; see Lancelot Blackford Diary, October 27, 1854, Blackford Family Papers, VHS; [Charles S. Stringfellow] "Fixed Purpose, and Fixed Principles of Action," *Virginia University Magazine* 3 (January 1859): 172–81; "Life and Its Mission," *Hampden Sydney Magazine* 2 (October 1860): 289–94; [James McDowell Graham], "Genius," *Virginia University Magazine* 5 (May 1859): 434–42; [William M. Radford], "Success in Life," *Virginia University Magazine* 4 (November 1859): 82–86; Archer Anderson to Mary Anne (Mason) Anderson, January 2, 1859, Mason Family Papers, VHS; William Cabell Diary, December 6, 1857, and March 20, 1859, Cabell Family Papers, AL; John Hampden Chamberlayne, "Essay on American Literature" (master's thesis, University of Virginia, 1858), in Student and Alumni Papers, UVA Master's Theses, AL.

9. William Blackford to Mary Blackford, May 8, 1853, Blackford Family Papers, SHC.

10. Henry Smith Carter, "Glory and Shame of Virginia," *Southern Repertory and College Review* 3 (June 1854): 203–4.

11. William R. Aylett, [no title or date], Aylett Family Papers, AL.

12. Hugh Blair Grigsby, *The Virginia Convention of 1776: A Discourse Delivered before the Virginia Alpha of the Phi Beta Kappa Society, in the Chapel of William and Mary College* (Richmond: J. W. Randolph, 1855), 38, 39, 40. A summary of Van Zant's speech can be found in "Editorial Correspondence," *Richmond Whig*, June 29, 1854, p. 2. For an additional critique of the cavalier image, see "How to Make Love," *Abingdon Democrat*, June 11, 1859, p. 1; Henry Wise, "Gov. Wise's Oration, at Lexington, Va., 4th July 1856," *Southern Literary Messenger* 23 (July 1856): 9. One older Virginian, James Baron Hope, insisted that young men should acknowledge their cavalier heritage as the source of Virginia exceptionalism in comparison to Northern Puritanism. Hope acknowledged that the rigid hierarchy and aristocratic ease long associated with the cavalier way of life had passed during the American Revolution. In other words, he did not employ the cavalier image to shape the morals and manners of young men. With an eye on the 1860 presidential election, he equated the cavalier tradition with states' rights and the defense of slavery. See his *Poem and Address: Delivered on the First Annual Meeting of the Society of the "Old Boys of Hampton Academy," July, 1860* (Richmond: Wm. H. Clemitt, 1861), 10, 13–14, 18.

13. "The Age of Chivalry," *Jefferson Monument Magazine* 2 (June 1851): 263; "Notes on Modern History," in University of Virginia Professor M. Schele de Vere Class, Notes by Don Peter Halsey of Lynchburg, Virginia, a student at the University of Virginia, 1854–56, in Student and Alumni Papers: Lecture Notebooks, 1827–1882, box 3, AL; "Notes on Modern History," in University of Virginia Professor M. Schele de Vere Class, Notes by David Watson of Louisa, Virginia, a student at the University of Virginia, 1852–55, in Student and Alumni Papers: Lecture Notebooks, 1827–1882, box 3, AL.

14. George B. Forgie, *Patricide in the House Divided: A Psychological Interpretation of Lincoln and His Age* (New York: W. W. Norton, 1979), 8.

15. James DeWitt Hankins to Virginia Wilson Hankins, March 29, 1857, and to John H. Hankins, July [?], 1858, Hankins Family Papers, VHS. For a similar view of ambition, see Robert T. Scott to Fanny (Carter) Scott, November 23, 1857, Keith Family Papers, VHS. For another favorable appraisal of ambition, see "Ambition," *Virginia University Magazine* 3 (November 1858): 80–83.

16. Henry Clay Pate, *The American Vade Mecum; or, The Companion of Youth and Guide to College* (Cincinnati: Morgan, 1852), 32–33.

17. Autograph book of James M. Foreman of Charlestown, Virginia, 1851–52, Student and Alumni Papers, AL; autograph book of Cary Selden Alexander of Jefferson County, Virginia, 1854–55, Student and Alumni Papers, AL.

18. Henry Coons, "The Noble and Ambitious Youth," June 8, 1858, Coons Family Papers, VHS.

19. Walter Monteiro, *Address Delivered before the Neotrophian Society of the Hampton Academy, on the Twenty-eighth of July, 1857* (Richmond: H. K. Ellyson, 1857), 20–21. For other members of the last generation who believed that ambition must come under the influence of Christianity, see [Camm Patterson], "Ideal Perfection," *Virginia University Magazine* 5 (February 1860): 262; Pate, *The American Vade Mecum*, 29–33; Ignatius E. Shumate, "The Victim of Passion," *Southern Repertory and College Review* 4 (December 1856): 216–17.

20. On the potential dangers of ambition for a society dedicated to reciprocal duties, see [Henry Herbert Harris], "New Preachment from an Old Text," *Virginia University Magazine* 3 (May 1859): 445–46.

21. [Radford], "Success in Life," 82–86. Autograph books from the University of Virginia also reveal the growing emphasis on individualism over duty in the last generation. A number of George William Neale's friends, for instance, reminded him to be true to himself, which, in their estimation, could only be done through professional success and a pious life; they did not make a single reference to duty or community obligation. See autograph book of George William Neale of Parkersburg, Virginia, 1857, Student and Alumni Papers, AL.

22. "Young Virginia," *The Kaleidoscope*, February 21, 1855, 44–45.

23. A writer for the *Hampden Sydney Magazine* insisted that young people should make their voices heard on political issues since they might have to guide "the ship of State" through the troubled waters of sectionalism. See "Facts to Be Considered," *Hampden Sydney Magazine* 2 (February 1860): 63–64.

24. "Young Virginia," *The Kaleidoscope*, 44–45.

25. "Moral Discipline in the Family," *Christian Intelligencer*, September 13, 1858, p. 1.

26. "The University of Virginia," *Southern Churchman*, September 24, 1858, p. 2. For those youth cultivators who understood the sins of gambling, drinking, and laziness as proof that young people were emotionally immature and morally stunted, see "Novel Reading: A Word to College Students," *Religious Herald*, January 21, 1858, p. 1; "To Our Young Readers," *Christian Intelligencer*, December 31, 1858, p. 3; "Think for One Hour," *Southern Churchman*, January 13, 1860, p. 1. On the day of prayer for Virginia colleges, see "Prayer for Colleges," *Southern Churchman*, February 27, 1857, p. 2; "Prayer for Colleges," *Religious Herald*, February 11, 1858, p. 2; "Prayer for Colleges," *Religious Herald*, February 17, 1859, p. 2; "Religion in Colleges," *Southern Churchman*, March 2, 1860, p. 2. Members of the adult community impressed upon the last generation to remember that they were at a stage of life that demanded moral vigilance. Pursuing vice and folly at college, young Virginians were told, would create a morally flawed foundation for adulthood. See Hugh Blair Grigsby, *Oration, Delivered before the Students of William and Mary College, July 4, 1859* (n.p.), 14; "Young Men's Christian Associations," *Southern Churchman*, October 19, 1855, p. 2; "A Young Man's Character," *Southern Churchman*, November 30, 1855, p. 4; "The Drinking Usages of Young Men at College," *Southern Churchman*, March 23, 1856, p. 2; "Idle Boys," *Christian Intelligencer*, September 13, 1858, p. 1. Examples of young Virginians who expressed concern about the potential dangers of college life include "Editors' Table," *Virginia University Magazine* 4 (May 1860): 465; David Watson, "The Formation of Character" (master's thesis, University of Virginia, 1855), in Student and Alumni Papers, UVA Master's Theses, AL.

27. Of the last generation, John Henry Stover Funk, a graduate of the Winchester Medical College, captured the defining role that mothers played in the religious upbringing of children. "When ever I am reflecting seriously," he wrote, "the chief thought is, if ever, a *christian*, '*I should like* to [be] *one like* my *mother*.' It was her who taught me to kneel & say 'Our Father in Heaven' nor have I forgot how to pray. & never has that verse been sent but what I thought of you—& ask our Heavenly Father, to lengthen your day in peace & hapiness [*sic*]." See his August 18, 1863, letter to his mother in John Henry Stover Funk Papers, FSNMP. For some young men, the religious influence of mothers was so strong that even death could not break the spiritual bond between parent and child. Lancelot Blackford reported that two University of Virginia students turned to Christ because they wanted to answer the prayers of their "departed mother." See his letter to his mother, March 21, 1859, Blackford Family Papers, SHC. William Cabell also felt the moral influence of his mother after she had gone to her grave. He turned to his sister as his maternal figure and spiritual counselor; [William Cabell] to his sister, September 5, 1858, Cabell Family Papers, AL. Motherly advice also centered on the development of proper secular habits. See Lancelot Blackford to his mother, February 10, 1855, Blackford Family Papers, SHC; Judith Page (Waller) Aylett to William R. Aylett, January 14, 1857, Aylett Family Papers, VHS. On the moral influence of mothers and its importance to young men in school, see "Editors' Table," *Virginia University Magazine* 4 (May 1860): 465.

28. The fathers of the last generation earned a reputation for scandalous behavior when they were young men and students. A Charlottesville newspaper detected a significant change in behavior between the two age groups. "Within the University, dissipation used to prevail to an alarming extent; there was gambling, cock-fighting, broils, and idleness. A Southern student rarely took a diploma. The village used to be nightly the scene of rows and disturbances; there used to be fights between the students and towns people; brickbats used to be actively in motion from dark alleys and corners; citizens' gates used to have [to] be locked; signs hung unsteadily over our merchants' doors: store boxes performed the most vexatious transmigrations; stables were broken up, and the horses after being almost ridden to death, turned loose—perhaps bereft of their toils; glass was broken; public performances were interrupted by volleys of bird-shot; the Square was frequently filled with armed students; they swaggered in bar-rooms; bullied the livery stables; visited the Ragged Mountains and the Shadwell cotton factory. Now—without going into a counter-description—our citizens will bear witness to the extraordinary changes. Not only is Charlottesville totally undisturbed by the young gentlemen of the University; but the University itself—with the occasional exception of a little noise—is one of the most quiet, orderly, peaceable communities that we know of." See "Religion in the University of VA.," *The Review* (Charlottesville), May 8, 1860, p. 2.

29. Maria Louisa Fleet and Benjamin Fleet to Alexander Frederick Fleet, April 29, 1861, in *Green Mount: A Virginia Plantation Family during the Civil War*, ed. Betsy Fleet and John D. P. Fuller, (Lexington: University of Kentucky Press, 1962), 54.

30. John Minor to Lancelot Blackford, December 1, 1859, Blackford Family Papers, SHC.

31. On the influence of Scottish moral philosophy on Southern education, see E. Brooks Holifield, *The Gentlemen Theologians: American Theology in Southern Culture, 1795–1860* (Durham: Duke University Press, 1978), chaps. 5–6.

32. Frederick Rudolph, *The American College and University* (New York: Alfred A. Knopf, 1965), 87, 104; Oscar Handlin and Mary F. Handlin, *The American College and American Culture: Socialization as a Function of Higher Education* (New York: McGraw-Hill, 1970), 3, 23.

33. Richard McIlwaine, *Memories of Three Score Years and Ten* (New York: Neale Publishing Co., 1908), 66.

34. In looking at the masculine experience in the nineteenth century, Donald Yacovone correctly points out the disturbing tendency to see men as having been incapable of forging meaningful relationships that did not involve fighting, drinking, or gambling. Like Yacovone's male abolitionists, young Virginians were not emotionally barren and hypermasculine. See Yacovone's "Abolitionists and the 'Language of Fraternal Love,'" in *Meanings for Manhood: Constructions of Masculinity in Victorian America*, ed. Mark C. Carnes and Clyde Griffen (Chicago: University of Chicago Press, 1990), 85–110. Historians who believe that Southern youth symbolized the rebellious, carefree student who frittered away his college years include Helen Lefkowitz Horowitz, *Campus Life: Undergraduate Cultures from the End of the Eighteenth Century to the Present* (New York:

Alfred A. Knopf, 1987), 27. For those scholars who emphasize aggressiveness and physical prowess as the basis of male friendship in the South, see n. 3 of the introduction.

35. Steven M. Stowe explores this issue in "The Rhetoric of Authority: The Making of Social Values in Planter Family Correspondence," *Journal of American History* 73 (March 1987): 928–30.

36. William S. White, *Sketches of the Life of Captain Hugh A. White of the Stonewall Brigade* (Columbia: South Carolinian Steam Press, 1864), 20–21; autograph book of Cary Selden Alexander of Jefferson County, 1854–55, Student and Alumni Papers, AL. For additional examples of the deep emotional bonds among young Virginians, see autograph book of Bennett Taylor of Jefferson County, 1859, Student and Alumni Papers, AL; Edward B. Smith to William Cabell, June 17, 1855, in Cabell Diary, Cabell Family Papers, AL. The dormitory and boarding houses placed students under the same roof where they tried to replicate aspects of their home life. Many felt at ease discussing spiritual issues within the confines of their own space, away from adult supervision. See Rudolph, *The American College and University*, 97.

37. Autograph book of Cary Selden Alexander, Student and Alumni Papers, AL. Wishes for professional success and warnings to fear God abound in student autograph books. See Edward B. Smith to William Cabell, June 17, 1855, in Cabell Diary, Cabell Family Papers, AL; autograph book of George William Neale, Student and Alumni Papers, AL.

38. George Washington Nelson to Carter Nelson Minor, March 27, 1861, in Carter Nelson Minor letter book, vol. 1, James Fontaine Minor Papers, AL.

39. Mothers, in particular, played a crucial role in fashioning how young Virginians understood the idea of the Christian gentleman. One University of Virginia student reported to his mother that he had befriended a classmate because "his mother must be something like you from the fact that we have been brought up so much alike in most respects." See Lancelot Blackford to Mary Blackford, February 8, 1860, Blackford Family Papers, SHC. In an 1854 public address on temperance, William R. Aylett proclaimed that "there is no influence which makes such good and lasting impression as the mothers—more which survives the lapse of years." See William R. Aylett, "Temperance Address," [1853], Aylett Family Papers, AL. On the role of mothers and the religious instruction of the young, see Philip Greven, *The Protestant Temperament: Patterns of Child-Rearing, Religious Experience, and the Self in Early America* (Chicago: University of Chicago Press, 1977); A. Gregory Schneider, *The Way of the Cross Leads Home: The Domestication of American Methodism* (Bloomington: Indiana University Press, 1993).

40. Focusing on whether Southern religion was becoming more masculine or feminine obscures the modern message of Christianity to young people who saw an intimate connection between elevating character and improving society. The experience of the last generation counters scholarly claims that young men turned to Southern religion once it merged with primal honor. An aggressive, militant expression of Protestantism did not appeal to young people trying to secure bourgeois respectability. Historians also make the mistake of assuming that values such as gentleness, emotion, and compassion were universally seen as distinctively women traits in the antebellum period. My argu-

ment takes issue with the work of Christine Leigh Heyrman; see her *Southern Cross: The Beginnings of the Bible Belt* (New York: Alfred A. Knopf, 1997), 248–49. I differ to a lesser degree with Kurt O. Berends; see his "'Wholesome Reading Purifies and Elevates the Man': The Religious Military Press in the Confederacy," in *Religion and the American Civil War*, ed. Randall M. Miller, Harry S. Stout, and Charles Reagan Wilson (New York: Oxford University Press, 1998), 136, 141.

41. Blackford Diary, December 30, 1854, Blackford Family Papers, SHC. In his memoirs, Blackford reinforced the point that his friend's letter from the University of Virginia played a crucial role in his religious awakening. See Lancelot Blackford Memoirs, Blackford Family Papers, SHC.

42. Blackford Diary, September 12, 1854, Blackford Family Papers, SHC. For other members of the last generation whose spiritual quest was part of a larger personal campaign of self-improvement, see William T. Kinzer Diary, January 1, 1857, William T. Kinzer Papers, VHS; Henry Wilkins Coons, "Early Rising," May 10, 1860, Coons Family Papers, VHS. In trying to build character, young Virginians could become hypercritical to the point of self-destruction. See James DeWitt Hankins to Virginia Wilson Hankins, February 8, 1858, Hankins Family Papers, VHS; undated excerpt from the diary of Randolph Fairfax in Philip Slaughter's *A Sketch of the Life of Randolph Fairfax* (Richmond: Tyler, Allegre and McDaniel, 1864), 10–11, 12, 13.

43. Lancelot Blackford to his mother, December 17, 1854, Blackford Family Papers, SHC. On Blackford's desire to make prayer a more "profitable exercise," see Blackford Diary, October 18, 1854, Blackford Family Papers, SHC. Southerners of all ages regarded time management as extremely important. See Mark M. Smith, *Mastered by the Clock: Time, Slavery, and Freedom in the American South* (Chapel Hill: University of North Carolina Press, 1997), 9.

44. Blackford Diary, November 2, 3, 1854, Blackford Family Papers, SHC.

45. William Blackford to Lancelot Blackford, November 19, 1854, Blackford Family Papers, SHC.

46. Blackford Diary, October 27, 1854, Blackford Family Papers, SHC.

47. Lancelot Blackford to his mother, January 19, 1859, and October 18, 1858, Blackford Family Papers, SHC.

48. "Collegiana," *Virginia University Magazine* 4 (November 1859): 104.

49. Ibid., 264. On the role of the YMCA at the University of Virginia, see Clarence P. Shedd, *Two Centuries of Student Christian Movements: Their Origin and Intercollegiate Life* (New York: Association Press, 1934), 98–100.

50. "Religion in the University of VA.," *The Review*, 2. A similar description of the missionary activity at the University of Virginia can be found in Slaughter, *A Sketch of the Life of Randolph Fairfax*, 14–15. The fascinating details of Hugh A. White's experiences as a religious tract salesman can be found in White, *Sketches of the Life of Captain Hugh A. White*, 17–20.

51. On Bledsoe's visit to Lynchburg, see Lancelot Blackford to his father, November 23, 1857, Blackford Family Papers, SHC.

52. On the secular and religious activities of various YMCAs throughout the state, see "Young Men's Christian Association," *Southern Churchman*, October 19, 1855, p.

2; "Bayard Taylor and the Richmond Young Men's Christian Association," *Richmond Daily Dispatch*, February 10, 1860, p. 2; "Lecture To-Night," *Daily Richmond Enquirer*, December 14, 1860, p. 2; "Young Men's Christian Association," *Lynchburg Daily Virginian*, February 8, 1861, p. 2; "The Young Men's Christian Association," *Richmond Dispatch*, January 4, 1861, p. 1; "Mr. Thompson's Lecture," *Richmond Daily Dispatch*, March 21, 1861, p. 1; "Young Men's Christian Association-Meeting To-Night," *Richmond Daily Dispatch*, February 12, 1861, p. 1; "The Young Men's Christian Association," *Richmond Dispatch*, January 4, 1861, p. 1; "Young Men's Christian Association," *Richmond Whig*, March 26, 1856, p. 3.

53. Beth Barton Schweiger, *The Gospel Working Up: Progress and the Pulpit in Nineteenth-Century Virginia* (New York: Oxford University Press, 2000), 65.

54. "Negro Sunday Schools," *Richmond Whig*, October 15, 1856, p. 3; "Confederation of Young Men's Christian Associations," *Richmond Whig*, July 23, 1856, p. 1. For additional coverage of the YMCA at the University of Virginia, see "Religious Intelligence," *Richmond Daily Dispatch*, February 13, 1860, p. 2; "Religious Intelligence," *Richmond Daily Dispatch*, July 10, 1860, p. 1.

55. "Religion in the University of VA.," *The Review*, 2.

56. Religious statistics for the University of Virginia can be found in "Collegiana," *Virginia University Magazine* 5 (April 1861): 380–81. On student efforts to build a university chapel, see W. F. Shepherd to Genl. Cocke, May 1, 1861, *Bulletin of Fluvanna County Historical Society* 38 (October 1984): 12.

57. Lancelot Blackford to his mother, January 21, 1856, Blackford Family Papers, SHC.

58. Aylett, "Temperance Address," Aylett Family Papers, AL.

59. On the origins and development of muscular Christianity, see Clifford Putney, *Muscular Christianity: Manhood and Sports in Protestant America, 1880–1920* (Cambridge, Mass.: Harvard University Press, 2001).

60. "Play," *Virginia University Magazine* 5 (December 1860): 113.

61. John Minor to Lancelot Blackford, March 4, 1860, Blackford Family Papers, SHC; Lancelot Blackford to his mother, October 18, 1858, Blackford Family Papers, SHC; Alexander Frederick Fleet to Benjamin Robert Fleet, October 3, 1860, and October 29, 1860, in *Green Mount*, 33, 39.

62. "Play," *Virginia University Magazine*, 113; "Collegiana," *Virginia University Magazine* 5 (January 1860): 202–3. On the rise of exercising in the 1850s, see Harvey Green, *Fit for America: Health, Fitness, Sport, and American Society* (New York: Pantheon Books, 1986), 95–100. The connection between sports and spiritual renewal is treated by Donald J. Mrozek, *Sport and American Mentality, 1880–1910* (Knoxville: University of Tennessee Press, 1983), 4–12.

63. "Religion in the University of VA.," *The Review*, 2.

64. Philip Alexander Bruce, *History of the University of Virginia, 1819–1919* (New York: Macmillan, 1920–21), 3:133–38; Charles Coleman Wall Jr., "Students and Student Life at the University of Virginia, 1825–1861" (Ph.D. diss., University of Virginia, 1978), 255–57. Granting students more autonomy, according to a Charlottesville newspaper, explained the improvement in their moral and manners. "The leaving to the

students themselves to regulate their own habits—has worked out its lesson. What are the results? In the first place, then, we affirm, that as regards [to] good morals, studious habits, the absence of dissipation, the University will compare favorably with any institution in the world." See "Religion in the University of VA.," *The Review*, 2. The strict, authoritarian system of governance broke down at universities across the country, giving way to student autonomy, particularly in regard to religious matters. See Rudolph, *The American College and University*, 104, 106.

65. Ollinger Crenshaw, "General Lee's College: Rise and Growth of Washington and Lee" (typescript, Washington and Lee University, 1973), 1:423.

66. George Junkin, *An Apology for Collegiate Education: Being the Baccalaureate Address, Delivered Commencement Day of Washington College* (Lexington, Va.: n.p. 1851); Francis H. Smith, *Introductory Address to the Corps of Cadets of the Virginia Military Institute, on the Resumption of Academic Duties, September 2, 1856* (Richmond: MacFarlane and Fergusson, 1856), 23; Quoted in Albea Godbold, *The Church College of the Old South* (Durham, N.C.: Duke University Press, 1944), 136. During his summer break from Randolph-Macon College, Richard Bagby, filled with religious enthusiasm, was eager to return home to distribute religious tracts. See his letter to Bennette M. Bagby, May 17, 1859, Bennette M. Bagby Letters, DU.

67. Wall, "Students and Student Life," 128. On student pranks in the 1850s, see "Religion in the University of VA.," *The Review*, 2.

68. William J. Bouwsma, "Christian Adulthood," in *Adulthood*, ed. Erik H. Erikson (New York: W. W. Norton, 1976), 91–92.

69. For those members of the last generation who insisted that an intimate relationship existed between morality, education, and material progress, see W. Dinwiddie, "Essay on the Province and Culture of the Imagination" (master's thesis, University of Virginia, 1854), in Student and Alumni Papers, UVA Master's Theses, AL; Philip B. Cabell, "Essay on Moral Intellectual Excellence" (master's thesis, University of Virginia, 1857), in Student and Alumni Papers, UVA Masters Theses, AL; Lancelot Blackford "Advantages of Fictitious Reading," (master's thesis, University of Virginia, 1860), in Student and Alumni Papers, UVA Master's Theses, AL; David Watson, "Essay on the Formation of Character" (master's thesis, University of Virginia, 1855), in Student and Alumni Papers, UVA Master's Theses, AL.

70. Charles M. Gibbons, "An Essay on Popular Education" (master's thesis, University of Virginia, 1859), in Student and Alumni Papers, UVA Master's Theses, AL.

71. Pate, *The American Vade Mecum*, 75.

72. Craig M. Simpson, *A Good Southerner: The Life of Henry A. Wise of Virginia* (Chapel Hill: University of North Carolina Press, 1985), 151–53; Berkeley Minor and James F. Minor, comps. *Legislative History of the University of Virginia as Set Forth in the Acts of the General Assembly of Virginia, 1802–1927* (n.p.: Rector and Visitors, 1928), 30–34.

73. Simpson, *A Good Southerner*, 152.

74. "Editors' Table," *Virginia University Magazine* 4 (March 1860): 333.

75. "Editors' Table," *Virginia University Magazine* 4 (May 1860): 461–62; Charles S. Venable, *An Address Delivered before the Society of Alumni, of the University of Virginia*,

at *Its Annual Meeting Held in the Public Hall, July 26, 1858* (Richmond: MacFarlane and Fergusson, 1859), 30.

76. Pendleton, "The Cincinnati Oration," July 2, 1857.

77. "College Education in America," *Jefferson Monument Magazine* 2 (May 1851): 228; "Editors' Table," *Virginia University Magazine* 4 (March 1860): 333. On the pressures of American colleges to demonstrate utility to society, see Rudolph, *The American College and University*, 218.

78. "Southern Education for Southern Youth," *Hampden Sydney Magazine*, 82.

79. Student, "University of Virginia," *Richmond Enquirer*, June 29, 1860, p. 1. Students at Virginia universities made frequent pleas for additional state funding for their respective institutions during the 1850s. They rooted their arguments in the assumption that the state's institutions of higher learning could no longer compete with Northern schools. See "State Aid to Our College," *Hampden Sydney Magazine* 2 (January 1860): 41–43; "Endowment of the University," *Virginia University Magazine* 4 (March 1860): 330–34; "The University and Its Politics," *Virginia University Magazine* 4 (May 1860): 461–64; Henry Clay Pate, "Patriotic Discourse on Local and General History," *Southern Repertory and College Review* 2 (December 1852): 143; "William and Mary College," *Southern Churchman*, August 9, 1855, p. 3.

80. I am drawing from Daniel Kilbride's valuable insights into the aspirations of Southern youth and how they fit within a national context. Kilbride, however, does not make the connection to the idea of a Christian gentleman, which I believe served as the vital linkage between Virginia and the North and the rest of the world. See his "Southern Medical Students in Philadelphia, 1800–1861: Science and Sociability in the 'Republic of Medicine,'" *Journal of Southern History* 65 (November 1999): 697–700.

CHAPTER FOUR

1. William R. Aylett, [no title], 1853, Speeches of William R. Aylett, Aylett Family Papers, AL.

2. *The Address of the Southern Rights' Association of the University of Virginia to the Young Men of the South* (Charlottesville: James Alexander, 1851), 4.

3. This argument corresponds with Robert Bonner's in his "Roundhead Cavaliers? The Context and Limits of a Confederate Racial Project," *Civil War History* 48 (March 2002): 36–39. For those historians who emphasize the creation of an ethnic nationalism based on the cavalier and Puritan typology, see Rollin G. Osterweis, *Romanticism and Nationalism in the Old South* (New Haven: Yale University Press, 1949), 42, 52–53, 63; William R. Taylor, *Cavalier and Yankee: The Old South and American National Character* (New York: George Braziller, 1961), 15–18; James M. McPherson, *Is Blood Thicker Than Water? Crises of Nationalism in the Modern World* (New York: Vintage Books, 1998), 45–51.

4. Matthew Page Andrews to Anna Robinson, December 4, 1859, Charles Wesley Andrews Papers, DU. Sentiments of devotion for family fill the letters of the last generation. See John Samuel Apperson Diary, March 9, 1861, John Samuel Apperson Papers, VT; William T. Kinzer Diary, September 26, 1857, William T. Kinzer Papers, VHS;

James DeWitt Hankins to Virginia Wilson Hankins, November 3, 1859, Hankins Family Papers, VHS.

5. William R. Aylett to Alice Roane (Brockenbrough) Aylett, [?] 1860, and May 20, 1860, Aylett Family Papers, VHS.

6. James E. B. Stuart to his cousin, May 7, [1853], in "J. E. B. Stuart's Letters to His Hairston Kin, 1850–1855," ed. Peter W. Hairston, *North Carolina Historical Review* 6 (July 1974): 293.

7. "Mensalia," *Virginia University Magazine* 1 (February 1857): 86–87; "Advantages of an Observatory," *Southern Repertory and College Review* 3 (June 1854): 248–49; "A Glimpse of Natural Wonders," *Southern Repertory and College Review* 3 (June 1854): 254; John Newton Lyle, *A Reminiscence of Lieutenant John Newton Lyle of the Liberty Hall Volunteers*, ed. Charles W. Turner (Roanoke, Va.: Virginia Lithography and Graphics Co., 1987), 5–6.

8. During his travels in Europe, Edwin L. Taliaferro made a point to visit the natural wonders that Byron had described in his writings. See Edwin L. Taliaferro Diary, August 26, 1856, White-Wellford-Taliaferro and Marshall Family Papers, SHC.

9. [James McDowell Graham], "The Worship of Nature," *Virginia University Magazine* 5 (May 1859): 506. For other young Virginians who saw God's supreme powers in nature, see Thomas Underwood Dudley Jr., "Atheism an Impossibility" (master's thesis, University of Virginia, 1858), Student and Alumni Papers, UVA Master's Theses, AL; F. T. Meriwether, "Comparative Philology" (master's thesis, University of Virginia, 1860), in Student and Alumni Papers, UVA Master's Theses, AL; William G. Strange, "The Study of Man, in the Formation of His Character" (master's thesis, University of Virginia, 1854), in Student and Alumni Papers, UVA Master's Theses, AL. See also Stapleton Crutchfield Jr., "July 4, 1855 Oration," Stapleton Crutchfield Jr. Papers, VMI; James DeWitt Hankins, "Essay," [n.d.], Hankins Family Papers, VHS. Young Virginians were reminded by the adult community that scientific discoveries about the inner workings of nature were part of the Creator's plan. See T. C. H., "Musings of a Naturalist: Read before the Young Men's Christian Association of Richmond," *Southern Literary Messenger* 24 (June 1857): 413.

10. William Allen, "Harmony of the Human Mind and the Material Universe" (master's thesis, University of Virginia, 1860), in Student and Alumni Papers, UVA Master's Theses, AL. Many of Allen's peers shared his concerns about the rise of utilitarianism and its detrimental effects on the soul. See John Hampden Chamberlayne, "Essay on American Literature" (master's thesis, University of Virginia, 1858), in Student and Alumni Papers, UVA Master's Theses, AL; Crutchfield, "July 4, 1855 Oration," Stapleton Crutchfield Jr. Papers, VMI; [Graham], "The Worship of Nature," *Virginia University Magazine*, 515–16.

11. Allen, "Harmony of the Human Mind and the Material Universe" (master's thesis, University of Virginia, 1860), in Student and Alumni Papers, UVA Master's Theses, AL. On Allen's military service, see Robert J. Driver Jr., *14th Virginia Cavalry* (Lynchburg: H. E. Howard, 1988), 96.

12. "Abstract of Lectures by Lancelot M. Blackford, 1857," Lancelot Blackford Papers, AL.

13. "Mensalia," *Virginia University Magazine*, 86–87; Archibald M. Smith, "A Republican Government [Is] Most Favorable to the Development of Literature" (master's thesis, University of Virginia, 1857), in Student and Alumni Papers, UVA Master's Theses, AL. For other members of the last generation who believed that imagination, if cultivated properly, could uplift the soul and improve the mind, see Robert T. Scott to Fanny Scott, May 6, 1856, Keith Family Papers, VHS; [Graham], "The Worship of Nature," *Virginia University Magazine*, 503–16; Thomas R. Price Jr., "The Augustan Era of English Literature" (master's thesis, University of Virginia, 1858), in Student and Alumni Papers, UVA Master's Theses, AL; Allen, "Harmony of the Human Mind and the Material Universe" (master's thesis, University of Virginia, 1860), in Student and Alumni Papers, UVA Master's Theses, AL; W. Dinwiddie, "Essay on the Province and Culture of the Imagination" (master's thesis, University of Virginia, 1854), in Student and Alumni Papers, UVA Master's Theses, AL.

14. Summerfield Smith, "The Development of Society" (master's thesis, University of Virginia, 1858), in Student and Alumni Papers, UVA Master's Theses, AL.

15. Lyle, *A Reminiscence of Lieutenant John Newton Lyle*, 5–6.

16. John Lee Buchanan, "Oration Delivered before the Calliopean Society of Emory & Henry College," June 9, 1858, in John B. May, "The Life of John Lee Buchanan" (Ph.D. diss., University of Virginia, 1937), 43; Crutchfield, "July 4, 1855 Oration," Stapleton Crutchfield Jr. Papers, VMI; William Cabell Diary, February 19, 1855, Cabell Family Papers, AL; Alexander S. Pendleton, "Cincinnati Oration," July 2, 1857, Ellinor Porcher Gadsden Papers, W&L. For other examples of nature instilling in the last generation a stronger attachment to Virginia, see John H. Chamberlayne to Lucy Parke (Chamberlayne) Bagby, October 24, 1859, Bagby Family Papers, VHS; Apperson Diary, May 5, 1862, John Samuel Apperson Papers, VT; Kinzer Diary, June 16, 1857, William T. Kinzer Papers, VHS; Edwin Taliaferro Diary, August 26, 29, 1856, White-Wellford-Taliaferro and Marshall Family Papers, SHC; James DeWitt Hankins to [?], [misc. prewar composition], Hankins Family Papers, VHS; Henry Wilkins Coons to [?], February 10, 1860, Coons Family Papers, VHS; Matthew Page Andrews to Anna Robinson, January 20, 1861, Charles Wesley Andrews Papers, DU; James E. B. Stuart to Bettie Hairston, March 23, 1853, in "J. E. B. Stuart's Letters to His Hairston Kin," *North Carolina Historical Review*, 290–91.

17. Jean B. Lee, "Historical Memory, Sectional Strife, and the American Mecca: Mount Vernon, 1783–1853," *Virginia Magazine of History and Biography* 109 (2001): 255–300. Elizabeth R. Varon, *We Mean to Be Counted: White Women and Politics in Antebellum Virginia* (Chapel Hill: University of North Carolina Press, 1998), 124–36.

18. "Jamestown Society," *Richmond Whig*, February 4, 1854, p. 2; "Monumental History and National Recollections," *Virginia University Magazine* 2 (May 1858): 199.

19. "The Grave of Jefferson," *Virginia University Magazine* 1 (February 1857): 83–84.

20. Henry Clay Pate, *The American Vade Mecum; or, The Companion of Youth and Guide to College* (Cincinnati: Morgan, 1852), 113; Lancelot Blackford to Mary Blackford, February 10, 1855, Blackford Family Papers, SHC.

21. Pate, *The American Vade Mecum*, 113.

22. For an example, see "Northern Fanaticism and Northern Colleges," *Richmond Whig*, March 15, 1854, p. 2.

23. Walter Monteiro, *Address Delivered before the Neotrophian Society of the Hampton Academy, on the Twenty-eighth of July, 1857* (Richmond: H. K. Ellyson, 1857), 8–10. For a similar perspective on the rivalry between Northern and Southern education, see "Editors' Table," *Virginia University Magazine* 3 (February 1859): 265–66.

24. Henry E. Shepherd, "The University of Virginia, October, 1860, to April, 1861," *Confederate Veteran* 28 (1920): 302; "Virginia," *Southern Churchman*, March 16, 1860, p. 3. For the most part, relations between students and professors were not contentious, but personal confrontations did arise on occasion, often when a young person perceived that he had been treated unfairly in front of his peers. Joseph Cabell complained in 1855 that Professor William H. McGuffey "is rather rude in [the] classroom in his question[ing]. I happened to be the one on that occasion, & took the opportunity to inform him that he had the 'wrong sow by the ear' — ever since he has been prejudiced against me." Joseph Cabell to William Cabell, May 15, 1855, Cabell Family Papers, AL. A more serious rupture occurred between a Baptist student who charged McGuffey with religious bigotry. See, "Rev. Dr. McGuffey," *Religious Herald*, March 17, 1859, p. 2; "Dr McGuffey — His Colleagues," *Religious Herald*, March 31, 1859, p. 1. In June 1860, students publicly complained that law professors James P. Holcombe and John B. Minor missed too many classes due to illness. See "To the Editors of the Enquirer," *Richmond Enquirer*, June 29, 1860, p.1.

25. Eugene D. Genovese, "Higher Education," in Genovese, *The Southern Front: History and Politics in the Cultural War* (Columbia: University of Missouri Press, 1995), 93.

26. George Junkin, *An Apology for Collegiate Education: Being the Baccalaureate Address, Delivered Commencement Day of Washington College* (Lexington, Va.: n.p., 1851), 3; Rev. C. P. Gadsden, *The Bible, the Only Safe Director of the Activity of the Day: An Address Delivered before the Cadets' Bible Society of the Virginia Military Institute, June 3, 1859* (Richmond: MacFarlane and Fergusson, 1859), 25.

27. Although philosophically a diverse group, all of these men rooted their arguments in traditional Christianity to explain the distinctive nature of Southern society. In his biography of George Fitzhugh, Harvey Wish called these intellectuals "the Virginia militants" because of their rejection of Jeffersonianism and the desire to resurrect religious conservatism in the Old Dominion and the South. Wish, *George Fitzhugh: Propagandist of the Old South* (Baton Rouge: Louisiana State University Press, 1943), 47–53. See also Elizabeth Fox-Genovese and Eugene D. Genovese, "The Divine Sanction of Social Order: Religious Foundations of the Southern Slaveholders' World View," *Journal of the American Academy of Religion* 55 (Summer 1987): 211–29; Eugene D. Genovese, *The Slaveholders' Dilemma: Freedom and Progress in Southern Conservative Thought, 1820–1860* (Columbia: University of South Carolina Press, 1992), 49–54; Neal C. Gillespie, *The Collapse of Orthodoxy: The Intellectual Ordeal of George Frederick Holmes* (Charlottesville: University Press of Virginia, 1972), 75–80; Anne C. Loveland, *Southern Evangelicals and the Social Order, 1800–1860* (Baton Rouge: Louisiana State University Press, 1980), 258–62.

28. Moncure Daniel Conway, *Autobiography, Memories and Experiences of Moncure Daniel Conway* (Boston: Houghton, Mifflin, 1904), 1:71, 224.

29. Edmund Ruffin, "Slavery and Free Labor Described and Compared," *Southern Planter* 20 (January 1860): 11–12.

30. "Notes on Modern History," in University of Virginia Professor M. Schele de Vere Class, Notes by Don Peter Halsey of Lynchburg, Virginia, a student at the University of Virginia, 1854–56, Student and Alumni Papers: Lecture Notebooks, 1827–1882, AL; "Notes on Modern History," in University of Virginia Professor M. Schele de Vere Class, Notes by David Watson of Louisa, Virginia, a student at the University of Virginia, 1852–55, Student and Alumni Papers: Lecture Notebooks, 1827–1882, AL. On the popularity of ancient history among Southerners as a defense of slavery, see Genovese, *The Slaveholders' Dilemma*, 4–5.

31. James DeWitt Hankins to George Duffield, January 24, 1860, Hankins Family Papers, VHS. Similar comparisons between Rome and the United States were made in [Carter M. Louthan], "Progress," *Virginia University Magazine* 3 (May 1859): 452. Powell Harrison argued that the analogy between the United States and Rome did not work. He believed the United States superior in morality, education, refinement, and form of government. See his "A Few Remarks on 'The Perpetuity of the Union'" (master's thesis, University of Virginia, 1855), in Student and Alumni Papers, UVA Master's Theses, AL.

32. "Notebook," by David Watson of Louisa, Virginia, a student at the University of Virginia, 1852–55, Student and Alumni Papers: Lecture Notebooks, 1827–1882, AL. The Christian sensibilities of young Virginians pervaded every aspect of their life. For those who believed that religion and education could not be divorced and that to do so would risk skepticism, see William D. Thomas, "Connections of Political Economy with Natural Theology" (master's thesis, University of Virginia, 1855), in Student and Alumni Papers, UVA Master's Theses, AL; J. B. Thompson, "Religion and Learning in the Middle Ages" (master's thesis, University of Virginia, 1854), in Student and Alumni Papers, UVA Master's Theses, AL; Lancelot M. Blackford, "Advantages of Fictitious Reading" (master's thesis, University of Virginia, 1860), in Student and Alumni Papers, UVA Master's Theses, AL; John H. Timberlake, "Tendency of Science" (master's thesis, University of Virginia, 1858), in Student and Alumni Papers, UVA Master's Theses, AL; Thomas Underwood Dudley Jr., "Atheism an Impossibility" (master's thesis, University of Virginia, 1858), in Student and Alumni Papers, UVA Master's Theses, AL.

33. Quoted in Clarence P. Shedd, *Two Centuries of Student Christian Movements: Their Origin and Intercollegiate Life* (New York: Association Press, 1934), 100.

34. William A. Smith, *Lectures on the Philosophy and Practice of Slavery as Exhibited in the Institution on Domestic Slavery in the United States: With the Duties of Masters to Slavery*, ed. Thomas O. Summers (Nashville: Stevenson and Evans, 1856). For a similar message, see Gadsden, *The Bible, the Only Safe Director of the Activity of the Day*, 25.

35. Apperson Diary, February 8, 1862, John Samuel Apperson Papers, VT; [Lancelot Minor Blackford], "The Past and the Present," *Virginia University Magazine* 4 (February 1860): 259–60. It was not uncommon for members of the last generation who professed faith in one church to attend the services of other denominations. William

T. Kinzer, for example, heard sermons at Methodist, German Reformed, Presbyterian, English Lutheran, Roman Catholic, and Episcopal churches between October 13, 1856, and March 1, 1857. See Kinzer Diary, William T. Kinzer Papers, VHS. On the spirit of interdenominational cooperation in the South, see Eugene D. Genovese and Elizabeth Fox-Genovese, "The Religious Ideals of Southern Slave Society," *Georgia Historical Quarterly* 70 (Spring 1986): 12–13.

36. "Evidence of Christianity," *Southern Literary Messenger* 18 (August 1852): 473.

37. [James M. Boyd], "Roman Catholicism and Free Institutions," *Virginia University Magazine* 4 (April 1860): 348; James M. Boyd, "Islamism: Its Beneficial Influences," master's thesis, University of Virginia, 1860), in Student and Alumni Papers, UVA Master's Theses, AL. For more examples of religious toleration among the last generation, see Lancelot Blackford to Mary Blackford, January 19, 1859, Blackford Family Papers, SHC; Thomas R. Price Jr., "The Edinburgh Reviewers," *Virginia University Magazine* 3 (February 1859): 236–37; W. B. Meredith, "Religious Intolerance" (master's thesis, University of Virginia, 1859), in Student and Alumni Papers, UVA Master's Theses, AL.

38. G. W. W. M. Simms, "The South," *Southern Repertory and College Review* 3 (June 1854): 223, 225.

39. Boyd, "Islamism: Its Beneficial Influences" (master's thesis, University of Virginia, 1860), in Student and Alumni Papers, UVA Master's Theses, AL; R. Rives, "Crusades—Some of Their Causes and Effects" (master's thesis, University of Virginia, [1859?]), in Student and Alumni Papers, UVA Master's Theses, AL.

40. John McCardell, *The Idea of a Southern Nation: Southern Nationalists and Southern Nationalism, 1830–1860* (New York: W. W. Norton, 1979), 226.

41. W. A. Smith, *Lectures on the Philosophy and Practice of Slavery*, vii–viii; Craig M. Simpson, *A Good Southerner: The Life of Henry A. Wise of Virginia* (Chapel Hill: University of North Carolina Press, 1985), 153.

42. "Notes on Moral Philosophy," in University of Virginia Professor William H. McGuffey by David Watson of Louisa, Virginia, a student at the University of Virginia, 1852–55, Student and Alumni Papers: Lecture Notebooks, 1827–1882, AL.

43. "Improvements—Lectures of George Fitzhugh and Oliver P. Baldwin," *Richmond Dispatch*, March 17, 1860, p. 2. On Fitzhugh's Unionism, see Wish, *George Fitzhugh*, 289.

44. John Minor to Lancelot Minor and Eugene Blackford, December 16, 1859, Blackford Family Papers, SHC.

45. Ibid.

46. Susan-Mary Grant, *North over South: Northern Nationalism and American Identity in the Antebellum Era* (Lawrence: University Press of Kansas, 2000), 79.

47. Francis H. Smith, *Introductory Address to the Corps of Cadets of the Virginia Military Institute, on the Resumption of Academic Duties, September 2, 1856* (Richmond: MacFarlane and Fergusson, 1856), 21. For additional examples of speeches that emphasize a rivalry between Virginia and the South, see "Virginia Medical College," *Richmond Whig*, March 18, 1854, p. 2; "Professor Holcombe's Discourse before the Virginia Historical Society," *Richmond Whig*, January 31, 1856, p. 1.

48. "Editors' Table," *Virginia University Magazine* 4 (March 1860): 332–33; John H.

Chamberlayne suggested that regional prejudices had reached ridiculous proportions, for they made Northerners and Southerners incapable of objectively evaluating literature. See Chamberlayne, "Essay on American Literature" (master's thesis, University of Virginia, 1858), in Student and Alumni Papers, UVA Master's Theses, AL.

49. James E. B. Stuart to George Hairston, March 6, 1851, in "J. E. B. Stuart's Letters to His Hairston Kin," *North Carolina Historical Review*, 270.

50. James E. B. Stuart to George Hairston, May 7 and October 28, [1853], ibid., 293, 304.

51. James E. B. Stuart to George Hairston, May 8, [1854], ibid., 310.

52. James E. B. Stuart to Bettie Hairston, December 20, 1852, ibid., 288.

53. James E. B. Stuart to Bettie Hairston, May 7, [1853], ibid., 294.

54. Stephanie McCurry, "The Two Faces of Republicanism: Gender and Proslavery Politics in Antebellum South Carolina," *Journal of American History* 78 (March 1992): 1251–52.

55. Daniel W. Crofts, *Reluctant Confederates: Upper South Unionists in the Secession Crisis* (Chapel Hill: University of North Carolina Press, 1989), 53–54, 277–83, 308–23; Henry T. Shanks, *The Secession Movement in Virginia* (Richmond: Garrett and Massie, 1934), 103–213.

56. "Discourse: Before the Young Men's Christian Association of Richmond, on the Ethics of Christianity, by William C. Rives," *Richmond Whig*, January 18, 1856, p. 2. In speaking at the 1854 William and Mary commencement, Democrat Roger Pryor echoed Rives's concerns, although his forecast for the future of the Union was not so dire. He did, however, caution that ruthless politicians cared more about satisfying personal ambition than saving the country. See "College of William and Mary," *Virginia Gazette* (Williamsburg), July 13, 1859, p. 2.

57. Members of the last generation who looked at the politics of slavery from the same framework as John Buchanan and James Hankins include Robert Beale Davis to Wilbur Davis, November 15, December 8, 1856, Beale and Davis Family Papers, SHC; William R. Aylett, [no title], 1853, Speeches of William R. Aylett, Aylett Family Papers, AL; Kinzer Diary, August 26, September 5, October 7, 1856, William T. Kinzer Papers, VHS; Thomas Gordon Pollock to his mother, November 25, 1859, Abram David Pollock Papers, vol. 4, pp. 204–5, SHC; Joseph M. Logan, "Young America," *Southern Repertory and College Review* 4 (December 1855): 147; J. P. Garland, "America—Her Glory and Her Shame," *Southern Repertory and College Review* 4 (December 1856): 233–34. Just before and immediately after Lincoln's election, members of the last generation were more inclined to articulate their concerns about ambitious politicians, the need to guarantee slavery expansion, and their suspicion of Republicans for associating with the abolitionists. For an elaboration of this point, see chapter 5.

58. James DeWitt Hankins to George Duffield, January 24, 1860, Hankins Family Papers, VHS.

59. John Lee Buchanan, "Address before Calliopean Society," November 25, 1855, in John B. May, "The Life of John Lee Buchanan" (Ph.D. diss., University of Virginia, 1937), 21; John L. Buchanan, "The Conflicts of Parties," *Southern Repertory and College Review* 4 (December 1855): 144.

60. Of the members of the last generation, William R. Aylett best articulated why the Western territories played a vital role in the development of the South and the nation. See his "American Progress," [1850–1853?], Aylett Family Papers, VHS. Enthusiasm for westward expansion among members of the last generation should not be confused with support for filibustering. Young Virginians were surprisingly silent on this issue, except for James Hankins who thought territorial aspirations should stay within national boundaries. See James DeWitt Hankins to George Duffield, January 24, 1860, Hankins Family Papers, VHS. On the Young America Movement and expansion, see Charles H. Brown, *Agents of Manifest Destiny: The Lives and Times of the Filibusters* (Chapel Hill: University of North Carolina Press, 1980), 95.

61. On the Southern reaction to the Compromise of 1850, see John Hope Franklin, *The Militant South, 1800–1861* (Cambridge, Mass.: Belknap Press of Harvard University Press, 1956), 223–26; William J. Cooper Jr., *The South and the Politics of Slavery, 1828–1856* (Baton Rouge: Louisiana State University Press, 1978), 301–21.

62. *The Address of the Southern Rights' Association of the University of Virginia to the Young Men of the South* (Charlottesville: James Alexander, 1851), 6–8. The formation of the Southern Rights' Association gained the students some immediate public recognition. See "Southern Rights' Associations," *Southern Literary Messenger* 17 (March 1851): 178–79.

63. "University of Virginia, Nov. 30th, 1853," *Richmond Whig*, December 5, 1853, p. 2.

64. William R. J. Pegram to John Pegram, January 23, 1860, Pegram-Johnson-McIntosh Papers, VHS.

65. "Editors' Table," *Virginia University Magazine* 4 (January 1860): 208.

66. For examples, see "Lecture To-Night," *Richmond Daily Enquirer*, December 14, 1860, p. 2. "Bayard Taylor and the Richmond Young Men's Christian Association," *Richmond Daily Dispatch*, February 10, 1860, p. 2; "Young Men's Christian Association-Meeting To-Night," *Richmond Daily Dispatch*, February 21, 1861, p. 1.

67. "Memoir of Robert T. Barton," in *Defend the Valley: A Shenandoah Family in the Civil War*, ed. Margaretta Barton Colt (New York: Orion Books, 1994), 48.

68. Debates in student literary societies dealt with a wide variety of issues. The politics of sectionalism and slavery did not receive an unusual amount of attention. See "Questions for Debate," [1852–57], Lancelot Blackford Papers, AL. W. G. Bean offers a brief survey of questions raised by the Graham Society at Washington College; see his *Stonewall's Man: Sandie Pendleton* (Chapel Hill: University of North Carolina Press, 1959), 9.

69. Buchanan, "Address before Calliopean Society," November 25, 1855, 23.

70. *The Address of the Southern Rights' Association*, 7.

CHAPTER FIVE

1. John H. Chamberlayne to George William Bagby, December 6, 1860, Bagby Family Papers, VHS.

2. Some of the finest scholarship on Virginia's attitude toward secession has unfor-

tunately overlooked the role of young people. See Daniel W. Crofts, *Reluctant Confederates: Upper South Unionists in the Secession Crisis* (Chapel Hill: University of North Carolina Press, 1989), 53–54, 277–83, 308–23; Henry T. Shanks, *The Secession Movement in Virginia* (Richmond: Garrett and Massie, 1934), 103–213; Charles B. Dew, *Apostles of Disunion: Southern Secession Commissioners and the Causes of the Civil War* (Charlottesville: University Press of Virginia, 2001).

3. In his discussion of Southern medical students in Philadelphia, Daniel Kilbride upholds the stereotype that Southern students, when offering their opinions on sectional issues, were essentially adolescent pranksters who were incapable of expressions of mature political thought. See his "Southern Medical Students in Philadelphia, 1800–1861: Science and Sociability in the 'Republic of Medicine,'" *Journal of Southern History* 65 (November 1999): 717.

4. My understanding of Southern honor and its relationship to the secession crisis draws heavily from Bertram Wyatt-Brown, *Southern Honor: Ethics and Behavior in the Old South* (New York: Oxford University Press, 1982). A more focused discussion of honor, submission, and secession can be found in Wyatt-Brown's "Shameful Submission and Honorable Secession," in Bertram Wyatt-Brown, *The Shaping of Southern Culture: Honor, Grace, and War, 1760s–1890s* (Chapel Hill: University of North Carolina Press, 2001), 177–202.

5. Members of the last generation did not associate themselves with the "fire-eater" mentality of the Deep South. For an example of the Unionist views of young Virginians, see Matthew Page Andrews to Anna Robinson, December 26, 1859, Charles Wesley Andrews Papers, DU.

6. James DeWitt Hankins, "Speeches," [n.d.], Hankins Family Papers, VHS.

7. Alexander Fleet to Benny, October 29, 1860, in *Green Mount: A Virginia Plantation Family during the Civil War: Being the Journal of Benjamin Robert Fleet and Letters of His Family*, ed. Betsy Fleet and John D. P. Fuller (Lexington: University of Kentucky Press, 1962), 38; "A Good Sign," *Staunton Spectator*, October 16, 1860, p. 2.

8. On Virginia and the 1860 presidential election, see Shanks, *The Secession Movement in Virginia*, 103–19; Crofts, *Reluctant Confederates*, 59–60; Craig M. Simpson, *A Good Southerner: The Life of Henry A. Wise of Virginia* (Chapel Hill: University of North Carolina Press, 1985), 234–38.

9. Quoted in Dew, *Apostles of Disunion*, 61.

10. Crofts, *Reluctant Confederates*, 104–5.

11. William R. J. Pegram to Virginia Johnson (Pegram) McIntosh, November 10, 1860, Pegram-Johnson-McIntosh Papers, VHS. For a similar perspective from the University of Virginia, see Alexander F. Fleet to Benny, October 29, 1860, in *Green Mount*, 40; James DeWitt Hankins to Virginia Wilson Hankins, November 21, 1860, Hankins Family Papers, VHS. Although he was not a member of the last generation, George Knox Miller's observations of Virginia students at the University of Virginia confirms the resignation that most young men felt toward the nation's political future. See George Knox Miller to his "dear friend," November 24, 1860, George Knox Miller Papers, SHC. The inevitability of disunion was also conveyed in a resolution passed by students at Emory and Henry College. See "Meeting of the Students of Emory and

Henry College," *Richmond Enquirer*, November 27, 1860, p. 3. A few men declared outright support for secession as soon as Lincoln was elected. See John W. Davis to Robert Beale Davis, November 25, 1860, Beale and Davis Family Papers, SHC.

12. William Goodwyn Ridley to Francis Thomas Ridley, December 5, 1860, The Ridley Family of Southampton Co., Va., Papers, VHS. The resolution that Ridley referred to can be found under "University of Virginia," *Richmond Enquirer*, November 16, 1860, p. 2; George Knox Miller to his "dear friend," November 24, 1860, George Knox Miller Papers, SHC.

13. Henry Lenoir to Fred, November 9, 1860, Lenoir Family Papers, SHC.

14. Hodijah Lincoln Meade to Jane E. Meade, December 9, 1860, Meade Family Papers, VHS. For a similar opinion, see Peter L. Kurtz to John Henry Stover Funk, November 19, 1860, John Henry Stover Funk Papers, FSNMP.

15. Crofts, *Reluctant Confederates*, 197.

16. Philip Alexander Bruce, *History of the University of Virginia, 1819–1919* (New York: Macmillan, 1920–21), 3:264–65; Peter L. Kurtz to John Henry Stover Funk, January 26, 1861, John Henry Stover Funk Papers, FSNMP. See also William R. J. Pegram to Mary Evans (Pegram) Anderson, February 18, 1861, Pegram-Johnson-McIntosh Papers, VHS.

17. George W. Grimm to John Henry Stover Funk, January 16, 1861, John Henry Stover Funk Papers, FSNMP; Charles W. Turner to George Wilmer Turner, February 18, 1861, George Wilmer Turner Papers, DU. Virginia's secondary role in the secession movement also disturbed Thomas Gordon Pollock. See Pollock's letter to his father, November 20, 1860, Abram David Pollock Papers, SHC.

18. Edwin Taliaferro to F. Bland B. Tucker, February 6, 1861, White-Wellford-Taliaferro and Marshall Family Papers, SHC. For additional examples of young Virginians who envisioned the Old Dominion's becoming the center of the Confederacy, see Alexander Fleet to his father, February 18, 1861, in *Green Mount*, 48.

19. "Affairs at the University of Virginia—General Scott Burnt in Effigy," *Richmond Daily Dispatch*, January 15, 1861, p. 1; George Washington Nelson to Carter Nelson Minor, January 19, 1861, James Fontaine Minor Papers, vol. 1, AL.

20. "Gen. Scott Burnt in Effigy," *Staunton Spectator*, January 29, 1861, p. 2.

21. Ollinger Crenshaw, "General Lee's College: Rise and Growth of Washington and Lee" (typescript, Washington and Lee University, 1973), 1:471, 488.

22. For some of the best examples of secessionist sentiment before 1861 expressed by members of the last generation who were not students, see George Woodville to George William Bagby, December 30, 1860, Bagby Family Papers, VHS; Matthew Page Andrews to Anna Robinson, December 2, 1860, Charles Wesley Andrews Papers, DU; Hodijah Lincoln Meade to James E. Meade, December 9, 1860, Meade Family Papers, VHS; Robert Beale Davis to John Davis, December 18, 1860, Beale and Davis Family Papers, SHC; John Samuel Apperson Diary, January 30, 1861, John Samuel Apperson Papers, VT; Edwin Taliaferro to F. Bland B. Tucker, January 11, 1861, White-Wellford-Taliaferro and Marshall Family Papers, SHC; Emily Coles Rutherford Aylett to William R. Aylett, February 28, 1861, Aylett Family Papers, VHS.

23. "Affairs in Albemarle," *Richmond Daily Dispatch*, January 26, 1861, p. 1; "Young

Virginia Chivalry," *Norfolk Day Book* reprinted in *Richmond Enquirer*, January 15, 1861, p. 2; Bruce, *History of the University of Virginia*, 3:265; Crenshaw, "General Lee's College," 2:971–72.

24. "Military Arrangements—Weather, &c.," *Richmond Daily Dispatch*, January 17, 1861, p. 1; Susan H. Godson, Ludwell H. Johnson, Richard B. Sherman, Thad W. Tate, and Helen C. Walker, *The College of William and Mary: A History* (Williamsburg: King and Queen Press, 1993), 1:289.

25. L. H. Minor to Carter Nelson Minor, January 30, 1861, James Fontaine Minor Papers, vol. 1, AL. The generational conflict over disunion extended beyond the public sphere and touched some of these young men on a more personal level. Although the secession crisis rarely divided families, bitter disputes did erupt in some households. A more serious and lasting rupture occurred between William Syndor Thomson and his father, Warner Alexander Thomson, an unconditional Unionist who lived in the lower Shenandoah Valley. When Warner Alexander Thomson learned that his son had spoken at a secessionist meeting, he wrote the young man on December 27: "If you join the fire-eating army, all I hope is that you will fight bravely, even should history regret that it was not in a better cause than the downfall of a glorious Union for the elevation of demagogues." Despite the reservations of his father, William Thomson enlisted in the "fire-eating army," an act that severed their relations. The younger Thomson regretted that "political differences should make me an enemy of my own father." See William Syndor Thomson to Warner Alexander Thomson, December 27, 1860, William Syndor Thomson Papers, EU; William Syndor Thomson to Josephine Thomson, December 8, 1863, William Syndor Thomson Papers, EU. For other examples of tension between fathers and sons over secession, see Matthew Page Andrews to Anna Robinson, May 27, 1861, Charles Wesley Andrews Papers, DU; Charles Wesley Andrews to Matthew Page Andrews, May 17, 1861, Charles Wesley Andrews Papers, DU; Richard Hobson Bagby to Bennette M. Bagby, March 8, 1861, Bennette M. Bagby Papers, DU.

26. John Newton Lyle, *A Reminiscence of Lieutenant John Newton Lyle of the Liberty Hall Volunteers*, ed. Charles W. Turner (Roanoke, Va.: Virginia Lithography and Graphics Co., 1987), 6.

27. "Public Notice," *Richmond Daily Dispatch*, January 7, 1861, p. 2.

28. "Public Meeting—College Military Companies," *Richmond Daily Dispatch*, January 23, 1861, p. 3; John Luster Brinkley, *On This Hill: A Narrative History of Hampden-Sydney College, 1774–1994* (Farmville, Va.: Hampden-Sydney, 1994), 273–74.

29. "To the Young Men of Lunenburg County," *Richmond Enquirer*, December 18, 1860, p. 2. For other militia groups formed exclusively for young men, see "Company 'B,' 1st Regiment," *Richmond Daily Dispatch*, January 22, 1861, p. 1; "New Military Company to Be Composed Chiefly of Christian Young Men," *Richmond Daily Dispatch*, January 10, 1861, p. 2; "The Young Guard," *Richmond Enquirer*, February 15, 1861, p. 3. General tension increased in Warrenton when the young men in the area formed a militia organization. A man from the last generation observed in the fall of 1860 that the "sudden outburst of the disunion feeling . . . is so powerful as to sweep all before it." He predicted "Virginia's leaving the Union with drums beating, colours flying and [?] it may be by the music of artillery." "The war fervor is moving," he added, "& the young

men feel like taking up those long unused arms with which their grandfathers whipt the British." The same man also reported that "the old people of the country were very much shocked when it was published in the papers that its Captain had tendered the services of 'The Black Horse' to Governor John Letcher." See [?] to Thomas Gordon Pollock, after October 5, 1860, Abram David Pollock Papers, SHC. By the content of the letter, it is apparent that the writer was a boyhood friend of Pollock, a confirmed member of the last generation.

30. Members of the last generation who described those against immediate secession as submissionists include William Goodwyn Ridley to Francis Thomas Ridley, [n.d.], Ridley Family of Southampton Co., Va., Papers, VHS; John H. Chamberlayne to George W. Bagby, February 12, 1861, Bagby Family Papers, VHS.

31. "Old Men's Meeting in Westmoreland," *Richmond Daily Whig*, January 30, 1861, p. 1.

32. "Flag Raising," *Valley Star*, April 18, 1861, p. 2.

33. Ibid.

34. Ibid.

35. Dew, *Apostles of Disunion*, 59–60. For the actions and attitudes of the members of Virginia's secession convention, see George H. Reese, ed., *Proceedings of the Virginia State Convention of 1861: February 13–May 1*, 4 vols. (Richmond: Virginia State Library, 1965).

36. Apperson Diary, March 13, 1861, John Samuel Apperson Papers, VT; Albert Davidson, "Lieutenant Albert Davidson: Letters of a Virginia Soldier," ed. Charles W. Turner, *West Virginia History* 39 (Fall 1977): 54. For other negative views of Virginia's secession convention, see Robert Beale Davis to Wilbur Davis, March 8, 1861, Beale and Davis Family Papers, SHC; Alexander S. Pendleton to Mary Pendleton, February 16, [1861], Ellinor Porcher Gadsden Papers, W&L; George Washington Nelson to Carter Nelson Minor, January 19, 1861, James Fontaine Minor Papers, vol. 1, AL; J. E. Celurke to "Dear Cousin Jane," April 12, 1861, Collection 283, Birmingham Public Library Archives, Birmingham, Ala. For the only favorable assessment of the convention, see Robert T. Scott to Fanny (Carter) Scott, March 3, 1861, Keith Family Papers, VHS. The fact that Robert Scott's father was a delegate to the convention probably explains why he trusted the delegates in Richmond, contrary to most of his peers.

37. Robert Beale Davis to John Davis, December 18, 1860, and to Wilbur Davis, March 8, 1861, Beale and Davis Papers, SHC.

38. "Editors' Table," *Virginia University Magazine* 5 (March 1861): 240.

39. George Woodville Latham to George William Bagby, March 9, 1861, Bagby Family Papers, VHS. For other members of the last generation who threatened to leave Virginia, see John Booton Hill to Anna Lee (Hill) Major, February 20, 1861, Hill Family Papers, VHS; John Hampden Chamberlayne to George W. Bagby, February 12, 1861, Bagby Family Papers, VHS.

40. "Editor's Table," *Southern Literary Messenger* 32 (March 1861): 240.

41. Apperson Diary, March 9, 1861, John Samuel Apperson Papers, VT; Richard Hobson Bagby to Bennette M. Bagby, March 8, 1861, Bennette M. Bagby Papers, DU; Charles Trueheart to Cally, March 1, 1861, in *Rebel Brothers: The Civil War Letters of*

the Truehearts, ed. Edward B. Williams (College Station: Texas A&M University Press, 1995), 21–22. Trueheart makes specific reference to Lincoln's inaugural in a letter that must have been misdated since Lincoln did not give his address until March 4. For a similar reaction to Lincoln's inaugural, see Matthew Page Andrews to Anna Robinson, March 10, 1861, Charles Wesley Andrews Papers, DU.

42. "University of Virginia," *Richmond Enquirer*, March 14, 1861, p. 4.

43. "Secession Flag at the University," *Richmond Daily Dispatch*, March 10, 1861, p. 3; Charles Trueheart to Henry, March 25, 1861, in *Rebel Brothers*, 23.

44. Charles Trueheart to Henry, March 25, 1861, in *Rebel Brothers*, 23.

45. Richard M. McMurry, *Virginia Military Institute Alumni in the Civil War* (Lynchburg: H. E. Howard, 1999), 35; W. Harrison Daniel, "Old Lynchburg College, 1855–1869," *Virginia Magazine of History and Biography* 88 (October 1980): 471; "Secession —Roanoke College—Politics," *Richmond Daily Dispatch*, April 9, 1861, p. 3. The students at the College of William and Mary also raised a Confederate banner over campus, but not until the end of March. See "Secession Flag on William and Mary," *Richmond Daily Dispatch*, April 1, 1861, p. 3. A professor at the school, Edwin Taliaferro, reported that "the Students are just raising a flag staff in the College Yard which will soon float the Flag of the New Confederacy. I wish we had a better right to claim it as our own than the mere effervescence of boyish patriotism—and yet I am right glad that, as in days of old the Students of Wm & Mary are willing to express themselves so decidedly in favor of resistance of oppression & so clearly in favor of State rights." See Edwin Taliaferro to F. Bland B. Tucker, April 5, 1861, White-Wellford-Taliaferro and Marshall Family Papers, SHC.

46. Morrison letter quoted in Crenshaw, "General Lee's College," 2:969.

47. Ibid., 970.

48. George W. Grimm to John Henry Stover Funk, January 16, 1861, John Henry Stover Funk Papers, FSNMP. Edwin Taliaferro also tried to organize secessionist activity through community meetings. See his letter to F. Bland B. Tucker, January 2, 1861, White-Wellford-Taliaferro and Marshall Family Papers, SHC.

49. Matthew Page Andrews to Anna Robinson, February 10, 1861, Charles Wesley Andrews Papers, DU; Edwin H. Harmon to Jennie Harmon, March 12, 1861, Edwin H. Harmon Papers, VT. During the nominating meeting for Virginia's secession convention in January, John H. Chamberlayne claimed that some "rowdies," principally "northern factory hands," interrupted the proceedings, prompting him and some friends to clear "the obnoxious gallery." "You never saw such dogs as they were," he exclaimed, "we could not excite them to resist & absolutely had to drag them bodily out with kicks & cuffs." The scrape bolstered Chamberlayne's faith in the ultimate success of the secessionist campaign: "Plug uglyism will have a hard road to travel here. We have the muscle on them & if necessary will have the weapons." See John H. Chamberlayne to George W. Bagby, January 31, 1861, Bagby Family Papers, VHS.

50. Apperson Diary, February 4, March 3, 1861, John Samuel Apperson Papers, VT.

51. Wayland F. Dunaway, *Reminiscences of a Rebel* (New York: Neale Publishing Co., 1913), 10; John B. Minor to Mary Blackford, April 8, 1861, Blackford Family Papers, SHC.

52. Davidson, "Lieutenant Albert Davidson," *West Virginia History*, 54. The two most prominent examples of anti-coercionists in the last generation are Peachy Breckinridge and Robert T. Scott. On Breckinridge, see John Lipscomb Johnson, *The University Memorial: Biographical Sketches of Alumni of the University of Virginia Who Fell in the Confederate War* (Baltimore: Turnbull Brothers, 1871), 744–47. On Scott, see Robert T. Scott to Fanny (Carter) Scott, March 3, 1861, Keith Family Papers, VHS.

53. James Keith to Isham Keith Sr., [?] 19, 1860, Keith Family Papers, VHS. Wayland F. Dunaway recorded a similar experience with Professor Minor. See Dunaway, *Reminiscences of a Rebel*, 10. An elaboration of Minor's views on secession can be found in his February 11, 1861, and April 18, 1861, letters to Lancelot Blackford, Blackford Family Papers, SHC. Not only did Virginia professors try to contain student militia organizations in an attempt to harness "youthful energy," but faculty and administration also preached moderation to their students and, in rare cases, even punished those who aligned themselves too closely with the fire-eaters. For Superintendent Francis Smith's advice to the cadets at Virginia Military Institute, see "Letter from Col. F. H. Smith to a Friend, on the Questions of the Day," *Richmond Daily Dispatch*, January 7, 1861, p. 1. President Junkin of Washington College condemned William L. Yancey as an anarchist during a religious service for the students. See Lyle, *A Reminiscence of Lieutenant John Newton Lyle*, 4. At Emory and Henry College, students who left campus to hear William Yancey speak in Abingdon in October 1860 received three demerits from the faculty. See John S. Dobbins to William Dobbins, October 13, 1860, and William H. Dobbins to John S. Dobbins, December 23, 1860, in John S. Dobbins Papers, EU.

54. "Flag Raising," *Valley Star* (Lexington, Va.), April 18, 1861, p. 2. For the near riot in Lexington, see McMurry, *Virginia Military Institute in the Civil War*, 36.

55. For typical reactions to Fort Sumter, see Apperson Diary, April 16, 1861, John Samuel Apperson Papers, VT; Charles W. Turner to George Wilmer Turner, April 17, 1861, George Wilmer Turner Papers, DU.

56. "Doings at the University—Effect of the News," *Richmond Daily Dispatch*, April 16, 1861, p. 4.

57. Richard Hobson Bagby to Bennette M. Bagby, April 21, 1861, Bennette M. Bagby Papers, DU. For additional examples of lingering hostility among young Virginians after the state's proclamation of disunion, see Giles B. Cooke Diary, April 19, 1861, Giles B. Cooke Papers, VHS; Edwin Taliaferro to F. Bland B. Tucker, April 19, 1861, White-Wellford-Taliaferro and Marshall Family Papers, SHC.

58. "Politics at School," *Richmond Whig*, April 19, 1861, p. 1.

59. Ibid.

60. Andrew C. L. Gatewood to his parents, April 18, 1861, Andrew C. L. Gatewood Papers, VMI; James Henry Langhorne to Margaret Louise Langhorne, Langhorne Family of Montgomery Co., Va., Papers, VHS. For other members of the last generation who saw enlisting in the Confederate army as the transition to manhood, see Richard H. Bagby to Bennette M. Bagby, April 21, 1861, Bennette M. Bagby Papers, DU.

61. Disillusionment with the political establishment, exclusion from positions of power and authority, and a sense of historical mission are factors commonly found in all youth movements. For comparative studies of youth movements, see F. Musgrove,

Youth and the Social Order (Bloomington: Indiana University Press, 1965), 126; John R. Gillis, *Youth and History: Tradition and Change in European Age Relations, 1770–Present* (New York: Academic Press, 1974), 95; Lewis S. Feuer, *The Conflict of Generations: The Character and Significance of Student Movements* (New York: Basic Books, 1969), 11–13.

62. John L. Buchanan, "The Conflict of Parties," *Southern Repertory and College Review* 4 (December 1855): 142; George C. Rable, *The Confederate Republic: A Revolution against Politics* (Chapel Hill: University of North Carolina Press, 1994), 300.

63. Matthew Page Andrews to Anna Robinson, March 10, 1861, Charles Wesley Andrews Papers, DU.

CHAPTER SIX

1. Richard Hobson Bagby to Bennette M. Bagby, April 21, 1861, Bennette M. Bagby Papers, DU.

2. On the place of nonslaveholders in a slaveholding society, see Eugene D. Genovese, "Yeomen Farmers in a Slaveholders' Democracy," in Elizabeth Fox-Genovese and Eugene D. Genovese, *Fruits of Merchant Capital: Slavery and Bourgeois Property in the Rise and Expansion of Capitalism* (New York: Oxford University Press, 1983), 249–64; J. Mills Thornton III, *Politics and Power in a Slave Society: Alabama, 1800–1860* (Baton Rouge: Louisiana State University Press, 1978), 155–60; Emory M. Thomas, *The Confederate Nation: 1861–1865* (New York: Harper and Row, 1979), 8–14. On race as cementing relationships among Southern whites, see U. B. Phillips, *The Slave Economy in the Old South: Selected Essays in Economic and Social History*, ed. Eugene D. Genovese (Baton Rouge: Louisiana State University Press, 1968); George M. Frederickson, *The Black Image in the White Mind: The Debate on Afro-American Character and Destiny* (New York: Harper and Row, 1971).

3. William Blair, *Virginia's Private War: Feeding Body and Soul in the Confederacy, 1861–1865* (New York: Oxford University Press, 1998), 5; U.S. War Department, *The War of the Rebellion: A Compilation of the Official Records of the Union and Confederate Armies*, 128 vols. (Washington, D.C.: U.S. Government Printing Office, 1880–1901), ser. 1,11 (3):614 (hereafter cited as *OR*).

4. My argument follows the lead of William A. Blair, who demonstrates how Confederate civil and military officials accommodated the demands from below. As a result, the war increasingly became a rich man's fight. While my emphasis is on the role of subordinate officers in Lee's army, Blair focuses his attention on Confederate officials and other Richmond policy makers. His research reveals that by 1863 the Confederacy's ruling class began to court "small slaveowners, nonslaveowning farmers, and soldiers' families" while eliminating exemptions that favored slaveholders. See Blair, *Virginia's Private War*, 81–107.

5. John Hampden Chamberlayne to Hartwell Macon Chamberlayne, October 11, 186[4], in John Hampden Chamberlayne, *Ham Chamberlayne—Virginian: Letters and Papers of an Artillery Officer in the War for Southern Independence, 1861–1865*, ed. C. G. Chamberlayne (Richmond: Press of the Dietz Printing Co., 1932), 276. For

additional members of the last generation who entertained a low opinion of enlisted men, see William R. J. Pegram to Mary Evans (Pegram) Anderson, February 11, 1864, Pegram-Johnson-McIntosh Papers, VHS; Greenlee Davidson to his father, May 13, 1862, in Greenlee Davidson, *Captain Greenlee Davidson, C.S.A.: Diary and Letters, 1851–1863*, ed. Charles W. Turner (Verona, Va.: McClure Press, 1975), 38; Richard W. Corbin to his mother, July 8, 1864, in Richard Corbin, *Letters of a Confederate Officer to His Family in Europe during the Last Year of the War of Secession* (1902; reprint, Baltimore: Butternut and Blue, 1993), 52.

6. Thomas Gordon Pollock to his sister, August 13, 1861, Abram David Pollock Papers, SHC. I take issue with Gerald Linderman, who believes that chaplains and men of piety were seen as being incapable of acting courageously. See his *Embattled Courage: The Experience of Combat in the American Civil War* (New York: Free Press, 1987), 253–56.

7. Drew Gilpin Faust cautions that "a view of the role of Confederate religion—as manipulative and hegemonic—is partial and one-dimensional." She contends that most religious leaders and Confederate officials "sincerely believed that their goals were above all to fulfill God's design and only secondarily to serve the needs of men." See her "Christian Soldiers: The Meaning of Revivalism in the Confederate Army," in Drew Gilpin Faust, *Southern Stories: Slaveholders in Peace and War* (Columbia: University of Missouri Press, 1992), 101–2. On religion and social control, see Lois W. Banner, "Religious Benevolence as Social Control: A Critique of an Interpretation," *Journal of American History* 60 (June 1973): 23–41.

8. Edwin Harmon to Jennie Harmon, June 14, 1863, Edwin Harmon Papers, VT. On the religious activities of the Army of Northern Virginia and the importance of religion to the common soldiers in general, see J. William Jones, *Christ in the Camp; or, Religion in the Confederate Army* (1887; reprint, Harrisonburg, Va.: Sprinkle Publications, 1986); Herman Norton, "Revivalism in the Confederate Armies," *Civil War History* 6 (December 1860): 410–24; John Shepard Jr., "Religion in the Army of Northern Virginia," *North Carolina Historical Review* 25 (July 1948): 341–76; Sidney J. Romero, *Religion in the Rebel Ranks* (Lanham, Md.: University Press of America, 1983); Gorrell Clinton Prim Jr., "Born Again in the Trenches: Revivalism in the Confederate Army" (Ph.D. diss., Florida State University, 1982). For a more analytical discussion of revivalism in Confederate armies, see Faust, "Christian Soldiers," 88–109.

9. Richard H. Bagby to Bennette M. Bagby, July 21, 1861, Bennette M. Bagby Papers, DU.

10. Richard Corbin to his mother, July 8, 1864, in Corbin, *Letters of a Confederate Officer*, 51.

11. The independent nature of Southern soldiers has been explored by a number of scholars; see, for example, Reid Mitchell, *Civil War Soldiers: Their Expectations and Experiences* (New York: Viking Press, 1988), 58. A more focused analysis of the relationship between Confederate soldiers and their officers can be found in Bell Irvin Wiley, *The Life of Johnny Reb: The Common Soldier of the Confederacy* (Indianapolis: Bobbs-Merrill, 1943), 235–43.

12. John M. Travers to Greenlee Davidson, March 25, 1862, James Dorman David-

son Collection, W&L; Peter S. Carmichael, *The Purcell, Crenshaw, and Letcher Artillery* (Lynchburg, Va.: H. E. Howard, 1990), 124–26.

13. Desertion did not contribute to the collapse of the army until the fall and winter of 1864. At that stage of the war, Richmond authorities had attacked the problem energetically and effectively. Manpower problems in the Confederacy stemmed from too few men, rather than an overabundance of shirkers.

On the varied reasons for absence without leave and desertion in the Confederate army, see Ella Lonn, *Desertion during the Civil War* (New York: Century, 1928), 16–19; Wiley, *The Life of Johnny Reb*, 135–38.

On the multiple and sometimes contradictory meanings of desertion in the Confederate army, see R. Mitchell, *Civil War Soldiers*, 170–71. Some of the most prominent works on desertion are Georgia Lee Tatum, *Disloyalty in the Confederacy* (Chapel Hill: University of North Carolina Press, 1934); Richard Bardolph, "Confederate Dilemma: North Carolina Troops and the Deserter Problem," *North Carolina Historical Review* 66 (January–April 1989): 61–86; Judith Lee Halleck, "The Role of Community in Civil War Desertion," *Civil War History* 29 (June 1983): 123–34; Maris A. Vinovskis, "Have Social Historians Lost the Civil War? Some Preliminary Demographic Speculations," *Journal of American History* 76 (June 1989): 34–58; Mark A. Weitz, *A Higher Duty: Desertion among Georgia Troops during the Civil War* (Lincoln: University of Nebraska Press, 2000). On Virginia in particular, see Blair, *Virginia's Private War*, 88–92, 127, 128, 130, 142, 149; Kenneth W. Noe, *Southwest Virginia's Railroad: Modernization and the Sectional Crisis* (Urbana: University of Illinois Press, 1994), 110, 117–18, 120, 128–29, 134; Rand Dotson, "'The Grave and Scandalous Evil Infected to Your People': The Erosion of Confederate Loyalty in Floyd County, Virginia," *Virginia Magazine of History and Biography* 108 (2000) 4: 203–15.

14. Kevin Confley Ruffner, "Civil War Desertion from a Black Belt Regiment: An Examination of the 44th Virginia Infantry," in *The Edge of the South: Life in Nineteenth-Century Virginia*, ed. Edward L. Ayers and John C. Willis (Charlottesville: University Press of Virginia, 1991), 101. Ruffner's important findings have been supported by Blair, *Virginia's Private War*, 62. A similar argument for Texas troops in Virginia has been made by Charles E. Brooks, "The Social and Cultural Dynamics of Soldiering in Hood's Texas Brigade," *Journal of Southern History* 67 (August 2001): 571–72. Rand Dotson discovered that men from Floyd County in southwest Virginia deserted because of the harsh treatment the home guard inflicted on civilians and other Confederate runaways. Contrary to what Ruffner found among men from the state's black belt, Dotson noticed a steady increase in desertion as the war progressed, leading him to conclude that disaffection with the Confederacy motivated most men to leave the ranks. See his "'Grave and Scandalous Evil,'" 393–434.

15. *OR*, ser. 1, 11 (3):614.

16. William Thomas Poague, *Gunner with Stonewall: Reminiscences of William Thomas Poague*, ed. Monroe F. Cockrell (1957; reprint, Wilmington, N.C.: Broadfoot Publishing Co., 1987), 32–33.

17. William R. Aylett to Alice Roane (Brockenbrough) Aylett, October 9, 1863, Aylett Family Papers, VHS.

18. Robert T. Scott to Fanny (Carter) Scott, March 13, 1862, Keith Family Papers, VHS; Carmichael, *The Purcell, Crenshaw, and Letcher Artillery*, 23; John H. Chamberlayne to Lucy Parke Chamberlayne, February 18, 1861, in Chamberlayne, *Ham Chamberlayne*, 280. See also William R. Aylett to John Bankhead Magruder, November 21, 1861, Aylett Family Papers, VHS.

19. James I. Robertson Jr., *Soldiers Blue and Gray* (Columbia: University of South Carolina Press, 1988), 13.

20. Hodijah Lincoln Meade to Jane E. Meade, November 6, 1863, Meade Family Papers, VHS. For a similar reaction to the electioneering process for officers, see James Henry Langhorne to Uncle Archer (Langhorne?), November 21, 1861, Langhorne Family of Montgomery Co., Va., Papers, VHS.

21. Robert T. Scott to Fanny (Carter) Scott, September 27, 1861, Keith Family Papers, VHS.

22. John Hampden Chamberlayne to Martha Burwell Chamberlayne, September 4, 1864, in Chamberlayne, *Ham Chamberlayne*, 268.

23. On the punishment of soldiers, see Orders and Circulars issued by the Army of Northern Virginia, C.S.A., July–August 1862, (M921), National Archives, Washington, D.C.; Jack A. Bunch, *Military Justice in the Confederate States Armies* (Shippensburg, Pa.: White Mane Books, 2000), 61–87.

24. Edwin Harmon to Jennie Harmon, December 15, 1862, Edwin Harmon Papers, VT.

25. John O. Casler, *Four Years in the Stonewall Brigade* (1893; reprint, Dayton, Ohio: Morningside Bookshop, 1982), 101–2.

26. Thomas Claybrook Elder to Anna Fitzhugh (May) Elder, August 21, 1863, Thomas Claybrook Elder Papers, VHS.

27. Thomas Claybrook Elder to Anna Fitzhugh (May) Elder, May 27, 1863, Thomas Claybrook Elder Papers, VHS. For other officers in the last generation who allowed their enlisted men to leave the ranks without formal permission, see Fanny (Carter) Scott to Robert T. Scott, March 15, 1862, Keith Family Papers, VHS; William R. Barham to James Dewitt Hankins, July 11, 1862, Hankins Family Papers, VHS. Not all common soldiers escaped punishment for leaving the ranks without permission, and some received preferential treatment because they came from wealthy families. In the summer of 1862, John James Reeve complained that some men convicted of desertion "were severely whipped" while "'the highly intelligent & gentlemanly' youth" of his company received milder punishments for the same crime. See John James Reeve to Lucy Parke (Chamberlayne) Bagby, June 8, 1862, Bagby Family Papers, VHS.

28. On the shift toward a policy of severity, see Blair, *Virginia's Private War*, 55–68. For the impact of wayward Confederates across the state, see Steven Elliott Tripp, *Yankee Town, Southern City: Race and Class Relations in Civil War Lynchburg* (New York: New York University Press, 1997), 125–33; Daniel W. Crofts, *Old Southampton: Politics and Society in a Virginia County, 1834–1869* (Charlottesville: University Press of Virginia, 1992), 204; Brian Steel Wills, *The War Hits Home: The Civil War in Southeastern Virginia* (Charlottesville: University Press of Virginia, 2001), 47–66; Ernest

B. Furgurson, *Ashes of Glory: Richmond at War* (New York: Alfred A. Knopf, 1996), 162–63.

29. [Letter from an officer in the 10th Virginia Infantry], *Rockingham Register* (Harrisonburg, Va.), August [29?], 1862, p. 1.

30. William R. J. Pegram to Virginia Johnson (Pegram) McIntosh, September 7, 1862, Pegram-Johnson-McIntosh Papers, VHS; [Letter from an officer in the 10th Virginia Infantry], *Rockingham Register*, August [29?], 1862, p. 1. Drew Gilpin Faust explores how Civil War soldiers constructed the right way to die. See her "The Civil War Soldier and the Art of Dying," *Journal of Southern History* 67 (February 2001): 3–38. Discussions of the psychological effects of ritual executions on the army include Linderman, *Embattled Courage*, 58–59, 174–77; Eric T. Dean Jr., *Shook over Hell: Post-traumatic Stress, Vietnam, and the Civil War* (Cambridge, Mass.: Harvard University Press, 1997), 68–69.

31. *OR*, ser. 4, 2:687. Lee reluctantly agreed to President Davis's proclamation of amnesty after Gettysburg. For the general's reaction, see R. E. Lee to Jefferson Davis, August 17, 1863, in *The Wartime Papers of R. E. Lee*, ed. Clifford Dowdey and Louis H. Manarin (Boston: Little, Brown, 1961), 591.

32. In his historiographical treatment of Civil War soldiers, Reid Mitchell notes that recent scholarly trend has emphasized the role of ideology and culture in trying to understand the rank and file. See his "'Not the General but the Soldier': The Study of Civil War Soldiers," in *Writing the Civil War: The Quest to Understand*, ed. James M. McPherson and William J. Cooper Jr. (Columbia: University of South Carolina Press, 1998), 81–95.

33. Notions of honor, duty, and courage have been explored by a number of Civil War scholars. For some of the finest work on this issue, see James M. McPherson, *For Cause and Comrades: Why Men Fought in the Civil War* (New York: Oxford University Press, 1997), 77–84; Michael Barton, *Goodmen: The Character of Civil War Soldiers* (University Park: Pennsylvania State University Press, 1981), 23–44; Earl J. Hess, *The Union Soldier in Battle: Enduring the Ordeal of Combat* (Lawrence: University Press of Kansas, 1997), 95–97.

34. The two best studies of Stuart's wartime career are John W. Thomason Jr., *Jeb Stuart* (New York: Charles Scribner's Sons, 1929); and Emory M. Thomas, *Bold Dragoon: The Life of J. E. B. Stuart* (New York: Harper and Row, 1986).

35. George Woodville Latham to George William Bagby, February 1, 1862, Bagby Family Papers, VHS. For a thoughtful discussion of the changing meaning of courage in Civil War armies, see Linderman, *Embattled Courage*. I disagree with Linderman's contention that by 1863 soldiers began to question the value of bold, aggressive behavior in the face of rifled weapons and entrenchments. While the men in the last generation might have avoided suicidal frontal attacks by the middle of the war, they still considered it their duty to behave bravely, even recklessly, in front of the enemy. As subordinate officers, young Virginians understood the inspiring effect of such behavior on their men. The meaning of courage changed little over the course of the war for the last generation. They continued to fight the war they had set out to fight in 1861. Testimony

from young Virginians who did not deviate from the early war code of battle includes William R. Aylett to Alice Roane (Brockenbrough) Aylett, May 23, 1864, Aylett Family Papers, VHS; William R. J. Pegram to Mary Evans (Pegram) Anderson, October 5, 1864, Pegram-Johnson-McIntosh Papers, VHS; William Gordon McCabe Diary, April 1, 1865, in Armistead Churchill Gordon, *Memories and Memorials of William Gordon McCabe* (Richmond: Old Dominion Press, 1925), 1:165. John H. Chamberlayne to Martha Burwell Chamberlayne, May 21, 1864, and August 10, 1864, in Chamberlayne, *Ham Chamberlayne*, 222, 252.

36. James Henry Langhorne to Margaret Louise Langhorne, May 7, 1861, Langhorne Family of Montgomery Co., Va., Papers, VHS; Richard Hobson Bagby to Bennette M. Bagby, Bennette M. Bagby Papers, DU.

37. James Henry Langhorne to Margaret Louise Langhorne, January 21, 1862, Langhorne Family of Montgomery Co., Va., Papers, VHS

38. John James Reeve to Lucy Parke (Chamberlayne) Bagby, January 11, 1862, and February 18, 1862, Bagby Family Papers, VHS.

39. John Warwick Daniel, *Character of Stonewall Jackson* (Lynchburg: Schaffter and Bryant, 1868), 53.

40. C. Jennings Wise, "Boy Gunners of Lee," in *Southern Historical Society Papers*, ed. J. William Jones et al., 52 vols. and 2-vol. index (1876–1959; reprint, Millwood, N.Y.: Kraus Reprint Co., 1977–80), 42:156.

41. John H. Chamberlayne to his mother, August 27, 1864, in Chamberlayne, *Ham Chamberlayne*, 264.

42. William S. White, *Sketches of the Life of Captain Hugh A. White* (Columbia: South Carolinian Steam Press, 1864), 94, 51.

43. Ibid., 3, 6. Similar themes can be found in other Confederate imprints commemorating fallen members of the last generation. See Robert L. Dabney, *The Christian Soldier: A Sermon Commemorative of the Death of Abram C. Carrington* (Richmond: Presbyterian Committee of Publications, 1863); Philip Slaughter, *A Sketch of the Life of Randolph Fairfax* (Richmond: Tyler, Allegre, and McDaniel, 1864); Cornelia Jane Matthews Jordan, *In Memoriam: John Tyler Waller of Virginia* ([Richmond?]: n.p., [1865?]).

44. White, *Sketches of the Life of Captain Hugh A. White*, 5.

45. Ibid., 5–6.

46. Ibid., 6.

47. Ibid., 12.

48. Ibid., 121, 119–20.

49. Ibid., 123–24.

50. Slaughter, *A Sketch of the Life of Randolph Fairfax*, 41.

51. Casler, *Four Years in the Stonewall Brigade*, 114.

52. On the revolution in gender roles during the Civil War, see George C. Rable, *Civil Wars: Women and the Crisis of Southern Nationalism* (Urbana: University of Illinois Press, 1989); Catherine Clinton and Nina Silber, eds., *Divided Houses: Gender and the Civil War* (New York: Oxford University Press, 1992); Drew Gilpin Faust, "Altars of Sacrifice: Confederate Women and the Narrative of War," *Journal of American History*

76 (March 1990): 1200–1228; Anne Firor Scott, *The Southern Lady: From Pedestal to Politics, 1830–1930* (Chicago: University of Chicago Press, 1970).

53. Not all young Virginians resigned themselves to the hardships placed on Southern women, and many lamented their inability to help those at home. See John Samuel Apperson Diary, February 22, 1863, John Samuel Apperson Papers, VT.

54. Walter H. Taylor to his sister, May 8, 1863, in Walter H. Taylor, *Lee's Adjutant: The Wartime Letters of Colonel Walter Herron Taylor, 1862–1865*, ed. R. Lockwood Tower (Columbia: University of South Carolina Press, 1995), 114.

55. Robert T. Scott to Fanny (Carter) Scott, March 10, 1861, Keith Family Papers, VHS. Also see Scott's letter of February 2, 1862. For other members of the last generation who found solace in the spiritual connection with those remaining at home, see John James Reeve to Lucy Parke (Chamberlayne) Bagby, December 9, 1861, Bagby Family Papers, VHS; James E. B. Stuart to his wife, November 6, 1862, in *The Letters of Major General James E. B. Stuart*, ed. Adele H. Mitchell (N.p.: Mosby Historical Society, 1990), 279; James Keith to Juliet (Chilton) Keith, May 28, 1864, and October 18, 1864, Keith Family of Woodburne, Fauquier Co., Va., VHS; Virginia Wilson Hankins to James DeWitt Hankins, [?] 15, 1861, Hankins Family Papers, VHS; William R. J. Pegram to Virginia Johnson (Pegram) McIntosh, August 1, 1864, Pegram-Johnson-McIntosh Papers, VHS; Elizabeth Norfleet (Goodwyn) Ridley to William Goodwyn Ridley, February 15, 1862, Ridley Family of Southampton Co., Va., Papers, VHS; Richard H. Bagby to Bennette M. Bagby, April 11, 1863, Bennette M. Bagby Letters, DU; Matthew Page Andrews to Anna Robinson, December 28, 1864, Charles Wesley Andrews Papers, DU.

56. Richard Corbin to his father, June 15, 1864, in Corbin, *Letters of a Confederate Officer*, 35–36. Before collecting a tax-in-kind in his own Lunenburg County, Thomas Elder wanted his family to alert the county's residents of his pending trip so that they could meet his requests. He did not want to put excessive demands on his neighbors and offered various means by which the tax could be paid. His conciliatory approach reveals how sensitive members of the last generation needed to be with those who stood outside the slaveholding class. See Thomas Claybrook Elder to Anna Fitzhugh (May) Elder, January 24, 1863, Thomas Claybrook Elder Papers, VHS. For examples of Virginia military units collecting money or rations for the poor, see "The Twelfth Virginia Regiment" (financial contribution to Fredericksburg's poor), *Richmond Daily Whig*, Jan. 6, 1863, p. 3; "The Fayette Artillery" (proceeds from a company ball for widows of deceased members of the unit), *Richmond Sentinel*, October 26, 1863, p. 2.

57. Apperson Diary, March 13, 1864, John Samuel Apperson Collection, VT.

58. On public relief efforts in the Confederacy, see Blair, *Virginia's Private War*, 70–71, 75–77, 81–82, 119–20; Charles W. Ramsdell, *Behind the Lines in the Southern Confederacy* (Baton Rouge: Louisiana State University Press, 1944), 40, 62–68; William F. Zornow, "Aid for Indigent Families of Soldiers in Virginia, 1861–1865," *Virginia Magazine of History and Biography*, 66 (October 1958): 454–58; Paul D. Escott, "'The Cry of the Sufferers': The Problem of Welfare in the Confederacy," *Civil War History* 23 (1977): 231–32.

59. Fanny (Carter) Scott to Robert Taylor Scott, September 20, 1861, Keith Family Papers, VHS.

60. For the best discussion of the factors affecting the morale of Confederate women, see Rable, *Civil Wars*, 202–20.

61. Matthew Page Andrews to Anna Robinson, March 21, 1865, Charles Wesley Andrews Papers, DU; Virginia Wilson Hankins to James DeWitt Hankins, July 11, 1864, Hankins Family Papers, VHS. For additional examples of Virginia women banding together to resist Union encroachments, see Mary D. Robertson, ed., *Lucy Breckinridge of Grove Hill: The Journal of a Virginia Girl, 1862–1864* (Kent, Ohio: Kent State University Press, 1979); 185–87; Nancy Chappelear Baird, ed., *Journals of Amanda Virginia Edmonds: Lass of the Mosby Confederacy, 1859–1867* (Stephens City, Va.: Commercial Press, 1984), 180–82.

62. William R. J. Pegram to Virginia Johnson (Pegram) McIntosh, July 14, 1864, Pegram-Johnson-McIntosh Papers, VHS: Virginia Wilson Hankins to James DeWitt Hankins, September 3, 1864, Hankins Family Papers, VHS.

63. William R. Aylett to Alice Roane (Brockenbrough) Aylett, July 20, 1863, Aylett Family Papers, VHS.

64. Greenlee Davidson to his father, December 9, 1862, in Davidson, *Captain Greenlee Davidson, C.S.A.*, 60–61; Thomas Claybrook Elder to Anna Fitzhugh (May) Elder, November 23, 1862, Claybrook Elder Papers, VHS. On the role of vengeance in motivating Confederate soldiers, see James M. McPherson, *What They Fought For* (Baton Rouge: Louisiana State University Press, 1994), 18, 21–24. Many young Virginians desired revenge during the Gettysburg Campaign and bitterly regretted that they did not make Northern civilians feel the brutality of war. See Robert T. Scott to Fanny (Carter) Scott, July 16, 1863, Keith Family Papers, VHS; Hodijah Lincoln Meade to Charlotte Randolph (Meade) Lane, July 19, 1863, Meade Family Papers, VHS; William R. Aylett to Alice Roane (Brockenbrough) Aylett, June 23, 1863, Aylett Family Papers, VHS. For other members of the last generation who demanded retaliation, see John James Reeve to Lucy Parke (Chamberlayne) Bagby, July 8, 1862, Bagby Family Papers, VHS; Thomas Claybrook Elder to Anna Fitzhugh (May) Elder, December 21, 1862, Thomas Claybrook Elder Papers, VHS; Richard Corbin to his mother, June 26, 1864, in Corbin, *Letters of a Confederate Officer*, 39.

65. Walter H. Taylor to Bettie Saunders, December 20, 1863, in W. H. Taylor, *Lee's Adjutant*, 100.

66. James E. B. Stuart to his wife, November 13, 1863, in *The Letters of Major General James E. B. Stuart*, 353. For other members of the last generation who encouraged women to see the war as a collective effort involving both soldiers and those on the home front, see Robert T. Scott to Fanny (Carter) Scott, March 19, 1862, Keith Family Papers, VHS; John James Reeve to Lucy Parke (Chamberlayne) Bagby, November 14, 1864, Bagby Family Papers, VHS; William R. J. Pegram to Virginia Johnson (Pegram) McIntosh, March 10, 1865, Pegram-Johnson-McIntosh Papers, VHS.

67. John Henry Stover Funk to his mother, December 13, 1863, John Henry Stover Funk Papers, FSNMP. For a summary of Blair's argument, see his *Virginia's Private War*, 5.

68. William R. J. Pegram to Mary Evans (Pegram) Anderson, September 1, 1864, Pegram-Johnson-McIntosh Papers, VHS.

69. Apperson Diary, February 1, 1864, John Samuel Apperson Papers, VT. For other members of the last generation who advocated a centralized Confederate government at the expense of the slaveholding class, see Richard H. Bagby to Bennette M. Bagby, August 23, 1864, Bennette M. Bagby Papers, DU; Thomas Claybrook Elder to Anna Fitzhugh (May) Elder, January 24, 1864, Thomas Claybrook Elder Papers, VHS; William R. J. Pegram to Mary Evans (Pegram) Anderson, December 16, 1863, Pegram-Johnson-McIntosh Papers, VHS.

70. William R. J. Pegram to James West Pegram Jr., March 17, 1865, Pegram-Johnson-McIntosh Papers, VHS; Richard Corbin to his father, December 9, 1864, in Corbin, *Letters of a Confederate Officer*, 88–89. For other positive assessments of slaves as potential soldiers, see Richard W. Oram, ed., "Harpers Ferry to the Fall of Richmond: Letters of Colonel John De Hart Ross," *West Virginia History* 45 (1984): 173; John H. Chamberlayne to Lucy Parke (Chamberlayne) Bagby, March 29, 1865, in Chamberlayne, *Ham Chamberlayne*, 316.

71. Berkeley Minor, *If Lee Could Have Stood at the Helm* (Staunton, Va.: n.p., 1911).

CHAPTER SEVEN

1. William Gordon McCabe to Mary Early, April 7, 1865, Early Family Papers, 1764–1956, VHS; John Hampden Chamberlayne, *Ham Chamberlayne—Virginian*, ed. C. G. Chamberlayne (Richmond: Press of the Dietz Printing Co., 1932), 322. For a similar reaction to Appomattox, see Carter Nelson Minor Diary, April [?], 1865, James Fontaine Minor Papers, vol. 3, AL; George S. Bernard Diary, April 10, 11, 1865, in *War Talks of Confederate Veterans*, ed. George S. Bernard (1892; reprint, Dayton, Ohio: Morningside House, 1981), 281–82.

2. Some of the most notable observations on weak Confederate morale and guilt over slavery appear in Ellis Merton Coulter, *The Confederate States of America, 1861–1865* (Baton Rouge: Louisiana State University Press, 1950), 566; Kenneth M. Stampp, *The Imperiled Union: Essays on the Background of the Civil War* (New York: Oxford University Press, 1980), 264, 252, 255; James Oakes, *The Ruling Race: A History of American Slaveholders* (New York: Alfred A. Knopf, 1982), 102, 119; Richard E. Beringer, Herman Hattaway, Archer Jones, and William N. Still Jr., *Why the South Lost the Civil War* (Athens: University of Georgia Press, 1986), 360–61; Drew Gilpin Faust, *The Creation of Confederate Nationalism: Ideology and Identity in the Civil War South* (Baton Rouge: Louisiana State University Press, 1988), 41–42; Clarence L. Mohr, *On the Threshold of Freedom: Masters and Slaves in Civil War Georgia* (Athens: University of Georgia Press, 1986), 235–71; Gardiner H. Shattuck Jr., *A Shield and Hiding Place: The Religious Life of the Civil War Armies* (Macon, Ga.: Mercer University Press, 1987), 9.

3. The literature that proceeds from the premise that the antebellum South must be understood as a religious society is voluminous. On the Confederacy's use of religion as a source of legitimation, see Faust, *The Creation of Confederate Nationalism*, 22–23;

George C. Rable, *The Confederate Republic: A Revolution against Politics* (Chapel Hill: University of North Carolina Press, 1994), 75–77.

4. On the Confederacy's use of the revolutionary tradition, see James M. McPherson, *What They Fought For, 1861–1865* (Baton Rouge: Louisiana State University Press, 1994), 9–12; Rable, *The Confederate Republic*, 65, 122–23, 134–35, 176; Faust, *The Creation of Confederate Nationalism*, 14–15.

5. George W. Koontz to Nellie Koontz, August 21, 1861, Koontz Family Papers, VT. For other members of the last generation who saw a parallel between the Confederate experiment and the American Revolution, see Thomas Claybrook Elder to Anna Fitzhugh (May) Elder, May 8, 1863, Thomas Claybrook Elder Papers, VHS; William R. J. Pegram to Charles Ellis Munford, April 18, 1861, Munford-Ellis Papers (George W. Munford Division), DU; Edwin Taliaferro to F. Bland B. Tucker, April 19, 1861, White-Wellford-Taliaferro and Marshall Family Papers, SHC; Robert T. Scott to Fanny (Carter) Scott, July 29, 1863, Keith Family Papers, VHS.

6. Drew Gilpin Faust, "Christian Soldiers: The Meaning of Revivalism in the Confederate Army," in Faust, *Southern Stories: Slaveholders in Peace and War* (Columbia: University of Missouri Press, 1992), 91–92. Other scholars who make a similar argument include Kurt O. Berends, "'Wholesome Reading Purifies and Elevates the Man': The Religious Military Press in the Confederacy," in *Religion and the American Civil War*, ed. Randall M. Miller, Harry S. Stout, and Charles Reagan Wilson (New York: Oxford University Press, 1998), 136, 141; Beth Barton Schweiger, *The Gospel Working Up: Progress and the Pulpit in Nineteenth-Century Virginia* (New York: Oxford University Press, 2000), 99.

7. William S. White, *Sketches of the Life of Captain Hugh A. White of the Stonewall Brigade* (Columbia: South Carolinian Steam Press, 1864), 5; Philip Slaughter, *A Sketch of the life of Randolph Fairfax* (Richmond: Tyler, Allegre, and McDaniel, 1864), 4. Alice Fahs demonstrates that the model of the sentimental soldier was widely popular throughout the North and South. Sentimentalism emphasized the power of emotion to prepare a soldier for death or to make him more caring and more sensitive to the suffering of others without taking away his heroic qualities. See her *The Imagined Civil War: Popular Literature of the North and South, 1861–1865* (Chapel Hill: University of North Carolina Press, 2001), 93–119.

8. James Keith to Juliet (Chilton) Keith, May 27, 1864, Keith Family Papers, VHS; William R. J. Pegram to Virginia Johnson (Pegram) McIntosh, August 14, 1862, Pegram-Johnson-McIntosh Papers, VHS; White, *Sketches of the Life of Captain Hugh A. White*, 77. For other young Virginians who believed God protected them in battle, see Hodijah Lincoln Meade to Richard Hardaway Meade, May 13, 1862, Meade Family Papers, VHS; James E. B. Stuart to his wife, November 6, 1862, in Stuart, *The Letters of Major General James E. B. Stuart*, ed. Adele H. Mitchell (N.p.: Mosby Historical Society, 1990), 279; Alexander S. Pendleton to Kate Corbin, July 16, 1863, William N. Pendleton Papers, SHC; Richard H. Bagby to Bennette M. Bagby, December 17, 1862, Bennette M. Bagby Letters, DU; Randolph Fairfax to [?], March, 1862, in Slaughter, *A Sketch of the Life of Randolph Fairfax*, 21.

9. White, *Sketches of the Life of Captain Hugh A. White*, 49, 92.

10. Thomas Claybrook Elder to Anna Fitzhugh (May) Elder, April 6, 1862, Thomas Claybrook Elder Papers, VHS.

11. Robert T. Scott to Fanny (Carter) Scott, August 15, 1861, Keith Family Papers, VHS.

12. Robert T. Scott to Fanny (Carter) Scott, March 10, 1862, Keith Family Papers, VHS. See also Robert T. Scott to Fanny (Carter) Scott, September 27, 1861, Keith Family Papers, VHS. Equating duty to God with duty to the Confederacy was common among young Virginians. See William R. J. Pegram to Virginia Johnson (Pegram) McIntosh, April 3, 1862, Pegram-Johnson-McIntosh Papers, VHS; Thomas Claybrook Elder to Anna Fitzhugh (May) Elder, April 27, 1862, Thomas Claybrook Elder Papers, VHS; James Keith to Juliet (Chilton) Keith, June 7, [1861], Keith Family Papers, VHS; Richard Hobson Bagby to Bennette M. Bagby, May 12, 1861, Bennette M. Bagby Papers, DU; Ted Barclay to his sister, May 2, [1864], in Barclay, *Ted Barclay, Liberty Hall Volunteers: Letters from the Stonewall Brigade*, ed. Charles W. Turner (Natural Bridge Station, Va.: Rockbridge Publishing Co., 1992), 143–45; A. B. Roler Diary, July 16, 1861, A. B. Roler Papers, VHS; Edwin Taliaferro to F. Bland B. Tucker, April 19, 1861, White-Wellford-Taliaferro and Marshall Family Papers, SHC; Walter H. Taylor to his sister, August 30, 1862, in W. H. Taylor, *Lee's Adjutant: The Wartime Letters of Colonel Walter Herron Taylor, 1862–1865*, ed. Tower R. Lockwood (Columbia: University of South Carolina Press, 1995), 41.

13. The fusion of Christian salvation and the promise of Confederate independence made it difficult for some soldiers to distinguish between the secular and the sacred. See Berends, " 'Wholesome Reading Purifies and Elevates the Man,' " 153–55. Reid Mitchell offers a different perspective on this subject. In a weakly argued and thinly documented paper, he suggests that revivals and religion in general might not have "tied southern faith in salvation to the Confederate cause as much as some postwar spokesmen assumed." See his "Christian Soldiers? Perfecting the Confederacy," in *Religion and the American Civil War*, Randall M. Miller, Harry S. Stout, and Charles Reagan Wilson (New York: Oxford University Press, 1998), 305–8. A similar but more sophisticated interpretation can be found in Faust, "Christian Soldiers," 88–109.

14. Randolph Fairfax to [?], March [?], 1862, in Slaughter, *A Sketch of the Life of Randolph Fairfax*, 21.

15. Fanny (Carter) Scott to Robert Taylor Scott, June 28 and September 20, 1861, Keith Family Papers, VHS. Not all Virginia women urged their husbands to uphold their duties to the Confederacy, believing that fatherly responsibilities remained paramount, even in war. For an example, see the correspondence of Julia Calvert Bolling to Philip Barraud Cabell in "The Bolling-Cabell Letters," ed. Richard T. Couture, *Goochland County Historical Society Magazine* 14 (1982): 25–29.

16. Robert T. Scott to Fanny (Carter) Scott, September 22, 1861, Keith Family Papers, VHS.

17. William Weldon Bentley to his mother, June 13, 1862, William Weldon Bentley Papers, VMI. The dangers of the battlefield elicited a similar opinion from Hugh A. White. See his letter to his brother, September 12, 1861, in White, *Sketches of the Life of Captain Hugh A. White*, 55. The formation of the Confederacy sparked the religious

interest of the young Virginians who continued to strive to live as Christians as they had before the war. See Thomas Claybrook Elder to Anna Fitzhugh (May) Elder, April 27, 1862, Thomas Claybrook Elder Papers, VHS; James Henry Langhorne to Margaret Louise Langhorne, May 2, 1861, Langhorne Family of Montgomery Co., Va., Papers, 1843–1863, VHS; Robert T. Scott to Fanny (Carter) Scott, September 22, 1861, and March 29, 1862, Keith Family Papers, VHS. On the importance of religion to Confederate soldiers, see Bell Irvin Wiley, *The Life of Johnny Reb: The Common Soldier of the Confederacy* (Indianapolis: Bobbs-Merrill, 1943), 36, 174–91; Michael Barton, *Goodmen: The Character of Civil War Soldiers* (University Park: Pennsylvania State University Press, 1981), 23–33; James I. Robertson Jr., *Soldiers Blue and Gray* (Columbia: University of South Carolina Press, 1988), 170–89; Reid Mitchell, *Civil War Soldiers: Their Expectations and Experiences* (New York: Viking Press, 1988), 173–74.

18. John James Reeve to Lucy Parke (Chamberlayne) Bagby, July 8, 1862, Bagby Family Papers, VHS.

19. For a typical letter from the last generation that describes the immorality of soldiering, see Hugh A. White to [?], June 24, 1861, in White, *Sketches of the Life of Captain Hugh A. White*, 50–51. On the hardening process of Civil War soldiers, see Gerald Linderman, *Embattled Courage: The Experience of Combat in the American Civil War* (New York: Free Press, 1987), and McPherson, *What They Fought For*.

20. Robert T. Scott to Fanny (Carter) Scott, February 4, 1862, Keith Family Papers, VHS. For others who complained about the immorality of army life, see Thomas Claybrook Elder to Anna Fitzhugh (May) Elder, April 2, 1862, Thomas Claybrook Elder Papers, VHS; Roler Diary, August 11, 1861, A. B. Roler Papers, VHS; John H. Chamberlayne to George W. Bagby, October 4, 1862, in Chamberlayne, *Ham Chamberlayne*, 118; John Booton Hill to Judith Frances (Booton) Hill, July 28, 1861, Hill Family Papers, VHS. Walter Taylor to Bettie Saunders, February 2, 1864, in W. H. Taylor, *Lee's Adjutant*, 113–14; John Samuel Apperson Diary, October 20, 1862, John Samuel Apperson Papers, VT.

21. Robert T. Scott to Fanny (Carter) Scott, February 4, 1862, Keith Family Papers, VHS.

22. I am in agreement with Reid Mitchell, who maintains that "just as divine displeasure could explain military defeat, the possibility of divine favor could lead men to continue the struggle long after it seemed rational." See his *Civil War Soldiers*, 173–74.

23. For a general treatment of "Confederate sins" behind the lines and the impact on the South's notion of divine favor, see Eugene D. Genovese, *A Consuming Fire: The Fall of the Confederacy in the Mind of the White Christian South* (Athens: University of Georgia Press, 1998), 45–55.

24. Philip B. Cabell to Julia Calvert Bolling Cabell, August 18, 1861, in "The Bolling-Cabell Letters," ed. Couture, 23. A similar view can be found in Hugh A. White to William Spottswood White, July 23, 1861, in White, *Sketches of the Life of Captain Hugh A. White*, 52.

25. William R. J. Pegram to Mary Evans (Pegram) Anderson, May 11, 1863, Pegram-Johnson-McIntosh Papers, VHS. On the lessons of Jackson's death for the Confederate people, see Daniel W. Stowell, "Stonewall Jackson and the Providence of God," in *Re-*

ligion and the American Civil War, ed. Randall M. Miller, Harry S. Stout, and Charles Reagan Wilson (New York: Oxford University Press, 1998), 187–207.

26. Richard H. Bagby to Bennette M. Bagby, August 24, 1863, Bennette M. Bagby Papers, DU; George W. Koontz to his mother, August 13, 1863, Koontz Family Papers, VT.

27. Recent scholarship suggests that Confederates in the Army of Northern Virginia did not interpret the battle of Gettysburg as a decisive defeat, let alone a turning point in the war. Most of Lee's soldiers considered the battle a draw. See Gary W. Gallagher, "Lee's Army Has Not Lost Any of Its Prestige: The Impact of Gettysburg on the Army of Northern Virginia and the Confederate Home Front," in *The Third Day at Gettysburg and Beyond*, ed. Gary W. Gallagher, (Chapel Hill: University of North Carolina Press, 1994), 1–30. For members of the last generation who support this contention, see Robert T. Scott to Fanny (Carter) Scott, July 16, 1863, and July 29, 1863, Keith Family Papers, VHS; James Keith to Isham Keith Sr., July 18, 1863, Keith Family Papers, VHS; Hodijah Lincoln Meade to Charlotte Randolph (Meade) Lane, July 19, 1863, Meade Family Papers, VHS; James E. B. Stuart to his wife, July 13, 1863, in Stuart, *The Letters of Major General James E. B. Stuart*, 327; Richard H. Bagby to Bennette M. Bagby, August 24, 1863, Bennette M. Bagby Papers, DU; William R. Aylett to Alice Roane (Brockenbrough) Aylett, July 19, 1863, Aylett Family Papers, VHS.

28. James DeWitt Hankins to Virginia Wilson Hankins, February 12, 1863, Hankins Family Papers, VHS. Other members of the last generation who lamented the sin of speculation include George Woodville Latham to Lucy Parke (Chamberlayne) Bagby, March 15, 1863, Bagby Family Papers, VHS; Robert T. Scott to Fanny (Carter) Scott, January 24, 1863, Keith Family Papers, VHS; John James Reeve to Lucy Parke (Chamberlayne) Bagby, March 31, 1863, Bagby Family Papers, VHS.

29. Apperson Diary, February 21, 1864, John Samuel Apperson Papers, VT. Apperson was careful not to label all civilians as speculators. He wrote: "I do not impeach all the citizens of Winchester with this penurious, merciless principle, for those there are some, I have no doubt, that are soul and body engrossed in the welfare of our soldiers and the cause of our country."

30. Ibid., April 3, 1863. Walter Taylor also twisted powerful evidence of lower-class dissatisfaction into declarations of support. "Speaking of deserters &c, we have one of the finest & most striking illustrations of the patriotism of the Southern women presented here today that I have ever heard of," he wrote in the spring of 1864. "A soldier deserted some five months ago, and this morning his wife brought him back like a true woman, pleading that his offence might be forgiven and he restored to duty." He thought she was "too good a woman indeed for such a man." See Walter Taylor to Bettie Saunders, March 25, 1864, in W. H. Taylor, *Lee's Adjutant*, 143.

31. Eugene Blackford to his mother, December 17, 1863, Blackford Family Papers, SHC.

32. William R. J. Pegram to Mary Evans (Pegram) Anderson, October 5, 1864, Pegram-Johnson-McIntosh Papers, VHS.

33. William R. J. Pegram to Mary Evans (Pegram) Anderson, March 14, 1865, Pegram-Johnson-McIntosh Papers, VHS.

34. James E. B. Stuart to Flora Stuart, February 8, 1864, in Stuart, *The Letters of Major General James E. B. Stuart*, 370–71.

35. Herman Hattaway and Archer Jones, *How the North Won: A Military History of the Civil War* (Urbana: University of Illinois Press, 1983), 671–72; James M. McPherson, "American Victory, American Defeat," in *Why the Confederacy Lost*, ed. Gabor S. Boritt (New York: Oxford University Press, 1992), 39–41.

36. John H. Chamberlayne to Martha Burwell Chamberlayne, October 9, 1864, in Chamberlayne, *Ham Chamberlayne*, 274. For a similar analysis of military affairs in the Confederacy, see Robert T. Scott to Fanny (Carter) Scott, October 3, 1864, Keith Family Papers, VHS.

37. For historians who have emphasized actions of the Union army as a unifying force among white Virginians, see William A. Blair, "Barbarians at Fredericksburg's Gate: The Impact of the Union Army on Civilians," in Gary W. Gallagher, ed., *Decision on the Rappahannock: Essays on the Fredericksburg Campaign* (Chapel Hill: University of North Carolina Press, 1995), 158; Stephen V. Ash, *Middle Tennessee Society Transformed, 1860: War and Peace in the Upper South* (Baton Rouge: Louisiana State University, 1988); Stephen V. Ash, *When the Yankees Came: Conflict and Chaos in the Occupied South, 1861–1865* (Chapel Hill: University of North Carolina Press, 1996); Mark Grimsley, "Conciliation and Its Failure, 1861–1862," *Civil War History* 39 (December 1993), 317–35.

38. William R. Aylett to Alice Roane (Brockenbrough) Aylett, June 23 and June 30, 1863, Aylett Family Papers, VHS.

39. William R. Aylett to Alice Roane (Brockenbrough) Aylett, July 20 and July 21, 1863, Aylett Family Papers, VHS.

40. Robert T. Scott to Fanny (Carter) Scott, December 31, 1862, Keith Family Papers, VHS. Northern depredations convinced the last generation that God would intervene on their side. No sermon or political speech evoked the same emotions as the behavior of Northern armies. It was inconceivable that God would punish Southerners when they had been victims of the enemy's brutal treatment. See James DeWitt Hankins to John H. Hankins, October 28, 1862, Hankins Family Papers, VHS; James Henry Langhorne to John Archer Langhorne, December 15, 1861, Langhorne Family of Montgomery Co., Va., Papers, VHS; Apperson Diary, July 4, 1861, and December 15, 1862, John Samuel Apperson Papers, VT; Matthew Page Andrews to Anna Robinson, August 25, 1861, Charles Wesley Andrews Papers, DU; Henry Wilkins Coons to Mary Dillard (Coons) Corbin, July 26, 1862, Coons Family Papers, VHS; Richard Corbin to his father, June 10, 1864, in Richard W. Corbin, *Letters of a Confederate Officer to His Family in Europe during the Last Year of the War of Secession* (1902; reprint, Baltimore: Butternut and Blue, 1993), 31.

41. Carter Nelson Minor Diary, October 14, 1864, James Fontaine Minor Papers, vol. 3, AL.

42. Alexander S. Pendleton to Kate Corbin, June 23, 1863, William Nelson Pendleton Papers, SHC. For a similar cultural interpretation of the differences between Northern character and Southern character, see Apperson Diary, May 9, 1862, John Samuel Apperson Papers, VT; Hodijah Lincoln Meade to Charlotte Randolph (Meade) Lane,

July 19, 1863, Meade Family Papers, VHS; James DeWitt Hankins to Virginia Wilson Hankins, July 11, 1862, Hankins Family Papers, VHS.

43. Alexander S. Pendleton to Kate Corbin, June 28, 1863, William Nelson Pendleton Papers, SHC.

44. Ibid.

45. Robert T. Scott to Fanny (Carter) Scott, July 16, 1863, Keith Family Papers, VHS.

46. Jefferson Davis, "Speech at Richmond," [January 5, 1863], in *The Papers of Jefferson Davis*, ed. Lynda Lasswell Crist et al. (Baton Rouge: Louisiana State University Press, 1997), 9:13.

47. William R. J. Pegram to Virginia Johnson (Pegram) McIntosh, August 1, 1864, Pegram-Johnson-McIntosh Papers, VHS.

48. Quoted in Steven E. Woodworth, *While God Is Marching On: The Religious World of Civil War Soldiers* (Lawrence: University Press of Kansas, 2001), 280. This point counters much of the current orthodoxy concerning Confederate reaction to battlefield reverses. For the best summary of the various arguments that religion caused Southerners to feel guilty over slavery, see Beringer et al., *Why the South Lost the Civil War*, 352–67. Genovese offers an effective rebuttal to the "guilt over slavery" school. He argues that Southerners did not condemn slavery as a sin of the Confederacy. Those parties concerned about the institution called for amelioration, not eradication, to earn divine favor. See his *A Consuming Fire*.

49. Members of the last generation overemphasized the fragmentation of Northern society as a way to make the tensions within their own communities seem less severe. If the Confederacy had a problem with profiteers, young Virginians consoled themselves with the belief that the situation behind Northern lines was far worse. They highlighted antigovernment riots to show the lack of support for the Northern cause and the festering of class resentment. See Apperson Diary, June 20 and 21, 1863, January 30, 1864, John Samuel Apperson Papers, VT. Thomas Claybrook Elder to Anna Fitzhugh (May) Elder, July 27, 1862, Thomas Claybrook Elder Papers, VHS; Hodijah Lincoln Meade to Charlotte Randolph (Meade) Lane, July 19, 1863, Meade Family Papers, VHS; Robert T. Scott to Fanny (Carter) Scott, July 16, 1863, Keith Family Papers, VHS. On resistance to the war in the North, see Iver Bernstein, *The New York City Draft Riots: Their Significance and Politics in the Age of the Civil War* (New York: Oxford University Press, 1990); William F. Hanna, "The Boston Draft Riot," *Civil War History* 36 (September 1990): 262–73; Frank L. Klement, *The Copperheads in the Middle West* (Chicago: University of Chicago Press, 1960). For the best overview of wartime society in the North, see Phillip Shaw Paludan, *"A People's Contest": The Union and Civil War, 1861–1865* (New York: Harper and Row, 1988).

50. Hodijah Lincoln Meade to Charlotte Randolph (Meade) Lane, July 19, 1863, Meade Family Papers, VHS.

51. James Keith to Juliet (Chilton) Keith, November 16, 1864, Keith Family Papers, VHS.

52. Richard Corbin to his father, June 10, 1864, in Corbin, *Letters of a Confederate Officer*, 28–29.

53. John H. Chamberlayne to Martha Burwell Chamberlayne, September 6, 1862, in Chamberlayne, *Ham Chamberlayne*, 102.

54. John James Reeve to Lucy Parke (Chamberlayne) Bagby, August 11, 1864, Bagby Family Papers, VHS.

55. William R. J. Pegram to Mary Evans (Pegram) Anderson, July 21, 1864, Pegram-Johnson-McIntosh Papers, VHS.

56. Walter H. Taylor to Bettie Saunders, March 25, 1864, in W. H. Taylor, *Lee's Adjutant*, 144; Berends, "'Wholesome Reading Purifies and Elevates the Man,'" 133. Examples of Lee's encouraging religious activity in the army appear in J. Tracy Power, *Lee's Miserables: Life in the Army of Northern Virginia from the Wilderness to Appomattox* (Chapel Hill: University of North Carolina Press, 1998), 4–5, 126. For other expressions of confidence in Lee, see Thomas Claybrook Elder to Anna Fitzhugh (May) Elder, November 22, 1862, May 8, 1863, and September 11, 1864, Thomas Claybrook Elder Papers, VHS; Richard H. Bagby to Bennette M. Bagby, August 24, 1863, Bennette M. Bagby Papers, DU; William T. Poague to his father, June 1, 1864, in Poague, *Gunner with Stonewall: Reminiscences of William Thomas Poague*, ed. Monroe F. Cockrell (1957; reprint, Wilmington, N.C.: Broadfoot Publishing Co., 1987), 133–35. On Lee's symbolic value to the Confederacy, see Gary W. Gallagher, "'Upon their Success Hang Momentous Interests': Generals," in *Why the Confederacy Lost*, ed. Gabor S. Boritt (New York: Oxford University Press, 1992), 100–103; Douglas Southall Freeman, *R. E. Lee: A Biography* (New York: Charles Scribner's Sons, 1934, 1936), 4:183–87; Power, *Lee's Miserables*, 286–87. For a more critical view of Lee, see Thomas L. Connelly, *The Marble Man: Robert E. Lee and His Image in American Society* (New York: Alfred A. Knopf, 1977); Alan T. Nolan, *Lee Considered: General Robert E. Lee and Civil War History* (Chapel Hill: University of North Carolina Press, 1991).

57. Slaughter, *A Sketch of the Life of Randolph Fairfax*, 45.

58. Alexander S. Pendleton to Kate Corbin, July 16, 1863, William N. Pendleton Papers, SHC. In his important article on the impact of the religious military press, Kurt Berends writes: "There is also a smattering of evidence within the religious military press that some soldiers over zealously identified with the worldview proclaimed by the editors. . . . It seems as if in their efforts to Christianize the cause and pay tribute to the 'martyred' heroes, editors fused the sacred and secular in the minds of some soldiers in an undesired way. . . . Perhaps all editors knew the difference between a Christian martyr and a noble patriot, but obviously not all soldiers made the same distinction." See his "'Wholesome Reading Purifies and Elevates the Man,'"154.

59. In his remarkable study of the Army of Northern Virginia in the final year of the war, J. Tracy Power argues that Lee's officers retained their allegiance to the Confederate cause throughout the winter of 1864–65, and that these same men were surprised that the war had so little support among civilians. Power also detects a gradual erosion in morale after the Crater on July 30, 1864. See Power, *Lee's Miserables*, 291, 303–4, 308–10.

60. James Keith to Sarah Agnes (Blackwell) Keith, December 2, 1864, Keith Family Papers, VHS.

61. Notebooks of David Watson, in Student and Alumni Papers, AL; James Keith to Juliet (Chilton) Keith, October 9, 1863, Keith Family Papers, VHS.

62. William T. Poague to his mother, March 15, 1865, in Poague, *Gunner with Stonewall*, 153–54.

63. James Keith to Sarah Agnes (Blackwell) Keith, November 16, 1864, Keith Family Papers, VHS.

64. Those scholars who argue that an impressive number of Confederates refused to believe that God would ever abandon the cause include Genovese, *A Consuming Fire*, 45; Berends, "'Wholesome Reading Purifies and Elevates the Man,'" 153–55; Woodworth, *While God Is Marching On*, 270–86. As students of the Bible and history, young Virginians were well aware of the plight and persecution of the Jews. In 1856, D. H. Conrad said of "those wonderful people the Jews" while speaking to the Virginia Military Institute's Bible Society: "There is hardly an event in their strange, eventful history, that is not predicted from Moses to the last apostle. Read, I pray you, at your leisure, the 28th chapter of Deuteronomy, and you will find their present status there depicted thirty-five centuries, nearly, ago. And this you will see followed up by the prophets, and confirmed by the great central anti-type of all prophecies—Christ." Conrad thought the Jews were "standing evidence" of God's justice and that in time they would serve a higher destiny for the world to see. The last generation readily identified with the historical experience of the Jews, drawing immense comfort and courage from this analogy, for they too believed they had inherited the mantle of God's chosen people. With such a distinction, they expected to be tried by the vicissitudes of war. See Conrad, *The Bible: In Some of Its Less Familiar Aspects* (Richmond: MacFarlane and Fergusson, 1856), 25.

65. James Keith to Sarah Agnes (Blackwell) Keith, December 29, 1864, Keith Family Papers, VHS. Also see Keith's letter to Juliet (Chilton) Keith, October 18, 1864, Keith Family Papers, VHS.

66. William R. J. Pegram to Virginia Johnson (Pegram) McIntosh, March 10, 1865, Pegram-Johnson-McIntosh Papers, VHS. For other members of the last generation who understood the war as a test of faith, see Robert T. Scott to Fanny (Carter) Scott, May 6, 1862, September 26, 1864, and November 3, 1864, Keith Family Papers, VHS; John Booton Hill to Anna Lee (Hill) Major, February 6, 1864, and January 9, 1865, Hill Family Papers, VHS; Richard H. Bagby to Bennette M. Bagby, April 11, 1863, and August 24, 1863, Bennette M. Bagby Papers, DU; Matthew Page Andrews Diary, October 28, 1864, and December 31, 1864, Charles Wesley Andrews Papers, DU; William Poague to his mother, March 17, 1865, in Poague, *Gunner with Stonewall*, 152–53.

67. James DeWitt Hankins to Virginia Wilson Hankins, October 9, 1863, Hankins Family Papers, VHS.

68. James DeWitt Hankins to Virginia Wilson Hankins, January [?], 1865, Hankins Family Papers, VHS. For a similar view of surrender, see James Keith to Juliet (Chilton) Keith, October 9, 1863, Keith Family Papers, VHS; Robert T. Scott to Fanny (Carter) Scott, March 29, 1862, Keith Family Papers, VHS; Jeb Stuart to his wife, March 2, 1862, in Stuart, *The Letters of Major General James E. B. Stuart*, 252.

69. Abraham Fulkerson to Selina Fulkerson, May 7, 1865, Fulkerson Family Papers, VMI.

CHAPTER EIGHT

1. John H. Chamberlayne to Sally Grattan, August 1, 1865, in John Hampden Chamberlayne, *Ham Chamberlayne — Virginian*, ed. C. G. Chamberlayne (Richmond: Press of the Dietz Printing Co., 1932), 333.

2. John Hampden Chamberlayne, *Public Spirit: An Address Delivered at Randolph-Macon College before the Washington Literary Society, June 23, 1875* (Norfolk: Virginian Book and Job Print, 1875), 14. Some partisan newspaper writers also believed that the end of slavery would unleash powerful economic forces that had been pent up in Virginia. See "Conservatives in the South," *Richmond Enquirer*, May 24, 1874, p. 2; "Domestic Economy," *Richmond Dispatch*, January 3, 1879, p. 2.

3. "Free Speech in Virginia!," *Cincinnati Commercial*, clipping in John Hampden Chamberlayne Scrapbook, 1846–1881, VHS. In his superb book on postwar Virginia politics, Jack P. Maddex Jr. detected a generational rift between young Virginia veterans and the old antebellum political guard. See his *The Virginia Conservatives, 1867–1879: A Study in Reconstruction Politics* (Chapel Hill: University of North Carolina Press, 1970), 287–92.

4. On Early and the Virginia contingent, see Gaines M. Foster, *Ghosts of the Confederacy: Defeat, the Lost Cause, and the Emergence of the New South* (New York: Oxford University Press, 1987), 56–61. The best treatment of Early's postwar activities can be found in Gary W. Gallagher, "Jubal A. Early, the Lost Cause, and Civil War History: A Persistent Legacy," in *The Myth of the Lost Cause and Civil War History*, ed. Gary W. Gallagher and Alan T. Nolan (Bloomington: Indiana University Press, 2000), 35–59. A summary of Dabney's postwar views can be found in David W. Blight, *Race and Reunion: The Civil War in American Memory* (Cambridge, Mass.: Harvard University Press, 2001), 262–63.

5. In his masterful study of the Lost Cause, Gaines Foster detects a sharp move toward reconciliation in the mid-1880s in Virginia. I disagree. I found that many members of the last generation, at least in public, avoided militant sectionalism and the war's issues shortly after Appomattox. This changed in the late 1890s. At that time, so I discovered, many Virginians who were junior officers in the war started to downplay reconciliation in favor of Confederate traditions. Even then, such expressions never called for political mobilization or renewed warfare against the North. This chapter seeks to chart the evolution of the last generation's ideas about reunion with the understanding that ideological transitions in Lost Cause thought were not marked by rigid demarcations but did follow generational lines.

6. "Editors' Drawer," *Virginia University Magazine* 6 (May and June 1868): 335. Members of the last generation helped contribute to a spirit of political moderation that generally prevailed in postwar Virginia politics. For a few examples from the partisan press, see "A Word of Advice," *Daily State Journal*, March 18, 1873, p. 1; "The Eyes

on Virginia," *Richmond Enquirer*, August 22, 1873, p. 2; "The Life of the Country," *Richmond Dispatch*, January 29, 1879, p. 2.

7. This realistic assessment of the postwar power relations between North and South transcended generational lines. See "What We Must Do," *Southern Opinion*, June 22, 1867, p. 2.

8. Historians who argue that the Southern impulse to industrialize originated during the Civil War include Maddex, *The Virginia Conservatives*; Paul M. Gaston, *The New South Creed: A Study in Southern Myth-Making* (New York: Alfred A. Knopf, 1970).

9. John Dooley Diary, April 30, 1865, in Dooley, *John Dooley, Confederate Soldier, His War Journal*, ed. Joseph T. Durkin (South Bend: University of Notre Dame Press, 1963), 205.

10. William Gordon McCabe, *Captain Robert Edward Lee* (Richmond: n.p., 1915), 9.

11. Chamberlayne, *Ham Chamberlayne*, ix.

12. See table 8 in the appendix.

13. See table 5 in the appendix.

14. John Warwick Daniel, "The People: An Address Delivered before the Jefferson Literary Society of the University of Virginia," in *Speeches and Orations of John Warwick Daniel*, comp. Edward M. Daniel (Lynchburg: J. P. Bell Co., 1911), 36. Six years after Daniel's speech at the University of Virginia, Edward A. Pollard articulated a postwar vision that follows Daniel's plan but with more details as to how the state should reconstruct itself. This article is quintessential New South boosterism. See Pollard, "New Virginia," *Old and New* 5 (March 1872): 279–90.

15. Daniel, "The People," 36.

16. For other members of the last generation who shared Daniel's postwar faith in the joint advance of Christianity and progress, see Thomas U. Dudley, *An Address Delivered before the Society of Alumni of the University of Virginia, July 2, 1879* (Charlottesville: Chronicle Steam Power Book and Job Print, 1879), 21; Robert Taylor Scott, *Address at the Unveiling of the Monument in Hollywood Cemetery, October 5, 1888* (Richmond: Whittet and Shepperson, 1888), 8. Eugene D. Genovese has found a great degree of moral confusion and doubt immediately following Appomattox. I did not find a similar response in the last generation. See his *A Consuming Fire: The Fall of the Confederacy in the Mind of the White Christian South* (Athens: University of Georgia Press, 1998), 63–66. Also on the rise of postwar skepticism, see Charles Reagan Wilson, *Baptized in Blood: The Religion of the Lost Cause, 1865–1920* (Athens: University of Georgia Press, 1980), 63–69.

17. Daniel, "The People," 36.

18. Ibid., 14.

19. John Warwick Daniel, *Character of Stonewall Jackson* (Lynchburg: Schaffter and Bryant, 1868), 63.

20. Maddex, *The Virginia Conservatives*, 291.

21. For a discussion of the last generation's critique of the Virginia cavalier and their desire to live as Christian gentlemen, see chapter 3.

22. "Virginia—Past and Present," *Southern Opinion*, July 27, 1867, p. 2.

23. "The Times That Were, the Times That Are, and the Times That Are to Be," *Richmond Enquirer*, February 7, 1873, p. 2; "Domestic Economy," *Richmond Dispatch*, January 3, 1879, p. 2. For a similar opinion, see "Thurman and Farnsworth," *Daily State Journal* (Richmond), January 21, 1870, p. 1.

24. The economic vision of Virginia's conservative party centered on massive internal improvements and diversification. See Maddex, *The Virginia Conservatives*, 276–83.

25. Ibid., 276.

26. Frank Ruffin to R. M. T. Hunter, January 13, 1874, Hunter-Garnett Collection, AL. Maddex, *The Virginia Conservatives*, 289.

27. Chamberlayne, *Public Spirit*, 12; John Warwick Daniel, "Conquered Nations," in *Speeches and Orations of John Warwick Daniel*, comp. Edward M. Daniel (Lynchburg: J. P. Bell, 1911), 146.

28. Armistead Churchill Gordon, *Memories and Memorials of William Gordon McCabe* (Richmond: Old Dominion Press, 1925), 1:325.

29. Chamberlayne, *Public Spirit*, 16. Edward Pollard offered a similar view of Virginia's antebellum past and its parallels to the state's postwar situation. See his "New Virginia," 283. This perspective can also be found in "The Times That Were, the Times That Are, and the Times That Are to Be," *Richmond Enquirer*, February 7, 1873, p. 2.

30. Archer Anderson, *Address Delivered before the Washington Literary Society of Randolph-Macon College* (Richmond: Evening News Steam Presses, 1873), 7.

31. For a discussion of how Lost Cause mythology was used to advance the goals of the New South, see Foster, *Ghosts of the Confederacy*, 79–85. Charles Reagan Wilson found less compatibility between the New South creed and Lost Cause orthodoxy. See his *Baptized in Blood*, 81–82.

32. Jubal A. Early, "The Campaigns of Gen. Robert E. Lee: An Address by Lieut. General Jubal A. Early, before Washington and Lee University, January 19th, 1872," in *Lee: The Soldier*, ed. Gary W. Gallagher (Lincoln: University of Nebraska Press, 1996), 71.

33. Gallagher, "Jubal A. Early," 40.

34. Fitzhugh Lee is the best example from the last generation of a young Virginian collaborating with Jubal Early. As members of the Association of the Army of Northern Virginia, both men worked tirelessly in attacking the reputation of James Longstreet, and they even fabricated evidence to claim that the general foiled Lee's plans at Gettysburg. Significantly, when it came to the question of reconciliation with the North, Early and Fitzhugh Lee parted ways. In 1875, Lee accepted a speaking invitation in Boston, and Early strenuously objected to his friend's travel plans. On their partnership in shaping Confederate historical memory and their divergent views on reunion, see Gary W. Gallagher's introduction to Fitzhugh Lee, *General Lee* (1894; reprint, Wilmington, N.C.: Broadfoot Publishing Co., 1989), xix–xx; Foster, *Ghosts of the Confederacy*, 100. Early's influence can also be found in the postwar writings of the last generation's William T. Poague. See Poague, *Gunner with Stonewall: Reminiscences of William Thomas Poague*, ed. Monroe F. Cockrell (1957; reprint, Wilmington, N.C.: Broadfoot Publishing Co., 1987), 70–73. John Warwick Daniel also had close ties with Early during the war

and after, but Early did not agree with Daniel's reconciliationist sentiments. See Foster, *Ghosts of the Confederacy*, 88.

35. Archer Anderson, "Robert Edward Lee: An Address Delivered at the Dedication of the Lee Monument," in *Southern Historical Society Papers*, ed. J. William Jones et al., 52 vols. and 2-vol. index (1876–1959; reprint, Millwood, N.Y.: Kraus Reprint Co., 1977–80), 17:315. A fine analysis of Anderson's address can be found in Blight, *Race and Reunion*, 267–70. A similar perspective on Lee can be found in John Hampden Chamberlayne, "Address on the Character of General R. E. Lee," *SHSP* 3 (1877): 36–37; F. Lee, *General Lee*; Walter H. Taylor, *General Lee: His Campaigns in Virginia, 1861–1865, with Personal Reminiscences* (Norfolk: Nusbaum Book and News Co., 1906); Edward A. Pollard, *Lee and His Lieutenants: Comprising the Early Life, Public Services, and Campaigns of General Robert E. Lee and His Companions in Arms, with a Record of Their Campaigns and Heroic Deeds* (New York: E. B. Treat, 1867); Poague, *Gunner with Stonewall*, 70–73. When editing the papers of Robert E. Lee, Robert E. Lee Jr. emphasized his father's nationalistic side in an attempt to portray the general as an American hero. See Gary W. Gallagher's introduction to Robert E. Lee Jr., *Recollections and Letters of General Robert E. Lee* (1904; reprint, Wilmington: Broadfoot Publishing Co., 1988). John Warwick Daniel also paid tribute to Lee as a great general, and he emphasized Lee's postwar actions as a model of sectional moderation. See his "Lee: An Oration Pronounced at the Unveiling of the Recumbent Figure at Lexington, Virginia, June 30, 1883," in *Speeches and Orations of John Warwick Daniel*, comp. Edward M. Daniel (Lynchburg: J. P. Bell, 1911), 187–237. Only Thomas U. Dudley of my sample group suggested that Lee's character demonstrated the superiority of the Old South. See his *The Memory of Robert E. Lee* (New York: Press of Andrew H. Kellogg, 1901), 15.

36. John Warwick Daniel, "Character of Stonewall Jackson," in *Speeches and Orations of John Warwick Daniel*, comp. Edward M. Daniel (Lynchburg: J. P. Bell, 1911), 45–46, 47.

37. Edward Pollard, "The Real Condition of the South," *Lippincott's Magazine of Literature, Science and Education* (Philadelphia: J. B. Lippincott, 1870), 5:614. Partisan papers generally confirmed Pollard's assessment that despite all the evils of Radical Reconstruction, Virginians should suffocate the flame of the secessionist past and place their faith in those Northerners who embraced a moderate policy toward the South that would ultimately pave the way for home rule. See "A Word of Advice," *Daily State Journal*, March 18, 1873, p. 1; "General Wise's Indictment of the Conservative Party," *Daily State Journal*, June 11, 1873, p. 2; "New Virginia," *Richmond Enquirer*, September 4, 1873, p. 2.

38. Eric Foner, *Reconstruction: America's Unfinished Revolution, 1863–1877* (New York: Harper and Row, 1988), 413.

39. Quoted in James L. Nichols, *General Fitzhugh Lee: A Biography* (Lynchburg: H. E. Howard, 1989), 119.

40. "North and South at Gettysburg," *Army and Navy Journal*, July 1887, 1001. William T. Poague also attended the 1887 Gettysburg reunion and wrote glowingly about

the spirit of Americanism that prevailed at that event. See his *Gunner with Stonewall*, 76–77. A superb discussion of the 1887 Gettysburg reunion and its role in promoting sectional healing can be found in Carol Reardon, *Pickett's Charge: In History and Memory* (Chapel Hill: University of North Carolina Press, 1997), 93–104.

41. William R. Aylett to Alice Roane (Brockenbrough) Aylett, July 20 and July 21, 1863, Aylett Family Papers, VHS.

42. On Northern sentimentality and reconciliation with the South, see Nina Silber, *The Romance of Reunion: Northerners and the South, 1865–1900* (Chapel Hill: University of North Carolina Press, 1993); Stuart McConnell, *Glorious Contentment: The Grand Army of the Republic, 1865–1900* (Chapel Hill: University of North Carolina Press, 1992).

43. Scott, *Address at the Unveiling of the Monument*, 19. For a similar perspective, see William Gordon McCabe, *Speech of Capt. W. Gordon McCabe, of Richmond, Virginia, Delivered Before the New England Society, New York City, at the Waldorf Astoria, on December 22, 1899* (Nashville: Brandon Printing Co., n.d.), 11; James Keith, "General Eppa Hunton: Presentation of His Portrait to Lee Camp," *Addresses on Several Occasions by James Keith of Fauquier* (Richmond: Appeals Press, 1917) 19.

44. William Gordon McCabe eulogized three of his contemporaries in the last generation, and in each publication he stressed that none of these men had reconciled themselves to defeat and that they thought the Southern cause was just. See his following publications: "Address of Colonel McCabe," *University of Virginia Bulletin* 5 (January 1905): 13; "A Brief Sketch of Andrew Reid Venable, Jr.," *SHSP* 37 (1909): 14; and *Captain Robert E. Lee*, 14.

45. On the politics of segregation in Virginia, see J. Douglas Smith, *Managing White Supremacy: Race, Politics, and Citizenship in Jim Crow Virginia* (Chapel Hill: University of North Carolina Press, 2002); Jeffrey R. Kerr-Ritchie, *Freedpeople in the Tobacco South: Virginia, 1860–1900* (Chapel Hill: University of North Carolina Press, 1999); Jane Dailey, *Before Jim Crow: The Politics of Race in Postemancipation Virginia* (Chapel Hill: University of North Carolina Press, 2000); James Tice Moore, *Two Paths to the New South: The Virginia Debt Controversy, 1870–1883* (Lexington: University Press of Kentucky, 1974).

46. Jane Turner Censer, *The Reconstruction of White Southern Womanhood, 1861–1895* (Baton Rouge: Louisiana State University Press, 2003), 261–63; James Keith, "William Smith," in *Addresses on Several Occasions by James Keith of Fauquier* (Richmond: Appeals Press, 1917), 23. Foster believes that at the beginning of the twentieth century power shifted along generational lines in Confederate organizations. See his *Ghosts of the Confederacy*, 163–64.

47. Foster, *Ghosts of the Confederacy*, 178.

48. Quoted from ibid., 151.

49. Archer Anderson to Captain Smith, May 12, 1916, Archer Anderson Papers, Eleanor Brockenbrough Library, Museum of the Confederacy, Richmond. Like Anderson, those members of the last generation who contested the reconciliationist message did not intend to reawaken sectional disharmony. See Charles L. C. Minor, "President

Lincoln," *SHSP* 27 (1899): 165–70; Charles L. C. Minor, "President Lincoln Further Arraigned," *SHSP* 27 (1899): 365–71; W. H. Taylor, *General Lee*, 1–14.

50. Charles L. C. Minor, "The South and the Union: To Whom Should the Southern People Build Monuments, to Lee or to Grant, to Lincoln or to Davis?" *SHSP* 30 (1902): 332.

51. Ibid., 337–38.

52. The role of the cavalier in Southern culture is brilliantly explored by Daniel Singal in *The War Within: From Victorian to Modernist Thought in the South, 1919 to 1945* (Chapel Hill: University of North Carolina Press, 1982), 11–33. John Esten Cooke offered a highly romantic interpretation of the Virginia Civil War experience from shortly after Appomattox until his death in 1886. His literary contributions show how a veteran could quickly become nostalgic about the glory days of military life. Unfortunately, I did not find a single reference to Cooke's writings by a member of the last generation in my sample. On Cooke's postwar influence, see Blight, *Race and Reunion*, 156–57.

53. Those members of the last generation who evoked the cavalier tradition and the "moonlight and magnolias" view of the South after the Spanish-American War include William Gordon McCabe. See three of his writings: *Speech of Capt. W. Gordon McCabe*, 9, 11; *Joseph Bryan: A Brief Memoir* (Richmond: Wm. Ellis Jones, 1909), iii–xxix; "A Brief Sketch of Andrew Reid Venable, Jr.," *SHSP* 37 (1909): 3. See also Charles L. C. Minor, "The Old System of Slavery: Its Compensations and Contrasts With Present Labor Conditions," 30 *SHSP* (1902): 125–29.

54. Holmes Conrad, "Virginia Mourning Her Dead," *SHSP* 38 (1910): 235–36, 240. Other members of the last generation expressed similar concerns about Virginia's place in a modern world but most still framed the Confederate experience as a truly American one. See James Keith, "The Supreme Court of Appeals: Before the 'Pewter Platter Club' of Norfolk, Virginia," in *Addresses on Several Occasions by James Keith of Fauquier* (Richmond: Appeals Press, 1917), 71; Thomas C. Elder, *Address of Major Thomas C. Elder: President of the Virginia State Bar Association at Its Fourteenth Annual Meeting Held at Hot Springs, Virginia, August 5th, 6th, and 7th, 1902* (Richmond: Everett Waddey Co., 1902), 3, 5.

Bibliography

MANUSCRIPTS

Atlanta, Ga.
  Special Collections, Emory University General Library
    John S. Dobbins Papers
    William Syndor Thomson Papers
Birmingham, Ala.
  Birmingham Public Library Archives
    J. E. Celurke Letters, Collection 283
Blacksburg, Va.
  Special Collections, Virginia Polytechnic Institute and State University
    John Samuel Apperson Papers, Ms74-003
    Edwin H. Harmon Papers, Ms90-019
    Koontz Family Papers
Chapel Hill, N.C.
  Southern Historical Collection, Wilson Library, University of North Carolina
    at Chapel Hill
    Beale and Davis Family Papers
    Blackford Family Papers
    John L. Johnson Papers
    Lenoir Family Papers
    George Knox Miller Papers
    William Nelson Pendleton Papers
    Abram David Pollock Papers
    White-Wellford-Taliaferro-Marshall Papers
Charlottesville, Va.
  Albert and Shirley Small Special Collections Library, Alderman Library,
    University of Virginia
    Aylett Family Papers
    Lancelot Blackford Papers
    Breckinridge Family Papers
    Cabell Family Papers
    Hunter-Garnett Collection
    James Fontaine Minor Papers

Student and Alumni Papers: Lecture Notebooks, 1827–1882, and Autograph
Books
University of Virginia Student Papers
Durham, N.C.
Rare Book, Manuscript, and Special Collections Library, Duke University
Charles Wesley Andrews Papers
Bennette M. Bagby Papers
Munford-Ellis Papers (George W. Munford Division)
George W. Turner Papers
Farmville, Va.
Special Collections, Hampden-Sydney College
Union Society Notes
Fredericksburg, Va.
Fredericksburg and Spotsylvania National Military Park
John Henry Stover Funk Papers
Lexington, Va.
Virginia Military Institute Archives, Preston Library, Virginia Military Institute
William Weldon Bentley Papers
Stapleton Crutchfield Jr. Papers
Fulkerson Family Papers
Andrew C. L. Gatewood Papers
Special Collections, James Graham Leyburn Library, Washington and Lee
University
Crenshaw, Ollinger. "General Lee's College: Rise and Growth of Washington
and Lee." 2 vols. Typescript, Washington and Lee University, 1973.
James Dorman Davidson Papers
Ellinor Porcher Gadsden Papers
Richmond, Va.
Eleanor Brockenbrough Library, Museum of the Confederacy
Archer Anderson Papers
Virginia Historical Society
Archer Anderson Papers
Aylett Family Papers
Bagby Family Papers
John Hampden Chamberlayne Scrapbook, 1846–1881
Giles B. Cooke Papers
Coons Family Papers
John Warwick Daniel Papers
Early Family Papers, 1764–1956
Thomas Claybrook Elder Papers
Gwathmey Family Papers
Hankins Family Papers
Hill Family Papers
Keith Family Papers

Keith Family of Woodburne, Fauquier Co., Va., Papers
William T. Kinzer Papers
Langhorne Family of Montgomery Co., Va., Papers
Mason Family Papers
Meade Family Papers
Pegram-Johnson-McIntosh Papers
Ridley Family of Southampton Co., Va., Papers
A. B. Roler Papers
Washington, D.C.
Library of Congress
Jubal A. Early Papers

DIARIES, LETTERS, JOURNALS, AND MEMOIRS

The Address of the Southern Rights' Association of the University of Virginia to the Young Men of the South. Charlottesville: James Alexander, 1851.

Allan, Elizabeth Randolph Preston. *A March Past: Reminiscences of Elizabeth Randolph Preston Allan.* Richmond: Dietz Press, 1938.

Anderson, Archer. *Address Delivered before the Washington Literary Society of Randolph-Macon College.* Richmond: Evening News Steam Presses, 1873.

Baird, Nancy Chappelear, ed. *Journals of Amanda Virginia Edmonds: Lass of the Mosby Confederacy, 1859–1867.* Stephens City, Va.: Commercial Press, 1984.

Barclay, Ted. *Ted Barclay, Liberty Hall Volunteers: Letters From the Stonewall Brigade.* Edited by Charles W. Turner. Natural Bridge Station, Va.: Rockbridge Publishing Co., 1992.

Bernard, George S., ed. *War Talks of Confederate Veterans.* 1892. Reprint, Dayton, Ohio: Morningside House, 1981

Casler, John O. *Four Years in the Stonewall Brigade.* 1893. Reprint, Dayton, Ohio: Morningside Bookshop, 1982.

Catalogue of the University of Virginia, Session of 1860–61. Richmond: Chas. H. Wynne, 1861.

Chamberlayne, John Hampden. *Ham Chamberlayne—Virginian.* Edited by C. G. Chamberlayne. Richmond: Press of the Dietz Printing Co., 1932.

———. *Public Spirit: An Address Delivered at Randolph-Macon College before the Washington Literary Society, June 23, 1875.* Norfolk: Virginian Book and Job Print, 1875.

W. F. Shepherd to Genl. Cocke, May 1, 1861. *Bulletin of Fluvanna County Historical Society* 38 (October 1984): 15.

Colt, Margaretta Barton, ed. *Defend the Valley: A Shenandoah Family in the Civil War.* New York: Orion Books, 1994.

Conrad, D. H. *The Bible: In Some of Its Less Familiar Aspects.* Richmond: MacFarlane and Fergusson, 1856.

Conway, Moncure Daniel. *Autobiography, Memories and Experiences of Moncure Daniel Conway.* 2 vols. Boston: Houghton, Mifflin, 1904.

Corbin, Richard W. *Letters of a Confederate Officer to His Family in Europe during the Last Year of the War of Secession.* 1902. Reprint, Baltimore: Butternut and Blue, 1993.

Couture, Richard T., ed. "The Bolling-Cabell Letters." *Goochland County Historical Society Magazine* 14 (1982): 25–29.

Dabney, Robert L. *The Christian Soldier: A Sermon Commemorative of the Death of Abram C. Carrington.* Richmond: Presbyterian Committee of Publications, 1863.

———. "Co-operation: Something for Virginians to Read." In *Discussions: Evangelical and Theological.* London: Banner of Truth Trust, 1967. First published in the *Central Presbyterian*, October 31, 1857.

Daniel, John Warwick. *Character of Stonewall Jackson.* Lynchburg: Schaffter and Bryant, 1868.

———. *Speeches and Orations of John Warwick Daniel.* Compiled by Edward M. Daniel. Lynchburg: J. P. Bell, 1911.

Davidson, Albert. "Lieutenant Albert Davidson: Letters of a Virginia Soldier." Edited by Charles W. Turner. *West Virginia History* 39 (Fall 1977): 49–71.

Davidson, Greenlee. *Captain Greenlee Davidson, C.S.A.: Diary and Letters, 1851–1863.* Edited by Charles W. Turner. Verona, Va.: McClure Press, 1975.

Davis, Jefferson. *The Papers of Jefferson Davis.* Edited by Lynda Lasswell Crist et. al. 10 vols. Baton Rouge: Louisiana State University Press, 1997.

Dooley, John. *John Dooley, Confederate Soldier: His War Journal.* Edited by Joseph T. Durkin. South Bend: University of Notre Dame Press, 1963.

Dudley, Thomas U. *An Address Delivered before the Society of Alumni of the University of Virginia, July 2, 1879.* Charlottesville: Chronicle Steam Power Book and Job Print, 1879.

———. *The Memory of Robert E. Lee.* New York: Press of Andrew H. Kellogg, 1901.

Dunaway, Wayland F. *Reminiscences of a Rebel.* New York: Neale Publishing Co., 1913.

Elder, Thomas C. *Address of Major Thomas C. Elder: President of the Virginia State Bar Association at Its Fourteenth Annual Meeting Held at Hot Springs, Virginia, August 5th, 6th, and 7th, 1902.* Richmond: Everett Waddey, 1902.

Early, Jubal A. "The Campaigns of Gen. Robert E. Lee: An Address by Lieut. General Jubal A. Early, before Washington and Lee University, January 19th, 1872." In *Lee: The Soldier.* Edited by Gary W. Gallagher. Lincoln: University of Nebraska Press, 1996.

Fleet, Betsy, and John D. P. Fuller, eds. *Green Mount: A Virginia Plantation Family during the Civil War: Being the Journal of Benjamin Robert Fleet and Letters of His Family.* Lexington: University of Kentucky Press, 1962.

Gadsden, C. P. *The Bible, the Only Safe Director of the Activity of the Day: An Address Delivered before the Cadets' Bible Society of the Virginia Military Institute, June 3, 1859.* Richmond: MacFarlane and Fergusson, 1859.

Gordon, Armistead Churchill. *Memories and Memorials of William Gordon McCabe.* 2 vols. Richmond: Old Dominion Press, 1925.

Grigsby, Hugh Blair. *Oration, Delivered before the Students of William and Mary College, July 4, 1859.* N.p.

————. *The Virginia Convention of 1776: A Discourse Delivered before the Virginia Alpha of the Phi Beta Kappa Society, in the Chapel of William and Mary College.* Richmond: J. W. Randolph, 1855.

Hairston, Peter W., ed. "J. E. B. Stuart's Letters to His Hairston Kin, 1850–1855," *North Carolina Historical Review* 51 (July 1974): 261–333.

Holcombe, James P. *An Address Delivered before the Society of Alumni of the University of Virginia, at Its Annual Meeting, Held in the Public Hall, June 29, 1853.* Richmond: MacFarlane and Fergusson, 1853.

Hope, James Baron. *Poem and Address: Delivered on the First Annual Meeting of the Society of the "Old Boys of Hampton Academy," July, 1860.* Richmond: Wm. H. Clemitt, 1861.

Johnson, John Lipscomb. *The University Memorial: Biographical Sketches of Alumni of the University of Virginia Who Fell in the Confederate War.* Baltimore: Turnbull Brothers, 1871.

Jones, J. William. *Christ in the Camp; or, Religion in the Confederate Army.* 1887. Reprint, Harrisonburg, Va.: Sprinkle Publications, 1986.

Jordan, Cornelia Jane Matthews. *In Memoriam: John Tyler Waller of Virginia.* [Richmond?]: n.p., [1865?].

Junkin, George. *An Apology for Collegiate Education: Being the Baccalaureate Address, Delivered Commencement Day of Washington College.* Lexington, Va.: n.p., 1851.

Keith, James. *Addresses on Several Occasions by James Keith of Fauquier.* Richmond: Appeals Press, 1917.

Lee, Fitzhugh Lee. *General Lee.* 1894. Reprint, Wilmington, N.C.: Broadfoot Publishing Co., 1989.

Lee, Robert E. *The Wartime Papers of R. E. Lee.* Edited by Clifford Dowdey and Louis H. Manarin. Boston: Little, Brown, 1961.

Lee, Robert E., Jr. *Recollections and Letters of General Robert E. Lee.* 1904. Reprint, Wilmington: Broadfoot Publishing Co., 1988.

Lyle, John Newton. *A Reminiscence of Lieutenant John Newton Lyle of the Liberty Hall Volunteers.* Edited by Charles W. Turner. Roanoke, Va.: Virginia Lithography and Graphics Co., 1987.

Massie, James W. *An Address Delivered before the Society of Alumni of the Virginia Military Institute, July 3rd, 1857.* Richmond: MacFarlane and Fergusson, 1857.

Maury, Matthew F. *Address Delivered before the Literary Societies of the University of Virginia of the 28th June, 1855.* Richmond: H. K. Ellyson, 1855.

McCabe, William Gordon. *Joseph Bryan: A Brief Memoir.* Richmond: Wm. Ellis Jones, 1909.

————. *Captain Robert Edward Lee.* Richmond: n.p., 1915.

————. *Speech of Capt. W. Gordon McCabe, of Richmond, Virginia, Delivered before the New England Society, New York City, at the Waldorf Astoria, on December 22, 1899.* Nashville: Brandon Printing Co., n.d.

McIlwaine, Richard. *Memories of Three Score Years and Ten.* New York: Neale Publishing Co., 1908.

Minor, Berkeley. *If Lee Could Have Stood at the Helm.* Staunton, Va.: n.p., 1911.

Monteiro, Walter. *Address Delivered before the Neotrophian Society of the Hampton Academy, on the Twenty-eighth of July, 1857.* Richmond: H. K. Ellyson, 1857.

Oram, Richard W., ed. "Harpers Ferry to the Fall of Richmond: Letters of Colonel John De Hart Ross," *West Virginia History* 45 (1984): 159–74.

Pate, Henry Clay. *The American Vade Mecum; or, The Companion of Youth and Guide to College.* Cincinnati: Morgan, 1852.

Poague, William Thomas. *Gunner with Stonewall: Reminiscences of William Thomas Poague.* Edited by Monroe F. Cockrell. 1957. Reprint, Wilmington, N.C.: Broadfoot Publishing Co., 1987.

Pollard, Edward A. *Lee and His Lieutenants: Comprising the Early Life, Public Services, and Campaigns of General Robert E. Lee and His Companions in Arms, with a Record of Their Campaigns and Heroic Deeds.* New York: E. B. Treat, 1867.

Reese, George H., ed. *Proceedings of the Virginia State Convention of 1861: February 13–May 1.* 4 vols. Richmond: Virginia State Library, 1965.

Robertson, Mary D., ed. *Lucy Breckinridge of Grove Hill: The Journal of a Virginia Girl, 1862–1864.* Kent, Ohio: Kent State University Press, 1979.

Scott, Robert Taylor. *Address at the Unveiling of the Monument in Hollywood Cemetery, October 5, 1888.* Richmond: Whittet and Shepperson, 1888.

Sherman, William T. *Sherman's Civil War: Selected Correspondence of William T. Sherman, 1860–1865.* Edited by Brooks D. Simpson and Jean V. Berlin. Chapel Hill: University of North Carolina Press, 1999.

Slaughter, Philip. *A Sketch of the Life of Randolph Fairfax.* Richmond: Tyler, Allegre, and McDaniel, 1864.

Smith, Francis H. *Introductory Address to the Corps of Cadets of the Virginia Military Institute, on the Resumption of Academic Duties, September 2, 1856.* Richmond: MacFarlane and Fergusson, 1856.

Smith, William A. *Lectures on the Philosophy and Practice of Slavery as Exhibited in the Institution of Domestic Slavery in the United States: With the Duties of Masters to Slavery.* Edited by Thomas O. Summers. Nashville: Stevenson and Evans, 1856.

Strother, David Hunter. *A Virginia Yankee in the Civil War: The Diaries of David Hunter Strother.* Edited by Cecil D. Eby Jr. Chapel Hill: University of North Carolina Press, 1961.

Stuart, J. E. B. *The Letters of Major General James E. B. Stuart.* Edited by Adele H. Mitchell. N.p.: Mosby Historical Society, 1990.

Taylor, Walter H. *General Lee: His Campaigns in Virginia, 1861–1865, with Personal Reminiscences.* Norfolk: Nusbaum Book and News Co., 1906.

———. *Lee's Adjutant: The Wartime Letters of Colonel Walter Herron Taylor, 1862–1865.* Edited by Tower R. Lockwood. Columbia: University of South Carolina Press, 1995.

U.S. War Department. *The War of the Rebellion: A Compilation of the Official Records of the Union and Confederate Armies.* 128 vols. Washington, D.C.: U.S. Government Printing Office, 1880–1901.

Venable, Charles S. *An Address Delivered before the Society of Alumni, of the Uni-*

versity of Virginia, at Its Annual Meeting Held in the Public Hall, July 26, 1858. Richmond: MacFarlane and Fergusson, 1859.

Williams, Edward B., ed. *Rebel Brothers: The Civil War Letters of the Truehearts.* College Station: Texas A&M University Press, 1995.

White, William S. *Sketches of the Life of Captain Hugh A. White of the Stonewall Brigade.* Columbia: South Carolinian Steam Press, 1864.

MASTER'S THESES AT THE UNIVERSITY OF VIRGINIA
(IN STUDENT AND ALUMNI PAPERS, ALDERMAN LIBRARY)

Allen, William. "Harmony of the Human Mind and the Material Universe." 1860.

Blackford, Lancelot. "Advantages of Fictitious Reading." 1860.

————. "Importance of Classical Education." 1860.

Boyd, James M. "Islamism: Its Beneficial Influences." 1860.

Cabell, Philip B. "Essay on Moral Intellectual Excellence." 1857.

Carroll, Gray. "Essay on the Utilitarian Spirit of the Present Day as Affecting Our Literature." 1859.

Chamberlayne, John Hampden. "Essay on American Literature." 1858.

Dinwiddie, W. "Essay on the Province and Culture of the Imagination." 1854.

Dudley, Thomas Underwood, Jr. "Atheism an Impossibility." 1858.

Fristoe, E. T. "The Wonders and Tendencies of Modern Science." [1854–1861?].

Gannon, Douglas. "A Discourse on the Soul." 1859.

Garnett, James M. [No title]. 1859.

Gibbons, Charles M. "An Essay on Popular Education." 1859.

Harris, R. Herbert. "Essay." 1860.

Harrison, Powell. "A Few Remarks on 'The Perpetuity of the Union,'" 1855.

Hunter, R. M. T., Jr., "On the Advantages of Historical Study." [1860?].

Latane, J. A. "The Value of Grecian History to the American Student." 1851.

Louthan, William P. "The Influence of Moral Principles on the Prosperity of Nations." 1859.

Magruder, John Brown. "The Greek Myths—Their Origins and Development." 1860.

Mathews, Henry M. "Poetry in America." 1854.

Meredith, W. B. "Religious Intolerance." 1859.

Meriwether, F. T. "Comparative Philology." 1860.

Minor, Charles L. C. "On the Danger of Repressing the Natural Emotions." 1858.

Price, Thomas R., Jr., "The Augustan Era of English Literature." 1858.

Rives, R. "Crusades—Some of Their Causes and Effects." [1859?].

Smith, Archibald M. "A Republican Government [Is] Most Favorable to the Development of Literature." 1857.

Smith, Summerfield. "The Development of Society." 1858.

Strange, William G. "The Study of Man, in the Formation of His Character." [1854].

Taliaferro, Edwin. "The Poetry of Greece." 1855.

Thomas, William D. "Connections of Political Economy with Natural Theology."
   1855.
Thompson, J. B. "Religion and Learning in the Middle Ages." 1854.
Timberlake, John H. "Tendency of Science." 1858.
Watson, David. "Essay on the Formation of Character." 1855.
Withrow, Charles H. "Southern Literature." 1859.

PERIODICALS

Army and Navy Journal
Christian Intelligencer (Richmond)
Cincinnati Commercial
Confederate Veteran
Daily State Journal (Richmond)
Hampden Sydney Magazine
Jefferson Monument Magazine (Charlottesville)
The Kaleidoscope (Petersburg)
Lexington Gazette and General Advertiser
Lippincott's Magazine of Literature, Science and Education
Lynchburg Daily Virginian
Old and New
Randolph-Macon Magazine
Religious Herald (Richmond)
The Review (Charlottesville)
Richmond Dispatch and *Richmond Daily Dispatch*
Richmond Enquirer and *Richmond Daily Enquirer*
Richmond Semi-Weekly Examiner
Richmond Sentinel
Richmond Whig and *Richmond Daily Whig*
Rockingham Register (Harrisonburg)
Southern Churchman (Richmond)
Southern Literary Messenger (Richmond)
Southern Historical Society Papers
Southern Opinion (Richmond)
Southern Planter (Richmond)
Southern Repertory and College Review (Emory and Henry College)
Staunton Spectator
University of Virginia Bulletin
Valley Star (Lexington, Va.)
Virginia Gazette (Williamsburg)
Virginia University Magazine

[Allen, William]. "The Progress of Literature." *Virginia University Magazine* 4 (December 1859): 128–33.

[Berkeley, W. R.]. "Religious Reform—Its Nature." *Virginia University Magazine* 4 (January 1860): 161–66.

[Blackford, Lancelot Minor]. "Importance of Classical Education." *Virginia University Magazine* 3 (December 1858): 106–12.

———. "The Past and the Present." *Virginia University Magazine* 4 (February 1860): 255–60.

[Boyd, James M.]. "Roman Catholicism and Free Institutions." *Virginia University Magazine* 4 (April 1860): 341–53.

Buchanan, John L. "The Conflicts of Parties." *Southern Repertory and College Review* 4 (December 1855): 140–44.

Carter, Henry Smith. "Glory and Shame of Virginia." *Southern Repertory and College Review* 3 (June 1854): 202–5.

Garland, J. P. "America—Her Glory and Her Shame." *Southern Repertory and College Review* 4 (December 1856): 232–35.

[Graham, James McDowell]. "Genius." *Virginia University Magazine* 5 (May 1859): 434–42.

———. "The Worship of Nature." *Virginia University Magazine* 3 (June 1859): 503–16.

Halley, J. H. "Proscription of the Clergy." *Southern Repertory and College Review* 4 (January 1855): 33–34.

[Harris, Henry Herbert]. "New Preachment from an Old Text." *Virginia University Magazine* 3 (May 1859): 443–48.

[Hunter, Robert M. T., Jr.]. "The Advantages of Historical Study." *Virginia University Magazine* 4 (November 1859): 57–66.

———. "Novels and Novel Reading." *Virginia University Magazine* 4 (October 1859): 19–28.

[Jones, Walter G.] "Women vs. Success." *Virginia University Magazine* 3 (November 1858): 60–65.

Logan, Joseph M. "Young America." *Southern Repertory and College Review* 4 (December 1855): 146–48.

[Louthan, Carter M.]. "Progress." *Virginia University Magazine* 3 (May 1859): 450–53.

———. "The Present and the Past." *Virginia University Magazine* 4 (January 1860): 170–79.

[Meade, Hodijah Lincoln]. "Legal Ethics." *Virginia University Magazine* 4 (November 1859): 87–90.

Pate, Henry Clay. "Patriotic Discourse on Local and General History." *Southern Repertory and College Review* 2 (December 1852): 135–43.

[Patterson, Camm]. "Effects of Circumstances upon Character." *Virginia University Magazine* 4 (January 1860): 192–94.

———. "Ideal Perfection." *Virginia University Magazine* 5 (February 1860): 261–63.

Pendleton, Albert G. "The Aspirations of the American Youth." *Southern Repertory and College Review* 4 (January 1855): 29–31.

[Pollard, Edward]. "Hints on Southern Civilization." *Southern Literary Messenger* 32 (March 1861): 310.

[Price, Thomas R., Jr.]. "The Edinburgh Reviewers." *Virginia University Magazine* 3 (February 1859): 235–43.

[Radford, William M.]. "Men of Thought vs. Men of Action." *Virginia University Magazine* 4 (October 1859): 30–35.

———. "Success in Life." *Virginia University Magazine* 4 (November 1859): 82–86.

Simms, G. W. W. M. "The South." *Southern Repertory and College Review* 4 (June 1856): 222–27.

[Stringfellow, Charles S.]. "The Christ of History." *Virginia University Magazine* 3 (November 1858): 68–77.

———. "Fixed Purpose, and Fixed Principles of Action." *Virginia University Magazine* 3 (January 1859): 172–81.

[Venable, Richard M.]. "College Law and Order." *Virginia University Magazine* 4 (March 1860): 311–17.

———. "Principles—Their Growth." *Virginia University Magazine* 4 (April 1860): 212–19.

BOOKS

Alley, Reuben E. *History of the University of Richmond.* Charlottesville: University Press of Virginia, 1977.

Altshuler, Glenn C., and Stuart M. Blumin. *Rude Republic: Americans and Their Politics in the Nineteenth Century.* Princeton: Princeton University Press, 2000.

Anderson, Benedict. *Imagined Communities: Reflections on the Origin and Spread of Nationalism.* New York: Verso, 1983.

Ash, Stephen V. *Middle Tennessee Society Transformed, 1860: War and Peace in the Upper South.* Baton Rouge: Louisiana State University, 1988.

———. *When the Yankees Came: Conflict and Chaos in the Occupied South, 1861–1865.* Chapel Hill: University of North Carolina Press, 1996.

Ayers, Edward L., and John C. Willis, eds. *The Edge of the South: Life in Nineteenth-Century Virginia.* Charlottesville: University Press of Virginia, 1991.

Barney, William L. *The Secessionist Impulse: Alabama and Mississippi in 1860.* Princeton: Princeton University Press, 1974.

Barton, Michael. *Goodmen: The Character of Civil Soldiers.* University Park: Pennsylvania State University Press, 1981.

Barzun, Jacques. *Classic, Romantic, and Modern.* Boston: Little, Brown, 1961.

Bean, W. G. *Stonewall's Man: Sandie Pendleton.* Chapel Hill: University of North Carolina Press, 1959.

Bederman, Gail. *Manliness and Civilization: A Cultural History of Gender and Race in the United States, 1880–1917.* Chicago: University of Chicago Press, 1995.

Beringer, Richard E., Herman Hattaway, Archer Jones, and William N. Still Jr. *Why the South Lost the Civil War*. Athens: University of Georgia Press, 1986.

Bernstein, Iver. *The New York City Draft Riots: Their Significance and Politics in the Age of the Civil War*. New York: Oxford University Press, 1990.

Bertelson, David. *The Lazy South*. New York: Oxford University Press, 1967.

Black, C. E., *The Dynamic of Modernization: A Study in Comparative History*. New York: Harper and Row, 1966.

Blair, William. *Virginia's Private War: Feeding Body and Soul in the Confederacy, 1861–1865*. New York: Oxford University Press, 1998.

Blight, David W. *Race and Reunion: The Civil War in American Memory*. Cambridge, Mass.: Harvard University Press, 2001.

Boritt, Gabor S., ed. *Why the Confederacy Lost*. New York: Oxford University Press, 1992.

Bradshaw, Herbert C. *History of Hampden-Sydney College*, 2 vols. Durham, N.C.: Fisher-Harrison, 1976.

Brinkley, John Luster. *On This Hill: A Narrative History of Hampden-Sydney College, 1774–1994*. Farmville, Va.: Hampden-Sydney, 1994.

Brown, Charles H. *Agents of Manifest Destiny: The Lives and Times of the Filibusters*. Chapel Hill: University of North Carolina Press, 1980.

Brown, Richard D. *Modernization: The Transformation of American Life, 1600–1865*. New York: Hill and Wang, 1976.

Brubacher, John S., and Willis Rudy. *Higher Education in Transition: A History of American Colleges and Universities, 1636–1976*. New York: Harper and Row, 1976.

Bruce, Dickson D., Jr. *Violence and Culture in the Antebellum South*. Austin: University of Texas Press, 1979.

Bruce, Philip Alexander. *History of the University of Virginia, 1819–1919*, 5 vols. New York: Macmillan, 1920–21.

Bunch, Jack A. *Military Justice in the Confederate States Armies*. Shippensburg, Pa.: White Mane Books, 2000.

Burton, Orville Vernon. *In My Father's House Are Many Mansions: Family and Community in Edgefield, South Carolina*. Chapel Hill: University of North Carolina Press, 1985.

Carmichael, Peter S. *Lee's Young Artillerist: William R. J. Pegram*. Charlottesville: University Press of Virginia, 1995.

———. *The Purcell, Crenshaw, and Letcher Artillery*. Lynchburg: H. E. Howard, 1990.

Censer, Jane Turner. *The Reconstruction of White Southern Womanhood, 1865–1895*. Baton Rouge: Louisiana State University Press, 2003.

Cash, W. J. *The Mind of the South*. 1941. Reprint, New York: Vintage Books, 1991.

Chudacoff, Howard P. *How Old Are You? Age Consciousness in American Culture*. Princeton: Princeton University Press, 1989.

Clinton, Catherine, and Nina Silber, eds. *Divided Houses: Gender and the Civil War*. New York: Oxford University Press, 1992.

Connelly, Thomas L. *The Marble Man: Robert E. Lee and His Image in American Society*. New York: Alfred A. Knopf, 1977.

Cooper, William J., Jr. *The South and the Politics of Slavery, 1828–1856*. Baton Rouge: Louisiana State University Press, 1978.

Coulter, E. Merton. *College Life in the Old South*. Athens: University of Georgia Press, 1928.

———. *The Confederate States of America, 1861–1865*. Baton Rouge: Louisiana State University Press, 1950.

Craigie, Sir William A., and James R. Hulbert, eds. *A Dictionary of American English on Historical Principles*. Chicago: University of Chicago Press, 1940.

Craven, Avery. *Soil Exhaustion as a Factor in the Agricultural History of Virginia and Maryland, 1606–1860*. 1926. Reprint, Gloucester, Mass.: Peter Smith, 1965.

Crofts, Daniel W. *Old Southampton: Politics and Society in a Virginia County, 1834–1869*. Charlottesville: University Press of Virginia, 1992.

———. *Reluctant Confederates: Upper South Unionists in the Secession Crisis*. Chapel Hill: University of North Carolina Press, 1989.

Dabney, Virginius. *Virginia: The New Dominion*. Garden City, N.Y.: Doubleday, 1971.

Dailey, Jane. *Before Jim Crow: The Politics of Race in Postemancipation Virginia*. Chapel Hill: University of North Carolina Press, 2000.

Daniel, W. Harrison. *History of the University of Richmond*. Richmond: Print Shop, 1991.

Davis, William C. *Look Away! A History of the Confederate States of America*. New York: Free Press, 2002.

Dean, Eric T., Jr. *Shook over Hell: Post-traumatic Stress, Vietnam, and the Civil War*. Cambridge, Mass.: Harvard University Press, 1997.

Degler, Carl N. *The Other South: Southern Dissenters in the Nineteenth Century*. New York: Harper and Row, 1974.

Dew, Charles B. *Apostles of Disunion: Southern Secession Commissioners and the Causes of the Civil War*. Charlottesville: University Press of Virginia, 2001.

Driver, Robert J., Jr. *14th Virginia Cavalry*. Lynchburg: H. E. Howard, 1988.

Durrill, Wayne K. *War of Another Kind: A Southern Community in the Great Rebellion*. New York: Oxford University Press, 1990.

Eaton, Clement. *The Civilization of the Old South: Writings of Clement Eaton*. Edited by Albert D. Kirwan. Lexington: University of Kentucky Press, 1968.

Escott, Paul D. *After Secession: Jefferson Davis and the Failure of Confederate Nationalism*. Baton Rouge: Louisiana State University, 1978.

Fahs, Alice. *The Imagined Civil War: Popular Literature of the North and South, 1861–1865*. Chapel Hill: University of North Carolina Press, 2001.

Faust, Drew Gilpin. *The Creation of Confederate Nationalism: Ideology and Identity in the Civil War South*. Baton Rouge: Louisiana State University Press, 1988.

———. *A Sacred Circle: The Dilemma of the Intellectual in the Old South, 1840–1860*. Baltimore: Johns Hopkins University Press, 1977.

———. *Southern Stories: Slaveholders in Peace and War*. Columbia: University of Missouri Press, 1992.

Feuer, Lewis S. *The Conflict of Generations: The Character and Significance of Student Movements*. New York: Basic Books, 1969.

Fischer, David Hackett. *Growing Old in America.* New York: Oxford University Press, 1977.

Foner, Eric. *Free Soil, Free Labor, Free Men: The Ideology of the Republican Party before the Civil War.* New York: Oxford University Press, 1970.

———. *Politics and Ideology in the Age of the Civil War.* New York: Oxford University Press, 1980.

———. *Reconstruction: America's Unfinished Revolution, 1863–1877.* New York: Harper and Row, 1988.

Ford, Lacy K., Jr. *Origins of Southern Radicalism: The South Carolina Upcountry, 1800–1860.* New York: Oxford University Press, 1988.

Forgie, George B. *Patricide in the House Divided: A Psychological Interpretation of Lincoln and His Age.* New York: W. W. Norton, 1979.

Foster, Gaines M. *Ghosts of the Confederacy: Defeat, the Lost Cause, and the Emergence of the New South.* New York: Oxford University Press, 1987.

Fox-Genovese, Elizabeth. *Within the Plantation Household: Black and White Women of the Old South.* Chapel Hill: University of North Carolina Press, 1988.

Fox-Genovese, Elizabeth, and Eugene D. Genovese. *Fruits of Merchant Capital: Slavery and Bourgeois Property in the Rise and Expansion of Capitalism.* New York: Oxford University Press, 1983.

Franklin, John Hope. *The Militant South, 1800–1861.* Cambridge, Mass.: Belknap Press of Harvard University Press, 1956.

Frederickson, George M. *The Inner Civil War: Northern Intellectuals and the Crisis of the Union.* New York: Harper and Row, 1965.

———. *The Black Image in the White Mind: The Debate on Afro-American Character and Destiny.* New York: Harper and Row, 1971.

Freehling, Alison Goodyear. *Drift toward Dissolution: The Virginia Slavery Debate of 1831–1832.* Baton Rouge: Louisiana State University Press, 1982.

Freehling, William W. *The Road to Disunion: Secessionists at Bay, 1776–1854.* New York: Oxford University Press, 1990.

Freeman, Douglas Southall. *R. E. Lee: A Biography.* 4 vols. New York: Charles Scribner's Sons, 1934–36.

Frost, Dan R. *Thinking Confederates: Academia and the Idea of Progress in the New South.* Knoxville: University of Tennessee Press, 2000.

Furgurson, Ernest B. *Ashes of Glory: Richmond at War.* New York: Alfred A. Knopf, 1996.

Gallagher, Gary W. *The Confederate War: How Popular Will, Nationalism, and Military Strategy Could Not Stave Off Defeat.* Cambridge, Mass.: Harvard University Press, 1997.

———, ed. *Decision on the Rappahannock: Essays on the Fredericksburg Campaign.* Chapel Hill: University of North Carolina Press, 1995.

———, ed. *The Third Day at Gettysburg and Beyond.* Chapel Hill: University of North Carolina Press, 1994.

Gallagher, Gary W., and Alan T. Nolan, eds. *The Myth of the Lost Cause and Civil War History.* Bloomington: Indiana University Press, 2000.

Gaston, Paul M. *The New South Creed: A Study in Southern Myth-Making*. New York: Alfred A. Knopf, 1970.

Geertz, Clifford. *The Interpretation of Cultures: Selected Essays*. New York: Basic Books, 1973.

Genovese, Eugene D. *A Consuming Fire: The Fall of the Confederacy in the Mind of the White Christian South*. Athens: University of Georgia Press, 1998.

———. *The Political Economy of Slavery: Studies in the Economy and Society of the Slave South*. New York: Vintage Books, 1965.

———. *Roll Jordan Roll: The World the Slaves Made*. New York: Pantheon Books, 1972.

———. *The Slaveholders' Dilemma: Freedom and Progress in Southern Conservative Thought, 1820–1860*. Columbia: University of South Carolina Press, 1992.

———. *The Southern Tradition: The Achievement and Limitations of an American Conservatism*. Cambridge, Mass.: Harvard University Press, 1994.

———. *The World the Slaveholders Made: Two Essays in Interpretation*. Middletown, Conn.: Wesleyan University Press, 1988.

Gillespie, Neal C. *The Collapse of Orthodoxy: The Intellectual Ordeal of George Frederick Holmes*. Charlottesville: University Press of Virginia, 1972.

Gillis, John R. *Youth and History: Tradition and Change in European Age Relations, 1770–Present*. New York: Academic Press, 1974.

Godbold, Albea. *The Church College of the Old South*. Durham, N.C.: Duke University Press, 1944.

Godson, Susan H., Ludwell H. Johnson, Richard B. Sherman, Thad W. Tate, and Helen C. Walker. *The College of William and Mary: A History*. 2 vols. Williamsburg: King and Queen Press, 1993.

Grant, Susan-Mary. *North over South: Northern Nationalism and American Identity in the Antebellum Era*. Lawrence: University Press of Kansas, 2000.

Green, Harvey. *Fit for America: Health, Fitness, Sport, and American Society*. New York: Pantheon Books, 1986.

Greven, Philip. *The Protestant Temperament: Patterns of Child-Rearing, Religious Experience, and the Self in Early America*. Chicago: University of Chicago Press, 1977.

Hahn, Steven. *The Roots of Southern Populism: Yeoman Farmers and the Transformation of the Georgia Upcountry, 1850–1890*. New York: Oxford University Press, 1983.

Handlin, Oscar, and Mary F. Handlin. *The American College and American Culture: Socialization as a Function of Higher Education*. New York: McGraw-Hill, 1970.

Harris, J. William. *Plain Folk and Gentry in a Slave Society: White Liberty and Black Slavery in Augusta's Hinterlands*. Middletown, Conn.: Wesleyan University Press, 1985.

Hattaway, Herman, and Archer Jones. *How the North Won: A Military History of the Civil War*. Urbana: University of Illinois Press, 1983.

Hess, Earl J. *The Union Soldier in Battle: Enduring the Ordeal of Combat*. Lawrence: University Press of Kansas, 1997.

Heyrman, Christine Leigh. *Southern Cross: The Beginnings of the Bible Belt.* New York: Alfred A. Knopf, 1997.

Hobsbawm, Eric J. *The Age of Capital, 1848–1875.* New York: Penguin Books, 1975.

———. *The Age of Revolution, 1789–1849.* New York: Mentor, 1962.

Holifield, E. Brooks. *The Gentlemen Theologians: American Theology in Southern Culture, 1795–1860.* Durham, N.C.: Duke University Press, 1978.

Horowitz, Helen Lefkowitz. *Campus Life: Undergraduate Cultures from the End of the Eighteenth Century to the Present.* New York: Alfred A. Knopf, 1987.

Irby, Richard. *History of Randolph-Macon College, Virginia: The Oldest Incorporated Methodist College in America.* Richmond: Whittet and Shepperson, n.d.

Johnson, Michael P. *Toward a Patriarchal Republic: The Secession of Georgia.* Baton Rouge: Louisiana State University Press, 1977.

Jordan, Ervin L., Jr. *Charlottesville and the University of Virginia in the Civil War.* Lynchburg: H. E. Howard, 1988.

Kerr-Ritchie, Jeffrey R. *Freedpeople in the Tobacco South: Virginia, 1860–1900.* Chapel Hill: University of North Carolina Press, 1999.

Kimball, Gregg D. *American City, Southern Place: A Cultural History of Antebellum Richmond.* Athens: University of Georgia Press, 2000.

Klement, Frank L. *The Copperheads in the Middle West.* Chicago: University of Chicago Press, 1960.

Lebsock, Susan. *The Free Women of Petersburg: Status and Culture in a Southern Town, 1784–1860.* New York: W. W. Norton, 1984.

Lighter, J. E., ed. *Random House Historical Dictionary of American Slang.* New York: Random House, 1994.

Linderman, Gerald. *Embattled Courage: The Experience of Combat in the American Civil War.* New York: Free Press, 1987.

Link, William. *Roots of Secession: Slavery and Politics in Antebellum Virginia.* Chapel Hill: University of North Carolina Press, 2003.

Lonn, Ella. *Desertion during the Civil War.* New York: Century, 1928.

Loveland, Anne C. *Southern Evangelicals and the Social Order, 1800–1860.* Baton Rouge: Louisiana State University Press, 1980.

Maddex, Jack P., Jr. *The Reconstruction of Edward A. Pollard: A Rebel's Conversion to Postbellum Unionism.* Chapel Hill: University of North Carolina Press, 1974.

———. *The Virginia Conservatives, 1867–1879: A Study in Reconstruction Politics.* Chapel Hill: University of North Carolina Press, 1970.

Majewski, John. *A House Dividing: Economic Development in Pennsylvania and Virginia before the Civil War.* Cambridge: Cambridge University Press, 2000.

Mathews, Donald G. *Religion in the Old South.* Chicago: University of Chicago Press, 1977.

McCardell, John. *The Idea of a Southern Nation: Southern Nationalists and Southern Nationalism, 1830–1860.* New York: W. W. Norton, 1979.

McConnell, Stuart. *Glorious Contentment: The Grand Army of the Republic, 1865–1900.* Chapel Hill: University of North Carolina Press, 1992.

McLoughlin, William G. *Revivals, Awakenings, and Reform: An Essay on Religion and Social Change in America, 1607–1977*. Chicago: University of Chicago Press, 1978.

McMurry, Richard M. *Virginia Military Institute Alumni in the Civil War*. Lynchburg: H. E. Howard, 1999.

McPherson, James M. *Battle Cry of Freedom: The Civil War Era*. New York: Oxford University Press, 1988.

———. *For Cause and Comrades: Why Men Fought in the Civil War*. New York: Oxford University Press, 1997.

———. *Is Blood Thicker Than Water? Crises of Nationalism in the Modern World*. New York: Vintage Books, 1998.

———. *What They Fought For, 1861–1865*. Baton Rouge: Louisiana State University Press, 1994.

McPherson, James M., and William J. Cooper Jr., eds. *Writing the Civil War: The Quest to Understand*. Columbia: University of South Carolina Press, 1998.

McWhiney, Grady, and Perry D. Jamieson. *Attack and Die: Civil War Military Tactics and the Southern Heritage*. University, Ala.: University of Alabama Press, 1982.

Minor, Berkeley, and James F. Minor, comps. *Legislative History of the University of Virginia as Set Forth in the Acts of The General Assembly of Virginia, 1802–1927*. N.p.: Rector and Visitors, 1928.

Mitchell, Reid. *Civil War Soldiers: Their Expectations and Experiences*. New York: Viking Press, 1988.

Mohr, Clarence L. *On the Threshold of Freedom: Masters and Slaves in Civil War Georgia*. Athens: University of Georgia Press, 1986.

Moore, Albert B. *Conscription and Conflict in the Confederacy*. New York: Hillary House, 1963.

Moore, James Tice. *Two Paths to the New South: The Virginia Debt Controversy, 1870–1883*. Lexington: University Press of Kentucky, 1974.

Moore, Winfred B., Jr., and Joseph F. Tripp, eds. *Looking South: Chapters in the Story of an American Region*. New York: Greenwood Press, 1989.

Morgan, Edmund. *American Slavery—American Freedom: The Ordeal of Colonial Virginia*. New York: W. W. Norton, 1975.

Mrozek, Donald J. *Sport and American Mentality, 1880–1910*. Knoxville: University of Tennessee Press, 1983.

Musgrove, F. *Youth and the Social Order*. Bloomington: Indiana University Press, 1965.

Nichols, James L. *General Fitzhugh Lee: A Biography*. Lynchburg: H. E. Howard, 1989.

Nolan, Alan T. *Lee Considered: General Robert E. Lee and Civil War History*. Chapel Hill: University of North Carolina Press, 1991.

Noe, Kenneth W. *Southwest Virginia's Railroad: Modernization and the Sectional Crisis*. Urbana: University of Illinois Press, 1994.

Oakes, James. *The Ruling Race: A History of American Slaveholders*. New York: Alfred A. Knopf, 1982.

O'Brien, Michael. *Rethinking the South: Essays in Intellectual History*. Athens: University of Georgia Press, 1993.

——, ed. *All Clever Men, Who Make Their Way: Critical Discourse in the Old South*. Fayetteville: University of Arkansas Press, 1982.

Olsen, Christopher J. *Political Culture and Secession in Mississippi: Masculinity, Honor, and the Antiparty Tradition, 1830–1860*. New York: Oxford University Press, 2000.

Osterweis, Rollin G. *Romanticism and Nationalism in the Old South*. 1949. Reprint, Gloucester, Mass.: P. Smith, 1964.

Ownby, Ted. *Subduing Satan: Religion, Recreation, and Manhood in the Rural South, 1865–1920*. Chapel Hill: University of North Carolina Press, 1990.

Paludan, Phillip Shaw. *"A People's Contest": The Union and Civil War, 1861–1865*. New York: Harper and Row, 1988.

Patton, John S. *Jefferson, Cabell and the University of Virginia*. New York: Neale Publishing Co., 1906.

Phillips, U. B. *The Slave Economy in the Old South: Selected Essays in Economic and Social History*. Edited and with an introduction by Eugene D. Genovese. Baton Rouge: Louisiana State University Press, 1968.

Potter, David M. *The South and the Sectional Conflict*. Baton Rouge: Louisiana State University Press, 1968.

Power, J. Tracy. *Lee's Miserables: Life in the Army of Northern Virginia from the Wilderness to Appomattox*. Chapel Hill: University of North Carolina Press, 1998.

Putney, Clifford. *Muscular Christianity: Manhood and Sports in Protestant America, 1880–1920*. Cambridge, Mass.: Harvard University Press, 2001.

Rable, George C. *Civil Wars: Women and the Crisis of Southern Nationalism*. Urbana: University of Illinois Press, 1989.

——. *The Confederate Republic: A Revolution against Politics*. Chapel Hill: University of North Carolina Press, 1994.

Ramsdell, Charles W. *Behind the Lines in the Southern Confederacy*. Baton Rouge: Louisiana State University Press, 1944.

Reardon, Carol. *Pickett's Charge: In History and Memory*. Chapel Hill: University of North Carolina Press, 1997.

Robertson, James I., Jr. *Soldiers Blue and Gray*. Columbia: University of South Carolina Press, 1988.

Romero, Sidney J. *Religion in the Rebel Ranks*. Lanham, Md.: University Press of America, 1983.

Rose, Anne C. *Victorian America and the Civil War*. New York: Cambridge University Press, 1992.

Rotundo, E. Anthony. *American Manhood: Transformations in Masculinity from the Revolution to the Modern Era*. New York: Basic Books, 1993.

Rudolph, Frederick. *The American College and University*. New York: Alfred A. Knopf, 1965.

Scanlon, James Edward. *Randolph-Macon College: A Southern History, 1925–1967*. Charlottesville: University Press of Virginia, 1977.

Schneider, A. Gregory. *The Way of the Cross Leads Home: The Domestication of American Methodism*. Bloomington: Indiana University Press, 1993.

Schweiger, Beth Barton. *The Gospel Working Up: Progress and the Pulpit in Nineteenth-Century Virginia*. New York: Oxford University Press, 2000.

Scott, Anne Firor. *The Southern Lady: From Pedestal to Politics, 1830–1930*. Chicago: University of Chicago Press, 1970.

Shamir, Milette, and Jennifer Travis, eds. *Boys Don't Cry: Rethinking Narratives of Masculinity and Emotion in the U.S.* New York: Columbia University Press, 2002.

Shanks, Henry T. *The Secession Movement in Virginia*. Richmond: Garrett and Massie, 1934.

Shattuck, Gardiner H., Jr. *A Shield and Hiding Place: The Religious Life of the Civil War Armies*. Macon, Ga.: Mercer University Press, 1987.

Shedd, Clarence P. *Two Centuries of Student Christian Movements: Their Origin and Intercollegiate Life*. New York: Association Press, 1934.

Silber, Nina. *The Romance of Reunion: Northerners and the South, 1865–1900*. Chapel Hill: University of North Carolina Press, 1993.

Singal, Daniel Joseph. *The War Within: From Victorian to Modernist Thought in the South, 1919 to 1945*. Chapel Hill: University of North Carolina Press, 1982.

Simpson, Craig M. *A Good Southerner: The Life of Henry A. Wise of Virginia*. Chapel Hill: University of North Carolina Press, 1985.

Simpson, Lewis P. *The Dispossessed Garden: Pastoral and History in Southern Literature*. Athens: University of Georgia Press, 1975.

Smith, Francis H. *History of the Virginia Military Institute*. Lynchburg: J. P. Bell, 1912.

Smith, J. Douglas. *Managing White Supremacy: Race, Politics, and Citizenship in Jim Crow Virginia*. Chapel Hill: University of North Carolina Press, 2002.

Smith, Mark M. *Mastered by the Clock: Time, Slavery, and Freedom in the American South*. Chapel Hill: University of North Carolina Press, 1997.

Stampp, Kenneth M. *The Imperiled Union: Essays on the Background of the Civil War*. New York: Oxford University Press, 1980.

Stevenson, George J. *Increase in Excellence: A History of Emory and Henry College*. New York: Appleton-Century-Crofts, 1963.

Stowe, Stephen M. *Intimacy and Power in the Old South: Ritual in the Lives of the Planters*. Baltimore: Johns Hopkins University Press, 1987.

Summers, Mark W. *The Plundering Generations: Corruption and the Crisis of the Union, 1849–1861*. New York: Oxford University Press, 1987.

Tatum, Georgia Lee. *Disloyalty in the Confederacy*. Chapel Hill: University of North Carolina Press, 1933.

Taylor, William R. *Cavalier and Yankee: The Old South and American National Character*. New York: George Braziller, 1961.

Thomas, Emory M. *The Confederate Nation: 1861–1865*. New York: Harper and Row, 1979.

———. *Bold Dragoon: The Life of J. E. B. Stuart*. New York: Harper and Row, 1986.

Thomason, John W., Jr. *Jeb Stuart*. New York: Charles Scribner's Sons, 1929.

Thornton, J. Mills, III. *Politics and Power in a Slave Society: Alabama, 1800–1860.* Baton Rouge: Louisiana State University Press, 1978.

Tolbert, Lisa C. *Constructing Townscapes: Space and Society in Antebellum Tennessee.* Chapel Hill: University of North Carolina Press, 1999.

Tripp, Stephen Elliott. *Yankee Town, Southern City: Race and Class Relations in Civil War Lynchburg.* New York: New York University Press, 1997.

Varon, Elizabeth R. *We Mean to Be Counted: White Women and Politics in Antebellum Virginia.* Chapel Hill: University of North Carolina Press, 1998.

Wallace, Lee A., Jr. *The Richmond Howitzers.* Lynchburg: H. E. Howard, 1993.

Walther, Eric H. *The Fire-Eaters.* Baton Rouge: Louisiana State University Press, 1992.

Watson, Ritchie Devon, Jr. *The Cavalier in Virginia Fiction.* Baton Rouge: Louisiana State University Press, 1985.

Weitz, Mark A. *A Higher Duty: Desertion among Georgia Troops during the Civil War.* Lincoln: University of Nebraska Press, 2000.

Widmer, Edward L. *Young America: The Flowering of Democracy in New York City.* New York: Oxford University Press, 1999.

Wiley, Bell Irvin. *The Life of Johnny Reb: The Common Soldier of the Confederacy.* Indianapolis: Bobbs-Merrill, 1943.

Wills, Brian Steel. *The War Hits Home: The Civil War in Southeastern Virginia.* Charlottesville: University Press of Virginia, 2001.

Wilson, Charles Reagan. *Baptized in Blood: The Religion of the Lost Cause, 1865–1920.* Athens: University of Georgia Press, 1980.

Wise, Jennings C. *The Military History of the Virginia Military Institute from 1839 to 1865.* Lynchburg: J. P. Bell, 1915.

Wish, Harvey. *George Fitzhugh: Propagandist of the Old South.* Baton Rouge: Louisiana State University Press, 1943.

Wohl, Robert. *The Generation of 1914.* Cambridge, Mass.: Harvard University Press, 1979.

Woodworth, Steven E. *While God Is Marching On: The Religious World of Civil War Soldiers.* Lawrence: University Press of Kansas, 2001.

Wyatt-Brown, Bertram. *The Shaping of Southern Culture: Honor, Grace, and War, 1760s–1890s.* Chapel Hill: University of North Carolina Press, 2001.

———. *Southern Honor: Ethics and Behavior in the Old South.* New York: Oxford University Press, 1982.

ARTICLES AND PARTS OF BOOKS

Ash, Stephen V. "White Virginians under Federal Occupation, 1861–1865." *Virginia Magazine of History and Biography* 98 (April 1990): 169–92.

Banner, Lois W. "Religious Benevolence as Social Control: A Critique of an Interpretation." *Journal of American History* 60 (June 1973): 23–41.

Bardolph, Richard. "Confederate Dilemma: North Carolina Troops and the Deserter Problem." *North Carolina Historical Review* 66 (January–April 1989): 61–86.

Berends, Kurt O. "'Wholesome Reading Purifies and Elevates the Man': The Religious Military Press in the Confederacy." In *Religion and the American Civil War*, edited by Randall M. Miller, Harry S. Stout, and Charles Reagan Wilson, 131–66. New York: Oxford University Press, 1998.

Blair, William A. "Barbarians at Fredericksburg's Gate: The Impact of the Union Army on Civilians." In *Decision on the Rappahannock: Essays on the Fredericksburg Campaign*, edited by Gary W. Gallagher, 147–70. Chapel Hill: University of North Carolina Press, 1995.

Bonner, Robert B. "Roundheaded Cavaliers? The Context and Limits of a Confederate Racial Project." *Civil War History* 48 (March 2002): 34–59.

Bouwsma, William J. "Christian Adulthood." In *Adulthood*, edited by Erik H. Erikson, 81–96. New York: W. W. Norton, 1976.

Brooks, Charles E. "The Social and Cultural Dynamics of Soldiering in Hood's Texas Brigade." *Journal of Southern History* 67 (August 2001): 535–72.

Daniel, W. Harrison. "Old Lynchburg College, 1855–1869." *Virginia Magazine of History and Biography* 88 (October 1980): 446–77.

Dotson, Rand. "'The Grave and Scandalous Evil Infected to Your People': The Erosion of Confederate Loyalty in Floyd County, Virginia." *Virginia Magazine of History and Biography* 108 (2000): 203–15.

Erikson, Erik H. "'Identity Crisis' in Autobiographic Perspective." In Erikson, *Life History and the Historical Moment*, 17–47. New York: W. W. Norton, 1975.

Escott, Paul D. "'The Cry of the Sufferers': The Problem of Welfare in the Confederacy." *Civil War History* 23 (1977): 228–40.

Faust, Drew Gilpin. "Altars of Sacrifice: Confederate Women and the Narrative of War." *Journal of American History* 76 (March 1990): 1200–1228.

———. "The Civil War Soldier and the Art of Dying." *Journal of Southern History* 67 (February 2001): 3–38.

Fields, Barbara J. "*Origins of the New South* and the Negro Question." In *"Origins of the New South" Fifty Years Later: The Continuing Influence of a Historical Classic*, edited by John B. Boles and Bethany L. Johnson, 261–77. Baton Rouge: Louisiana State University Press, 2003.

Fox-Genovese, Elizabeth, and Eugene D. Genovese. "The Cultural History of Southern Slave Society: Reflections on the Work of Lewis P. Simpson." In *American Letters and the Historical Consciousness: Essays in Honor of Lewis P. Simpson*, edited by J. Gerald Kennedy and Daniel Mark Fogel, 15–41. Baton Rouge: Louisiana State University Press, 1987.

———. "The Divine Sanction of Social Order: Religious Foundations of the Southern Slaveholders' World View." *Journal of the American Academy of Religion* 55 (Summer 1987): 201–23.

Gallagher, Gary W. "Jubal A. Early, the Lost Cause, and Civil War History: A Persistent Legacy." In *The Myth of the Lost Cause and Civil War History*, edited by Gary W. Gallagher and Alan T. Nolan, 35–59. Bloomington: Indiana University Press, 2000.

———. "Lee's Army Has Not Lost Any of its Prestige: The Impact of Gettysburg on the Army of Northern Virginia and the Confederate Home Front." In *The Third Day at Gettysburg and Beyond*, edited by Gary W. Gallagher, 1–30. Chapel Hill: University of North Carolina Press, 1994.

———. "'Upon their Success Hang Momentous Interests': Generals." In *Why the Confederacy Lost*, edited by Gabor S. Boritt, 94–108. New York: Oxford University Press, 1992.

Genovese, Eugene D. "The Chivalric Tradition in the Old South." *Sewanee Review* 108 (Spring 2000): 180–98.

———. "Higher Education." In Genovese, *The Southern Front: History and Politics in the Cultural War*, 92–106. Columbia: University of Missouri Press, 1995.

Genovese, Eugene D., and Elizabeth Fox-Genovese. "The Religious Ideals of Southern Slave Society." *Georgia Historical Quarterly* 70 (Spring 1986): 1–16.

———. "The Social Thought of Antebellum Southern Theologians." In *Looking South: Chapters in the Story of an American Region*, edited by Winfred B. Moore Jr. and Joseph F. Tripp, 31–40. New York: Greenwood Press, 1989.

Grimsley, Mark. "Conciliation and Its Failure, 1861–1862." *Civil War History* 39 (December 1993): 317–35.

Halleck, Judith Lee. "The Role of Community in Civil War Desertion." *Civil War History* 29 (June 1983): 123–34.

Hanna, William F. "The Boston Draft Riot." *Civil War History* 36 (September 1990): 262–73.

Jordan, Winthrop D. "Searching for Adulthood in America." In *Adulthood*, edited by Erik H. Erikson, 189–200. New York: W. W. Norton, 1976.

Kilbride, Daniel. "Southern Medical Students in Philadelphia, 1800–1861: Science and Sociability in the 'Republic of Medicine.'" *Journal of Southern History* 65 (November 1999): 697–700.

Lee, Jean B. "Historical Memory, Sectional Strife, and the American Mecca: Mount Vernon, 1783–1853." *Virginia Magazine of History and Biography* 109 (2001): 255–300.

Lowenberg, Peter. "The Psychohistorical Origins of the Nazi Youth Cohort." *American Historical Review* 76 (December 1971): 1457–1502.

Luraghi, Raimondo. "The Civil War and the Modernization of American Society: Social Structure and Industrial Revolution in the Old South before and during the War." *Civil War History* 18 (September 1972): 230–50.

Maddex, Jack P., Jr. "Proslavery Millennialism: Social Eschatology in Antebellum Southern Calvinism." *American Quarterly* 31 (1979): 46–62.

———. "'The Southern Apostasy' Revisited: The Significance of Proslavery Christianity." *Marxist Perspectives* 2 (Fall 1979): 132–41.

Mannheim, Karl. "The Problem of the Generations." In Mannheim, *Essays on the Sociology of Knowledge*, edited by Paul Kecskemeti. New York: Oxford University Press, 1952.

McCurry, Stephanie. "The Two Faces of Republicanism: Gender and Proslavery Politics in Antebellum South Carolina." *Journal of American History* 78 (March 1992): 1245–64.

Mitchell, Reid. "Christian Soldiers? Perfecting the Confederacy." In *Religion and the American Civil War*, edited by Randall M. Miller, Harry S. Stout, and Charles Reagan Wilson, 297–309. New York: Oxford University Press, 1998.

———. " 'Not the General but the Soldier': The Study of Civil War Soldiers." In *Writing the Civil War: The Quest to Understand*, edited by James M. McPherson and William J. Cooper Jr., 81–95. Columbia: University of South Carolina Press, 1998.

Norton, Herman. "Revivalism in the Confederate Armies." *Civil War History* 6 (December 1960): 410–24.

Rintala, Marvin. "Generations: Political Generations." In *International Encyclopedia of the Social Sciences*, edited by David L. Sills, 5:92–95. New York: Macmillan, 1973.

Ruffner, Kevin Conley. "Civil War Desertion from a Black Belt Regiment: An Examination of the 44th Virginia Infantry." In *The Edge of the South: Life in Nineteenth-Century Virginia*, edited by Edward L. Ayers and John C. Willis, 79–108. Charlottesville: University Press of Virginia, 1991.

Ryder, Norman B. "The Cohort as a Concept in the Study of Social Change." *American Sociological Review* 30 (August 1965): 843–61.

Shepard, John, Jr. "Religion in the Army of Northern Virginia." *North Carolina Historical Review* 25 (July 1948): 341–76.

Snay, Mitchell. "American Thought and Southern Distinctiveness: The Southern Clergy and the Sanctification of Slavery." *Civil War History* 35 (December 1989): 321–28.

Spitzer, Alan B. "The Historical Problem of Generations." *American Historical Review* 78 (December 1973): 1353–85.

Stowe, Steven M. "The Rhetoric of Authority: The Making of Social Values in Planter Family Correspondence." *Journal of American History* 73 (March 1987): 916–33.

Stowell, Daniel W. "Stonewall Jackson and the Providence of God." In *Religion and the American Civil War*, edited by Randall M. Miller, Harry S. Stout, and Charles Reagan Wilson, 187–207. New York: Oxford University Press, 1998.

Sutton, Robert P. "Nostalgia, Pessimism, and Malaise: The Doomed Aristocrat in Late–Jeffersonian Virginia." *Virginia Magazine of History and Biography* 76 (January 1986): 41–55.

Vinovskis, Maris A. "Have Social Historians Lost the Civil War? Some Preliminary Demographic Speculations." *Journal of American History* 76 (June 1989): 34–58.

Yacovone, Donald. "Abolitionists and the 'Language of Fraternal Love.' " In *Meanings for Manhood: Constructions of Masculinity in Victorian America*, edited by Mark C. Carnes and Clyde Griffen, 85–110. Chicago: University of Chicago Press, 1990.

Zornow, William F. "Aid for Indigent Families of Soldiers in Virginia, 1861–1865." *Virginia Magazine of History and Biography* 66 (October 1958): 454–58.

DISSERTATIONS

Holland, Lorraine Eva. "Rise and Fall of the Ante-bellum Virginia Aristocracy:
   A Generational Analysis." Ph.D diss., University of California at Irvine, 1980.
May, John B. "The Life of John Lee Buchanan." Ph.D. diss., University of Virginia,
   1937.
Prim, Gorrell Clinton, Jr. "Born Again in the Trenches: Revivalism in the Confed-
   erate Army." Ph.D. diss., Florida State University, 1982.
Wall, Charles Coleman, Jr. "Students and Student Life at the University of Virginia,
   1825–1861." Ph.D. diss., University of Virginia, 1978.

Index

(n. 32); desires vengeance against
North, 198; at 1887 Gettysburg Reunion, 1–3, 229–30; loyalty to Union,
89–90; praises Southern women, 173;
sense of honor violated, 91–92; supports temperance, 80

82; model of behavior at Virginia universities, 12; represented by Lancelot Blackford, 75–78, 80; symbol of reform in Virginia, 75. *See also* Chivalry; Christianity; Manliness

Christian Intelligencer, 55, 70

Christianity: beginnings of "muscular Christianity," 80–81; draws attention away from military defeats, 191–92, 207; feminizing effects of, 244, 265 (n. 40); found in nature, 93, 95; fuels sectionalism, 103–4, 105; function in Confederate army, 151–52, 171, 284 (n. 7); impact on understanding military defeats, 190–91; influences ideas of masculinity, 6, 12, 59–60, 64–65; informs last generation's view of progress, 21–22, 72; inspires challenge to adult authority, 83–84; inspires Confederate nationalism, 14–15, 180–86, 205–7, 293 (n. 13), 299 (n. 64); instills professional drive, 76–78; interdenominational cooperation among young, 106–7; last generation against religious fanaticism, 108; last generation believes orthodoxy under attack, 105–6; martyrdom during war, 207–10; not seen as feminizing by last generation, 81–82; profound influence in classroom, 102–3; refusal to question God's authority, 251 (n. 16); relationship to cavalier myth, 234–35; shapes loyalty to Union and South, 90; stirs student activism, 73–75; supports last generation's belief in human inequality, 22–23

Clothing: symbolizes secessionist activity, 125, 139–40

College of William and Mary, 63–64; flag raising at, 139; militia organizations at, 130, 132

Combat: soldiers make sense of, 188. *See also* Army of Northern Virginia

Compromise of 1850: reaction of University of Virginia students, 116–17

Confederacy: collapse of, 177; connected to American Revolution, 181–82; determination of Southern women, 172–73; devotion of last generation, 13, 14–15, 18, 79–80, 197, 205–11; historical memory of, 220–21; importance of last generation to, 8; independent nature of enlisted soldier, 152–53, 155; last generation as martyrs for, 165–66, 168–70; last generation desires centralized authority, 174–77; limits of political dissent, 186; morale boosted by Northern dissent, 203–4; need for lower-class support, 149–50; problems on home front, 192–94, 196; religious foundations of, 180–86; resilient nature of nationalism, 185–90, 205–11; symbolic value of Lee, 204–5; last generation's relationship with home front, 170–75

Conrad, Holmes: idealization of Virginia soldiers, 235

Conscription: views of last generation, 175–76

Conservative Party: last generation supports, 222–23

Conway, Moncure, 20; on Southern education, 103

Coons, Henry Wilkins: belief in power of youth, 24, 68; belief in human inequality, 23

Corbin, Richard, 171–72; on arming of slaves, 176; opinion of Confederate rank and file, 152; questions Northern patriotism, 204

Courage: buttressed by religion, 182–83; last generation's notion of, 194, 287 (n. 35); last generation's reputation for, 8; unites soldiers of all classes, 161–62. *See also* Combat

Crater, battle of the, 203

Crittenden Compromise: alienates last generation, 126

Crusades, 26–27

Crutchfield, Stapleton: believes Virginia nurtures greatness, 97–98

Dabney, Robert Lewis, 19, 103, 182; encourages young people to stay in Virginia, 53–54; on meaning of death in Confederacy, 166, 168; religious instruction to troops, 185–86
Daniel, John W.: admires Stonewall Jackson's ambition, 227–28; believes Virginians have industrial talents, 224; critical of army's promotional system, 163–64; vision for postwar Virginia, 218, 220–21
Davidson, Albert: feels isolated as Unionist, 141–42
Davidson, Greenlee: relations with soldiers, 152–54, 156
Davis, Robert Beale: criticizes Virginia's Secession Convention, 135; reverence for family, 91
Death: meaning in Confederate army, 165–66, 168–70
Delta Kappa Epsilon, 74
Democracy: last generation's critique of, 21
Depredations: impact on Confederate morale, 197–98
Desertion, 154–56, 157–61. See also Army of Northern Virginia
Dew, Thomas Roderick, 19
Dickinson College, 44
Dooley, John: demoralized after Appomattox, 216–17
Dunaway, Wayland F.: influenced by professors, 141

Early, Jubal A.: challenges last generation after Civil War, 214–15, 226; criticizes promoters of progress, 39; offers enduring interpretation of Lee, 226–27
Education: emphasis on Southern training, 85–86, 88; last generation possesses great faith in, 84–86; purpose of Southern educational movement, 101–2; relations between professors and students, 102–3
Elder, Thomas: 74; believes deserters should be pardoned, 158–59; opinion on bread riots, 193; religious perspective on war, 184–85
Emancipation: last generation's reaction to, 203
Emory and Henry College: secessionist activity among students, 139
Emotion: adults see last generation as too emotional, 145; among young men, 6, 73, 265 (n. 40); released by nature, 11, 96, 97; role in secession, 121–22

Fairfax, Randolph: as martyred Confederate, 170
Family: disagreements between fathers and sons, 47–48; basis of identity, 91
Fathers: role in raising last generation, 264 (n. 28). See also Adults
Faust, Drew Gilpin, 182
Femininity: relationship to Christianity, 81–82
First Families of Virginia: ridiculed, 63–64
Fitness: advocated by last generation, 81–82. See also Christian Gentleman
Fitzhugh, George, 103; speaks to young people, 108–9
Flag raisings: during secession, 138–39, 142–43
Fleet, Alexander, 71, 123; exercise regime at University of Virginia, 81
Founders: connected to idea of Christian gentleman, 59, 61, 65, 67; historical memory of during Reconstruction, 220–21; last generation's admiration for, 4, 55, 85; memory evoked during secession, 130; shape sense of Southern identity, 93
Fredericksburg, Va.: activities of YMCA in, 79

Fulkerson, Abraham: tries to understand Confederate defeat, 211

Funk, John Henry Stover: on conscription, 175

Gadsden, C. P., 103

Gallagher, Gary W.: on Confederate nationalism, 14

Gaston, Paul, 15

Gatewood, Andrew C. L.: sees himself as man, 145

Generations: construction of, 7–8, 243 (n. 1); differences between young and old, 5–6, 9, 10–11, 12, 53–54, 57–58, 62–63, 70, 96, 98–99, 254 (n. 2), 255 (n. 10); differences over 1860 election, 124; different perspectives on secession, 119–20, 121–22, 128–29, 130, 133–34, 144–45; difficulties between age groups during Reconstruction, 225; disagree over ambition, 11–12; disagree over progress, 35, 37–42; postwar tensions, 214–15; sense of mission among young people, 72; shape wartime experience, 206–7; similar views on progress, 44–45

Genovese, Eugene D., 103; on Southern chivalry, 61

Gettysburg, battle of: last generation's reaction to, 192, 198–202

Gettysburg reunion (1887), 1–3, 229–31

Gibbons, Charles M.: support for common schools, 84

Graham, James McDowell: celebrates nature, 95; denounces utilitarianism, 28

Grant, Susan-Mary, 109

Grigsby, Hugh Blair: questions cavalier image, 63–64

Grimm, George W.: supports secession, 127, 139–40

Halsey, Don Peter, 104

Hampden-Sydney College, 64; secessionist activity, 139; student militia activity, 132

Hankins, James DeWitt: admiration for Founders, 65, 67; considers leaving Virginia, 49; contemplates meaning of military defeat, 210; criticizes speculators, 192; representative of last generation's views on sectionalism, 114–15; studies history of Rome, 104–5; support for John Bell, 123; weary of partisan bickering, 42

Harmon, Edwin: campaigns for secession, 140–41; relations with soldiers, 151, 157–58

Harrison, Powell: on Union, 26

Hicks, Rebecca Brodnax: denounces morality of young Virginians, 69–70, 83

Historical memory: last generation calls for reunion, 215, 229–32; last generation creates mythical Confederate world, 234–36; last generation questions reconciliation, 232–34; of Revolutionary heroes during Reconstruction, 220–21

History: importance of historical sites to last generation, 96, 98–99; last generation's understanding of, 104; validates progress, 25–26

Holcombe, James P., 103; influences students' political beliefs, 141

Holmes, George Frederick, 102, 103

Honor: connected to progress, 33, 39–40, 58; desire for military reputation, 163–65; last generation rejects violent aspects of, 83; needed from former enemies, 230–31; leads to fanaticism during Civil War, 208–9; role during secession crisis, 133, 136, 138, 140; shapes last generation's political action, 125–26, 127; as understood by last generation, 91

Household: last generation's desire to control, 48–50

Hughes, Thomas, 88
Hunter, Robert W., 73

Identity: last generation's construction of, 33. *See also* Southern identity
Imagination: celebrated after Civil War, 227–28; creates tension between community and self, 68–69; importance to last generation, 23, 96, 271 (n. 13)
Islam: analyzed by last generation, 25–26; defended by last generation, 107

Jackson, Alfred H.: implores peers to stay in Virginia, 52
Jackson, Thomas J. "Stonewall": admired for his ambition by last generation, 227–29; last generation interprets death of, 190–91
Jamestown, Va., 98
Jefferson Medical College, 88
Jefferson Society, 41
John Brown's raid (1859), 109; radicalizes Virginia students, 117–18
Junkin, George, 103; applauds religious work of students, 83; confronts secessionist students, 139

Kaleidoscope, The, 69
Keith, James: clings to Civil War memories, 232; connects courage and godliness, 182; considers Unionist professor obsolete, 142; denounces Northern war effort, 204; extreme devotion to Confederacy, 207–10
Kinzer, William: compares material progress of North and South, 44
Know-Nothing Party, 107
Koontz, George W., 181–82; interprets Gettysburg, 191
Koran, 107
Kurtz, Peter: criticizes Crittenden Compromise, 126–27

Langhorne, James H.: enlists in Confederate army, 145
Last Generation, members of: activity in student organizations, 72, 74–75, 77–80, 82–83; advocate secession, 12–13, 121–23, 124, 128–30, 134–44, 279 (n. 25), 281(n. 45); adult criticism of, 56–57, 69–71; aspire to be Christian gentlemen, 10–11, 30, 32–34, 59–60, 64–65, 72, 77–84, 226–27; attacked by old fogies and youth cultivators, 41, 133–34, 144–45; become old fogies, 232–36; belief in antebellum Virginia's decline, 35, 37, 42–43, 223–26; belief in inequality, 22–23; believe they live in distinctive Christian community, 102–8, 180–81; cavalier ideal and aristocratic ease rejected by, 60, 61–64, 71–72, 260 (n. 3); champion New South creed, 214, 215, 223–28; champion progress, 19–22, 30–34, 57–58, 218–22; committed to slave expansion, 113–16, 126–27, 275 (n. 57), 276 (n. 60); condemn sins of Confederacy, 190–91; as Confederate nationalists, 13–15, 179–81, 193–94, 197–211; confusion over age status, 257 (n. 32); courageous in battle, 161–62, 287 (n. 35); critical of "old fogyism" and adult authority, 10, 22, 38–41, 85–86, 123, 128–29, 136–37, 214–15, 223, 255 (n. 10); critical of partisan politics, 43–44, 114–16, 255 (n. 12); critical of utilitarianism, 28–29; defend ambition and individualism, 11–12, 67–69, 227–28; defense of slavery, 249 (n. 3), 252 (23); desire for fame, 54–56, 163–65; desire for self-improvement, 75–78, 88; devotion to Union, 89–90; education of, 47–48; 102–6; emotional bonds among, 72–75; exerting authority over soldiers, 14, 150–60; expressions of

Christian faith, 74–75, 76, 79–83, 165–66, 182–90, 265 (n. 40); expressions of manliness, 13, 123, 145–47, 227–28, 244 (n. 3); faith in power of youth, 23–25; feel connected to Revolutionary generation, 60, 61, 65, 67, 127–28, 181; generational makeup and consciousness, 6–7, 18, 119–20, 121–23, 223, 243 (n. 1); guided by honor, 91–92, 208–10, 230–31; importance to Army of Northern Virginia, 8–9, 149–50, 205; inspired by nature, 92–93, 95–98; lobby for education, 84–86, 88; Lost Cause defenders, 15, 226–28, 231–36; migrate westward, 52–53; moderation during Reconstruction, 214–15, 218–22, 228–29; motherly influence on, 263 (n. 27), 265 (n. 39); need for honor, 57–58, 145–47; perception of North, 44–46, 110–12, 199–202, 205–6; professional lives during Reconstruction, 217–18; question whether they can become slaveholders, 30, 48–50; racial perspective, 202–3; reaction to Appomattox, 213–14, 216–17; relationship with civilians, 171–74, 192–94, 196; relationship with Southern intellectual class, 108–10, 130, 132, 282 (n. 53); religious perspective on Confederacy, 182–90, 198–99, 205–7, 209–11, 299 (n. 64) response to Northern cultural attacks, 26–28, 29–30, 85–86; sense of being a Virginian, 89–90, 92–93, 95–101, 110–12, 127–28, 234–35; Southern identity of, 9–10, 16–18, 29–30, 57–58, 86, 88, 89–91, 100–102, 107–8, 110–12, 114–18, 129, 180–81, 205–7; struggles in becoming lawyers, 51–52, 258 (n. 36); study of past, 25–26; support Confederate centralization, 174–77; tout reunification, 1–3, 218–22, 228–31, 300 (n. 5); turned into Con-

federate martyrs, 165–66, 168–70, 205–7; uphold ideas of Victorianism, 234–35

Latane, J., challenges old fogies, 22

Latham, George Woodville: condemns secession convention, 136; defends courage of unit, 162

Law: difficult career route for last generation, 51–53

Lee, Fitzhugh: calls for national loyalty, 229

Lee, Robert E.: as postwar symbol, 226–28; symbolic value to Confederacy, 14, 204–5

Lee, Robert E., Jr.: life after Appomattox, 217

Leesburg, Va.: activities of YMCA in, 79

Letcher, John, 223

Lexington, Va.: Unionists and secessionist students fight in, 133, 142–43

Lincoln, Abraham: inaugural address angers last generation, 136–40; last generation's expectation of, 126

Logan, Joseph M.: believes in power of youth, 24

Lost Cause: based on last generation's wartime experience, 210–11; collaboration between generations, 302 (n. 34); last generation adopts militant expression of, 15, 231–35; last generation's move toward reconciliation, 300 (n. 5). See also Reconstruction

Louthan, William P.: sees progress dependent on young people, 25

Lunenburg County: militia activity in, 132–33

Lyle, John Newton: organizes military company, 132

Lynchburg College: flag raising, 139

Maddex, Jack P., Jr.: on Virginia Reconstruction politics, 223

Manliness: beginnings of "muscular

Christianity," 80–81; challenged after Appomattox, 208–9, 216–17; desire for fame, 54–56; Confederate portrayed as perfect embodiment of, 235; influenced by Christianity, 6, 10–11, 59–60, 74–75, 171; intimate bonds of student organizations, 72–75; language employed during secession, 145; proven on battlefield, 162–64; and reconciliation movement, 230–32; related to age status, 49–50; relationships among men, 264 (n. 34); role of ambition, 67–69; shapes behavior during secession, 123, 133, 138, 140; shift toward individualism, 68–69; slaveholder ideal of, 48; Southern stereotype of, 6, 70, 244 (n. 3). *See also* Christian gentleman

Marye, Lawrence S.: pessimism about law, 51–52

Massie, James: questions advocates of progress, 39

Masturbation, 82

Mathews, Henry Mason: on utilitarianism, 29

Maupin, Socrates, 138

Maury, Matthew Fontaine, 39, 45–46, 54–55

Mayer, Francis Blackwell, 32

McCabe, William Gordon: believes Virginians apathetic after Civil War, 224; faith in Confederacy, 179

McCardell, John: on Southern education, 108

McGuffey, William H., 82; holds Bible study with students, 102; views on slavery, 108

McIlwaine, Richard, 73

Meade, Hodijah Lincoln: mocks older attorneys, 51–52; rewards soldiers, 156; on secession, 126

Military executions, 160–61. *See also* Army of Northern Virginia

Militia organizations: increased genera-

tional tension, 279 (n. 29); organized by young people, 129–31, 132

Minor, Berkeley: on Confederate defeat, 177

Minor, Carter Nelson, 74, 130, 132; describes Northern army, 199

Minor, Charles L. C.: condemns reconciliation movement, 233–34

Minor, Franklin: criticizes "Young America," 41

Minor, John B., 72, 82; criticizes secessionist students, 141; considered out of touch by students, 142; encourages young people to exercise, 80–81; preaches Union, 109

Monteiro, Walter: boasts about Southern educational movement, 102; calls for controlled ambition, 68

Monticello: last generation laments poor condition of, 98–99

Morrison, Henry R.: supports secession, 139

Mothers: role in raising last generation, 263 (n. 27), 265 (n. 39). *See also* Adults

Mount Vernon Ladies Association, 98

Nature: celebrated by last generation, 93, 95, 96–97; last generation's attachment to, 271 (n. 16); potential for economic development, 37; proves superiority of Virginia, 97–98; shapes sense of identity, 93, 95; realm for youthful freedom, 95–96

Nelson, George Washington, 74

New South: endorsed by last generation, 215–16, 224–26; last generation comes to question, 234, 235–36; last generation's vision not cut off from antebellum moorings, 228; Lee and Jackson symbols of, 226–28. *See also* Reconstruction

Newton, Willoughby: warns against lure of fame, 55–56

Nonslaveholders: place in Confederate army, 149–50

North: considers South backward, 26–29, 109–12; cultural unity with South, 110; last generation's perception of, 23, 103–4; monopolizes Southern economy, 45–46; perceived religious differences with South, 107–8; ridicules Southern education, 86

Old fogies: blame young people for abandoning Virginia, 53–54; critiqued after Civil War, 214; definition of, 10, 245 (n. 7); disagree with last generation over progress, 22; explanatory device during Reconstruction, 225–26; last generation achieves status as, 232; mock young people, 56–57; source of generational tension, 10, 12, 39–40. *See also* Generations

Parents: advise sons, 71, 130, 132; worried that sons are too emotional, 96. *See also* Adults

Partisan politics: blamed for sectionalism, 114, 115, 146; criticized by last generation, 13, 42–43, 85–86, 255 (n. 12)

Pate, Henry Clay, 21; attacks Northern capitalists, 45–46; calls for educational reform, 84; celebrates local environs, 100, 101; celebrates youthful ambition, 67–68; criticizes older Virginians, 35, 37

Paternalism: shapes last generation, 60–61

Peaks of Otter, Va., 100

Pegram, William R. J.: believes Lee should rule Confederacy, 205; disenchanted with civilians, 194, 196; claims God's protection, 182–83; on 1860 election, 124; fanatical devotion to Confederacy, 210; on John Brown's raid, 117; laments Stonewall Jackson's

death, 190–91; on military executions, 160–61; rise in ranks, 164; sanctions killing of black troops, 203; supports arming of slaves, 176

Pendleton, Alexander "Sandie": believes Virginians should study past, 98; calls for education reform, 85; describes Christian gentleman, 59–60; experience during Gettysburg campaign, 199–202; seeks Christian martyrdom, 207

Pendleton, William Nelson, 214–15

Plymouth Rock: spurs resentment among members of last generation, 98

Poague, William Thomas: devotion to Confederacy, 209; difficulties with soldiers, 155

Pollard, Edward: considers Reconstruction moderate, 222, 228–29

Pollock, Thomas G.: religious sensibility of, 151; seeks professional success outside Virginia, 5–53

Potter, David: on construction of Southern identity, 17

Prayer: connects last generation to home front, 171, 289 (n. 55). *See also* Christianity

Pride: considered debilitating trait of Confederacy, 190–91

Prince Edward County, Va.: militia activity in, 132

Princeton University, 88

Professors: prevent students from joining militia, 132–33; relations with students during secession, 272 (n. 24), 282 (n. 53)

Progress: causes generational tension, 22, 24–25, 35, 37–42, 56–57; comparison to North, 44–45; convergence of Northern and Southern thinking, 30; creates unrealistic expectations for last generation, 33–34; impulse awakened by Civil War, 224; instills a belief in economic diversity, 31–33; last generation's postwar vision of, 15, 215–16, 218, 220–21, 223, 235; last generation's prewar vision of, 10–12, 19, 21, 253 (n. 24); related to honor, 33; shapes ideas about manliness, 11–12; validated by history, 25–26

Providence: as part of last generation's belief system, 25. *See also* Christianity old, 128–29, 130, 132–33; Unionist students feel alienated, 141–42; University of Virginia students proclaim support for, 137; young people criticized for being too emotional, 129, 144–45; young people organize militias, 129–31, 132–33

Sectionalism: caused by partisan politics, 114, 115; connected to Virginia history, 98–99; economic rivalry between North and South, 45–46; encourages faith in progress, 26–27; heightened by Christianity, 105–6; last generation believes in Southern political equality, 101; promoted through education, 84–86, 88, 103–5; rivalry between Northern and Southern universities, 54. *See also* Southern identity

Shepherd, W. F., 47

Sherman, William T.: describes young Confederates, 8–9

Simms, G. W. W. M.: sees South as Christian bastion, 107–8

Slaughter, Philip: on Christian martyrdom, 182, 207

Slaveholders: last generation members aspire to become, 48–49, 51; last generation's perception of, 10

Slavery: criticized after Civil War, 214, 225; defended by last generation, 11, 18, 29–30, 32, 248 (n. 3), 252 (n. 23); important to class position of last generation, 113; last generation demands guarantees for western expansion, 113, 115; principles of as part of college curriculum, 101–2, 108; understood by last generation as South's social system, 105; shapes ideas about manliness, 60–61; shapes secessionist sentiments, 129

Smith, Archibald M.: defends importance of imagination, 96

Smith, Francis H.: praises religious activity of VMI cadets, 83; sectionalizes cultural issues, 110

Smith, Summerfield: values historical sites, 96

Smith, William, 103, 223

Smith, William Andrew: believes students should learn about slavery, 106, 108

Smyth County, Va.: secessionist activity in, 141

Southern Churchman, 71

Southern education: considered inferior, 27

Southern identity: coalesces around expansion of slavery, 116; Confederate expression of, 147, 201–2, 203, 209; connected to generational tensions, 57–58; defined in opposition to North, 109–10; draws from Christian and parental traditions, 72; grounded in locale, 91, 92–93, 100–101; imparts political moderation, 116–17; intersects with state and national interests, 46, 110–12, 147; last generation's expression of, 2–3, 9–10, 14, 16–18, 234–35, 253 (n. 24); as part of loyalty to Union, 89–90, 101; perceived as a Christian community, 105–6, 107–8; trapped between slavery and bourgeois world, 60

Southern intellectuals: influence on last generation, 19–20, 29

Southern Planter, 55

Southern Repertory and College Review, 62

Southern rights: affirmed unintentionally by professors, 109; employed by last generation, 37. *See also* Sectionalism; Southern identity

Southern Rights' Association (University of Virginia), 90, 116–17, 119

Speculation, last generation's denounces sin of, 192–93, 196

Stringfellow, Charles: on ambition, 50

Strother, David H.: ridicules Virginia, 27
Stuart, James Ewell Brown "Jeb": attachment to local community, 92–93;
compliments Southern women, 174;
condemns civilian society as corrupt,
196; critique of North, 110–12; ponders career choices, 50–51; representative of courageous soldiers, 162
Students: attracted to "muscular Christianity," 80–81; embrace religion, 12,
75–76, 79–80, 82–83, 102–3, 106;
last generation's counter-stereotype of,
146–47; literary societies of, 72–75,
119; obsessed with achieving fame,
54–56; paying for college, 47; relations with professors, 102–3, 105, 106,
108–9, 141; rioting, 82; secession debate between Deep South and Upper
South students, 125–26; spiritual
bond between, 74; stereotype of, 56–
57, 71; support of educational reform,
84–86; taught to love Union, 90; and
time management, 76; visits to historical and natural sites, 96–97. *See also*
Last generation, members of

Taliaferro, Edwin: desires disunion,
127–28
Taylor, Walter H.: admires Southern
women, 173–74; applauds Lee's devotion, 205; use of prayer, 171
Tazewell County, Va.: secessionist activity
in, 140–41
Temperance association: popularity at
University of Virginia, 80
Thornwell, James Henley, 19
Tom Brown's School Days, 88
Travers, John M., 153
Tucker, Beverley, 103
Tucker, Henry St. George, 82
Turner, Charles W., 45; on secession, 127

Union: last generation's reverence for, 9,
26, 89–90; last generation's sense of

doom about, 119. *See also* Southern
identity
United States Military Academy, 83
University of Virginia, 19, 84; condemned as a godless place, 82; dream
of becoming intellectual center of
South, 85–86; example of religious
toleration, 106; flag raising during secession, 138–39; improved relations
between professors and students, 82;
increase in number of religious students, 77–80, 82–83; low reputation,
27; militia organizations, 130; rejection
of endowment fund, 85; student revivals, 75–76, 79–80; students advocate
secession, 137; students vote in 1860
election, 123; tuition costs of, 47
Utilitarianism: critiqued by last generation, 28–29, 95, 252 (n. 21)

Venable, Richard M.: faith in progress,
21–22
Vengeance: motivator during Civil War
for last generation, 198–200, 290
(n. 64)
Victorianism: importance of cavalier
myth, 234–35; last generation's desire
for moral perfection, 95–96; shapes
manliness, 10–11. *See also* Christian
gentleman; Manliness
Virginia: belief that state created superior leaders, 39–40, 93; controlled by
Northern capitalists, 45–46; defect
in state character, 61–63; distinctive
identity, 99–100; economic changes in
1850s, 11, 17, 20, 247 (n. 15); economic
frustrations of young people, 34, 37,
48–49; educational debates, 84–86;
emigration of young people, 35, 37, 49,
52–53; last generation believes secession could redeem state, 8, 10, 12–13,
127–28, 145–46; last generation envisions diversified economy, 31–33; last
generation's attachment to, 111–12,

33, 58; memorialization of state's soldiers, 235–36; nature and history celebrated, 96–98; perception of decline, 10, 26, 27, 38–39, 59, 254 (n. 3); Reconstruction and last generation, 15, 218, 220–26, 228–29; shift in generational power relations after Civil War, 221, 222–23; state support for John Bell, 123; student protests after Lincoln's inaugural, 137–40; tension between generations, 12, 35, 37–42, 57–58, 254, (n. 2), 255 (n. 10)

Virginia Military Institute, 84, 129, 134; cadet religious activities, 83; confrontation between cadets and Unionists, 142–43; flag raising, 139; students vote in 1860 election, 123

Virginia's Secession Convention, denounced by last generation, 134–37

Virginia State Agricultural Society, 41

Virginia University Magazine, 79; editors criticize Virginia's Secession Convention, 135–36; on John Brown's raid, 117–18

Washington, George, 85

Washington College, 85, 129; flag raising, 139; militia organizations, 130; student excursions, 97; student religious activities, 83; students fight Lexington Unionists, 134

Washington Society (University of Virginia), 126

Watson, David, 104

Westmoreland County, Va.: militia activity in, 133

Whig Party: influences economic thought of last generation, 21; source of political moderation, 114, 115

White, Hugh A.: on college friendships,

73; ideas about death, 183; as martyred Confederate, 165–66, 168–70; punishes soldiers, 158

Wise, Henry A., 12, 125, 223; educational policies of, 84–85

Women: last generation's perception of, 110; loyalty to Confederate cause, 295 (n. 30); relations with soldiers, 170–75, 186–87. *See also* Mothers

Wyatt-Brown, Bertram: on honor, 91

Yale Literary Magazine: insults Virginia students, 117–18

Young Men's Christian Association, 12, 74–75, 77–79, 105, 118

Young Men's Literary Society of Fredericksburg, 108–9

Youth: advice from parents, 71; aspirations of becoming slaveholders, 60–61; believed to be growing up too quickly, 70–71; desire for fame, 54–56; difficult transition to adulthood, 49–51, 257 (n. 32); disillusionment with older generation, 282 (n. 61); drawn to nature, 96–97; embrace ambition, 67–69; dreams for professional success, 73–74; instructed to reject cavalier ideal, 63–64; lack of respect for adult authority, 41–42; language of honor used to discredit last generation, 144–45; natural landscape as unique space for, 96; "nature" of, 5, 54–55, 243 (n. 1); pressure to live up to departed ancestors, 92; secession a rite of passage for, 145–46; sense of mission, 99; stereotype of Southern youth, 56–57, 70; rhetoric of youth used to justify secession, 137, 140. *See also* Generations; Last generation, members of; Manliness